Series 7
Registered Representative Study Program
Volume I

D1287376

PASS PERFECT

www.PassPerfect.com

This page intentionally left blank

SERIES 7 GENERAL SECURITIES REGISTERED REPRESENTATIVE STUDY PROGRAM

ABOUT THE SERIES 7 EXAMINATION

The Series 7 General Securities Registered Representative Examination qualifies an individual to sell any type of security. The exam is administered by FINRA – the Financial Industry Regulatory Authority at test sites across the country.

In the United States, the examination is administered each work day on computer through the FINRA "PROCTOR" system at either Prometric (www.prometric.com) or Pearson VUE (www.pearsonvue.com) Centers. The exam consists of 250 multiple choice questions to be completed within 6 hours. The test is divided into two 3-hour segments of 125 questions each, with an extra 5 questions included in each segment for use in preparing future tests. The "extra questions" do not count in the grading. The questions in each segment are arranged in random order.

ABOUT THIS STUDY PROGRAM

The PassPerfect Series 7 Study Program is designed to cover all items that are tested on the examination while making the most efficient use of a candidate's time. The preparer of this material, Edward Fleur, has spent 30 years developing and writing training materials for all securities examinations and has personally trained thousands of individuals in class for the Series 7 examination. His in-depth knowledge of the material is presented in this course in an organized, concise, and clear format.

The course is divided into 10 chapters. Each chapter and the approximate number of questions included on the Series 7 test for that chapter are:

Equity Securities	10
Debt Securities	40
Options	25
Trading Markets	20
Customer Accounts	25
New Issues	15
Investment Companies	25
Taxes and Tax Shelters	20
Regulations	50
Analysis	20
Total Number of Questions	**250**

Each chapter is divided into sections. Each section is followed by a section examination with detailed answers and explanations. Separate from the course material is a book of Chapter Exams with Explanations, for final review of each chapter. In addition, the "Final Examinations" book contains eleven practice tests. Finally, a detailed Glossary is included for help mastering industry terminology.

HOW TO USE THE STUDY PROGRAM

The passing grade on the Series 7 examination is 72%, or 180 questions correct out of the total of 250 graded questions. To prepare for the examination, each chapter must be studied within the text. The examinations are very important because they reinforce your knowledge of the material and highlight any weak areas that you might have. Before proceeding to the next section, review those areas where questions were answered incorrectly.

Certain areas of the examination are weighted more heavily than others. The chart below shows the weighting of each tested chapter:

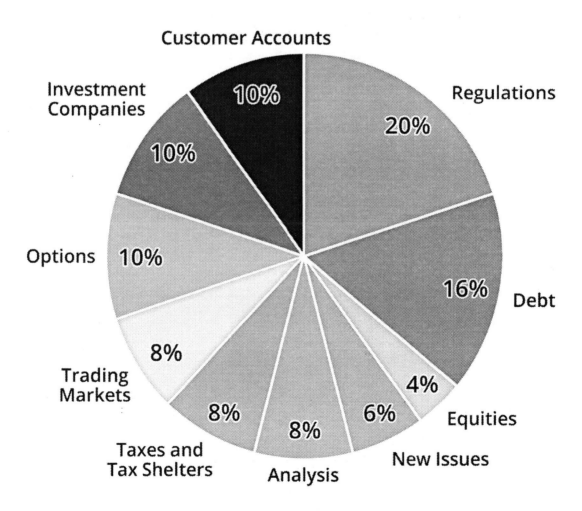

Just two of the chapters – Debt Securities and Regulations – comprise 90 out of 250 questions – slightly more than 35% of the examination. It is important that you emphasize these chapters.

Also note that Equities and New Issues are proportionately much less important on the examination. A weakness in any one of these is not critical, and the examination can still be passed.

For those who are using the material on a self-study basis, after completing each chapter in the text (including section examinations), a separate Chapter Exam must be taken. This can either be done in our online programs or in a separate printed Chapter Exam book, depending on which package you purchased. Each Chapter Exam question should be carefully reviewed, whether or not the question was answered correctly. This reinforces the information that must be mastered for the examination.

After completing the text and Chapter Exams, go on to the Final Examinations. The Final Examinations can either be completed online or in a printed book, depending on which package you purchased. The Final Examinations are weighted in the same manner as the actual examination and are of a similar difficulty level. Each Final Examination is equal to half of a real Series 7 test and is to be completed within 3 hours. A minimum of 10 Final Examinations must be completed with a grade of 75-80% to be prepared for the actual exam.

The total study time needed to complete the course is about 110 hours for the text and 40 hours for the Final Examinations. Since a person can only study effectively for about 4 hours a day, about 38 days of study are needed to complete the material.

CLASSROOM PROGRAMS

Training for all securities examinations is offered across the United States through our affiliates. Instructor led virtual training is also offered monthly.

Our instructors are experts in both the industry and the classroom, their enthusiasm and expertise makes a difficult learning test easy. Contact us for more information.

A schedule of virtual classes is posted on our website.

OTHER COURSES

Pass Perfect training materials are available for other examinations that you may need in the future. The current list includes:

Registered Representative Courses

    3 - Commodities / Future Representative
    6 - Investment Company / Variable Annuities Representative
    7 - General Securities Representative
   11 - Assistant Representative / Order Processor
   50 - Municipal Financial Advisor
   57 - Securities Trader
   63 - Uniform State Law Agent
   65 - Registered Investment Adviser
   66 - Combined State Agent and Investment Adviser
   82 - Private Securities Offerings Representative
   99 - Operations Professional

Principal Courses

     4 - Registered Options Principal
  9/10 - FINRA Branch Manager / General Sales Supervisor
   24 - FINRA General Securities Principal
   26 - Investment Companies / Variable Annuities Principal
   27 - Financial and Operations Principal
   51 - Municipal Fund Securities Principal
   53 - Municipal Securities Principal

In addition, many of our programs are available in various computer-based formats, including virtual classroom training. A schedule of virtual classes is posted on our website.

Our instructors are experts in both the industry and the classroom, their enthusiasm and expertise makes a difficult learning task easy.

For more information about our products or classes, call toll free:

 1-800-349-3396

Or visit our website at:

 www.passperfect.com

COMMENTS AND QUESTIONS

We welcome your comments on the material and any recommendations you may have for improving this product.

Email us at: info@passperfect.com

Our address is:
EFFE Corp. / Pass Perfect
176 Bedford Road
Greenwich, CT 06831

This page intentionally left blank

EQUITIES

EQUITIES

SECTION 1: COMMON STOCK

1a. ISSUANCE OF COMMON STOCK

Common Is Equity

Issued By Regular Corporations And Investment Companies

A common stockholder is an "owner" of a corporation. Owners are considered to have an equity position in the corporate structure. Therefore, common stock is an "equity" security. Aside from regular corporations, issuers of common stock include investment companies, such as mutual funds and real estate investment trusts.

Authorized Stock

Arbitrary Low Par Value

When a corporation is formed, its corporate charter authorizes that a fixed number of common shares may be issued. This is called "authorized" stock. The stock is assigned an arbitrary par value, which is typically set quite low. For example, common stock might be assigned a par value of 10 cents a share or $1 per share. Sometimes, par value is even set at zero, which is termed no par common stock. Par value for common has no bearing on the market price of the stock. Market value is based on investor expectations about the future of the company. The reason why par value is set so low is that many states tax corporations based on the par value of their shares.

Issued Stock

Assume that a corporation is authorized under its charter to sell 1,000,000 common shares with a $1 par value. The corporation does not "issue" all of its authorized shares. It sells only part of the authorized amount to the public so that it has the ability to sell more shares at a later date without having to amend its corporate charter. If this corporation issues 400,000 shares, it still has 600,000 shares available for issuance at a later date. This looks as follows:

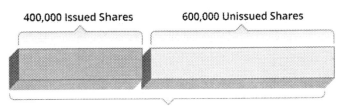

400,000 Issued Shares   600,000 Unissued Shares

1,000,000 Authorized Shares

Outstanding Shares

Treasury Stock - Repurchased Shares

This corporation now has 400,000 shares outstanding in the hands of the public. These are the shares that trade in the market. After issuance, the corporation may "buy back" shares that are trading in the market. Repurchased shares are called "Treasury Stock" and are no longer outstanding in the hands of the public.

Equity Securities

Corporations will repurchase shares because:

- The market price is low and the corporation feels that the stock is a "good buy" at that price.

- As Treasury stock is repurchased, the number of outstanding shares is reduced. Because earnings per share is based on outstanding shares, with fewer shares outstanding, earnings per share will rise.

- The shares can be used to fund pension plan and stock option plan obligations.

- The shares can be used at a later date as "payment" for an acquisition or merger.

Treasury Stock Does Not Vote Or Receive Dividends

Treasury shares do not have the usual privileges accorded to outstanding common shares. For example, Treasury shares cannot vote and do not receive dividends. (These rights of a common shareholder are covered later.)

Assume that our sample corporation has repurchased 100,000 common shares for its Treasury. The common stock structure is:

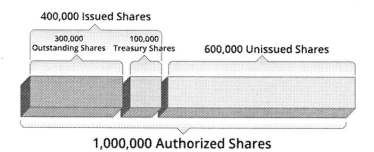

1b. SHAREHOLDER RECORDKEEPING

Registered In Owner's Name

The corporation must keep detailed records of the number of shares outstanding and the names and addresses of the owners of the shares. These shares are "registered" in the name of the owner. All equity securities are registered, so that the corporation can send dividends and other mail to the proper owners.

Registrar

The corporation hires an outside firm (usually a bank or trust company) to act as registrar. The registrar maintains the integrity of the list of all shareholder names and addresses and is given the responsibility to make sure that the company does not issue more shares than authorized under its charter.

Transfer Agent

Record Book Of Shareholders

The corporation also hires an outside firm, a bank or trust company, to act as transfer agent. Every day, as trades of the stock settle (meaning payment takes place), a report is made to the transfer agent. The transfer agent then cancels old shares which have been sold and issues new shares in the name of new buyers of the stock. The transfer agent keeps an accurate record of the shareholders updated daily. Because it maintains the shareholders' names and addresses, the transfer agent usually handles the mailings to shareholders (e.g., dividends, corporate reports, and voting materials).

The registrar acts as a watchdog over the transfer agent. Transfer agents can, and have, made mistakes, such as canceling 100 shares and transferring those shares to the new owner as 1,000 shares. The registrar is supposed to catch these mistakes and assure correction.

Book-Entry Certificate

Instead of physically issuing and canceling certificates, a newer method of recording owners is through "book-entry" certificates. When securities are issued "book-entry," no certificates are issued. Instead, the ownership record is simply kept by the transfer agent and by the clearing corporation that settles trades.

1c. RIGHTS OF A COMMON SHAREHOLDER

Common shareholders enjoy limited liability as owners of the company (the most they can lose is their investment) and have a number of rights. These rights are:

- Right to vote
- Right to inspect books and records
- Right to transfer ownership
- Preemptive right
- Right to corporate distributions
- Right to corporate assets upon dissolution

Right To Vote

Common stockholders vote at the company's annual meeting. They vote for the Board of Directors (most corporate charters have half the Board come up for election each year) and on matters that affect the shareholder's "ownership interest." For example, the common shareholders must approve the issuance of convertible bonds, since these securities can be converted into more common shares. If conversion occurs, with more shares outstanding, each existing shareholder's "ownership interest" will be diluted. Shareholders do not vote on management or dividend decisions - these are made by the Board.

Items That Require A Shareholder Vote

Voting rules may vary, to some degree, from state to state. However, the New York Stock Exchange has very specific voting rules for companies that wish to list their shares.

Voting rules may vary to some degree, from state to state. Generally, shareholder approval is required if the corporation wishes to:

- Declare a stock split;
- Declare a reverse stock split;
- Issue convertible bonds or preferred stock;
- Issue stock options to officers on a preferential basis.

The logic for shareholder approval of a stock split or reverse stock split is that these change the par value of the company's stock. Since the original par value was legally established in the corporate charter, any change to this par value must be approved by the shareholders.

The logic for shareholder approval of convertible securities is that such an action is highly "dilutive," resulting in the issuance of many more common shares, reducing each existing shareholder's ownership interest. Issuing "preferential" stock options to officers benefits a select group of individuals, and could be viewed as "self-dealing" by these persons - hence shareholder approval is required.

Items That Do Not Require A Shareholder Vote

Generally, shareholder approval is **not** required if the corporation wishes to:

- Declare a cash dividend;
- Declare a stock dividend;
- Declare a rights distribution (discussed later in this section);
- Repurchase shares for its Treasury.

Dividend decisions are made at the sole discretion of the Board of Directors - no shareholder vote is required. This is true for both cash dividends and stock dividends (defined as any stock distribution that is less than 25% of the outstanding shares). Any dividend distribution, even a stock dividend, had no effect on the stock's par value, so there is no requirement for a shareholder vote. Rights distributions preserve a shareholder's ownership interest, so no voting is required. Finally, repurchase of Treasury shares results in fewer common shares outstanding, increasing each shareholder's percentage ownership, so no voting is required.

1 Vote Per Share

Each shareholder gets 1 vote per share. An owner with 100 shares gets 100 votes on each item being voted on that year. The corporation will use one of two voting methods - either statutory voting or cumulative voting. Assume that 6 directorships are open (6 voting items), with a choice of one of three persons for each directorship. Voting for a 100 share owner works as follows:

Statutory Voting

Statutory Voting: 100 votes maximum are allowed for **each** directorship. In total, 600 votes are cast

Cumulative Voting

Cumulative Voting: 6 directorships x 100 votes = 600 votes which may be cast in **any manner**. For example, 300 could be cast for one director, 200 for a second, 100 for a third, with no votes for the remaining three directors.

Most corporations use statutory voting. Cumulative voting is considered to be an advantage for the "small investor" since he or she can vote disproportionately and can achieve more influence in the election of "selected" directors.

If a shareholder does not attend the annual meeting, he or she cannot vote. For this reason, many companies are infamous for having the meetings in places like East Gulch, Texas. If the only people who show up at the meeting are management (who usually hold large positions) and only they vote, they get to do whatever they want with the company.

Proxies - Completed By Shareholders Who Do Not Attend Annual Meeting

To stop this, shareholders not attending the meeting are required to receive voting cards from the company. By filling out these cards and mailing them to the company, at the annual meeting these votes will be counted. These cards are called "proxies" since a person at the annual meeting is acting as the shareholder's "proxy" (stand-in) and voting for them. Many shareholders receiving proxies do not respond. If this happens, management controls the voting at the annual meeting.

Common Stock With Different Classes

Some companies issue different classes of stock with different voting rights. For example, a family-owned company may go public by issuing Class A stock for family members and Class B stock for the public. Class A stock will have all voting privileges or "concentrated" privileges. Class B stock does not vote or has limited voting ability.

Right To Inspect Books And Records

Right To Inspect Books And Records: Common shareholders may inspect the books and records of a company. In practice, this doesn't happen since audited financial statements are required to be sent to shareholders annually by the Securities and Exchange Commission under the Securities Exchange Act of 1934.

Right To Transfer Ownership

Negotiable

Non-Negotiable

Right To Transfer Ownership: Common shareholders have the right to sell their shares to anyone else without restriction. The shares are "negotiable" securities. They can be traded. Certain securities are "non-negotiable." They cannot be traded. As an example, mutual fund shares are non-negotiable. Savings bonds are non-negotiable. These securities are redeemed with the issuer at a calculated value.

Preemptive Right

Preemptive Right: If the corporation wishes to issue more shares, common stockholders have the right to buy these shares before anyone else. Thus, they can maintain their proportionate ownership interest in the company. The offer of these shares to existing shareholders is called a "rights offering" and is discussed in the Rights Distributions section.

Right To Corporate Distributions

Right To Corporate Distributions: The Board of Directors decides if the corporation will pay a cash dividend, a stock dividend, or if it will "split" its stock (usually done when the market price of the stock rises too high for an average investor to buy the shares; by splitting the stock, the number of shares is increased and the price reduced, making the issue more accessible to investors). The common shareholder has the right to his pro-rata share of these distributions. Most corporations declare and pay common dividends quarterly.

Right To Corporate Assets Upon Dissolution

Right To Corporate Assets Upon Dissolution: If the corporation goes bankrupt or is dissolved, the common stockholder is paid **last** (if any assets remain).

1d. CORPORATE DISTRIBUTION PROCEDURES

When a corporation decides to make a distribution (for example, a cash dividend) or if the corporation is going to issue "preemptive rights" to its existing shareholders, it makes an announcement in the news media. Below is a sample announcement:

> **Monday, March 31, 20XX**
>
> The Board of Directors of Acme Manufacturing Company today declares a dividend of 50 cents per share to stockholders of record on April 15, 20XX. The dividend will be paid on April 30th, 20XX.

The Board of Directors has set the:

- **Declaration Date**: The date the dividend is declared.

- **Record Date**: The date on the which the corporation takes the shareholder names and addresses from the transfer agent records for mailing the dividend.

- **Payable Date**: The date the dividend checks will be mailed by the corporation's transfer agent.

These dates show on the calendar as:

APRIL

S	M	T	W	T	F	S
30	31	1	2	3	4	5
6	7	8	9	10	11	12
13	14	15	16	17	18	19
20	21	22	23	24	25	26
27	28	29	30	1	2	3

Declaration Date → 31

Record Date → 15   Payable Date → 30

Regular Way Settlement - 2 Business Days

Must Settle By Record Date To Receive Dividend

If Trade Settles After Record Date, Do Not Receive Dividend

Once the distribution is announced, the exchange where the stock trades has some work to do. To be an owner of record for the distribution, a customer must have paid for the stock by the close of business on the 15th (the record date). If the trade settles on the record date or before, the buyer will be on record as of the evening of the 15th and will be mailed the dividend.

Regular way settlement occurs 2 business days after trade date, so that the last day to buy and get the dividend is 2 business days prior to the record date. If the stock is bought after this date, the trade will settle after the record date and no dividend is received.

APRIL

S	M	T	W	T	F	S
30	31	1	2	3	4	5
6	7	8	9	10	11	12
13	14	15	16	17	18	19
20	21	22	23	24	25	26
27	28	29	30	1	2	3

Last day to buy stock regular way and receive dividend → 11

Record Date → 15

Cum-Dividend

If a customer buys on the 11th or before in a regular way trade, he or she will get the dividend. The stock is trading with the dividend - "cum dividend."

Ex-Dividend

If the customer buys on the 14th or later, he or she does not get the dividend - the stock is now trading "ex-dividend."

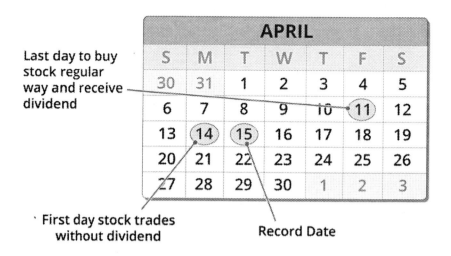

Last day to buy stock regular way and receive dividend

First day stock trades without dividend

Record Date

If a customer buys on the 10th, the trade will settle on the 14th, regular way, and the customer will get the dividend. If the customer buys on the 11th, the trade will settle on the 15th, and since the record book list is taken that night, the customer will get the dividend. If the customer buys on the 14th, the trade will settle on the 16th, and the customer will not be on the record book for the dividend, since the list was taken the previous night.

On Ex-Date The Exchange Reduces Price Of Stock

As of April 14th, any purchaser in a regular way trade does not get the dividend. FINRA sets this date as the "ex dividend" date and directs the exchange where the stock trades to reduce the price by the amount of the distribution when the stock opens for trading, since purchasers no longer qualify for the payment.

Last day to buy stock regular way and receive dividend

Ex-Date

Record Date

Ex-Date For Cash Dividends Is 1 Business Day Prior To Record Date

The "ex-date" is set by FINRA as the business day prior to the record date. (Remember, if one buys the stock 2 business days prior to the record date, the trade will settle on the record date and that person will get the distribution.)

Assume that Acme stock was trading at $20 on the 11th. As of the 14th (the "ex"- date), the stock will open for trading at a price reduced by the $.50 dividend, so it opens at $19.50. Reduction on ex-date is done for a very simple reason. It stops traders from making windfall profits. If there was no reduction, a day trader could buy the stock on the 11th (getting on the record book for the 15th) and then sell on the 14th (going off the record book on the 16th) and be on the record book for the one day necessary to get a $.50 dividend check. If there is no reduction, the trader could buy at $20 and then sell at $20 the next day and get a $.50 check for 1 day's investment.

With the reduction, the trader buys at $20 and sells at $19.50, but receives the $.50 dividend, so the end result is a "wash."

Ex-Dates For Cash Dividends, Stock Dividends And Splits, And Rights Offerings

Ex-dates (adjustment dates) are set not only for cash dividends, but also for stock dividends, stock splits, and rights offerings (discussed in the next section). For example, a corporation is splitting its stock 2 for 1. Just prior to the ex-date, the stock is trading at $44. As of the morning of the ex-date, the exchange will open the stock at $22 ($44 / 2).

As another example, a corporation declares a 20% stock dividend. Just prior to the ex-date, the stock is trading at $48. As of the ex-date, the exchange will open the stock at $40 ($48 / 1.20).

1e. RIGHTS DISTRIBUTIONS

We know that shareholders have the "preemptive" right to maintain proportionate ownership in the company. If a company wants to issue new shares, it gives its existing shareholders "first chance" on the issue.

Existing Owners Can Subscribe At A Lower Price

The existing shareholders are able to buy these shares for less than the current market price. The discount reflects the amount that would have to be paid to an underwriter to handle the offering if the issue were being sold to the general public. By selling directly to its existing shareholders, the company avoids using an underwriter and can pass the savings on to the existing shareholders.

Rights Agent

To handle the mechanics of the offering, the corporation hires a "rights agent." This is usually the existing transfer agent of the issuer. The rights agent issues the additional shares upon presentation of the rights certificates with the appropriate dollar subscription amount.

Rights Offering Performed With A Stand-By Underwriter

If all of the issue is not subscribed to by existing shareholders, the issuer will have an underwriter "stand-by" to pick up the unsubscribed shares. The underwriter then resells these shares to the public. This is known as a "stand-by" underwriting and ensures that the issuer sells the entire issue and gets the needed funding.

Rights Expire In 30 - 60 Days

Since the existing shareholders can buy the stock for less than the current market price, their subscription rights have value. Shareholders are free to exercise their subscription rights or they can sell them to someone else. Since these rights typically last for 30 to 60 days and then expire, shareholders must decide quickly. Below is a sample rights announcement:

> **Monday, March 31, 20XX**
>
> The Board of Directors of Acme Manufacturing Corporation today declares a rights distribution to stockholders of record on April 15th, 20XX. The rights will be distributed on April 30, 20XX.
>
> Under the terms of the offer, 5 rights are necessary to subscribe to one new share at a price of $14 per share. Any residual rights totaling less than 5 can be rounded to 5 rights to purchase 1 additional share. The offer expires Midnight May 31, 20XX.
>
> The current market price of Acme stock is $20.

1 Right Per Share

Assume that a customer owns 100 shares of Acme stock. He will receive 100 rights from Acme on April 30th. These come as a physical certificate which can be sent to Acme with money to buy ("subscribe") more shares or they can be traded in the open market until expiration.

Cum Rights

Assume that it is March 31st and the customer wants to know how much the rights will be worth in the market. The stock is still trading "cum rights," since any purchaser will settle before the record date of April 15th and will receive the rights.

Value Of Right (Cum Rights)

In theory the value of the right is included in the current market price of the stock. The formula for the value of the right is:

$$\text{Value of Right (Cum Rights)} = \frac{\text{Market Price - Subscription Price}}{N + 1}$$

where N = number of rights to buy 1 share

$$= \frac{\$20 - \$14}{5 + 1} = \frac{\$6}{6} = \$1 \text{ Value Per Right}$$

The right is worth $1 and theoretically can be sold for this amount.

Value Of Right (Ex-Rights)

When the stock trades "ex-rights," any purchaser will no longer get the distribution. The market price will be reduced by $1 ($20 - $1 = $19 new market price). As of the ex-date, the formula to calculate the value of a right is:

$$\text{Value of Right (Ex)} = \frac{\text{Adjusted Market Price - Subscription Price}}{N}$$

$$= \frac{\$19 - \$14}{5} = \frac{\$5}{5} = \$1 \text{ Value Per Right}$$

Please notice that the theoretical value did not change. This is not an accident - the values must always be the same.

This shareholder receives 100 rights which are worth $100. He can send his certificate for 100 rights to Acme with a check for $280 and receive 20 shares of stock (remember, it takes 5 rights to buy 1 share, so 100 rights buys 20 shares at $14 subscription price = $280). Or the rights can be traded in the market and the customer should get about $100 for them. The shareholder must act fast though, since the rights expire in 2 months.

Fractional Shares Rounded To Whole Shares

If the customer had 104 shares, he or she would get 104 rights. Under the terms of the offer, the customer can "round up" to 105 rights and buy 21 shares at $14.

Equity Securities

COMMON STOCK
SECTION EXAMINATION

1.

The definition of Treasury Stock is:

   a.   issued stock minus authorized stock

   b.   issued stock minus outstanding stock

   c.   authorized stock minus outstanding stock

   d.   outstanding stock minus authorized stock

2.

Which of the following are equity security holders of a company?

   I   Common shareholders

   II   Preferred Shareholders

   III   Convertible Bondholders

   IV   Warrant Holders

   a.   I and II

   b.   II and III

   c.   I, II, IV

   d.   I, II, III, IV

3.

The market price of common stock will be influenced by which of the following?

   I   The par value of the shares

   II   Expectations for future earnings of the company

   III   Expectations for future dividends to be paid by the company

   IV   Book value of the company

   a.   I and IV

   b.   II and III

   c.   I, II, III

   d.   II and IV

4.

Which of the following are **TRUE** statements regarding the activities of the registrar?

   I   The registrar cancels old shares

   II   The registrar transfers shares to new owners

   III   The registrar accounts for the number of shares issued

   IV   The registrar keeps the integrity of the shareholder record

   a.   I and II

   b.   II and IV

   c.   III and IV

   d.   I, II, III, IV

5.

Cumulative voting is considered to be an advantage to the:

   a.   large investor

   b.   institutional investor

   c.   small investor

   d.   novice investor

6.

Which of the following are functions of the transfer agent?

   I   Mailing dividend payments to shareholders

   II   Canceling old shares and issuing new shares

   III   Preparing and mailing proxies

   IV   Setting the Declaration Date

   a.   I and II

   b.   III and IV

   c.   I, II, III

   d.   I, II, III, IV

7.
Which of the following terms describes common stock?

a. negotiable
b. redeemable
c. non-negotiable
d. callable

8.
The Board of Directors of a company will set all of the following **EXCEPT**:

a. declaration date
b. record date
c. ex date
d. payable date

9.
ABC Corporation has declared a cash dividend to stockholders of record on Friday, December 10th. The last day to buy ABC shares **BEFORE** they go ex dividend is?

a. Tuesday, December 7th
b. Wednesday, December 8th
c. Thursday, December 9th
d. Friday, December 10th

10.
In a rights offering, shareholders who subscribe make payment to the:

a. stand-by underwriter
b. rights agent for the issuer
c. brokerage firm
d. trustee

11.
A customer gives a power of attorney to a caretaker to vote his shares on his behalf at the company's annual meeting. This is called (a):

a. discretionary authority
b. voting trust
c. proxy
d. trading authorization

12.
ABC Corporation has declared a rights offering to stockholders of record on December 10th. Under the offer, shareholders need 10 rights to subscribe to 1 new share at a price of $19. Fractional shares can be rounded up to purchase 1 full share. A customer owning 111 shares wishes to subscribe. The market price of the stock is currently $30. The customer can buy:

a. 11 shares for $209
b. 12 shares for $228
c. 11 shares for $341
d. 12 shares for $372

13.
ABC Corporation has declared a rights offering to stockholders of record on Friday, December 10th. Under the offer, shareholders need 10 rights to subscribe to 1 new share at a price of $19. Fractional shares can be rounded up to purchase 1 full share. As of Thursday, December 1st, the stock is trading at $30. The value of the right is:

a. $.90
b. $1.00
c. $1.10
d. $1.25

14.
ABC Corporation has declared a rights offering to stockholders of record on Friday, December 10th. Under the offer, shareholders need 10 rights to subscribe to 1 new share at a price of $19. Fractional shares can be rounded up to purchase 1 full share. As of the ex date, the stock is trading at $29. The value of the right is:

a. $.90
b. $1.00
c. $1.10
d. $1.25

15.

Stockholder approval is needed if a corporation wishes to do all of the following **EXCEPT**:

a. split its stock 1 for 2
b. split its stock 2 for 1
c. repurchase shares for Treasury
d. issue convertible securities

16.

Which of the following statements are **TRUE** regarding Treasury Stock?

I   Treasury Stock receives dividends
II   Treasury Stock votes
III Treasury Stock reduces the number of shares outstanding
IV Treasury Stock purchases are used to increase reported Earnings Per Share

a. I and II
b. III and IV
c. II, III, IV
d. I, II, III, IV

17.

All of the following are rights of a common shareholder **EXCEPT** the:

a. right to vote
b. right to receive a dividend
c. right to manage
d. right to transfer shares

18.

Common dividends are usually paid:

a. monthly
b. quarterly
c. semi-annually
d. annually

19.

A customer owns 200 shares of ABC stock. ABC is having a rights offering where 20 rights are needed to subscribe to 1 new share. The customer will receive:

a. 1 right
b. 10 rights
c. 100 rights
d. 200 rights

20.

In a corporate liquidation, common stockholders are paid:

a. before bondholders and preferred stockholders
b. after bondholders and preferred stockholders
c. after bondholders but before preferred stockholders
d. before all creditors

COMMON STOCK EXAMINATION EXPLANATIONS

1. The best answer is **b**. Treasury stock consists of issued shares that have been repurchased by the corporation. Repurchased shares are no longer "outstanding," so the definition of Treasury Stock is issued shares minus outstanding shares.

2. The best answer is **a**. "Owners" have an equity position - and the only owners of a company are shareholders - both common and preferred. Convertible bondholders are creditors of a company. Their position only becomes equity if they convert to common shares. Warrant holders have long term options to buy stock. They only become equity holders if they exercise their options.

3. The best answer is **b**. The market price of common stock is determined by investor expectations about the future of the company. Par value and book value have no bearing on the market price of the common.

4. The best answer is **c**. The transfer agent cancels old shares and issues new shares, keeping a record of current shareholder names and addresses. The registrar ensures that all shares are properly accounted for and also verifies the integrity of the record of shareholders' names and addresses.

5. The best answer is **c**. Cumulative voting allows a disproportionate voting weight to be placed on selected directors and is considered to be an advantage for the small investor who wishes to have specific directors elected.

6. The best answer is **c**. The declaration date is set by the Board of Directors of the company. The transfer agent cancels old shares and issues new shares; and mails voting materials (proxies), annual reports, and dividend payments to the shareholders.

7. The best answer is **a**. Common stock is a negotiable (transferable) security. It is not redeemable with the issuer nor is it callable by the issuer.

8. The best answer is **c**. The ex-date is set by FINRA (the self regulatory organization or SRO that oversees the securities markets in the U.S.) once the Board of Directors sets the Record date. The Board of Directors, when it announces a dividend, sets the Declaration date, Record date, and Payable date.

9. The best answer is **b**. The regular way ex date is 1 business day prior to the record date for cash dividends. The record date is Friday, December 10th, therefore the ex date is Thursday, December 9th. To buy the shares before they go ex dividend, the shares must be purchased before December 9th, meaning they must be purchased on Wednesday, December 8th.

10. The best answer is **b**. In a rights offering, a company is attempting to sell additional shares directly to its existing shareholders. The company hires a "rights agent" to handle the mechanics of the offer, typically a commercial bank.

11. The best answer is **c**. When a shareholder cannot attend the annual meeting and vote, the shareholder can give a power of attorney to another individual or the management of the company to "stand in" and cast that shareholder's votes as directed. This is called a "proxy," where the individual granted the power of attorney acts as the shareholder's proxy. The "caretaker" wording used in the question is a little odd, but that individual granted the proxy must act in the shareholder's interests, so this person could be viewed as a caretaker.

12. The best answer is **b**. The subscription offer allows fractional shares to be rounded up to buy 1 whole share. Since 10 rights are needed to buy 1 new share, the customer receiving 111 rights can buy 111 / 10 = 11.1 shares which rounds up to 12 shares at $19 each = $228 total for 12 shares.

13. The best answer is **b**. Since the record date is Friday, December 10th, a customer buying on Thursday, December 1st would settle on Monday, December 5th (2 business days later) and would be on the record books for the distribution. Therefore, the stock is trading cum rights. The value of a right "cum rights" is:

$$\frac{\text{Market Price - Subscription Price}}{N + 1} = \text{Value "Cum Rights"}$$

$$\frac{\$30 - \$19}{10 + 1} = \frac{\$11}{11} = \$1 \text{ Value "Cum Rights"}$$

14. The best answer is **b**. The value of a right "ex rights" is:

$$\frac{\text{Adjusted Market Price - Subscription Price}}{N} = \text{Value "Ex Rights"}$$

$$\frac{\$29 - \$19}{10} = \frac{\$10}{10} = \$1 \text{ Value "Ex Rights"}$$

Notice that the market price of $29 was already adjusted on the ex date by the exchange where the stock trades. Do not try and reduce the price again!

15. The best answer is **c**. Stockholder approval is needed for a stock split, because it changes the par value of the stock. The State in which the company is incorporated typically requires shareholder approval of a par value change. In contrast, dividend decisions, either in cash or stock, do not require shareholder approval because they are "paid" out of retained earnings and do not affect par value per share. They are made solely by the Board of Directors of the company.

Issuance of convertible securities requires shareholder approval because it is potentially "dilutive" (if the securities are converted, there will be more common shares outstanding, and earnings per common share will fall). The repurchase of shares for Treasury will boost earnings per share, because there will be fewer shares outstanding. This boosts the value of the existing common shares, so no shareholder approval is required. This is another decision that is made solely by the Board of Directors.

16. The best answer is **b**. Treasury stock does not vote nor receive dividends. Treasury stock is deducted from outstanding shares, and since outstanding shares are reduced, Earnings Per Share increases.

17. The best answer is **c**. The common shareholder does not manage the company - this is the domain of the Board of Directors and corporate officers. The common shareholder does have the right to vote, receive a dividend, and to sell his shares.

18. The best answer is **b**. Common dividends are usually declared and paid quarterly.

19. The best answer is **d**. The customer receives a right for each common share held. Since he or she owns 200 shares, he or she gets 200 rights. 20 rights are needed to buy 1 new share, so 200 rights / 20 rights per share allows the purchase of 10 new shares.

20. The best answer is **b**. In a liquidation, common shareholders are paid last, after creditors, bondholders, and preferred stockholders.

This page intentionally left blank

SECTION 2: PREFERRED STOCK

2a. ISSUANCE OF PREFERRED STOCK

Senior Security

Priority Of Claim To Dividend And Corporate Assets

Preferred stock is termed a "senior" security because it has priority over the common stock issued by the company. If the company declares a dividend, preferred shareholders must receive the dividend before the common dividend can be paid. If the company liquidates, preferred shareholders are paid before common shareholders.

$100 Par

Fixed Dividend Rate

Semi-Annual Or Quarterly Payments

Preferred stock is typically issued at $100 par with a stated dividend rate. For example, a company issues $100 par 10% preferred stock. The annual dividend is 10% of $100 par = $10 per year. Preferred dividends are paid semi-annually by many companies (similar to bond interest payments), so each 6-month payment will be $5. Please note that there are a large number of companies that pay preferred dividends in a similar fashion to common dividends. These companies pay both common and preferred dividends quarterly, if declared by the Board.

Recent Issues Of Preferred Stock Are $50 Par Or $25 Par

A recent trend in preferred stock issuance is the offering of $50 par preferred stock and $25 par preferred stock. Many issuers are using these lower par values because they make a "round lot" (100 shares) more affordable to investors ($5,000 for a round lot of $50 par preferred or $2,500 for a round lot of $25 par preferred, as opposed to $10,000 for a round lot of $100 par preferred).

Preferred differs from common in that it pays a **fixed** dividend rate. Common dividends are a discretionary decision made by the Board of Directors. If the company's earnings improve, the Board may vote to increase the common dividend. Preferred shareholders do not enjoy this increase - they always get the same dollar dividend - a fixed percentage of par value.

The benefit for preferred shareholders is the known dividend rate and the priority of claim over common shareholders. But if the Board of Directors votes to omit a dividend, the preferred dividends are **not** paid and the preferred shareholders have no recourse.

Bought By Corporations With Excess Funds - 70% Of Dividends Received Are Not Taxable To Smaller Corporate Investor

The typical purchaser of preferred shares is a corporate treasurer with excess funds on hand. The tax code gives the corporate treasurer a big incentive to invest in stock. If the treasurer were to buy bonds, all of the interest income is taxable to the corporate owner of the bonds. But if the corporation buys stock and receives dividends, 70% of the dividends received are excluded from tax. (This applies if the position held is less than 20% of the outstanding stock. If 20% or more is held, the exclusion increases to 80%.) Unfortunately, individuals do not get this loophole, but they do get the benefit of a lower tax rate on both common and preferred dividends received (15%, raised to 20% for high-earning individuals).

Price Of Preferred Influenced By Interest Rate Moves

Once the preferred shares are issued, they trade in the market as does any other negotiable security. Unlike common stock, preferred stock price movements are not based on future expectations for the company. This makes sense since preferred does not share in earnings increases. Because preferred gets a fixed return, its price movement is influenced by interest rate movements.

2b. INTEREST RATE MOVEMENTS AND PREFERRED STOCK PRICES

Preferred Is Priced At Par At Issuance

When preferred stock is issued, the dividend rate printed on the issue is set at a level comparable with the market rate of interest at the time. For example, assume that the market rate of interest for similar securities is 10%. The market is "pricing" these securities to give a 10% rate of return. Therefore, a new preferred issue will be priced in the market to give a yield of 10%.

Current Yield

For preferred shares we can derive the theoretical market price from the Current Yield formula:

$$\text{Current Yield} = \frac{\text{Annual Income from Security}}{\text{Market Price of Security}}$$

$$10\% = \frac{\$10 \text{ Annual Dividends}}{? \text{ Market Price}}$$

Theoretical Market Price

Restated, the formula for the theoretical market price of the preferred stock is:

$$\text{Theoretical Market Price} = \frac{\text{Annual Income}}{\text{Market Yield}} \qquad = \frac{\$10}{10\%} = \$100$$

Therefore, this issue should sell in the market for $100. Since the issuer prints "$100 par" on the preferred shares, the issue sells at its par value.

Interest Rates Rise, Theoretical Price Must Fall

Once the issue is outstanding in the market, assume that interest rates in general rise to 20%. If this occurs, any new preferred issues will be sold with 20% dividend rates. To be competitive with the market, a holder of the old 10% preferred wishing to sell, must drop his price. The price must fall to a level where the old preferred will give a current yield of 20%. The new theoretical price is:

$$\text{Theoretical Market Price} = \frac{\text{Annual Income}}{\text{Market Yield}} \qquad = \frac{\$10}{20\%} = \$50$$

If interest rates double (as in this example), the price of the issue drops in half.

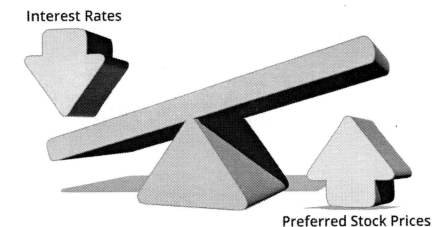

Preferred Stock Prices

Interest Rates

Interest Rates Fall, Theoretical Price Must Rise

On the other hand, assume that market interest rates fall to half the original level and are now at 5%. If this occurs, any newly issued preferred shares will be sold with 5% dividend rates. To be competitive with the market, a holder of old 10% preferred shares wishing to sell will get more than par. The price will rise to a level where the issue gives a current yield of 5%. The new theoretical price is:

$$\text{Theoretical Market Price} = \frac{\text{Annual Income}}{\text{Market Yield}} = \frac{\$10}{5\%} = \$200$$

If interest rates drop in half (as in this example), the price of the issue doubles.

Interest Rates

Preferred Stock Prices

The inverse relationship between interest rate movements and preferred stock prices also holds true for bond prices since they also make fixed payments.

2c. PREFERRED STOCK FEATURES

No Voting Or Preemptive Rights

Unlike common stock, preferred stock does not vote and does not have preemptive rights (since issuance of additional preferred shares does not dilute existing preferred holders' returns). We already know that the owner has preference to dividend distributions (paid semi-annually, though many preferred issues now pay dividends quarterly), and to company assets upon liquidation.

Preferred Stock Has Similar Features To Bonds

In reality, preferred stock is very similar to a bond. Bondholders also receive a fixed interest rate, paid semi-annually, and do not have voting or pre-emptive rights. The differences are:

- Bonds mature on a set date while preferred stock has an indefinite life;

- Bondholders have priority of claim to interest payments and corporate assets upon liquidation before preferred shareholders;

- Bondholders have a legal right to the interest payments; preferred dividends are only paid if declared by the Board of Directors.

Preferred stock features are very similar to bond features (covered in the Bonds chapter in detail). These features are:

- Cumulative
- Callable
- Convertible
- Participating
- Adjustable rate

Cumulative

Cumulative Preferred: If the issuer omits dividend payments, they "accumulate" and are paid **if** the issuer can ever resume making dividend payments. All accumulated preferred dividends must be paid, of course, in order to make a common dividend distribution.

Callable

Callable Preferred: The issuer has the right to "call in" the shares after a set date, usually at par. Issuers will call in the shares if interest rates have fallen. After retiring the old high rate shares, new preferred shares can be issued at the current lower rates (Call features are covered in detail in the Debt Securities chapter).

Convertible

Convertible Preferred: The preferred shareholder can "convert" his shares into the common stock of the issuer based on a predetermined price. If the market price of the common rises, the convertible's value is pushed up as well (since it can be turned into the common stock). In addition to the fixed dividend rate, convertible holders can enjoy capital gains if the price of the common stock moves up. The issuer can sell convertibles at lower dividend rates because of the value of the conversion feature.

Conversion Ratio

For example, an issuer sells $100 par convertible preferred stock, convertible at $25, when the market price of the common is $10 per share. The preferred stockholder has the right, at any time, to convert 1 preferred share at $100 par, into common at a price of $25 per share. Thus, the conversion ratio is: $100 par preferred / $25 conversion price = 4 common shares per preferred share.

To summarize, the formula for the conversion ratio is:

$$\text{Conversion Ratio} = \frac{\text{Par}}{\text{Conversion Price}}$$

Thus, this preferred stockholder can always convert into 4 shares of common. Also note that at issuance, the conversion feature has no value, since the preferred stockholder can convert based upon a common price of $25 per share; and the common is worth $10 per share at issuance. For the conversion feature to have value, the price of the common must rise above $25 in the market.

Parity Price

If the price of the common rises above $25 per share, the price of the preferred will rise; not because interest rates have fallen; but because the preferred is equivalent to 4 of those common shares. Thus, the preferred will trade at "parity" with the common.

Continuing from the previous example, if the common stock price rises to $30 per share, the preferred must be trading at a price equal to 4 times this amount, since each preferred share can be converted into 4 common shares. Thus, the preferred will be trading at 4 x $30 = $120 per share, not because interest rates have fallen, but because the price of the common has increased.

To summarize, the formula for the parity price of the preferred stock is:

Parity Price of Preferred = Market Price of Common x Conversion Ratio

Forced Conversion

When the price of the convertible preferred stock rises due to an increase in the market value of the common, if the issuer originally made the convertible preferred stock callable, then the issuer can "force conversion" of the preferred.

Continuing from the previous example, assume that the convertible preferred stock is callable at $110 per share by the issuer; and that the preferred is trading in the market at the current parity price of $120. If the issuer calls in the preferred stock, the preferred stockholder who tenders his or her shares will get $110 per share. If the preferred stockholder converts, he or she will get 4 shares of common, currently worth $30 each, receiving common stock with a total value of $120. This is the better deal for the customer, who is "forced" to convert, since if he does nothing, once the preferred is called, dividend payments cease.

By forcing conversion, the issuer eliminates the preferred stock on which it pays a higher fixed dividend rate; and replaces it with common shares on which it pays a lower dividend rate. Note that conversion can only be forced if the convertible preferred is trading at a premium to the call price.

Participating

Participating Preferred: In addition to the fixed dividend rate, the preferred "participates" in any "extra" dividends declared by the Board of Directors. For example, assume that ABC pays a $1.50 quarterly common dividend. After having an exceptionally strong year, the Board declares a special year-end dividend of $5.00. The preferred as well as the common will receive this dividend if the preferred has a "participating" feature.

Also Known As Performance Preferred Stock

Market Price Influenced Up If Extra Dividends Are Paid

Sometimes, participating preferred stock is referred to as "performance preferred," because the preferred shareholders are able to receive a higher dividend amount if the company's performance is better than usual. Note that the market price of performance preferred will not be directly interest rate sensitive, as is the case with straight preferred stock. If the company does well and pays an extra preferred dividend above the stated rate, this will tend to push the preferred stock price up - and this increase does not occur because market interest rates have fallen.

Adjustable Rate (Reset)

Adjustable Rate Preferred: This is a relatively new type of preferred stock. Instead of paying a "fixed" dividend rate, the dividend rate is "reset" periodically (usually once a year) to an index of market rates. If interest rates rise, the rate will increase at the reset date. If interest rates fall, the rate will decrease at the reset date. Sometimes this type of issue is called "reset" preferred.

Variable Rate Security Price Stays At, Or Close To, Par

Please note that with any "variable rate" security, because the interest or dividend rate is continually reset to the market, the price of the security stays at, or very close to, par. The inverse relationship between preferred stock prices and market interest rate levels does not hold for a variable rate security because as market interest rates move, the rate on the security is moved in tandem, so the price stays at par.

PREFERRED STOCK SECTION EXAMINATION

1.
Which of the following statements are **TRUE** about preferred stock?

I   Dividends are paid before common
II   Dividends are paid monthly
III   Dividends are based on corporate earnings
IV   Preferred shareholders have a prior claim to common shareholders

a.   I and II
b.   I and IV
c.   II, III, IV
d.   I, II, III, IV

2.
A customer buys 100 shares of preferred at $80 per share. The par value is $100. The dividend rate is 10%. The customer will receive how much in each dividend payment?

a. $400
b. $500
c. $800
d. $1,000

3.
Which statements are **TRUE** regarding the taxation of dividends received by investors?

I   Individuals cannot exclude any dividends received from taxation
II   Individuals can exclude 70% of dividends received from taxation
III   Corporations cannot exclude any dividends received from taxation
IV   Corporations can exclude 70% of dividends received from taxation

a.   I and III
b.   I and IV
c.   II and III
d.   II and IV

4.
All of the following are terms associated with preferred stock **EXCEPT**:

a.   callable
b.   cumulative
c.   redeemable
d.   convertible

5.
ABC Company has issued 8%, $100 par, cumulative preferred stock. Two years ago, ABC paid a 4% preferred dividend. Last year, ABC paid a 5% preferred stock dividend. This year, ABC wishes to pay a common dividend. If the preferred stock is now trading at $94, a customer who owns 100 shares of the company's preferred stock will receive:

a. $700
b. $800
c. $1,000
d. $1,500

6.
ABC 10% $100 par preferred is trading at $120 in the market. The current yield is:

a.   5%
b.   8.33%
c.   10%
d.   125

7.
As interest rates rise, preferred stock prices will:

a.   remain unaffected
b.   rise
c.   fall
d.   fluctuate

8.

Which statement is **BEST** regarding participating preferred stock?

- a. The dividend rate is fixed
- b. The dividend rate varies depending on the decision of the Board of Directors
- c. The dividend rate is fixed as to maximum but not as to minimum
- d. The dividend rate is fixed as to minimum but not as to maximum

9.

Callable preferred stock is likely to be redeemed by the issuer if:

- a. interest rates rise
- b. interest rates fall
- c. the common stock price rises
- d. the common stock price falls

10.

All of the following features are common to both preferred stock and bonds **EXCEPT**:

- a. fixed rate
- b. periodic payments
- c. can be callable
- d. fixed maturity date

PREFERRED STOCK EXAMINATION EXPLANATIONS

1. The best answer is **b**. Preferred stock dividends are paid before common dividends can be paid and preferred shareholders have a prior claim to assets in a liquidation before common shareholders. Whereas common dividends are typically paid quarterly, preferred dividends are typically paid semi-annually - similar to bond interest payments (remember, both preferred and bonds are fixed income securities; common stock is not).

2. The best answer is **b**. Preferred dividends are based on a stated percentage of par value. The stated rate is 10% of $100 par = $10 annual dividend per preferred share. Since there are 100 shares, the annual dividend is $1,000. Remember, though, that preferred dividends are paid twice a year, so each payment will be for $500.

3. The best answer is **b**. Corporations that receive dividends from investments held generally are allowed to exclude 70% of the dividends received from taxation. This exclusion does not apply to individual investors (however, individual investors get the benefit of taxation of cash dividends received at a substantially lower rate - 15% (or 20% for very high earners) - than do corporate investors). Thus, a corporation that receives dividends from common stock holdings, preferred stock holdings, or mutual fund holdings where the fund's income is from common and/or preferred stock investments, is allowed to exclude 70% of that income from taxation.

4. The best answer is **c**. Preferred stock is not a redeemable security - it is a negotiable security. The stock cannot be redeemed with the issuer - an investor who wishes to liquidate must sell the stock in the market. Preferred stock can be callable, cumulative, and convertible.

5. The best answer is **d**. Since this is cumulative preferred stock, all missed dividends must be paid before a common dividend can be paid. Two years ago, 4% was missed; last year 3% was missed; and this year's preferred dividend of 8% must be paid before the common dividend is paid. The total preferred dividend to be paid is 15%.

6. The best answer is **b**. The formula for current yield is:

$$\frac{\text{Annual Income}}{\text{Market Price}} = \text{Current Yield}$$

$$\frac{\$10}{\$120} = 8.33\%$$

7. The best answer is **c**. Preferred stock is a fixed income security whose prices move inversely with interest rates. As interest rates rise, preferred stock prices fall, so that the preferred will give a yield that is competitive with the current market.

8. The best answer is **d**. Participating preferred pays a fixed dividend rate but also participates with common in "extra" dividends declared by the Board of Directors. Therefore, the dividend rate is fixed as to minimum but not as to maximum.

9. The best answer is **b**. If interest rates fall, issuers can "call in" old high rate preferred and replace it by selling new preferred at the lower current rates. Thus, calls take place when interest rates have fallen.

10. The best answer is <u>**d**</u>. Preferred stock has no maturity - its life is indefinite. Bonds have a stated maturity date. Both preferred and bonds are fixed rate, can be callable, and typically make semi-annual payments to holders.

SECTION 3: SPECIAL SECURITIES AND FINANCIAL LISTINGS

3a. WARRANTS

Warrant Attached To New Stock Or Bond Issue

A warrant is a long term option to buy stock at a fixed price. Warrants are typically attached to the sale of a new stock or bond issue as a "sweetener" to make the issue more attractive.

Long Term Option To Buy Stock

For example, a new issue is being sold as a "unit" consisting of 1 common share and 1 warrant to purchase an additional common share. The common stock is valued at $20 and the warrant allows the purchase of the additional share at $30. The warrant expires in 5 years.

The warrant usually has a "wait" period before it can be exercised (e.g. 1 year). After the wait period, it can be exercised at the set price until expiration. It makes no sense to exercise unless the market price of the stock rises, in this case to at least $30.

Thus, warrants have an indeterminate value at issuance. But they are worth something and allow the issuer to raise the price (if it is stock) or lower the interest rate (if it is debt) of the issue to which the warrant is attached.

Exercise Price Set At Premium To Market Price At Issuance

Warrants are almost always issued at a substantial premium to the stock's current market price and only gain additional value if the common stock price rises. For example, assume that this warrant is valued in the market at $1. If the market price of the stock moves to $35, the warrant will be worth at least $5 since it allows the purchase of the stock at $30 per share.

Perpetual Warrant

Warrants usually have a life of 5 years, but sometimes perpetual warrants are issued. They trade separately from the common stock on the exchange where the stock is listed.

3b. RIGHTS

Very Short Term

A right is a short-term option to buy stock at a fixed price. Typically, rights are issued for 30-60 days and then expire. Rights are issued under an offering of new common shares to existing shareholders under their pre-emptive rights.

Rights offerings were covered in the Equities section. Rights trade separately from the stock on the exchange where the stock is listed.

3c. AMERICAN DEPOSITARY RECEIPTS (ADRs)

ADRs Are A Vehicle For Trading Foreign Securities In U.S.

Foreign companies can "list" their shares for trading on stock exchanges in the U.S. For example, one can buy Sony stock or British Telecom stock. When one buys these "shares," instead of getting stock certificates, the buyer gets American Depositary Receipts.

Foreign companies do not want their actual shares traded in the U.S. because the shares have to be registered in the U.S. with the Securities and Exchange Commission, and the company must follow SEC reporting rules. This is time consuming and expensive.

Bank Holds Foreign Securities In Country Of Origin And Then Issues Receipts In U.S. Backed By The Foreign Securities

These companies let someone else bother with all of these requirements - usually J. P. Morgan Chase or another large bank with offices in the country where the company is headquartered. The bank will buy up blocks of the stock and place it in trust in the country of origin. The bank then issues American Depositary Receipts which are backed by the securities held in trust. The ADRs are registered with the SEC and sold in the U.S.

Holder Has Dividend Rights

No Voting Or Preemptive Rights

As dividend payments are received, the bank passes these on to the receipt holder. When doing this, the bank converts the dividend received in the foreign currency into U.S. dollars (and banks make big money on the conversion fee charged, which is the economic reason why banks sponsor ADR programs). But the receipt holder does not have voting or preemptive rights. The bank votes the shares that it owns and it will sell off preemptive rights and remit the money to the receipt holder.

Sponsored ADRs

Commonly Known As American Depositary Shares

Sponsored ADRs Trade On Exchanges

An ADR can represent one share of the underlying stock, multiple shares, or fractional shares. All exchange listed ADRs are "sponsored," that is, the foreign company "sponsors" the issue to increase its worldwide ownership base. Sponsored ADRs only use one depositary bank (such as J. P. Morgan Chase), which is appointed by the issuer. Issuers that sponsor ADRs provide quarterly and annual financial reports to shareholders in English. Sponsored ADRs are often called American Depositary Shares or ADSs. Sponsored ADRs are listed and trade on the NYSE, AMEX-MKT (the "new" name for the AMEX), and NASDAQ exchanges.

Non-Sponsored ADRs

Non-Sponsored ADRs Trade OTC

Non-sponsored ADRs are assembled by banks and broker-dealers without the issuer's participation. An unsponsored program may have more than one depositary bank, since the issuer does not participate in any way. Holders of non-sponsored ADRs receive annual reports only in the language of the issuer. Non-sponsored ADRs trade "over-the-counter."

Dividends Declared In Foreign Currency

Dividends Converted And Paid In Dollars

Also, please note, dividends on ADRs are declared by the foreign company in the local currency, and are then converted into U.S. dollars and remitted to the receipt holders by the intermediary bank. The market prices of ADRs will therefore be influenced not only by the performance of the company's stock, but also by foreign currency exchange fluctuations.

Exchange Rate Risk

The risk of currency exchange fluctuation is called "exchange rate risk." For the holder of a security denominated in a foreign currency, the risk is that the foreign currency weakens against the U.S. dollar (this is the same as the U.S. dollar strengthening). In such a case, when the foreign holding is converted to its value in U.S. dollars, because the weaker foreign currency buys "fewer" U.S. dollars, it is worth less in U.S. dollar terms.

Foreign Taxes Withheld - Credit On U.S. Return

On dividends received from ADRs, the country of origin can withhold local taxes, but such taxes can be claimed as a credit against U.S. taxes due on dividends received.

3d. SAMPLE STOCK EXCHANGE LISTING

Equities Quoted In Dollars And Cents Per Share

Equity securities are quoted in dollars and cents, in minimum price movements of $.01.

(Also note that listed options are also quoted in decimals, but instead of a minimum price movement of $.01, the minimum price change is $.05. However, please note that, in contrast, quotes for U.S. Government, corporate bonds, and municipal bonds are **NOT** decimalized. Quotes for debt instruments are covered in the Debt chapter.)

New York Stock Exchange Composite Transactions

| 52 Week | | | | | Yld | P-E | Sales | | | | Net |
High	Low	Stock	SYM	Div.	%	Ratio	100s	High	Low	Close	Chg.
35.50	13.13	PG&E	PGE	.52	3.2	15	1190	16.50	16.25	16.38	+.13
25.00	12.75	PG&E pf		1.37	8.9	...	2	15.50	15.38	15.38	...
5.50	2.38	ParTch	PTC	...	...	...	4722	2.75	2.50	2.75	+.25
1.88	.44	ParTch wt		...	...		25	.57	.57	.57	+.06
31.38	13.00	ParkerHan x	PH	.58	2.2	13	120	23.00	22.75	22.75	-.25
33.38	16.50	Pearson ADS	PSD	1.08e	5.8	8	372	18.75	18.50	18.63	+.13

The first 2 columns give the highest and lowest prices for the stock during the past year. For example, Pacific Gas and Electric (PGE) traded as high as $35.50 per share and as low as $13.13 per share during the past year.

"pf," "wt," "x," ADR, ADS

The third column gives the name of the security. For example, the second Pacific Gas and Electric listing is "pf"- preferred stock. The second Par Technology listing is "wt"-warrant. The Parker Hanifen listing is "x" - this is the "ex" date and the price of the stock was reduced that morning for the distribution. Pearson is a British publishing company - these are not common shares but are ADSs - American Depositary Shares.

Stock Symbol

The fourth column gives the stock's listing symbol. For example, the symbol for Pacific Gas and Electric is "PGE." NYSE listed stocks use a maximum of 3 letters in their symbols; NASDAQ stocks use 4 letters.

However, in 2007, in a move to make it easier for companies to move their stock listings from one market to another, the SEC permitted companies to move from NASDAQ to NYSE; or from the NYSE to NASDAQ, without having to change their ticker symbol. The NYSE and NASDAQ compete fiercely for stock listings and companies often move.

Ticker Symbol For NYSE Listed Companies Is Usually 3 Letters Or Less

Ticker Symbol For NASDAQ Listed Companies Is Usually 4 Letters

So now, you will find 3 letter symbol stocks traded on NASDAQ (these were companies that moved from the NYSE) and 4 letter symbol stocks traded on the NYSE (these were companies that moved from NASDAQ). To further the blurring here, new companies listing on either market can now pick their symbol using 1, 2, 3, or 4 letters. However, the vast majority of NYSE listed issues still have ticker symbols with 3 letters or less; and the vast majority of NASDAQ stocks have 4 letter symbols.

Stock Symbol Sources

Currently, the easiest way to find a stock symbol is to go to the finance section of any internet portal such as MSN or AOL and do a search. The Wall Street Journal only includes the "bigger" stocks in the printed newspaper - however, all domestic stock symbols can be found on its web site. Investor's Business Daily still includes the stock symbol in its listings. Other general interest newspapers usually don't include the stock symbol. Finally, to find a stock symbol, one can go to the Internet.

The fifth column gives the annual dividend rate; an "e" next to the rate means the amount is estimated. Pacific Gas and Electric (PG&E) common pays $.52 per share in common dividends. PG&E preferred pays $1.37 per share in preferred dividends.

The sixth column gives the dividend yield. The formula for dividend yield is the same as current yield:

Current Yield

$$\text{Dividend or Current Yield} = \frac{\text{Annual Income}}{\text{Market Price}}$$

For example, the current yield of Pacific Gas and Electric common is 3.2% from the table. This is computed as:

$$\frac{\text{Annual Income}}{\text{Market Price}} = \frac{\$.52}{\$16.38} = 3.2\%$$

P/E Ratio

The seventh column gives the Price-Earnings ratio for the stock. The Price-Earnings Ratio is:

$$\text{Price / Earnings Ratio} = \frac{\text{Market Price of Security}}{\text{Earnings per Share}}$$

Earnings Per Share

For Pacific Gas and Electric common, the ratio is 15, and the stock is said to be selling at a "multiple" of 15 times earnings. From the information presented, the earnings per share can also be computed. We know that the multiple is 15 and the stock closed at $16.38. To find the Earnings per Share, divide the price by the multiple.

The Earnings per Share (EPS) for Pacific Gas and Electric common is:

$$\text{Earnings per Share} = \frac{\text{Market Price}}{\text{"Multiple"}} = \frac{\$16.375}{15} = \$1.09$$

Trading Unit - 100

The eighth column gives the number of shares traded that day. Stocks, warrants and rights are traded in round lots of 100. 1,190 units of 100 Pacific Gas and Electric common shares were traded this day, so a total of 119,000 shares traded.

The ninth column gives the highest price the security traded at that day.

The tenth column gives the lowest price the security traded at that day.

The eleventh column gives the closing price that day. For example, Par Technology warrants closed at $.57 per warrant.

The twelfth column gives the change in price from the preceding day's close. Today, Pacific Gas and Electric common closed at $16.38, up $.13 from yesterday's close. This means that Pacific Gas and Electric closed $.13 **lower** yesterday at $16.25.

3e. SAMPLE STANDARD AND POOR'S DIVIDEND RECORD / STOCK GUIDE

Standard and Poor's Corporation compiles corporate dividend announcements and publishes a monthly report.

As dividends are announced quarterly, they are added to the listing. By the end of the year, 4 quarterly common dividends would show for companies that are making regular distributions. If at year end, the company has announced a dividend to be paid in the next year, this is also included in the listing.

At the beginning of the new year, the listing starts over with the dividends for that year. The listing also includes any stock dividends or special (extra year end) dividends.

Following is a sample of the Standard and Poor's Dividend Record:

DIVIDEND PAYMENTS 2017
STANDARD and POOR'S DIVIDEND RECORD

Div$.	Dec.	Ex.	Stk Rec.	Pay.
Acme Mot. - Cmn p$1				
Rate - .75Q Pd '17 3.00 '16 2.50				
.75	Dec 9	Jan 19	Jan 20	Jan 30 '17
.75	Mar 17	Apr 18	Apr 19	Apr 28
.75	Jun 16	Jul 20	Jul 21	Jul 31
.75	Sep 15	Oct 19	Oct 20	Oct 30
.75	Dec 8	Jan 18	Jan 19	Jan 29 '18

Reading from left to right, the report gives the Dividend Amount, Declaration Date, Ex-Dividend Date, Record Date and Payable Date.

The stock is Acme Motor Company $1 par common. The current dividend rate is $.75 quarterly. During 2017, $3.00 of dividends were paid. In 2016, $2.50 in dividends were paid, so the dividend rate was raised during 2016.

This is a listing from December 2017. Notice that the four dividends paid in 2017 are included as well as the dividend of $.75 to be paid on Jan 29th, 2018.

To see if you understand the listing, answer the following questions:

In order to receive the dividend payable Jan 29th, 2018, a customer must settle a purchase of the stock by which date?

Answer: The customer must be on record as of Jan 19th, so the purchase must settle by this date.

In order to receive the dividend payable July 31st, the stock must be purchased in a regular way trade before which date?

Answer: The stock must be purchased before the ex-date of July 20th.

How much in dividends were paid in 2016?

Answer: $2.50 per share was paid in 2016.

How much in dividends are expected to be paid in 2018?

Answer: The current rate is $.75 per quarter, so the indicated annual rate in 2018 is $3.00.

Standard And Poor's "Stock Guide"

Migrated To The Internet - Now Part S&P Net Advantage

Aside from the "Dividend Record," Standard and Poor's ("S&P") also produces the "Stock Guide" for equity securities (both common and preferred) of Exchange listed and large corporations traded "Over the Counter," the Stock Guide used to be printed monthly, but has been migrated to the Internet by S&P Net Advantage. The Stock Guide gives the following information:

- Ticker Symbol And Name Of Issue;
- Standard & Poor's Issuer Rating;
- Par Value;
- Shares Held By Institutions;
- Principal Business;
- Price Range Of Stock For Last 16 Years;
- Sales For That Month;
- High Price, Low Price, Closing Price For Month;
- If There Has Been A Recent Stock Split;
- Dividends Paid (Last Payment Only);
- Dividends Paid Year To Date And In Prior Year;
- Financial Position Of Corporation;
- Earnings Per Share (Past 5 Years);
- If The Stock Is In the S&P 500 Average.

Finding Ticker Symbol

Investors use the "Stock Guide" as a general information source for equity issues. For example, the Guide is an easy source to find the symbol under which a stock is traded. As another example, to quickly find a company's earnings per share, the Guide is the good place to look.

SPECIAL SECURITIES AND FINANCIAL LISTINGS SECTION EXAMINATION

1.
All of the following statements about warrants are true **EXCEPT**:

    a.   warrants have a longer term than rights

    b.   warrants are issued to make corporate senior securities offerings more attractive to investors

    c.   warrants give the holder a perpetual interest in the issuer's underlying common stock

    d.   warrants trade separately from the stock of the company

2.
American Depositary Receipts pay dividends in:

    I   U.S. Dollars
    II   Eurodollars
    III   European Currency Units
    IV   Foreign Currency

    a.   I only
    b.   I and II
    c.   III and IV
    d.   I, II, III, IV

3.
Which statement is **TRUE** about the time value and intrinsic value of rights and warrants when issued?

    a.   Both have time value and intrinsic value at issuance

    b.   Warrants have time value and rights have intrinsic value at issuance

    c.   Warrants have intrinsic value and rights have time value at issuance

    d.   Neither has time value or intrinsic value at issuance

4.
Which statements are **TRUE** regarding ADRs?

    I   ADRs are vehicles for trading United States securities in foreign countries

    II   ADRs are vehicles for trading foreign securities in the United States

    III   ADR market prices are influenced by foreign currency exchange fluctuations

    IV   ADR market prices are not influenced by foreign currency exchange fluctuations

    a.   I and III
    b.   I and IV
    c.   II and III
    d.   II and IV

5.
Which of the following sources could be consulted to find the symbol of an NYSE listed security?

    I   Federal Register
    II   NYSE web site
    III   Standard and Poor's Stock Guide

    a.   I only
    b.   I and II
    c.   II and III
    d.   I, II, III

6.
ABC Corp. has a market price of $15 and a Price/Earnings multiple of 10. What was the corporation's Earnings Per Common Share?

    a. $.67
    b. $1.50
    c. $10
    d.   This cannot be determined

7.

A corporation is offering a new issue consisting of 100,000 units at $200 each. Each unit consists of 2 shares of preferred stock and a warrant to buy one half additional common share. A full warrant allows the purchase of an additional common share at $5. If all the warrants are exercised, the corporation will have outstanding:

a. 100,000 preferred shares and 100,000 common shares

b. 200,000 preferred shares and 100,000 common shares

c. 200,000 preferred shares and 50,000 common shares

d. 50,000 preferred shares and 100,000 common shares

8.

The exercise price of a warrant is set at issuance at:

a. a discount to the market price of the common stock

b. a premium to the market price of the common stock

c. the market price of the common stock

d. any price designated by the issuer

9.

ADRs are used to:

a. facilitate trading of domestic securities in foreign countries

b. facilitate trading of foreign securities in the United States

c. allow trading of rights on exchanges

d. allow trading of warrants on exchanges

10.

All of the following statements are true about ADRs **EXCEPT:**

a. ADRs trade on national stock exchanges

b. ADR holders receive dividends

c. ADR holders can vote for the Board of Directors

d. ADR holders receive the cash value of pre-emptive rights

SPECIAL SECURITIES AND FINANCIAL LISTINGS
EXAMINATION EXPLANATIONS

1. The best answer is **c**. Warrants are long term options to buy a company's shares at a fixed price. They are typically attached to debt and preferred stock offerings (securities that are "senior" to the common stock of the issuer) to make the securities more attractive to purchasers. This is accomplished because the warrant gives growth potential to these senior security holders if the common stock price should rise in the future. Warrants typically have a fixed life of 5 years or less and then expire. Companies can issue perpetual warrants, but rarely do so.

2. The best answer is **a**. American Depositary Receipts pay dividends in U.S. Dollars only. The dividends are declared and paid in the foreign currency by the issuer. The bank that issues the ADR exchanges the dividend that was received in the foreign currency into U.S. Dollars and pays this to the U.S. ADR holders.

3. The best answer is **b**. Warrants are long term options (usually 5 years) that allow the holder to buy the stock at a substantial premium to the current market price. Therefore, the stock's price must rise substantially over time for the warrant to have any real monetary value. They have no intrinsic value at issuance; but they have 5 years of "time value."

Rights are very short term options (30-60 days) granted to existing shareholders that allow them to buy the stock at a discount to the current market price. The discount is the "intrinsic value" of the right. However, because they are so short term, they have virtually no "time value."

4. The best answer is **c**. ADRs are vehicles for trading foreign securities in the United States. Foreign companies do not want their actual shares traded in the U.S. because the shares would then have to be registered with the SEC (and what time and money would have to be spent on that!) Since dividends on ADRs are declared by the foreign company in local currency, and are then converted into U.S. dollars and remitted to the receipt holders by the depositary bank, market prices of ADRs will be influenced not only by the performance of the company's stock, but also by foreign currency exchange fluctuations.

5. The best answer is **c**. To find the symbol of a stock, one could consult (among other sources) the Standard and Poor's Stock Guide, which is now part of an S&P web service called Net Advantage. It gives capsule summaries of company history and performance. Of course, the easiest way is just to "Google" the stock symbol or go to a finance portal on the web. The exchange web site on which the security is traded also will have a search function for stock symbols. The Federal Register is where newly enacted regulations are published by the Federal Government, and has nothing to do with stock symbols.

6. The best answer is **b**. The Earnings per Share can be found by taking the:

$$\frac{\text{Market Price}}{\text{Multiple}} = \text{Earnings Per Share}$$

$$\frac{15}{10} = \$1.50$$

7. The best answer is **c**. Each unit consists of 2 preferred shares x 100,000 units equals 200,000 preferred shares issued and a warrant for 1/2 common share. If the warrants are exercised, 100,000 units x 1/2 common share = 50,000 common shares issued.

8. The best answer is **b**. At issuance, the exercise price of a warrant is set at a premium to the stock's current market price.

9. The best answer is **b**. American Depositary Receipts are the means by which foreign securities are traded in the United States.

10. The best answer is **c**. ADRs do not vote. The bank that actually owns the shares votes. The bank passes through dividends to receipt holders and sells off pre-emptive rights, sending the cash to the receipt holders. ADRs are listed on stock exchanges and trade like any other stock.

This page intentionally left blank

DEBT

Debt Securities

DEBT

DEBT

Debt Securities

DEBT

SECTION 1: BOND BASICS

1a. BASIC BOND TERMS

Bond Definition

A bond is a debt security which obligates the issuer to pay interest (usually semi-annually) and to repay the principal amount when the debt matures.

Par Value

Stated Interest Rate

Bonds are issued with a stated par value (usually $1,000 minimum) and a stated rate of interest on the debt. For example, a $1,000 par value bond is issued with a stated rate of interest of 8% by ABC Corporation in 2017. The maturity on the debt is 2037. ABC must pay $80 of interest annually to the bondholder for each of the 20 years the bond is outstanding.

Redemption

At maturity, ABC Corporation must repay the $1,000 principal amount to the bondholder. The bond is redeemed by the issuer at par.

Zero-Coupon Bond

Bonds can also be issued with a stated par value (usually $1,000 minimum) but without a stated rate of interest. No semi-annual interest payments are made on these "zero-coupon" bonds. Instead the bonds are purchased at a discount from par and are redeemed at maturity at par value.

1b. BOND ISSUE STRUCTURE

Term Bonds

A bond issue where every bond has the same interest rate and maturity is called a term bond issue. Corporate bond issues and U.S. Government bond issues are typically term bonds.

> For example, in 2017, ABC Corporation issues $1,000,000 of 8%, $1,000 par bonds, all maturing in 2037. Each and every $1,000 bond within the issue is identical - same maturity and interest rate.

Serial Bonds

A bond issue with differing maturities is a serial bond issue. Because of the nature of interest rates, differing maturities require different interest rates. Thus, both the maturities and stated interest rates differ for the bonds in the issue. Most municipal bond issues and corporate equipment trust certificates are serial bonds.

> For example, in 2017, the City of Los Angeles issues $10,000,000 of serial bonds with the following schedule:

Debt Securities

Maturity	Interest rate	Amount
2023	5.20%	$1,000,000
2024	5.30%	$1,000,000
2025	5.40%	$1,000,000
2026	5.50%	$1,000,000
2027	5.60%	$1,000,000
2028	6.00%	$5,000,000

Balloon Maturity

Each maturity has a different interest rate on the bond. This is natural because the longer the maturity, the higher the interest rate that investors demand. Note in this example that the majority of the bonds will mature in 2028 - this is called a balloon maturity.

Series Bonds

A bond issue where the bonds have the same maturity but different dates of issuance is a series bond issue. Series bonds are rarely issued, and are used to finance long-term construction projects where all of the money is not needed at once. Instead of floating a $10,000,000 bond issue today to build a new plant, a corporation could float a series bond issue, selling $5,000,000 of bonds this year, $3,000,000 next year, and $2,000,000 the following year, for a total issue of $10,000,000. By phasing in the bonds, the total interest cost to the issuer is reduced.

1c. BOND PRICE QUOTES

Term bonds are quoted on a percentage of par basis. This is the same as quoting the bonds on a dollar price basis. Because of this, term bonds are also known as dollar bonds.

Corporate Bonds % Of Par In 1/8ths

Corporate bonds are quoted as a percentage of par value; with minimum changes of 1/8th point.

For example, ABC Corporation debentures are quoted at 101 3/8. The dollar price of a $1,000 par bond is 101.375% of $1,000 par = $1,013.75

Government Bonds % Of Par In 1/32nds

U.S. Government bonds are quoted as a percentage of par value, with minimum changes of 1/32nd point.

For example, a U.S. Treasury Bond is quoted at 99.24. The dollar price of a $1,000 par bond is 99 and 24/32% of par = 99 and .75 % = 99.75% of $1,000 par = $997.50.

Both corporate bonds and government bonds are quotable on a percentage of par basis because they are term bonds. Each and every bond within a term issue is identical and therefore has the same dollar price. The reason why governments are quoted in 32nds whereas corporates are quoted in 1/8ths is because the government trading market is much more active and traders are willing to trade on narrower margins (known as spreads). Some government dealers quote in 1/64ths instead of 32nds.

Note that bond quotes are a throwback to the "good old days." Before the year 2000, stocks and corporate bonds were quoted in minimum increments of 1/8th point - which dates back to silver coins used in the American colonies in the 1700's that were made in Spain that could be fractioned into 1/2s, 1/4s, and 1/8ths. The term used was "pieces of eight." (There's some worthless history for you!)

As stock trading volumes skyrocketed in the 1980s with the introduction of computerized trading, the SEC pressed the stock exchanges to narrow their spreads, which makes the market more "efficient" and lowers costs to end users. Of course, the market makers did not want this, because wider spreads meant that they could earn bigger profits. The resistance of the market makers was finally overcome in the year 2000, when stock prices were first required to be quoted in pennies. However, the bond markets were never in the SEC's crosshairs - the corporate bond market has never had high trading volumes; and the SEC has no authority to regulate the Treasury bond market (this is covered in a later chapter). Thus, these markets are still quoted in 1/8ths (corporate bonds) or 32nds (Treasury bonds).

Municipal Serial Bonds - Basis Quotes

Municipal bond issues are generally serial bonds. In a serial bond offering, each maturity has a different interest rate. This means that each maturity has a different value, and therefore has a different market price. It would be very cumbersome to quote different market prices for each of the maturities within an issue. Instead, serial bonds are quoted on a "yield basis," also known as a basis quote.

> For example, a municipal dealer quotes the 2026 5.50% bond of Los Angeles (listed in the preceding section) on a 5.50 basis. This means he or she is offering the bond to the purchaser at a price to yield 5.50%. Since the coupon is 5.50%, this bond will be priced at par.

Basis Points

Basis quotes are in "yields." A quote of 5.50% is a bond priced to yield 5.50%. If the quote were 5.60, the bond is priced to yield 5.60%. The difference between the 5.50 and 5.60 quotes is a change of 10 basis points. One basis point equals .01% on a bond. Ten basis points equal .1%. One hundred basis points equal one full point or 1%.

To convert a basis quote into a dollar price requires the use of a bond calculator. The use of such a calculator is not permitted in the exam. Instead, the relationship between the coupon rate and the basis must be known.

When bonds are originally issued, the interest rate placed on the bonds is set at the current market rate, so that the issue will be priced at par. If market interest rates stay the same after the issuance date, the bonds will trade at par.

Price At Par

Assuming that it is now 2017, a bond maturing in 2026 has nine years to maturity. The coupon rate on the bond is 5 1/2% - this is the rate of interest that is printed on the $1,000 par bond certificate. If the bond is being offered at a price quoted to a 5.50% yield, or "basis," the price will be 100.00% of par.

Since the amount of interest received per $1,000 par bond does not change (the holder receives 5.50% of $1,000 = $55 of annual interest), if market interest rates move up after the bond has been issued, the price of the bond must fall below par, so that the bond gives a competitive yield to the current market.

Price At Discount

If the 5.50% coupon bond were quoted on a 6.00% basis, then the price would be 96.56% of par value, or $965.60 for every $1,000 par bond (this is from a bond calculator). This bond is selling at a discount. In order to increase the yield on the bond, above the stated coupon rate, the dealer had to lower the price below par.

Since the amount of interest received per $1,000 par bond does not change (the holder receives 5.50% of $1,000 = $55 of annual interest), if market interest rates move down after the bond has been issued, the price of the bond must rise above par, so that the bond gives a competitive yield to the current market.

Price At Premium

If the 5.50% bond were quoted on a 5.00% basis, then the price would be 103.59% of par value, or $1,035.90 for every $1,000 par bond (this is from a bond calculator). This bond is selling at a premium. In order to decrease the yield on the bond below the stated coupon rate, the dealer had to raise the price above par.

To summarize, corporate and government bonds are quoted on a percentage of par basis because they are term bonds. Any municipal issues which are term bonds are also quoted on a percentage of par basis, and are known as dollar bonds.

To Find Approximate Price Of Long Term Bond Quoted On A Yield Basis = Coupon / Basis

Municipal serial bonds are quoted on a yield basis. In order to find the dollar price from a basis quote, a bond calculator must be used. When a municipal serial bond is quoted on a yield basis, a "rough" approximation of the dollar price can be made, but it is only valid for long-term (20 year+ maturity) bonds.

To find the approximate price of a long-term municipal serial bond quoted on a yield basis, just divide the coupon by the basis.

For example, a municipal bond dealer quotes a 30 year 4% General Obligation bond on a 5.00 basis. The approximate price of this bond is:

$$\frac{4\% \text{ Coupon}}{5\% \text{ Basis}} = 80\% \text{ of } \$1,000 \text{ Par} = \$800$$

For example, a municipal bond dealer quotes a 30 year 6% General Obligation bond on a 5.00 basis. The approximate price of this bond is:

$$\frac{6\% \text{ Coupon}}{5\% \text{ Basis}} = 120\% \text{ of } \$1,000 \text{ Par} = \$1,200$$

Thus, if the "basis" is higher than the coupon, the bond is trading at a discount; and if the "basis" is lower than the coupon, the bond is trading at a premium.

1d. THE EFFECT OF INTEREST RATE MOVEMENTS ON BOND PRICES

In the previous section, basis quotes were used to show bonds selling at a discount and bonds selling at a premium.

Discount Bond

By definition, a bond sells at a discount when par value is in excess of the bond's purchase price.

For example, a $1,000 par corporate bond quoted at 90 is selling at a discount of 10 points ($100) from par.

Premium Bond

By definition, a bond sells at a premium when the bond's purchase price is in excess of par value.

For example, a $1,000 par corporate bond quoted at 110 is selling at a premium of 10 points ($100) over par.

When a bond is issued, the coupon rate on the bond is set at a level that is comparable to the market rate of interest at that time. If the yield that is demanded by the market is the same as the bond's coupon rate, then the bond will sell in the market at par value.

Interest Rates Up - Bond Prices Down

The bond is now trading in the secondary market. Assume that the bond has a 5.50% coupon rate. As long as market yields for this type of bond are at 5.50%, the dollar price will be par. But what happens if interest rates rise in general? Assume that interest rates in general rise to 6%. This bond yields only 5.50% if it is priced at par. To be competitive with the market, the price of the bond must drop to a level where this bond yields 6%. Therefore, when interest rates rise, the prices of bonds trading in the secondary market must drop.

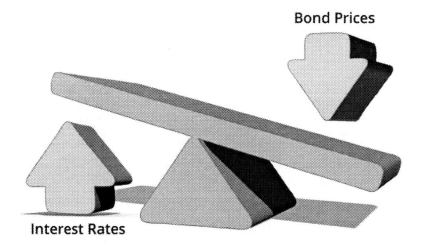

Bond Prices

Interest Rates

Interest Rates Down - Bond Prices Up

On the other hand, what happens if interest rates fall in general? Assume that interest rates in general fall to 5%. This bond yields 5.50% if it is priced at par. To be competitive with the market, the price of the bond will rise to a level where this bond yields 5%. Therefore, when interest rates fall, the prices of bonds trading in the secondary market must rise.

Interest Rates

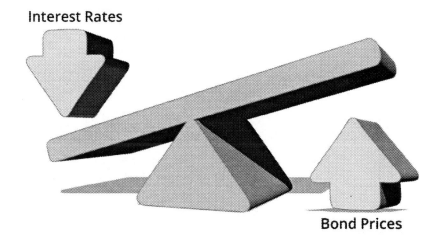

Bond Prices

To summarize:

- When interest rates **RISE**, bond prices **FALL**;
- When interest rates **FALL**, bond prices **RISE**.

Longer Maturity - Greater Volatility

Another factor to consider is that, as interest rates move, bond prices do not move by equal amounts. The longer a bond's maturity, the faster the bond's price will move in response to interest rate changes. This is due to the compounding effect of interest rates on the bond's value.

A bond can be visualized as having 2 components - these are:

- The stream of interest payments over the life of the bond; and
- The final principal repayment.

The actual current market price of the bond is the "present value" of the stream of future interest payments and the final principal repayment, discounted by the current market rate of interest (this is essentially the reverse of interest compounding).

Shorter Maturity - Lower Volatility

Most Of Bond's Value Is In Final Principal Repayment

Most of a bond's value is in the big final principal repayment. If the repayment will happen soon (a short maturity), then the price cannot move much from par as market interest rates move. If repayment is far in the future, then the "present value" of that large principal payment is greatly discounted to today's value, compounded over many years. Due to this greater compounding effect, the current price of the bond can move greatly as market interest rates move.

Lower Coupon - Greater Volatility

The lower the coupon rate on a given bond, the greater the price volatility of that bond in response to market interest rate movements. Again, bonds can be visualized as having 2 components:

- the stream of interest payments over the life of the bond: and
- the final principal repayment.

Bonds with low interest rates have more of the bond's "present value" in the final principal repayment; and less of the bond's value in the interest stream that is received sooner. If most of a bond's value is in the big final principal repayment that is received at the end of a bond's life, then the "present value" of that large principal payment is greatly discounted to today's value, compounded over many years. Due to this greater compounding effect, the current price of the bond can move greatly as market interest rates move.

Higher Coupon - Lower Volatility

Conversely, bonds with high interest rates have more of the bond's "present value" in the interest payment stream that is received sooner; and less of the bond's value in the final principal repayment that happens at the end of a bond's life. Because most of the value is in the high interest payments that are received sooner, the "present value" of these cannot be discounted as greatly since they are received much earlier. Due to this lesser compounding effect, the current price of the bond cannot move greatly as market interest rates move. To summarize, as market interest rates move:

- Long Maturity bond prices move more rapidly than do short maturity issues.

- Short Maturity bond prices move less rapidly than do long maturity issues.

- Low Coupon (Discount) bond prices move more rapidly than do high coupon (premium) bond prices.

- High Coupon (Premium) bond prices move less rapidly than do low coupon (discount) bond prices.

As market interest rates move up, the percentage downward price movement of bonds, ranked from greatest percentage movement to lowest, is:

- Large Discount Bond (lowest coupon)
- Small Discount Bond
- Par Bond
- Small Premium Bond
- Large Premium Bond (highest coupon)

Long Term Zero Coupon Issues Are Most Volatile

Thus, the most volatile bonds are deep discount long-term maturities. Bonds with low coupon rates will tend to trade at discounts - with the most steeply discounted issues being zero-coupon bonds. Such bonds have no interest payments - the entire value is in the final principal repayment at maturity. Long-term zero coupon issues are the most volatile of all bond issues.

Macaulay Duration

A formalized measure of bond price volatility is called "duration" - invented by Frederick Macaulay in the 1930s. Duration is defined as the weighted average term-to-maturity of a security's cash flows. Translated into "plain English," duration is the length of time it takes for the price of the bond to be repaid by its internal cash flows.

The formula to compute duration does not have to be known. However, when duration is computed, it turns out that:

- The longer the maturity, the greater the duration; and;
- The lower the coupon, the greater the duration.

This should sound familiar. Bonds with the biggest duration numbers are those with long maturities and low coupons - these are the most volatile bonds. Bonds with the lowest duration numbers are those with short maturities and high coupons - these are the least volatile bonds.

Following is a comparison of bonds with the same coupon but different maturities, with their durations:

Bond	Duration
5 year; 6% coupon	4.39
20 year; 6% coupon	11.90

As an example, this is telling us that if interest rates rise by 1/2% (50 basis points), then the price of the:

5 year bond will fall by: .5% x 4.39 = 2.20%.

20 year bond will fall by: .5% x 11.90 = 5.95%

Thus, the longer maturity bond moves faster in price, as market interest rates move.

Below is a comparison of bonds with the same maturities but different coupons, with their durations:

Bond	Duration
5 year; 0% coupon	5.00
5 year; 6% coupon	4.39
5 year; 9% coupon	4.19

As an example, this is telling us that if interest rates rise by 1/2% (50 basis points), then the price of the:

0% coupon bond will fall by: .5% x 5.00 = 2.50%
6% coupon bond will fall by: .5% x 4.39 = 2.20%
9% coupon bond will fall by: .5% x 4.19 = 2.09%

Thus, the lower coupon bond moves faster in price as market interest rates move.

Zero-Coupon Bond Duration Is The Time To Maturity

As a final note, for a zero-coupon bond, the number of years to maturity is the bond's duration, because the bondholder receives all cash at that point in time. In contrast, bonds that make periodic interest payments return cash faster, so their duration will be lower.

1e. BOND YIELDS

Assume that a corporate bond dealer is offering a 10 year, 10% bond at a price of 90. This bond is being offered at a discount, therefore the true yield of the bond is higher than the stated yield. The relevant yields are:

Nominal Yield

Nominal Yield, which is the stated rate of interest on the bond. The bond's stated rate of interest is 10% of $1,000 par.

Current Yield

Current Yield, which takes into account the market price of the bond. The formula for current yield is:

$$\text{Current Yield} = \frac{\text{Annual Interest in Dollars}}{\text{Bond's Market Price}} = \frac{\$100}{\$900} = 11.11\%$$

Note that the current yield is higher than the nominal yield, since the discount price is taken into account.

Yield To Maturity

Yield to Maturity, which takes into account both the market price of the bond as well as any capital gains or losses on the bond if held to maturity.

When a bond is bought at a discount from par, the discount is "earned" over the life of the bond. This capital gain is pro-rated over the bond's life to include the effect of the annual capital gain on the bond's yield. The annual capital gain for this bond can be visualized as follows:

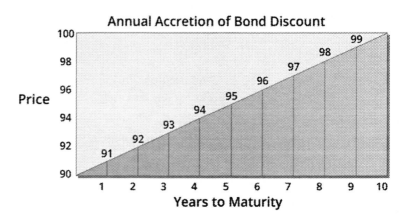

This bond is being purchased at a discount price of 90% of $1,000 par, or $900. The bond will mature at par in 10 years. The discount of $100 is being earned over 10 years, so each year $10 of the discount is earned. This is termed the annual accretion of the bond discount.

The formula for yield to maturity is:

$$\text{Yield to Maturity} = \frac{\text{Annual Income} \quad \begin{array}{c} \text{+ Annual Capital Gain (Discount Bond)} \\ \text{or} \\ \text{– Annual Capital Loss (Premium Bond)} \end{array}}{(\text{Purchase Price + Redemption Price})/2}$$

In this case, the yield to maturity for this discount bond is:

$$\frac{\$100 + \$10 \ (\$100 \text{ discount over 10 years} = \$10/\text{year})}{(\$900 + \$1,000)/2}$$

$$\frac{\$110}{\$950} = 11.58\%$$

Note that the yield to maturity is higher than the current yield. This is due to the inclusion of the capital gain arising from the discount in the YTM formula.

Discount Bond Yield Order   Thus, arranging the yields for discount bonds from lowest to highest shows:

> **Nominal Yield;**
> **Current Yield;**
> **Yield to Maturity (Basis).**

For the examination, you do not need to calculate Yield To Maturity. However, you must understand that the YTM is the highest for a discount bond because it not only reflects the fact that the bond is being purchased for less than par; but it also reflects the annual earning of the bond discount as part of the investment return.

Now, let's compute the nominal yield, current yield and yield to maturity for a premium bond. Assume that a 10-year, 10% corporate bond quoted at 110.

$$\text{Nominal Yield} = 10\%$$

$$\text{Current Yield} = \frac{\$100}{\$1,100} = 9.09\%$$

This is a premium bond. When a bond is bought at a premium over par, the premium is "lost" over the life of the bond. This capital loss is pro-rated over the bond's life to include the effect of the annual capital loss on the bond's yield. The annual capital loss for this bond can be visualized as follows:

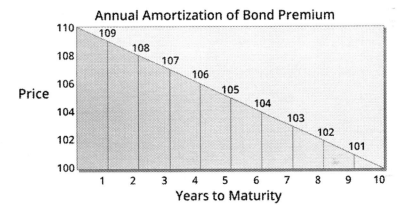

This bond is being purchased at a premium price of 110% of $1,000 par, or $1,100. The bond will mature at par in 10 years. The premium of $100 is being lost over 10 years, so each year $10 of the premium is lost. This is termed the amortization of the bond premium.

$$\text{Yield to Maturity} = \frac{\$100 - \$10 \text{ annual premium loss}}{(\$1,100 + \$1,000)/2} = \frac{\$90}{\$1,050} = 8.57\%$$

Note that in this example, the yield to maturity is lower than the current yield. This is due to the inclusion of the capital loss arising from the premium in the YTM formula.

Premium Bond Yield Order

Thus, arranging the yields for premium bonds from lowest to highest shows:

> **Yield to Maturity (Basis);**
> **Current Yield;**
> **Nominal Yield.**

For the examination, you do not need to calculate Yield To Maturity. However, you must understand that the YTM is the lowest for a premium bond because it not only reflects the fact that the bond is being purchased for more than par; but it also reflects the annual loss of the bond premium as a reduction of the investment return.

1f. CALL AND PUT FEATURES

Call Definition

An issuer may include features in a bond other than simply paying interest and promising to pay back the principal amount at maturity. The issuer may include "call provisions" in the bond contract. When a bond is callable, the issuer has the right to redeem (to "call in") the bond at a predetermined price at a date prior to maturity. However, the issuer is not obligated to do so.

For example, a 20-year bond is issued in 2017 with the following call schedule:

Call Schedule

Redemption Date	Redemption Price
2027	105
2028	104
2029	103
2030	102
2031	101
2032 and after	100

This issue is first callable in 2027 at a price of 105. The issuer will pay a 5 point call premium if it calls the bonds in 2027. Notice that the later the issuer calls the bonds, the less the call premium that will be paid. After 2031, no call premium will be paid if the issuer redeems.

Calls Occur When Interest Rates Drop

An issuer is likely to call a bond early if interest rates have dropped in the market subsequent to the bonds' issuance. The cost to the issuer for doing this is the call premium. The issuer can then sell new bonds to replace the old at a lower interest rate. From the investor's standpoint, a call is never welcome. The bonds will be called early and the investor will receive the call premium (if any). When the investor reinvests the proceeds, he or she will find that the new interest rate will be lower.

Call Protection

Clearly, investors are not happy when bonds are called. To make these issues marketable to the public, investors are protected from calls for a stated period after the bonds' issuance. In this example, the bonds issued in 2017 are first callable in 2027. An investor has 10 years of "call protection" with this issue.

Call Protection Is Typically 10 Years

The typical call protection period for new issues of bonds is 10 years; investors are reluctant to buy bonds with shorter initial periods of call protection.

Call Price Sets Ceiling On Market Price	If interest rates drop, it is more likely that an issuer will call in bonds. We also know that as interest rates drop, prices in the market will rise. The price will not rise by as much as that for a non-callable issue. For example, in 2027 the price of this issue will not go much above 105, no matter how far interest rates drop. The reason why is obvious; why would someone pay more than 105 for an issue that is likely to be called at that price? If he paid more, he would suffer a capital loss when the bond is called. Therefore, the call price tends to set a ceiling on the market price of the bond during periods of falling interest rates.
Zero-Coupon Bonds Callable At Accreted Value Plus Call Premium	Also note that zero-coupon bonds can be issued that are callable. Unlike conventional bonds which are called at par plus a call premium, zero-coupon bonds are called at their current accreted value (the purchase price plus compounded growth-to-date) plus a call premium.
Put Definition	The issuer may also include "put" provisions in the bond contract. This gives the investor the right to tender the bond (he or she can "put" the bond) to the issuer after a specified date for a price set in the bond contract. The price is usually par.
	For example, a 20-year bond is issued in 2017 with a tender option at par. The schedule included with the bond is:

Put Schedule

Tender Date	Tender Price
2027 and after	100

	The bondholder has the right to tender the bond to the issuer at any time starting in 2027 and will receive par for the bond.
Put/Tender Option Given To Bondholder When Interest Rates Are Low	During periods when interest rates for long term bonds are very low, any purchaser of a new bond with a low coupon rate is highly susceptible to "interest rate risk," - the risk that a rise in interest rates will cause the bond to fall sharply in value. To eliminate this risk and make the bond more marketable, the issuer might give the bondholder a put option instead of placing a somewhat higher coupon rate on the bond.
Put Exercised When Interest Rates Rise	The bondholder is likely to exercise the tender option if interest rates have risen during the period following the bonds' issuance. As interest rates rise, bond prices fall. If the bond's price were to drop below par, the bondholder can always tender the bond (as of 2027) to the issuer and receive par value. The bondholder is only too happy to exercise the option when interest rates rise because the proceeds of the redemption can be reinvested at higher current interest rates.

Debt Securities

**Put Price Sets Floor On
Market Price**

The price set by the tender option puts a floor under the market price of the bond during periods of rising interest rates. The price will never drop much below par once the option is exercisable, because if it did, traders would buy as many of the bonds as possible and "put" them to the issuer at par for a capital gain. This buying action would force the market price back up to par.

1g. YIELD TO CALL - YIELD TO PUT

Yield To Call

Yield To Put

If a bond is called prior to maturity, or a put option is exercised, the yield for that bond will change. Calculating yield to call or yield to put is similar to the yield to maturity formula.

$$\text{Yield to Call Date or Put Option} = \frac{\text{Annual Income} \quad \begin{array}{c} + \text{Annual Capital Gain (Discount Bond)} \\ \text{or} \\ - \text{Annual Capital Loss (Premium Bond)} \end{array}}{(\text{Purchase Price} + \text{Call or Put Price})/2}$$

Differences in the computation from YTM arise when the redemption (call or put) price is other than par, and because redemption occurs in a shorter time frame.

For example, a corporation issues a 20 year 10% bond at par. The bond is currently trading at par. The bond is callable in 5 years at 105 and is puttable in 5 years at 100. What are the yield to maturity, yield to call and yield to put for this bond?

$$\text{Yield to Maturity} = \frac{\$100 \text{ annual income} + 0 \text{ annual gain}}{(\$1,000 \text{ purchase price} + \$1,000 \text{ redemption})/2} = \frac{\$100}{\$1,000} = 10\%$$

$$\text{Yield to 5 Year Call} = \frac{\$100 \text{ annual income} + \$10 \text{ annual gain*}}{(\$1,000 \text{ purchase price} + \$1,050 \text{ redemption})/2} = \frac{\$110}{\$1,025} = 10.73\%$$

* The annual gain of $10 comes from earning the $50 premium over 5 years = $10 per year

$$\text{Yield to 5 Year Put} = \frac{\$100 \text{ annual income} \pm \$0 \text{ annual gain or loss}}{(\$1,000 \text{ purchase price} + \$1,000 \text{ redemption})/2} = \frac{\$100}{\$1,000} = 10\%$$

Note that the yield to call is higher than the yield to maturity due to the earning of the call premium over a shorter time period. The yield to put is the same as the yield to maturity because the redemption price was set at par.

Disc. Bond = YTC > YTM

Prem. Bond = YTC < YTM

For the examination, you do not have to compute yield to call or yield to put. What you must know is that yield to call is higher than yield to maturity for a discount bond (since the discount is earned faster); and yield to call is lower than yield to maturity for a premium bond (since the premium is lost faster).

1h. SUMMARY OF YIELDS AND BOND PRICE MOVEMENTS

We already know that there is an inverse relationship between interest rate movements and bond price movements. As interest rates increase in the market, the yield to maturity of outstanding bonds must increase to be competitive. This forces bond prices down. At the same time, the yield to call on the bond also must increase, due to the drop in the bond's price. This can be pictured as follows:

When the bond is issued, market interest rates and the stated interest rate on the bond are the same.

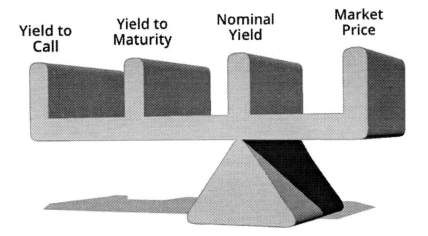

As interest rates rise in the market, yields are pushed up and the bond's market price is pushed down:

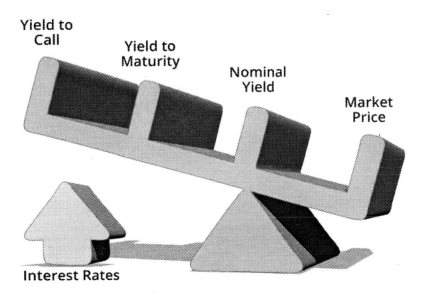

Conversely, as interest rates fall in the market, yields are pushed down as the market price of the bond rises.

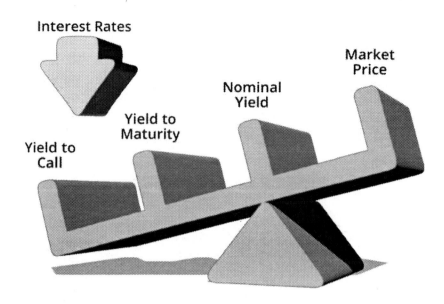

1i. RISKS ASSOCIATED WITH BONDS

Bondholders are subject to a variety of risks. An evaluation of a bond should take into consideration the risks to which the security is subject. The risks are:

Credit Risk

Credit Risk: The risk that the issuer cannot make interest and principal payments on an issue. The ratings agencies rate bonds only for credit risk, not for any other risks.

Moody's / Standard & Poor's

The two main agencies are Moody's and Standard & Poor's. A much smaller third rating's agency is Fitch's.

Treasury Debt - AAA Rated

Treasury bonds are rated AAA (top rating) by Moody's and Fitch's because they are considered to have no credit risk. Note that this is true, even with the Standard & Poor's "questionable" downgrade of U.S. Government debt mid-2011 to a "AA" rating because of the ballooning Federal debt. The other credit ratings agencies maintained their AAA ratings, since the U.S. Government is highly unlikely to ever default on its debt. This is the rating that must be known for the exam.

Long-Term Bond Ratings

Long term corporate and municipal bonds are rated under the "ABC" system.

The ratings used by the two largest agencies for long-term bonds are:

	Standard and Poor's	Moody's
Investment Grade	AAA AA A BBB	Aaa Aa A Baa
Speculative Grade	BB B CCC CC C	Ba B Caa Ca C

Investment Grade

The top 4 ratings are considered "investment" grade. The highest investment grade is AAA (there is no AAA+), while the lowest is BBB. Generally, institutions will restrict their investments to bonds of these grades.

Speculative Grade ("Junk")

Below this level, (the gray shaded area) the bonds become speculative. BB is the highest speculative rating, while the lowest is C. Speculative bonds are commonly referred to as "junk bonds." Thus, a "BB" rated bond is the highest "junk rating" available.

+ Or - Ratings

1-2-3 Ratings

Standard & Poor's can adjust a rating slightly without making a letter change by adding a + or - to the rating. For example, A+ is better than A. Moody's adjusts ratings by adding "1, 2, 3" rankings. For example, within an A rating A-1 is higher than A-2; A-2 is higher than A-3.

Short-Term Note Ratings

Moody's also rates short-term corporate and municipal issues for credit risk. The ratings used for short term issues are:

Commercial Paper	Municipal Notes
P1	MIG 1
P2	MIG 2
P3	MIG 3
NP	SG

The P ratings stand for "prime" paper with P 1 being the highest and P 3 the lowest. NP means "not prime," the lowest rating. The MIG ratings stand for "Moody's Investment Grade," with MIG 1 being the highest and SG ("Speculative Grade") the lowest.

Debt Securities

Standard & Poor's uses a different rating scale for commercial paper. It rates the paper of companies using a version of the "ABC" ratings.

Standard and Poor's Commercial Paper Ratings		
A Rated	B Rated	C Rated
A - 1	B	C
A - 2		
A - 3		

Only Top 2 Grades Of Paper Are Actively Traded (P1, P2; A1, A2)

Under the Standard and Poor's Ratings, investment grade paper carries an "A" rating. In the commercial paper market, institutional investors generally limit their purchases to the top 2 grades of paper (P1 or P2; and A1 and A2). For example, money market mutual funds will only buy paper of these grades.

Interest Rate Risk

Market Risk

Interest Rate Risk: The risk that rising interest rates will cause bond prices to fall. Long-term maturities, low coupon rate bonds and deep discount bonds are most susceptible to this risk, as discussed previously in this section. Another name for interest rate risk when talking about bonds is "market risk." It is the risk that market interest rates will rise, forcing bond prices lower.

Greater Risk For Longer Maturities And Lower Coupon Issues

Below is a chart that illustrates the price changes that will occur if market interest rates move by 1 percentage point, for bonds of varying maturities and coupon rates. The chart shows that as maturities lengthen, as well as when coupon rates are lower, percentage price changes are greater in response to market interest rate movements.

Years To Maturity	8% Coupon		10% Coupon		12% Coupon	
	If Rates		If Rates		If Rates	
	Rise ⬆	Fall ⬇	Rise ⬆	Fall ⬇	Rise ⬆	Fall ⬇
1	-.09	+1.0	-.09	+0.9	-.09	+0.9
2	-1.8	+1.8	-1.8	+1.8	-1.7	+1.8
3	-2.6	+2.7	-2.5	+2.6	-2.4	+2.5
4	-3.3	+3.4	-3.2	+3.3	-3.0	+3.2
5	-4.0	+4.2	-3.8	+4.0	-3.6	+3.8
10	-6.5	+7.1	-6.0	+6.5	-5.5	+6.0
15	-8.1	+9.2	-7.3	+8.1	-6.5	+7.3
20	-9.2	+10.7	-8.0	+9.2	-7.1	+8.0
30	-10.3	+12.5	-8.7	+10.3	-7.5	+8.7

Interest Rate Risk Applies Only To Fixed Rate Securities

Also note that interest rate risk only exists for fixed income securities, which include bonds with fixed coupon rates and preferred stock with fixed dividend rates. As market rates rise, the prices of these securities fall. This direct inverse relationship does not exist between common stock prices and market interest rate movements; nor does it exist for "variable rate" bonds.

Variable Rate Bonds Do Not Have Interest Rate Risk

A "variable rate" bond has an interest rate that is periodically reset to a market index. Thus, as market interest rates move up, so will the interest rate on the bond; and as market interest rates move down, so will the interest rate on the bond. Because the interest rate on these bonds moves with market rates, the price stays very close to par. Thus, variable rate bonds do not have market (interest rate) risk.

Purchasing Power Risk

Purchasing Power Risk: The risk that inflation will lower the value of bond interest payments and principal repayment, thereby forcing prices to fall. When there is significant inflation, market interest rates rise and this forces bond prices down. This risk is most significant for long term bonds (when market interest rates rise, long term bond prices fall faster). Another name for purchasing power risk is "inflation" risk. The only bond that gives protection against purchasing power risk is a "TIPS" - a Treasury Inflation Protection Security - covered later in this chapter.

Marketability Risk

Marketability Risk: The risk that the security will be difficult to sell. Many factors affect marketability: the issue's size, the number of traders in the market, etc. Marketability risk is virtually non-existent for Treasury bonds because the market is so large and liquid; while it is a major concern in the fragmented, illiquid municipal bond market (this is covered later in this chapter).

Liquidity Risk

Liquidity Risk: The risk that the security can only be sold by incurring large transaction costs. Generally, short-term high quality issues are liquid; the longer the term and lower the quality, the lesser the liquidity.

Legislative Risk

Legislative Risk: The risk that new laws reduce the value of a security, such as a change in the tax laws increasing tax rates on interest received from debt investments.

Call Risk

Call Risk: The risk that the bonds may be redeemed prior to maturity, forcing reinvestment of the proceeds at a lower interest rate. Call risk increases as interest rates fall, since issuers are able to call in existing higher rate issues and can "refund" them at lower current market rates.

The bonds most susceptible to call risk are those that an issuer is likely to call - these are bonds with high coupon rates and low call premiums. Conversely, the bonds that an issuer is least likely to call are those with low coupon rates and high call premiums.

Debt Securities

Reinvestment Risk	Reinvestment Risk: The risk for a long-term bond investor that market interest rates are falling over that investment's time horizon. A bond investor receives semi-annual interest payments, which must be "reinvested" in additional bond purchases to maintain the overall return on that bond portfolio. As these semi-annual payments are received, they are reinvested at lower and lower interest rates - hence the term "reinvestment risk."
Zero-Coupon Bond Avoids Reinvestment Risk	The only bond that avoids this risk is a "zero-coupon bond." The rate of return is established by the deep discount price at which the bond is purchased. The bond grows in value towards par at maturity and there are no payments received during the investment's time horizon that must be reinvested
Risks Of International Investing	There are other risks that affect bond investors (and equity investors as well) when investments are made outside the United States. The risks of international investing are:
Exchange Rate Risk	Exchange Rate Risk: The risk that the value of the foreign currency in which the investment is denominated weakens, which is the same as the U.S. dollar strengthening. When the value of the investment is converted into U.S. dollars, it buys "fewer" U.S. dollars, and is now worth less than before. Protection against this risk can be purchased by using foreign currency options, covered in a later chapter.
Political Risk	Political Risk: Not to be confused with legislative risk, this is the risk of investing in foreign countries that have weak political and legal systems - typically 3rd world countries. If one buys the bonds of, say, Indonesia and, Indonesia declares unilaterally that it is cutting the interest rate it will pay on the bonds from 8% to 4%, those bondholders don't have much in the way of legal recourse.

1j. THE YIELD CURVE

The direction which interest rates are taking determines what will happen to bond prices. To evaluate the interest rate environment, analysts use the yield curve. The curve shows the market rates of interest for bonds of different maturities with similar credit ratings.

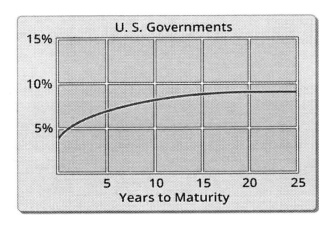

Normal Yield Curve (Ascending)

The "normal" shape of the yield curve shows that as maturities lengthen, yields increase. This curve is typical during periods of economic expansion, when monetary policy is loose. Above is an ascending yield curve. As a general statement, yields increase as maturities lengthen because investors demand a premium for the extra risk associated with longer term maturities (both interest rate risk and purchasing power risk).

Short Term Rates Move Faster Than Long Term Rates

During periods when economic expansion is peaking, monetary policy is tightened by the Federal Reserve (this will be covered more fully in the Analysis chapter). The effect is to increase short-term rates, since the Federal Reserve exerts its influence on short-term rates. This also forces long-term rates up, but they do not rise as much. This occurs because the market for short-term funds is much larger than that for long-term funds, and the greater activity causes rate changes to show rapidly.

Flat Yield Curve

The yield curve now "flattens out" as short-term rates rise closer to long-term levels.

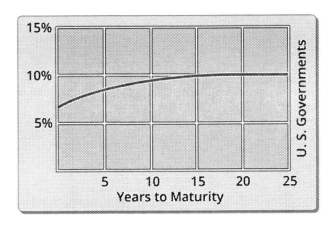

Inverted Yield Curve (Descending)

If the Federal Reserve really tightens short-term credit to slow the economy, then short-term rates can rise above long-term rates. This is called an "inverted" yield curve, and rarely occurs in the business cycle. It happens when the economy appears to be "overheating," increasing inflation fears. To slow things down, the Fed raises short-term rates to extremely high levels. Below is an inverted curve.

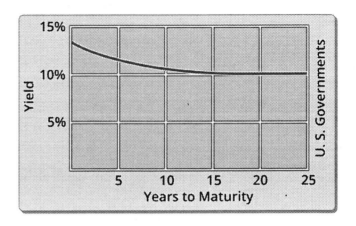

Yield Curve Shape Reflects Economic Cycle

One can see, as the economic cycle progresses, the shape of the yield curve changes.

An ascending curve occurs during periods of normal economic expansion;

A flat curve occurs when the economy is peaking;

An inverted curve occurs when short-term credit is severely tightened if the economy is "overheating."

Yield Curve Theories

There are various theories that attempt to explain yield curve shapes in a more precise manner. These are:

Liquidity Preference

Liquidity Preference: states that investors prefer liquidity; and that because of this, short term issues (which are more liquid) should trade at lower yields than long term issues. Thus, the "normal" curve under this theory is an ascending yield curve.

Market Segmentation

Market Segmentation: states that individual and institutional investors are restricted to making investments in specific maturity sectors. For example, pension funds will tend to buy long term bonds (to fund future pension liabilities); whereas money funds will buy short term maturities only. Under this theory, the yield curve simply shows the relative supply and demand for issues in each maturity range.

Expectations

Expectations: states that the shape of the yield curve shows investor expectations as to the future direction of interest rates.

A positive curve indicates that investors expect interest rates to rise. An ascending yield curve is typical when the economy is growing. When the economy is growing, it is "expected" that the Fed will try to slow down growth by raising interest rates, since an overheating of the economy could lead to inflation. Thus, an ascending yield curve is a predictor that interest rates will rise in the future.

A negative curve indicates that investors expect interest rates to fall. A descending yield curve is typical when the Fed has tightened credit greatly to slow the economy. When the economy is slowing, it is "expected" that the Fed will try to re-stimulate growth by lowering interest rates. This is also a low inflation type of environment, so the Fed can lower rates without worrying about igniting inflationary pressures. Thus, a descending yield curve is a predictor that interest rates will fall in the future.

A flat curve would indicate that investors expect no change in interest rate levels.

Yield Curve Shape Is Actually A Combination Of All Theories

In reality, yield curve shapes are driven by a combination of all of these factors. Yield curves, over time, tend to be ascending, showing investors' liquidity preference. If the curve shows unusual dips or humps, it means that the yield and hence the demand for that maturity is unusually low or high, as compared to other bonds. For example, there may be a big demand for 10 year Treasury Bonds by Japanese investors, causing yields for that maturity to drop below those of less popular 15 year bonds. This validates the market segmentation theory. Finally, inflation fears tend to steepen the yield curve, while disinflation would flatten or invert the yield curve, validating the expectations theory.

Comparative Yield Curves

Yield curves can also be compared for issuers in different risk categories. The base for comparison is the risk-free securities of the U.S. Government. These are often compared to the yields of AAA rated corporate bonds. Below is a sample comparative yield curve chart.

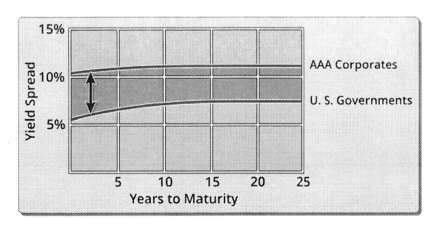

Yield Spread

Notice that corporates have a higher yield for all maturities than governments due to the higher default risk. The "spread" between the "risk-free" government yield and corporate yield is about 5% in this example. This is the "risk premium" component of interest rates.

Widening Spread Indicates Coming Recession

The yield spread is an indicator of future economic trends. Assume that the "normal" yield spread is 5%. If investors expect a recession, they will "flee to safety." They will sell corporate bonds (raising yields) and buy government bonds (lowering yields). Thus, when a recession is expected, the yield spread will **WIDEN**.

Narrowing Spread Indicates Coming Expansion

Conversely, when investors expect an economic expansion, they will sell governments (raising yields) and buy corporates (lowering yields). Thus, when an expansion is expected, the yield spread will **NARROW**.

BOND BASICS
SECTION EXAMINATION

1.

A customer wishes to invest in corporate bonds that offer minimum market risk. Which recommendation is appropriate?

  a. Bonds with short term maturities

  b. High yield bonds

  c. Guaranteed bonds with medium term maturities

  d. Bonds with long term maturities and high call premiums

2.

A corporation will call its debt when:

  a. interest rates are stable

  b. interest rates are falling

  c. interest rates are rising

  d. interest rates are volatile

3.

An investor is most likely to put a bond with a tender option at par when:

  a. interest rates are stable

  b. interest rates are falling

  c. interest rates are rising

  d. interest rates are volatile

4.

A customer has purchased three different bonds, each yielding 9%, with 5 year, 10 year, and 15 year maturities. If prevailing interest rates drop by 20 basis points, which will show the greatest percentage price change?

  a. 5 year maturity

  b. 10 year maturity

  c. 15 year maturity

  d. The bonds will all move by the same percentage

5.

Which of the following are **TRUE** statements about discount bonds?

  I   Discount bonds will appreciate more rapidly as interest rates fall than will similar premium bonds

  II A bond trading at a discount can indicate that market interest rates have risen

  III A bond trading at a discount can indicate that the issuer's credit rating has deteriorated

  IV Bonds trading at a discount are more likely to be called than bonds trading at a premium

  a. I and IV only

  b. II and IV only

  c. I, II, III

  d. I, II, III, IV

6.

Corporate bonds are quoted on what basis?

  a. Yield to maturity

  b. Dollar price

  c. Discount yield

  d. Nominal yield

7.

A corporation has issued 10% AA rated sinking fund debentures at par. Three years later, similar issues are being offered in the primary market at 8%. Which of the following are **TRUE** statements about the outstanding 10% issue?

   I   The current yield will be higher than the nominal yield

   II   The current yield will be lower than the nominal yield

  III The dollar price of the bond will be at a premium to par

  IV The dollar price of the bond will be at a discount to par

   a.   I and III
   b.   I and IV
   c.   II and III
   d.   II and IV

8.

During a period when the yield curve has a normal ascending shape, which statement is **TRUE**?

   a.   Short term bond prices are more volatile than long term bond prices
   b.   Long term bond prices are more volatile than short term bond prices
   c.   Both short term and long term prices are equally volatile
   d.   No relationship exists between long term and short term bond price movements

9.

When the price of a bond increases, which of the following statements regarding yields are **TRUE?**

   I   Yield to call increases
   II   Yield to call decreases
  III Yield to maturity increases
  IV Yield to maturity decreases

   a.   I and III
   b.   I and IV
   c.   II and III
   d.   II and IV

10.

Municipal dollar bonds are generally:

   a.   term bonds
   b.   series bonds
   c.   serial bonds
   d.   short term maturities

11.

The yield to maturity of a bond:

   a.   increases as bond market prices decline
   b.   increases as bond market prices increase
   c.   is unaffected by changes in market interest rates
   d.   will vary with the earnings of the issuer

12.

In 2017, a customer buys 5 GE 10% debentures, M '37, at 85. The interest payment dates are Feb 1st and Aug 1st. The bonds are callable as of 2027 at 103. The current yield on the bonds is:

   a.   10.00%
   b.   10.81%
   c.   11.76%
   d.   12.43%

13.

Yield curve analysis is useful for an investor in debt securities because:

   I   the curve shows market expectations for interest rates
   II   investors can compare rates of return relative to changing maturities
  III the yield of a specific security can be compared to the market expectation for similar securities
  IV the curve can show relative demand for differing maturities by comparing the change in yield to the change in maturity

   a.   I, II only
   b.   II, III only
   c.   I, III, IV
   d.   I, II, III, IV

14.

In 2017, a customer buys 5 GE 10% debentures, M '27, at 85. The interest payment dates are Feb 1st and Aug 1st. The bonds are callable as of 2022 at 103. The yield to maturity on the bonds is:

a. 10.00%
b. 10.81%
c. 11.76%
d. 12.43%

15.

In 2017, a customer buys 5 GE 10% debentures, M '27, at 85. The interest payment dates are Feb 1st and Aug 1st. The bonds are callable as of 2019 at 103. If the bonds are called prior to maturity, which statement is **TRUE**?

a. The yield to call will be higher than the yield to maturity
b. The yield to call will be lower than the yield to maturity
c. The yield to call will be the same as the yield to maturity
d. The yield to call will depend on the current market price of the bond at the time of the call

16.

During periods when the yield curve is inverted, investors wishing to maximize current income would buy:

a. short term maturities
b. medium term maturities
c. long term maturities
d. high yield bonds

17.

At which Standard and Poor's rating is a bond considered to be speculative ("junk bond")?

a. AA
b. BBB
c. BB
d. C

18.

A "call premium" on a bond is the:

a. amount by which the purchase price of the bond exceeds par
b. amount by which the redemption price prior to maturity exceeds par
c. amount which the redemption price at maturity exceeds par
d. maximum premium at which the bond can trade over its life

19.

Regarding bonds with put options, which of the following statements are **TRUE**?

I Exercise of the put is at the option of the bondholder
II Once the option is exercisable, the bond's price will not fall below the option price if interest rates rise
III Yields on bonds with put options are higher than similar bonds without this feature

a. I only
b. I and II
c. II and III
d. I, II, III

20.

Which of the following ratings applies to commercial paper?

a. MIG 1
b. P3
c. Bb
d. A+

BOND BASICS EXAMINATION EXPLANATIONS

1. The best answer is **a**. Market risk for a bondholder is the risk of rising interest rates forcing the price of a bond to drop. As interest rates rise, the price of a long term bond falls faster than that of a short term bond. To avoid market risk, a bondholder would want to invest in the shortest maturity possible.

2. The best answer is **b**. An issuer will call its debt when interest rates have fallen sufficiently. The issuer must pay call premiums to the bondholders to "call in" the debt. In order for the call to make economic sense, the issuer must be able to issue new bonds at a lower interest rate to cover the cost of the call premiums and the costs associated with calling the old debt and issuing new debt.

3. The best answer is **c**. A put option at par allows the bondholder to "put" the bond back to the issuer at par value. Usually, such an option can only be exercised after the issue has been outstanding in the market for 5 to 10 years, depending on the specifics of the trust indenture.

A bondholder purchases a bond with such an option because it protects him from market risk. If interest rates rise, the value of a typical bond without this option would drop. The option allows the bondholder to "put" the bond back to the issuer, receiving par for each bond. Thus, in a period of rising interest rates, the holder of a "puttable" bond is protected from market risk once the option is exercisable.

4. The best answer is **c**. As interest rates move, long term maturities will change in price at a faster rate than will short term obligations. This is due to the fact that the "compounding effect" is more acute as maturities lengthen. As interest rates move up, long term maturities fall faster in price than do short term maturities.

5. The best answer is **c**. As interest rates fall, discount bonds will appreciate at a faster rate than will premium bonds. The change in value of the bond's price is a result of an increased "present value" of the remaining interest payments to be received. This increase in the "value" of the remaining interest payments is a larger percentage of a discount bond's price than of a premium bond's price. Thus, as interest rates drop, discount bond prices rise faster than premium bond prices. Similarly, as interest rates rise, discount bond prices fall faster than premium bond prices.

If a bond is trading at a discount, it can indicate that interest rates have risen after the issuance of the bond. One reason why bonds trade at a discount is because the interest rate that the bond is paying is less than the "market" rate of interest. A bond may be trading at a discount because the issuer's credit rating has slipped, forcing prices down and subsequently, yields up. Bonds trading at a premium are most likely to be called. An issuer calls debt when interest rates have fallen so it can refund at a lower interest cost.

6. The best answer is **b**. Corporate bonds are usually term bonds - all bonds of an issue having the same interest rate and maturity. Term bonds are quoted on a percentage of par basis in 1/8ths, which is the same as a "dollar" quote.

7. The best answer is **c**. The bond was issued with a coupon of 10%. Currently, the yield for a similar issue is 8%. Therefore, interest rates have dropped subsequent to the issuance of the bond; or the credit quality of the bond has improved. When interest rates drop, yields on bonds already trading must also drop. What causes this is a rise in the dollar price of the issue - the bond now trades at a premium.

8. The best answer is **b**. Long term bond prices are more volatile than short term bond prices as interest rates move. Thus, short term bond prices are more stable (move more slowly) as interest rates change compared to long maturities.

9. The best answer is **d**. When the price of a bond increases, yield to maturity drops. Similarly, because the bond is more expensive, yield to call will also fall.

10. The best answer is **a**. Municipal dollar bonds (quoted on a percentage of par basis) are term bonds. Municipal bonds quoted in basis points (yield quotes) are serial bonds.

11. The best answer is **a**.

$$\frac{\text{Annual Interest + Annual Capital Gain}}{\text{(Bond Cost + Redemption Price) / 2}} = \begin{array}{l}\text{Yield to Maturity}\\ \text{for a Discount Bond}\end{array}$$

Since both the Annual Interest and Annual Capital Gain are fixed, as the cost of the bond falls, the Yield to Maturity must rise.

$$\frac{\text{Annual Interest - Annual Capital Loss}}{\text{(Bond Cost + Redemption Price) / 2}} = \begin{array}{l}\text{Yield to Maturity}\\ \text{for a Premium Bond}\end{array}$$

Since both the Annual Interest and Annual Capital Gain are fixed, as the cost of the bond rises, the Yield to Maturity must fall.

12. The best answer is **c**. The formula for current yield is:

$$\frac{\text{Annual Interest}}{\text{Bond Market Price}} = \text{Current Yield}$$

$$\frac{\$100}{\$850} = 11.76\%$$

13. The best answer is **d**. All of the statements are true regarding yield curve analysis. The curve shows market expectations for interest rates. Because it shows all the rates for all maturities, investors can compare rates against differing maturities. The yield curve is an average for securities of a given risk class. An investor can compare the yield on a specific security to the curve for the risk class to evaluate the attractiveness of that investment. If there is a great demand for a specific maturity, the price will be pushed up and the yield lowered. One can pick this out in a yield curve since the curve would drop for that specific maturity.

14. The best answer is **d**.   The formula for yield to maturity for a discount bond is:

$$\frac{\text{Annual Interest} + \text{Annual Capital Gain}}{(\text{Bond Cost} + \text{Redemption Price}) / 2} = \text{Yield to Maturity for a Discount Bond}$$

$$\frac{\$100 + (\$150 \text{ discount} / 10 \text{ years to maturity})}{(\$850 + \$1,000) / 2} = \frac{\$100 + \$15}{\$925} =$$

$$\frac{\$115}{\$925} = 12.43\%$$

15.   The best answer is **a**.   If the bonds are called prior to maturity, the yield to call will be higher than the yield to maturity since the discount will be earned faster **and** the bondholder will receive the call premium. Assume that the bonds are called in 2019. Yield to call uses the same formula as YTM computed to the call date. The Yield to Call will be:

$$\frac{\$100 + \$90 \ (\$150 \text{ discount} + \$30 \text{ premium}/2 \text{ years to call})}{(\$850 + \$1,030) / 2} =$$

$$\frac{\$190}{\$940} = 20.21\%$$

Note for the exam that you do not have to compute yield to call; but you must know that yield to call will be higher than yield to maturity if the bond is trading at a discount; and yield to call will be lower than yield to maturity if the bond is trading at a premium.

16.   The best answer is **a**.   When the yield curve is inverted, short term rates are higher than long term rates. To maximize income, invest in short term securities. This curve is typical during periods of tight credit.

17.   The best answer is **c**.   The top 4 ratings are "investment grade" - AAA, AA, A, and BBB. Bonds below these ratings are speculative. The best speculative rating is, therefore, BB.

18.   The best answer is **b**.   A call premium is the excess over par value that the issuer will pay the bondholder to call in the bonds prior to maturity.

19.   The best answer is **b**.   Put options are exercisable at the option of the bondholder; once the option is exercisable, the bond price cannot fall below the option price, since the bondholder can always "put" the bond to the issuer for this amount. The put price represents a floor on the market price of the bond. Because the put option removes some of the market risk from the bond, this feature is valued by bondholders, who will accept lower yields on bonds having this option.

20.   The best answer is **b**.   Commercial paper is rated P1, P2, P3, NP (highest to lowest) by Moody's. P stands for prime. NP means "not prime" and is the lowest rating. The "ABC" ratings are used for long term corporate and municipal bonds. The MIG ratings are used for municipal short term notes.

SECTION 2: CORPORATE DEBT

2a. CHARACTERISTICS OF CORPORATE DEBT

Corporations issue debt in order to raise capital. The debt can take the form of long-term bonds, intermediate-term notes or short-term notes known as commercial paper.

Bearer Bond

Bonds have evolved over time. The very first bonds issued were "bearer" bonds. Such bonds are not registered in an owner's name. They are payable to the "bearer" and have rows of coupons attached to the bond. Each semi-annual coupon has a payment date and amount on it. The bearer of the bond clips the coupon at the due date and sends it to the paying agent for cash payment.

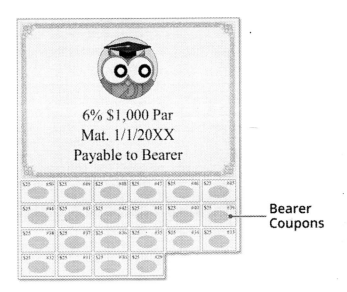

6% $1,000 Par
Mat. 1/1/20XX
Payable to Bearer

Bearer Coupons

In essence, a bearer bond is really no different than holding paper currency. Because there is no record of the owner, if the bond is lost or destroyed, it cannot be replaced

Registered To Principal Only Bond

The next version of the bond is the "registered to principal only" bond. The $1,000 face amount of the bond is now registered in the owner's name, but the bond still has bearer coupons attached.

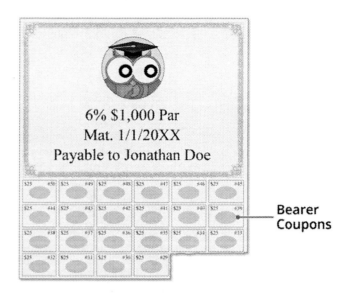

Bearer
Coupons

Both bearer bonds and registered to principal only bonds were convenient vehicles for people to hide money from the IRS, so they have not been allowed to be issued since mid-1983. Note, however, that these issues still trade (until the last of these issues mature), and are still tested and also note that bearer bonds are still issued outside of the U.S.

Fully Registered Bond

The next version of the bond gets rid of bearer coupons. This is a bond that is "registered to principal and interest," also called a fully registered bond.

Fully registered bonds have the bondholder registered with the transfer agent as the owner of record and a physical certificate is issued to the bondholder. The paying agent sends the semi-annual interest payments directly to the registered owner and, at maturity, sends the final $1,000 principal repayment to the registered owner.

Book Entry Bond

The problem with all of these bonds is that they are very expensive to print. The final solution comes in the form of the "book entry" bond. With book entry securities, no physical certificates are issued; but the holder's name, address, and purchase amount are registered with the transfer agent. All new issues of bonds coming out in the United States are now book entry only.

Transfer Agent **Paying Agent**	The transfer agent keeps the record of the owners of the debt outstanding, and when the debt is traded, "transfers" the ownership record to the new owner. The same financial institution usually acts as paying agent for the issuer as well. The paying agent makes the actual interest payments to the owners of record and handles debt redemptions.
Trust Indenture	The bonds are issued under a bond contract called an indenture. The indenture spells out the interest rate, maturity, collateral, call or put provisions, and all other relevant features of the bonds. The indenture may also call for the corporation to maintain specific protections for the bondholders such as insurance coverage, audit by an independent accountant, and certain ratios of assets to liabilities. To ensure that the corporation adheres to the indenture, an independent trustee is appointed to monitor compliance with the provisions of the indenture. The trustee reports annually to the bondholders, and is expected to inform the bondholders if he finds non-compliance. The trustee is usually a commercial bank.
Trust Indenture Act Of 1939	All corporate issues of $50,000,000 or more must have a Trust Indenture as specified by the Trust Indenture Act of 1939.
Funded Debt	Sometimes, long-term corporate debt is referred to as "funded" debt since the issuer has use of the funds for a long time period before repayment is due. (Obviously, this term would not be applicable to commercial paper.)

2b. SECURED CORPORATE DEBT

Corporate bonds can be secured or unsecured. When a bond is secured, specific collateral is pledged to back the bond issue. If the corporation defaults, the bondholders have claim to the collateral. Because of the extra protection afforded by the collateral, secured bonds can be sold at lower interest rates than unsecured bonds. Secured bonds are typically long-term maturities. These bonds are:

Mortgage Bond **Lien On Real Assets**	Mortgage Bond: Real estate such as a factory is pledged as collateral for the bond issue. The bondholder has a lien on the real estate. Under a "lien," the bondholder has the legal right to sell the mortgaged property if the bondholders' claims are not satisfied. The real estate that is pledged is worth more than the bonds that are issued, so the bondholders have a collateral "cushion."

Debt Securities

Open End

Additional Bonds Test

If the trust indenture is open-end, the corporation can sell additional bonds having equal status against the real estate. However, open-end trust indentures will typically include an "additional bonds test" requirement that must be met before new bonds may be sold. This test usually requires that earnings before interest expense for the preceding period or number of periods must exceed both the current interest expense **plus** the projected interest expense on the additional bonds to be sold by a stated multiple. For example, it might be required that earnings before interest expense be at least 2 times the current interest cost, plus projected interest cost on the new bond issue, before that issue can be sold.

Closed-End

If the trust indenture is closed-end, new bonds can be issued against the real estate only if they are junior (have lower status in a liquidation) to the existing bonds.

Senior/Junior Lien

Therefore, there can be senior lien mortgage bonds and junior lien mortgage bonds. Another way of showing the status of a mortgage bond is by calling the senior issue a first mortgage bond; junior issues are second and third mortgage bonds.

Mortgage Bonds Issued By Utilities

Mortgage bonds are the most common form of corporate debt, and are the principal financing source for public utilities. These issues generally get high credit ratings due mainly to the quality of the collateral backing the issue, and can be sold at lower interest rates than unsecured debt.

Equipment Trust Certificate

Commonly Issued By Transportation Companies

Equipment Trust Certificate: Equipment owned by the corporation is pledged as collateral. This is the typical form of financing for common carriers such as airlines, trucking companies and railroads. For example, if United Airlines wants to buy new planes, it will finance the purchase by issuing equipment trust certificates. The planes are the collateral backing the issue.

Serial Issues

Equipment trust certificates are issued in serial form (unlike most other corporate debts which are term issues). Serial bonds obligate the issuer to repay a portion of principal each year until the bonds are retired. In effect, the equipment is bought under a "pay as you use it" plan. The life of the issue coincides with, or is less than, the equipment's life.

Equipment trust certificates are rated highly, because if the issuer defaults, the equipment can easily be sold to repay the bondholders. Furthermore, because the principal amount of the loan is "paid down" each year due to the loan's serial structure, if the collateral has depreciated, it is unlikely that the depreciated value of the asset will be less than the outstanding loan balance. These issues are generally non-callable, making them attractive to investors who want to avoid call risk.

Collateral Trust Certificate

Collateral Trust Certificate: A portfolio of marketable securities is placed in trust as collateral. The typical use of this type of financing is when a parent company (Proctor and Gamble) pledges the securities of a subsidiary (Gillette, which is owned by P & G) as collateral.

Collateral trust certificates are also highly rated because the trust indenture requires that additional collateral be given if the securities drop in value, protecting investors.

2c. UNSECURED CORPORATE DEBT

Unsecured corporate debt is simply backed by the issuer's promise to pay. There is no collateral backing the issue.

Unsecured debt is issued in short term, intermediate term and long-term maturities.

Commercial Paper

Very Short Term Maturities - 30 Days Most Popular

Commercial Paper: Very short-term corporate financing needs are met by issuing commercial paper. Maturities typically range from 14 days to 90 days, with 30 days being the most common maturity. The maturity will never exceed 270 days, because the issue would then have to be registered with the SEC, an expensive and time consuming process.

Discount Instrument

Because of the short term nature, obviously semi-annual interest payments cannot be made as with longer term debt. Instead, commercial paper is sold at a discount and matures at face value. The difference is the earned interest income, which is effectively received at maturity. Unlike longer term debt sold in $1,000 units, commercial paper is sold in large units - $100,000 is the minimum denomination and it is often sold in multiples of $1,000,000.

Book Entry Form

Limited Trading

Commercial paper is sold in book entry form. The purchasers are not small investors because of the large denominations. They are large institutions with excess cash to invest and money market mutual funds. There is very limited trading of these instruments - most investors simply hold them to maturity.

Debenture

Debentures: Intermediate and long-term corporate debt which is backed solely by the full faith and credit of the issuer. There is no collateral backing the issue. Debentures are issued by "blue chip" corporations with high credit ratings who do not have to back the issue with assets, and also by lower credit rated companies in the form of high yield or "junk" bonds. Compared to a secured bond, credit risk is higher for a debenture holder.

Subordinated Debenture

Debentures can also be issued as "subordinated" debt. Subordinated debenture holders agree to a lower status in a corporate liquidation. If a company liquidates, subordinated debtholders are paid after all other creditors. In order to induce customers to buy subordinated debentures, another feature would have to be given to bondholders to compensate for the extra risk. This usually takes the form of a "conversion" feature - which allows the bondholder to convert the bond into a fixed number of common shares. This is covered in the following section.

Guaranteed Bond	Debentures can be guaranteed. In this case, bonds are typically issued by a subsidiary company; with the corporate parent company guaranteeing payment of interest and principal as due. Such bonds take on the credit rating of the guarantor.
Income Bonds **Termed "Adjustment Bonds"**	Income Bonds (Adjustment Bonds): When a corporation goes bankrupt, the issuer defaults on the outstanding debt. The company then tries to reorganize and emerge from bankruptcy. Part of the reorganization is getting the existing bondholders to give up any claims under the old bonds and accept a new type of bond. This new bond is an "income" bond, that only obligates the issuer to pay if it has sufficient "earnings." The bondholders are likely to accept this new instrument since they are receiving nothing anyway. To induce the bondholders to accept the new issue, they are often given a greater principal amount than they had before. Therefore, the principal amount is "adjusted" on these bonds.
Income Bonds Trade Flat	Interest accrues on the bonds but is only paid if the corporation returns to profitability. In theory, if the corporation is profitable, all missed interest payments will be made up. Because these bonds are not currently paying interest, they trade "flat" in the market - without any accrued interest.

2d. CONVERTIBLE CORPORATE DEBT

Convertible Debentures	Convertible bonds are corporate debentures which can be converted, at the option of the owner, into the common stock of the issuer. At the time of issuance, a conversion price is set per share. The bond can then be converted, based on its par value, into a fixed number of common shares.

At the time of issuance, the conversion price is set at a premium to the stock's current market price. In order for the conversion feature to benefit the bondholder, the stock's price must rise in the market above the conversion price.

> For example, a $1,000 par bond is issued, convertible into stock at $50 per share. As of the date of issuance, the market price of the stock is $40. This bond is convertible into 20 shares of stock ($1,000 par/$50 conversion price = 20 shares per bond). In order for the shareholder to benefit, the market price must rise above $50.

In order to handle convertible bond problems, two formulas are needed. Let's use the example of the $1,000 par bond convertible at $50. The current market price of the stock is $40. The bond is currently selling for $900. The first formula is the Conversion Ratio.

$$\text{Conversion Ratio} = \frac{\text{Par Value of Bond}}{\text{Conversion Price}} \qquad = \frac{\$1,000}{\$50} = 20:1$$

This bond is convertible into 20 shares of stock. The second formula is for the parity price. In theory, the bond and the stock should always be trading at equivalent values (since the bond is convertible into the stock).

In reality, this doesn't always happen. There are thousands of convertible issues outstanding and traders do not closely follow all of them. If there is a disparity between the parity price and the stock's market price, there can be a profitable trading opportunity. The formula for the parity price of a bond is:

$$\text{Parity Price of Bond} = \text{Conversion Ratio} \times \text{Stock's Market Price}$$

= 20 x $40 = $800

In order for the bond to be of equal value to the stock, it must trade for $800. The current market price is $900. Therefore, the bond is trading above its parity price.

The formula for the parity price of stock is:

$$\text{Parity Price of Stock} = \frac{\text{Bond Market Value}}{\text{Conversion Ratio}} = \frac{\$900}{20} = \$45$$

The market price of the stock must be $45 (it is currently $40) for the stock to be at parity. Therefore, the stock is selling below its parity value.

Trading Above Parity

When a convertible security trades above parity, the conversion feature does not have any value. There is no reason to convert into stock which is valued at less ($40 market) than the effective conversion price ($45). Therefore, the bond trades like any other debt security and its price movements respond inversely to interest rate swings.

Trading Below Parity

However, when a convertible security trades below parity, the conversion feature is valuable. Assume this $1,000 par bond is trading at $1,100. The market price of the stock is $60 while the conversion price is $50. The bond can be converted into 20 shares of stock worth $60 each or $1,200. Since the market price is $1,100, a large profit ($1,200 conversion - $1,100 purchase = $100 profit) can be made by purchasing the bond and converting it into stock. Any astute investor will take advantage of this opportunity. When a convertible security is trading below parity, the profit can be quickly realized through arbitrage.

Arbitrage

In an arbitrage, a trader buys the lower price security and simultaneously sells the equivalent higher priced security to lock in the profit before someone else does. In this case, the trader will buy the lower priced security (the bond at $1,100) and sell the equivalent number of shares of the higher priced security (the stock - 20 shares at $60 = $1,200)

The arbitrage trade is:

Buy 1 Convertible Bond = $1,100

Sell 20 shares of Stock at $60 = $1,200

The trader then converts the bond into 20 shares of stock through the transfer agent and delivers them to satisfy the sale. A quick profit of $100 was made. Arbitrage only works when the convertible security trades below parity. If the security is trading at or above parity, there is no profit potential.

Above Par - Acts Like Stock

Below Par - Acts Like Bond

When a convertible security trades above par, its price is usually being pulled up by the rising market price of the common stock. Thus, interest rate movements are not causing the bond's price changes; rather, the common stock price movements are the cause. When trading below par, convertible bonds act in the trading market like normal bonds, where price changes are primarily caused by interest rate movements.

2e. CONVERTIBLE BONDS ADVANTAGES - DISADVANTAGES

Lower Interest Rate

The benefit to the issuer of convertible bonds is that investors will accept a lower interest rate since there is potential price appreciation based on converting the bond if the stock price rises.

If the bond is callable, the issuer has a second advantage. We know that bonds are called if interest rates fall. Assume that falling interest rates over the five years following issuance have forced the price of our sample bond to $1,200. The stock price has also increased to $60. Since the conversion ratio is 20, there is no advantage to converting currently - the security is at parity (20 shares per bond x $60 market price = $1,200 bond parity price. The market price is also $1,200).

Assume that the issuer can call the bonds at 105. If the bonds are called, the bondholder tendering the bonds will receive $1,050 per bond. This is a loss of $150 from the current market value of $1,200. Once a call notice is announced, the bondholder has 3 choices; tender the bonds for 105, convert the bonds or do nothing. Doing nothing is not a solution because once the bonds are called, interest payments will cease. If the bonds are redeemed, the bondholder receives $1,050. If the bond is converted, the bondholder receives 20 shares valued at $60 = $1,200. Clearly, the best choice is to convert.

Forced Conversion

What the issuer has done by calling in the bonds is termed a forced conversion. A forced conversion allows the issuer to replace the bonds with equity securities and relieves the issuer of the interest payment burden. Instead, the issuer will now pay dividends on the stock. Remember, interest payments are a legal obligation; dividend payments are discretionary.

Dilution Of Earnings	The disadvantage to the issuer of convertible bonds is that when conversion occurs, existing stockholder's equity is diluted (since more shares have been issued). Because earnings are spread over a greater number of shares, reported earnings per share can fall.
Tax-Deductible Interest Payments Replaced By Non-Deductible Dividends	Conversion also causes debt to be replaced with equity. The corporation no longer makes tax-deductible interest payments to bondholders. Instead, it makes dividend payments which are paid "after tax."
Capital Gains	The advantages to the convertible bondholder are the possibility of capital gains if the stock price goes up, and the fact that bondholders have priority over stockholders if the company is liquidated. The disadvantages to the convertible bondholder are the lower interest rates on these issues, and the possible dilutive effect of a large conversion.
Issuance Of Convertible Bonds - Shareholder Approval Needed	Existing shareholders tend to have a problem with a new convertible issue proposed by a corporation. The reason is if the securities are converted, new common shares are issued. The earnings of the company are then spread over more shares, causing a dilution of earnings per share. This can depress the stock's market price. In order to issue convertible securities, approval of the existing shareholders is required.
Anti-Dilutive Covenant	Once convertible securities are issued, the bondholder is protected by an "anti-dilutive" covenant in the Trust Indenture. Assume that the market price of the stock is now $50 and the conversion price is $50. Both are at parity. If the company issues 25% more shares, the market price of the stock will fall since the earnings are spread over a greater number of shares. In theory, the new market price will be $50/1.25 = $40.
Conversion Price Is Adjusted For Stock Dividends And Stock Splits	If the conversion price is not adjusted, the stock will now be valued below parity. To keep the bondholder whole, the conversion price will also be adjusted (divided by the factor of 1.25) to get a conversion price of $40. In this way, the bondholder is protected from dilution affecting the value of the bond. Therefore, the conversion price will be adjusted for stock dividends, stock splits, and for the issuance of new shares.

Debt Securities

2f. CORPORATE DEBT RETIREMENT PROVISIONS

Retiring Debt

Sinking Fund

Corporate bonds may be redeemed at maturity, or, if a call provision is included in the Trust Indenture, may be called under the terms of the provision. In this manner, debt is retired. The indenture can also call for the establishment of a "sinking fund." Money is deposited into the fund periodically (usually annually) and the funds are used to retire the bonds at maturity or to retire a portion of the issue each year after a specified date. This is an extra protection measure for bondholders. The terms of a sinking fund provision allow the issuer to retire portions of the issue by either calling the bonds or buying them in the open market if the price is lower than the call price.

Tender Offer

Another way for a corporation to retire debt is to make a tender offer for the outstanding bonds. In such a case, the corporation makes an offer to buy the bonds from any of the bondholders, typically at a better than market price. Such offers may be for part of the bonds outstanding; so not all of the bondholders who tender may actually sell their bonds back to the corporation. The issuer will fill tenders of bonds on a first come, first served basis, until the issuer has retired the desired amount of debt. Any bonds tendered in excess of the amount repurchased by the company are returned to the holders.

Refunding Debt

Instead of retiring debt, a corporation may simply roll it over in part or in full. It does this by issuing a refunding bond issue and using the proceeds to call or retire debt. A corporation issues refunding bonds when interest rates have dropped (to retire expensive debt and replace it with lower interest rate debt) or when it simply doesn't have the funds or the desire to retire bonds.

2g. TRADING OF CORPORATE DEBT

Corporate debt is traded principally in the over-the-counter market. In addition, the New York Stock Exchange trades very small amounts of bonds of those companies listed on the exchange (less than $10,000,000 per day).

Over-The-Counter Trading

Most corporate debt is traded in the over-the-counter market. The NASDAQ Stock Market quotes convertible corporate bonds, since they are an "equivalent" security to common stock, but does not quote non-convertible bonds. This is a dealer-to-dealer market, with trading conducted over the phone and through electronic trading systems. A round lot trade of bonds is five $1,000 par value bonds ($5,000 face amount).

Corporate Bond Quotes **Bloomberg**	Electronic dealer quotes (bids and offers) for corporate bonds are posted by services such as Bloomberg and Reuters. The larger bond dealers, such as Goldman Sachs, Morgan Stanley, and Barclays, have their own internal trading systems that can access these quotes and trade against them. For trades that are too large for these proprietary systems, bond traders will simply pick up the phone and trade manually. Corporate bonds are quoted in this market as a percentage of par value in 1/8ths.
TRACE Reports Of Corporate Bond Trades	Trades of corporate, government, and agency bonds are reported by a FINRA system called TRACE (Trade Reporting and Compliance Engine). Any dealer that executes a trade in these securities must report the trade to TRACE "as soon as practicable, but no later than 15 minutes after execution." Once TRACE receives the report, it publishes the trade on the TRACE tape immediately.
FINRA	(A general note: In mid-2007, the NYSE and NASD merged their regulatory units into a new single regulator called "FINRA" - Financial Industry Regulatory Authority. The marketplaces, NYSE and NASDAQ, are completely separate from this regulator. FINRA intends to eliminate unneeded duplication between NYSE and NASD rules, and is developing a single harmonized set of rules for dealing with the public. Until this is finished (it is still a work-in-progress), FINRA is enforcing the separate sets of NYSE and NASD rules. In the text, we refer to these rules as either "FINRA/NYSE," "FINRA/NASD," or FINRA for the completed harmonized rule.)
Dealer Paper	Commercial paper also is sold over-the-counter through dealers and, more and more can be bought directly from the issuing corporation. Paper bought from the issuer is termed "direct" paper. Paper bought from a dealer who has purchased the security from the issuer is called "dealer" paper. If the dealer is simply acting as an agent in selling paper for the issuer, the paper is "bought as sold." There is little trading of commercial paper - it is usually held to maturity. Commercial paper is sold at a discount and matures at par. It is quoted on a discount yield basis.
NYSE Trading	The New York Stock Exchange has a separate bond trading area where a computerized system matches trades. Bonds of companies that are listed on the exchange trade here, but volume is comparatively light - averaging less than 10,000 bonds per day. A round lot trade is 5 - $1,000 par value bonds, quoted as a percentage of par in 1/8ths.

2h. SETTLEMENT AND ACCRUED INTEREST

Regular Way	Corporate bond trades settle "regular way" unless special delivery terms are required. A regular way trade settles 2 business days after trade date.

Debt Securities

Cash

If a seller does not want to wait for a number of business days to be paid, a trade can be done "for cash." Cash settlement occurs the same day as trade date before 2:30 PM. The downside for the seller is, to induce someone to pay today, the bonds would have to be sold at a lower price than in a regular way trade.

Seller's Option

A seller who does not feel that he or she can have the securities for delivery in 2 business days can specify that the trade be done "seller's option." The seller specifies how many days are needed for delivery at the time of the trade (e.g., 5M Ford 4 ½s of '29 offered at 90, seller's 15). The seller is specifying that 15 days are needed for delivery. The seller must deliver the bonds by the 15th business day but is allowed to deliver earlier at 24 hours' notice. Of course, to obtain a buyer for this unusual delivery, the price must be dropped.

When Issued

An unusual situation arises when a corporation announces it will issue new securities. The exchanges allow trading in the securities before they exist. These trades are settled on a "when, as and if issued" basis. There is no established settlement date. If the issue is canceled, the trades are canceled. The actual settlement date is set by the exchange once the securities are physically issued.

Trades Of Corporate Bonds Settle In Clearing House Funds At NSCC

Corporate bond trades are settled through clearing houses owned by the exchanges and their member firms. The clearing house for corporate bond trades (and also for municipal bond trades and all equity trades) is NSCC - the National Securities Clearing Corporation. NSCC is responsible for clearing virtually all domestic corporate (and municipal) securities trades. The deposits at NSCC are known as "clearing house funds."

Trades Of Treasury Bonds Settle In Federal Funds At FICC

In contrast, trades of U.S. Government, Government Agency securities, and mortgage-backed securities (all covered in the next section) clear through FICC - the Fixed Income Clearing Corporation. The majority of government bond trading is done by commercial banks that are members of the Federal Reserve Banking system. The deposits maintained at FICC by member banks are known as "Federal funds."

Accrued Interest

When a bond trade settles, the buyer must pay to the seller the purchase price of the bond plus any commissions due to the broker. In addition, the seller has earned any interest on the bond for the period that it has been held between interest payment dates. When the bond changes hands, the ownership record is changed with the transfer agent. The new holder of the bond will receive the entire 6-month interest payment coming due. However, the new holder has not earned this entire payment and is obligated to pay the portion of interest earned to the seller on settlement date.

For example, assume a customer purchases a 10% bond at 90 which pays interest on Jan 1st and Jul 1st. The trade settles on Feb 1st. The new owner will receive the 6-month interest payment on Jul 1st, but has only earned 5 months of the interest payment (Feb through Jun). The buyer must pay to the seller the accrued interest due for the month of January on settlement date.

Interest Accrues Until Settlement / 30 / 360 Basis

Interest accrues up to, but not including, settlement date. This makes sense because as of settlement, the buyer has paid for the bond and should get interest from that day forward. For corporate bonds, interest accrues on an arbitrary 30 day month / 360 day year basis.

A customer buys a 10% $1,000 par corporate bond at 90 in a regular way trade. The trade date is Tuesday, March 7th. The bond pays interest on Jan 1st and Jul 1st. How many days of accrued interest are due to the seller? How much accrued interest will be paid?

The trade date is Tuesday, March 7th. Regular way settlement is 2 business days, and so settlement takes place on Thursday, March 9th. Interest accrues up to, but not including settlement, therefore, interest accrues through March 8th.

The number of days of accrued interest is:

January	30 days
February	30 days
March	8 days
Total	68 days

$$\text{Amount Paid} = \frac{68 \text{ days}}{360 \text{ days}} \times \$100 \text{ annual interest} = \$18.88$$

Odd First Interest Payment - New Issue

When a new issue of bonds comes out, the issue date may not be a psychologically "convenient" date for investors. Isn't it comforting and easy to remember that your bond pays interest on Jan 1st and Jul 1st? If the issue date is Feb 4th, six-month interest payments would be due on Aug 4th and next Feb 4th. To make life easier, the first interest payment will be designated as "odd" and cover either the period from Feb 4th to Jul 1st or Feb 4th - Jan 1st. Thereafter, interest payments are made on Jan 1st and July 1st.

Trading "Flat"

The buyer is expected to pay the accrued interest only if the bond is currently making interest payments. If the bond is not making interest payments, then the buyer would be paying interest to the seller that would not be received on the interest payment date. Bonds that trade without accrued interest are said to trade "flat."

Types Of Bonds That Trade Flat

Defaulted bonds trade flat; income bonds trade flat since they are not currently paying interest; zero coupon bonds trade flat because no periodic interest payments are made; commercial paper trades flat because no interest payments are made - the paper is bought at a discount and redeemed at par. The increase in value is the "interest." Finally, if a bond trade settles on the interest payment date, no accrued interest is due since this is the exact cut-off date for the seller to receive his 6-month payment and the buyer to pick up the next 6-month period.

2i. CORPORATE DEBT FINANCIAL LISTINGS

Corporate Bond Financial Listing

Information in the news media is presented below:

NEW YORK EXCHANGE BONDS
Total Volume $11,690,000
CORPORATION BONDS

Bonds	Cur Yld	Vol	Close	Net Chg.
ANR 8 5/8 19	9.0	5	96 1/8	- 1 7/8
AVX 8 1/4 23	cv	10	107	- 1
Advst 9s 19	cv	30	87	+ 1 1/2
AirbF 7 1/2 22	cv	151	86 3/4	+ 1/4
AlaP 8 3/4 18	9.8	26	89 1/4	+ 1 1/2
AlaP 12 5/8 21	11.8	13	107	+ 2 1/2
viAlgl 10 3/4 20 f	----	35	59 5/8	- 3/8
AlldC zr 18	----	5	49 1/4	- 1

The first column gives the corporate name, the stated interest rate and the maturity. The ANR Corporation has issued 8 5/8% bonds maturing in 2019. Advest has issued 9% bonds maturing in 2019 ("9s" means "Nines" or nine % bonds). Alger International has issued 10 3/4% bonds maturing in 2020 that are trading flat (f) because they have defaulted (symbol vi). Allied Chemical has issued zero coupon (zr) bonds maturing in 2018. Remember, zero coupon bonds also trade flat.

The second column gives the bond's current yield. The symbol cv means convertible bond - no yield is shown for these. There is no yield shown for defaulted or zero coupon bonds since no interest payments are being made.

The third column gives the trading volume for that day. 5 ANR bonds traded that day ($5,000 face amount). Remember, corporate bond trading is very limited when compared to trades of common stock.

The fourth column gives the day's closing price. Airbus closed at 86 3/4, i.e., at 86 3/4% of par = $867.50 per bond. Alger closed at 59 5/8, i.e., 59 5/8% of par = $596.25.

The fifth column gives the change in closing price from the preceding day. Allied Chemical closed at 49 1/4, down 1 from the preceding day. This indicates that on the preceding day the bond closed at 50 1/4.

Commercial Paper Quotations

Commercial paper is not listed in the newspapers like bonds since there is almost no trading. Instead, representative discount yields are given each day in The Wall Street Journal for prime paper. A sample listing is:

COMMERCIAL PAPER; High grade unsecured notes sold through dealers by major corporations: 1.85% 30 days; 2.95% 60 days; 3% 90 days

Dealers are offering 30-day paper priced to yield 1.85%; 60-day paper to yield 2.95%; and 90-day paper to yield 3.00%.

Information Source - Standard And Poor's Bond Guide

Migrated To The Internet - Now Part Of S&P Net Advantage

For summarized bond (and preferred stock) financial information, Standard and Poor's publishes a "Bond Guide," giving capsule summaries for every corporate fixed income issue, including recent price, yield, and rating. The Bond Guide used to be printed monthly, but has been migrated to the Internet by S&P through a service called S&P Net Advantage (Moody's publishes a similar guide).

2j. TAX STATUS OF CORPORATE DEBT INTEREST

Interest Income Subject To Both Federal And State Tax

The interest income derived from corporate obligations is fully taxable by both the federal government and by state and local government. The interest income is taxable in the year the payment is made. Since most bonds pay interest semi-annually, two interest payments are included on each year's tax return.

Interest Income Taxed At Rates Up To 39.6%

Also note that interest income received from bonds held by individuals is taxed by the federal government at ordinary income tax rates (up to a maximum of 39.6%). In contrast, cash dividend income received by holders of common and preferred stock is taxed at maximum 20% rate for very high earners.

Discount On Original Issue Discount Bonds Is "Interest Income"

Original issue discount obligations, such as commercial paper and zero-coupon obligations, are unusual in that interest "payments" are not made. The securities are purchased at a discount and mature at par. The Internal Revenue Service considers the discount to be interest income earned over the life of the security. Since commercial paper matures in 270 days or less, the entire discount is included as interest income for that tax year.

Portion Of The Discount Is Accreted And Taxed Each Year

For obligations maturing over 1 year, the IRS requires that the pro-rata portion of the discount earned that year be taken as interest income on the tax return. This is called the "accretion" of the discount. Each year, the portion of the discount that is earned is added to the cost basis of the bond. At maturity, the bond will have a tax cost basis of par; since it is redeemed at par, there is no capital gain.

Zero-Coupon Bonds Held In Tax Deferred Accounts To Avoid Current Taxation

The problem for the holder of a zero-coupon bond is that every year tax must be paid on the "earned" portion of the discount even though no payment is made by the issuer. Because of this, zero-coupon bonds are generally not purchased unless they will be placed in a tax-deferred retirement account (IRA or Keogh).

2k. CLAIM PRIORITY IN A LIQUIDATION

If a corporation liquidates in bankruptcy, the following is the priority of making payments to creditors:

1st: Secured creditors such as mortgage bondholders and equipment trust certificate holders receive the proceeds from the sales of the property pledged;

2nd: Unpaid wages, taxes, and trade creditors are paid (in the order just presented);

3rd: Debenture bondholders are paid;

4th: Subordinated debenture bondholders are paid;

5th: Preferred stockholders are paid; and finally

6th: Common stockholders are paid anything that remains.

Note that a point of confusion that exists about the priority of claim in a liquidation is the status of secured creditors. Secured creditors are "carved out" in a liquidation and get the proceeds from the sale of any assets pledged as collateral before any other creditors are paid. That is why they are "secured" and accept a lower interest rate than other creditors.

The balance of the assets left in the bankruptcy estate are then distributed to the unsecured creditors, with workers' claims being the first unsecured claim to be paid.

CORPORATE DEBT
SECTION EXAMINATION

1.
Dealer offerings of corporate bonds found in Bloomberg are:

I   retail quotes
II   wholesale quotes
III   new issue offerings sold under a prospectus
IV   secondary market offerings

a.   I and III
b.   I and IV
c.   II and III
d.   II and IV

2.
A corporation is going to tender for 75% of its 10% subordinated debentures, M '25. The price of the offer will be decided by the:

a.   bond trustee
b.   issuer
c.   paying agent
d.   underwriter

3.
Zero coupon bonds:

I   pay interest semi-annually
II   pay interest at maturity
III   are bought at a discount and mature at par
IV   are bought at a par and mature at a premium

a.   I and III
b.   I and IV
c.   II and III
d.   II and IV

4.
Which of the following bonds trades "flat"?

a.   Unsecured bonds
b.   Income bonds
c.   Reset bonds
d.   Mortgage bonds

5.
Standard and Poor's Bond Guide:

a.   reports completed corporate bond trades on a real-time basis
b.   lists dealer offerings of corporate bonds in the secondary market
c.   gives capsule summaries of every outstanding corporate issue, including recent price, rating, and yield
d.   gives the details of each corporate new issue that is coming to market

6.
TRACE reports trades of all of the following **EXCEPT:**

a.   corporate bonds
b.   municipal bonds
c.   government bonds
d.   agency bonds

7.
In a corporate liquidation, the priority of claim to corporate assets is:

a.   Unpaid wages and taxes, debenture holders, mortgage bond holders, preferred stockholders
b.   Unpaid wages and taxes, preferred stockholders, debenture holders, mortgage bondholders
c.   Mortgage bond holders, debenture holders, unpaid wages and taxes, preferred stockholders
d.   Mortgage bond holders, unpaid wages and taxes, debenture holders, preferred stockholders

8.

The term "Funded Debt" applies to:

  I   Commercial Paper
  II   Corporate Bonds
  III Municipal Notes
  IV   Treasury Bills

  a. I only
  b. II only
  c. I and II
  d. II, III, IV

9.

All of the following bonds trade "flat" **EXCEPT:**

  a. defaulted bonds
  b. zero coupon bonds
  c. market discount bonds
  d. adjustment (income) bonds

10.

A customer buys 10 PDQ Corporation 10% debentures, M '35, at 93 on Friday, June 12th in a regular way trade. The interest payment dates are March 1st and September 1st. The trade settles on:

  a. Monday, June 15th
  b. Tuesday, June 16th
  c. Wednesday, June 17th
  d. Friday, June 19th

11.

A corporate bond which is backed solely by the full faith and credit of the issuer is a:

  a. debenture
  b. collateral trust certificate
  c. mortgage bond
  d. general obligation bond

12.

A customer purchases a convertible bond at 90, convertible into the common stock at $40. The common stock is currently trading at $36. The company declares a 25% stock dividend. The bond trust indenture includes an anti-dilution clause. Which statements are true **BEFORE** the stock dividend was declared?

  I   There is a bona fide arbitrage opportunity
  II   The conversion ratio is 25:1
  III The bond and the stock are trading at parity
  IV   If the bond is purchased and the equivalent number of common shares are sold short, there is an immediate profit

  a. I and IV only
  b. II and III only
  c. II and IV only
  d. I, II, III, IV

13.

A customer purchases a convertible bond at 90, convertible into the common stock at $40. The common stock is currently trading at $36. The company declares a 25% stock dividend. The bond trust indenture includes an anti-dilution clause. After the ex date for the stock dividend, the conversion price for this bond issue will be:

  a. $30
  b. $32
  c. $36
  d. $40

14.

All of the following are true statements regarding convertible bond issues **EXCEPT:**

a. at the time of issuance, the conversion price is set at a premium to the stock's current market price

b. the yield on convertible issues is higher than the yield for similar non-convertible issues

c. when the stock price is at a premium to the conversion price, bond price movements are usually caused by those of the stock

d. when the stock price is at a discount to the conversion price, bond price movements are usually caused by interest rate changes

15.

Accrued interest on a new issue corporate bond is calculated from:

a. dated date to settlement date

b. dated date to first interest payment

c. settlement date to first interest payment

d. trade date to settlement date

16.

A customer has bought a fully registered Exxon-Mobil debenture. The customer will receive interest payments:

a. from the paying agent once a year

b. from the paying agent twice a year

c. by clipping coupons once a year

d. by clipping coupons twice a year

17.

A customer buys 10 Allied Corporation 8% debentures, M '35, at 90 on Monday, October 8th. The interest payment dates are Feb. 1st and Aug. 1st. The trade settled on Wednesday, October 10th. How many days of accrued interest will the buyer pay to the seller?

a. 62

b. 63

c. 69

d. 70

18.

A customer buys 10M of Allied Corporation 8% debentures, M '35, at 90 on Tuesday, October 8th. The interest payment dates are Feb. 1st and Aug. 1st. The trade settled on Thursday, October 11th. The amount of the next interest payment will be:

a. $400

b. $444

c. $800

d. $888

19.

A customer buys 10M of Allied Corporation 8% debentures, M '41, at 90 on Tuesday, October 12th. The interest payment dates are Feb. 1st and Aug. 1st. The trade settled on Thursday, October 14th. The customer will receive how many months of interest in the next payment?

a. 2 1/2

b. 3 1/2

c. 6

d. 12

20.

All of the following statements are true regarding corporate zero coupon bonds **EXCEPT:**

a. zero coupon bonds do not offer investors a current return

b. zero coupon bonds are usually suitable investments for Individual retirement Accounts and Self Employed Retirement Plans

c. the interest income on such obligations is not taxable until maturity

d. the rate of return for zero coupon bonds is not subject to reinvestment risk associated with interest paying issues

21.

A corporation has posted a large financial loss for this year. It has a legal obligation to pay interest on all of the following bonds **EXCEPT:**

a. debentures

b. subordinated debentures

c. adjustment bonds

d. equipment trust certificates

22.

Which of the following affect the marketability of corporate bonds?

I   Bond rating
II Maturity
III Block size
IV Bond denominations

a. I only

b. II only

c. I, II, III

d. II, III, IV

23.

A guaranteed corporate bond is one which is:

a. insured by a private agency such as FGIC

b. guaranteed by the Federal Government

c. guaranteed by another corporation

d. funded through mandatory sinking fund payments

24.

All of the following corporate bonds are secured **EXCEPT:**

a. equipment trust certificates

b. second mortgage bonds

c. sinking fund debentures

d. collateral trust certificates

25.

The maximum maturity on commercial paper is:

a. 14 days

b. 30 days

c. 90 days

d. 270 days

26.

A short term corporate debt which is backed solely by the full faith and credit of the issuer is:

a. commercial paper

b. an income bond

c. a mortgage bond

d. a general obligation bond

27.

Ford Motor Company has issued 8% convertible debentures, convertible at a 12.5:1 ratio. Currently the debenture is trading at 90. The stock is trading at $72. What is the conversion price of the stock?

a. $72

b. $75

c. $80

d. $90

28.

Ford Motor Company has issued 8% convertible debentures, convertible at a 12.5:1 ratio. Currently the debenture is trading at 90. The stock is trading at $72. Which statement is **TRUE?**

   a.   The bond is trading at parity with the stock

   b.   The stock is trading above the bond's parity price

   c.   The stock is trading below the bond's parity price

   d.   The parity price is based on the market price of the stock

29.

All of the following are true statements regarding corporate obligations **EXCEPT:**

   a.   debentures are usually term issues

   b.   commercial paper is usually sold at a discount

   c.   corporate yields are higher than municipal yields

   d.   most corporate bonds are traded through the New York Stock Exchange

30.

Equipment trust certificates would most likely be issued by a(n):

   a.   manufacturer

   b.   utility

   c.   airline

   d.   bank

Debt Securities

CORPORATE DEBT EXAMINATION EXPLANATIONS

1. The best answer is **d**. Quote providers such as Bloomberg and Reuters give dealer to dealer prices (the "wholesale" market) for corporate bonds daily. These are bonds that are trading in the secondary market.

2. The best answer is **b**. In a tender offer, the issuer of the securities is offering to buy back either a portion or all of the issue at a stated price. These offers are usually conditioned upon a minimum percentage of the issue being tendered, otherwise the issuer cancels the offer. The price of the tender offer is set by the issuer, typically using the advice of a securities firm acting as "financial advisor" in the offer. Choice **D** is technically incorrect - an underwriter does not set the price; rather, a firm advises the issuer in setting a price, and this firm may, as part of its business, participate in underwritings.

3. The best answer is **c**. Zero-coupon bonds are often called "capital appreciation bonds" since the bondholder does not receive annual interest payments from the issuer. Instead, the bonds are bought at a discount from par, and are redeemed at par at maturity (similar to savings bonds). The discount is earned over the life of the bond and is the "income" from this type of investment.

4. The best answer is **b**. When a bond is trading "flat," it is trading without accrued interest. Income bonds trade flat since they do not pay interest unless the corporation meets a specific earnings target. The other bonds make periodic interest payments. Unsecured bonds, such as corporate debentures, trade with accrued interest. (They only trade flat if they have defaulted.) Reset bonds establish dates when the interest rate can be reset to a given index value. Mortgage bonds pay interest semi-annually, and have a lien on real property as collateral.

5. The best answer is **c**. Standard and Poor's Bond Guide is published on the web, and gives capsule summaries of every outstanding corporate issue, including recent price, rating, and yield. Reports of corporate bond trades are made through TRACE (FINRA's Trade Reporting and Compliance Engine). Dealer offerings of corporate bonds are found on Bloomberg and Reuters, as well as each bond dealer's web site. The Bond Guide does not include corporate new issue information.

6. The best answer is **b**. TRACE is FINRA's Trade Reporting and Compliance Engine. It reports trades of corporate, government, and agency bonds. Municipal bond trades are reported via RTRS - the Real Time Reporting System - operated by the MSRB.
Trades must be reported to TRACE "as soon as practicable," but no later than 15 minutes after execution. TRACE disseminates the trade report immediately.

7. The best answer is **d**. The priority of claim to corporate assets in a liquidation is: Secured creditors, unpaid wages and taxes, trade creditors, unsecured bondholders, preferred stockholders, common stockholders.

8. The best answer is **b**. "Funded debt" is a term that applies to long term corporate obligations. This debt is "funded," indicating that the monies are long term and do not have to be repaid shortly. Short term debt is termed "unfunded" debt - these are not a long term funding. All of the other choices - commercial paper, municipal notes, and Treasury bills are short term obligations.

9. The best answer is **c**. Market discount bonds are simply bonds trading at a discount in the secondary market because interest rates have risen. These bonds are meeting their interest payments and trade with accrued interest. Defaulted bonds trade flat; zero coupon bonds trade flat (since no interest payments are made); and adjustment bonds trade flat since interest is only paid if the issuer earns enough income to service the debt.

10. The best answer is **b**. Regular way trades of corporate bonds and stocks settle 2 business days after trade date (effective September 5, 2017).

11. The best answer is **a**. A debenture is corporate debt which is backed solely by the full faith and credit of the issuing corporation. Collateral trust certificates are backed by marketable securities held in trust; mortgage bonds are backed by real property owned by the issuing corporation. General obligation bonds are issued by municipalities; they are not issued by corporations.

12. The best answer is **b**. Arbitrage can only work if the equivalent number of shares of stock are selling for more than the bond. The bond is convertible into stock at $40 per share. Conversion always takes place with the bond valued at par so the conversion ratio is:

$$\frac{\text{Par Value of Bond}}{\text{Conversion Price}} = \text{Conversion Ratio}$$

$$\frac{\$1,000}{\$40} = 25 : 1$$

The bond is currently selling for $900. The stock is selling at $36. The bond is convertible into 25 shares of stock worth $36 = $900. The bond and the stock are at parity. Arbitrage cannot be successful at parity; the stock must be selling above parity to have an arbitrage opportunity between a convertible security and the equivalent common shares.

13. The best answer is **b**. If the company issues additional shares, each of the existing shares is worth "less" since the company's earnings are spread over a greater number of shares. Thus, the market price will adjust downward to reflect this. If a company issues 25% more shares (after the dividend, there will be 1.25 times the old number of shares), then the earnings and consequently the share price will drop by a factor of 1/1.25.

The bondholder bought the issue based on a conversion price of $40. The market price of the stock is being diluted by the additional shares, reducing or eliminating the value of the bondholder's conversion feature. To protect the bondholder from this occurrence, trust indentures include an anti-dilution covenant. The conversion price of the stock is adjusted downwards by the same factor, so that the convertible bondholder experiences no loss from the issuance of the new shares.

$$\frac{\text{Old Price}}{\text{New Factor}} = \text{New Conversion Price}$$

$$\frac{\$40}{1.25} = \$32 \text{ per share}$$

14. The best answer is **b**. When convertible bonds are issued, it is normal for the conversion price to be at a premium to the current market price. Thus, for the conversion feature to be worth something, the stock's price must move up in the market. Due to the value of the conversion feature (or rather, the potential value if the stock price goes up), convertible bonds are saleable at lower yields than bonds without the conversion feature.

When the stock price is at a discount to the conversion price, the conversion feature is worthless. The bond is valued based on interest rate movements. On the other hand, when the stock price is at a premium to the conversion price, the conversion feature now has intrinsic value. For every dollar that the stock now moves, the bond will move as well, since the securities are "equivalent."

15. The best answer is **a**. Accrued interest on a new issue is calculated from the dated date till settlement date. A new issue is bought from the underwriter. The customer pays the underwriter the price of the bond plus any accrued interest. This interest accrues from the dated date of the issue (the date of legal issuance) until the date the customer settles the purchase with the underwriter.

16. The best answer is **b**. All new issues of U.S. Government bonds, municipal bonds and corporate bonds are book entry. A "book entry" bond is a fully registered bond where no paper certificate is issued. Instead, the owner simply receives that confirmation that he or she bought the bond. On such bonds, the paying agent mails the semi-annual interest payments to the registered owner.

Note, however, that there are still many issues of long term corporate bonds still outstanding that have paper certificates. These bonds have not yet matured. Book entry bonds did not really come to dominate bond issuance until the 1990s, so 30-year bond certificates issued, say in 1995, do not mature until 2025. A fully registered bond is one issued with a physical certificate. The paying agent has the record of the owner's name and mails the interest payments semi-annually to the registered owner.

Also note that no bearer bonds have been sold since 1983, but 40-year bearer bonds still exist (at least until 2023!). Bearer bondholders receive interest payments by clipping coupons and submitting them to the paying agent.

17. The best answer is **c**. Interest accrues on a 30 day month / 360 day year basis for corporate bonds. The bonds were purchased on Monday, October 8th. Settlement takes place on Wednesday, Oct 10th. Interest accrues up to but does not include settlement date. Thus, 30 days are due for Aug; 30 for Sept; and 9 for Oct; for a total of 69 days.

18. The best answer is **a**. 10M stands for 10 - $1,000 bonds (M is Latin for $1,000) = $10,000 face amount of bonds. The bonds pay 8% interest annually. 8% of $10,000 is $800 annual interest. Since payments are made semi-annually, $400 is the amount of each payment. Note that the accrued interest paid from buyer to seller on settlement has no effect on the payments made by the issuer to the bondholder of record.

19. The best answer is **c**. The buyer pays the seller any accrued interest due at settlement. The buyer then shows as the owner of record for the next 6 month interest payment.

20. The best answer is **c**. Zero coupon bonds do not offer a current return; instead, the holder earns the discount on the bond over its life. This "earning" of the discount is taxed annually as interest income to the bondholder even though no physical payment is made.

Zero coupon bonds are usually invested in IRAs and retirement plans since these vehicles are tax deferred, thus avoiding paying tax on interest income that isn't actually received.

With bonds that make interest payments, the holder is subject to "reinvestment risk" on the interest payments. Rates may fall, causing the bondholder to reinvest the interest payments at lower rates. This risk is not present in zero coupon bonds since no interest payments are made.

21. The best answer is **c**. Adjustment (also known as "income") bonds obligate the issuer to pay interest only if the company meets a specified earnings test. If the earnings are not sufficient, no interest payment is legally required. All other bonds obligate the issuer to pay interest, regardless of events.

22. The best answer is **c**. The higher rated a bond, the more marketable it is. The shorter the maturity, the more marketable it is. For corporate bonds, the most marketable blocks are 5 bonds up to 100 bonds. Under 5 is an odd lot; over 100 is a large block which is more difficult to trade. The bond denominations have no effect on marketability.

23. The best answer is **c**. A guaranteed corporate bond is one guaranteed by another corporation. For example, a corporation may want to issue bonds through a subsidiary. The subsidiary may have a lower credit rating than the parent company. The parent can guarantee the issue, which then takes on the parent's higher credit rating.

24. The best answer is **c**. A secured bondholder has a lien on a specific asset of the company - such as equipment (an equipment trust certificate), real property (a mortgage bond) or securities given as collateral (a collateral trust certificate). A debenture is a promise to pay without any liens on corporate assets.

25. The best answer is **d**. Commercial paper is an exempt security under the Securities Act of 1933. It doesn't have to be registered and sold with a prospectus if its maturity is 270 days or less.

26. The best answer is **a**. Commercial paper is simply backed by the issuer's full faith and credit (the promise to pay). The maturities are short, most typically 30 days or less, though legally the maturity can extend to 270 days maximum (9 months). All of the other debts listed are long term (over 1 year) obligations. Income bonds are long term corporate obligations that require the issuer to pay interest only if it has sufficient income. Mortgage bonds are backed by real property owned by the issuing corporation. General obligation bonds are issued by municipalities; they are not issued by corporations.

27. The best answer is **c**. The bond is convertible into common at a 12.5:1 ratio, based on the par value of the bond. The conversion price formula is:

$$\frac{\text{Par Value of Bond}}{\text{Conversion Ratio}} = \text{Conversion Price}$$

$$\frac{\$1,000 \text{ par}}{12.5} = \$80 \text{ conversion price}$$

28. The best answer is **a**. The bond is convertible into 12.5 shares of stock, now trading at $72, for a conversion value of $900 ($72 x 12.5 = $900). Since the bond is trading at 90 ($900), the stock and the bond are trading at parity to each other.

29. The best answer is **d**. Debentures are usually term issues - all bonds having the same interest rate and maturity. Commercial paper is sold at a discount and matures at par - note that this is true for almost all money market securities. Corporate yields are higher than municipal yields because the interest income is fully taxable. Though a very small amount of corporate bonds are traded on the NYSE (in a separate trade matching computer), most of the trading volume takes place over-the-counter between corporate bond dealers such as Goldman Sachs and other firms.

30. The best answer is **c**. Equipment trust certificates are issued by common carriers such as airlines, railroads, and trucking companies. The rolling (or flying) stock is the collateral for the debt.

This page intentionally left blank

SECTION 3: U.S. GOVERNMENT DEBT

3a. CHARACTERISTICS OF U.S. GOVERNMENT DEBT

Largest Debt Market

The U.S. Government issues debt in order to finance the running of the government. The market for U.S. Government debt is the largest and most active trading market in the world. Currently, there is over $20 trillion in debt outstanding (our accumulated federal deficit). Negotiable government debt issues take the form of long-term bonds, intermediate-term notes, and short-term notes, known as Treasury Bills

U.S. Government Securities Are Exempt From The Securities Acts

Note that U.S. Government bonds and the market participants are exempt from regulation under the Securities Act of 1933; and the Securities Exchange Act of 1934. Thus, the Securities and Exchange Commission does not oversee U.S. Government bond trading. However, the Federal Reserve, in its regulation of banks (who are large participants in this market), does have an oversight role.

Also note that savings bonds (EE Bonds) are **NOT** part of this market - they are non-negotiable and cannot be traded. They are bought from the government and can only be redeemed with the government.

New Issues - Book Entry

Short-term Treasury Bills, intermediate-term notes and long-term bonds are typically issued in "book entry" form. No certificates are issued for book entry securities; the only ownership record is the "book" of owners kept by the transfer agent. No physical certificates have been issued since 1983. Prior to that date, notes and bonds were available in fully registered form - physical certificates were issued. These outstanding securities continue to trade until their redemption date.

T-Bill - Weekly Auction

All Other Treasury Debt - Monthly Auction

U.S. Government debt is sold by competitive bidding at a weekly auction conducted by the Federal Reserve. At the weekly auction, Treasury Bills are sold. This is, by far, the largest amount of debt issued by the government. Every four weeks, notes, bonds, and TIPS (Treasury Inflation Protection Security) are sold at auction.

The actual amount of debt for sale at each auction depends on the financing needs of the government. For example, right after April 15th, sales are reduced since the government has just received that year's tax receipts. (Auction procedures are covered in detail in the New Issues chapter.)

Agency Debt Highest Rating

Debt is also issued by agencies of the U.S. Government. Agency debt is not backed directly by the Government's promise to pay. Instead, there is an implicit promise on the part of the government to pay if the debt defaults. (One agency debt is directly backed by the government - Government National Mortgage Association.)

Direct Treasury Debt Highest Rating	U.S. Government debt is considered to be the highest rated debt - essentially free of credit risk. (Note that this is still the case, regardless of the Standard and Poor's credit downgrade to AA that occurred in 2011 - the other credit ratings agencies kept the rating at AAA). Agency debt is also highly rated (AAA) but is considered less safe than the direct debt.

3b. U.S. GOVERNMENT OBLIGATIONS

Treasury Bonds **30 Year Maturity** **Quoted In 32nds**	Treasury Bonds: Long-term securities issued with maturities of 30 years. The bonds are issued in minimum denominations of $100 and pay interest semi-annually to registered holders. Note that the $100 minimum is atypical - corporate and municipal bonds are sold in $1,000 minimums. The Treasury reduced the minimum from $1,000 to $100 in 2008 to expand investor interest. For the exam, bond quotes will still be in $1,000 amounts. Treasury bonds are quoted as a percentage of par, in minimum increments of 1/32nd.
Non-Callable	Long-term Treasury bonds are non-callable. In the past, the Treasury issued long bonds that were callable in the last 5 years of their lives, but they all matured in 2009. Now, all long bonds are non-callable. Over the years, the Treasury introduced variations on Treasury Bonds to meet specific investor needs.
STRIPS	For investors that wished to avoid reinvestment risk, the Treasury introduced Treasury STRIPS.
TIPS	For investors that wished to avoid purchasing power risk, the Treasury introduced TIPS.
STRIPS Is A Treasury Bond That Is Stripped Of Coupons	"STRIPS" - STRIPS are Treasury Bonds that have been "stripped" of their coupons. These are "zero coupon" Treasury Obligations. The full name is actually a "Separate Trading of Registered Interest and Principal Security," which is a fairly indecipherable phrase. To understand where the name "STRIPS" came from, let's take the picture of a coupon bond shown earlier in this chapter and use it to show what is happening here.

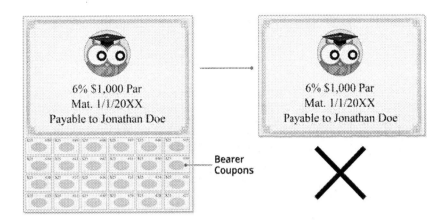

Bearer
Coupons

Remember that a bond really has 2 components - the semi-annual interest payments, represented by the coupons on the bond and the final principal repayment at maturity. In concept, a STRIP bond "strips" off the coupons from the bond, leaving just the final principal repayment of $1,000 that will occur years in the future. By stripping the coupons off the bond, we have created a "zero-coupon" Treasury bond.

If the bond is a 6%, 30 year STRIPS, the bond could be purchased right now for about $175 (rounded). Its principal value grows at a rate of 6% a year, and at maturity, the bond will be redeemed at $1,000.

No Reinvestment Risk

This investment is designed for pension fund managers who want a safe, long term investment and who do not want to worry about having to reinvest semi-annual interest payments that could be subject to reinvestment risk (if market interest rates fall during this time period).

High Level Of Interest Rate Risk

Because these are long-term zero-coupon (deep discount) obligations, price swings are very volatile as interest rates move. This security is highly susceptible to interest rate risk. But, purchasers are not too worried about this since STRIPS are usually held to maturity.

Predecessor To STRIPS Is A Treasury Receipt

The Treasury first started selling STRIPS in 1986. Before this, brokerage firms would buy conventional Treasury bonds and "strip" them to sell to pension fund investors. These broker-created zero-coupon bonds are generically called Treasury Receipts. They are no longer created (because the Treasury cut out the middleman by stripping bonds itself) but they still trade in the market. For the exam, Treasury Receipts must still be known - remember that they are zero-coupon Treasury bonds.

Treasury Inflation Protection Securities ("TIPS")

Interest Payment Adjusts With Inflation

"TIPS" - "Treasury Inflation Protection Securities" have a fixed interest rate over the life of the bond; however, the principal amount is adjusted every 6 months by an amount equal to the change in the Consumer Price Index. The bond pays interest semi-annually, and the interest amount (the fixed rate x the adjusted principal amount) will increase if the principal amount is adjusted upwards due to inflation; and will decrease if the principal amount is decreased due to deflation.

Principal Repayment The Higher Of Par Or The Inflation Adjusted Amount

If the principal amount is adjusted upwards due to inflation, the bondholder receives the higher amount at maturity. Thus, the bond is protected against purchasing power risk. On the other hand, if the principal amount is decreased due to deflation, the bondholder will always receive par at maturity.

Lower Interest Rate Than Regular Treasury Issues

TIPS have a lower interest rate than similar maturity regular Treasury issues because of this inflation protection feature. TIPS are only available for long-term Treasury issues.

To really understand the concept behind TIPS, consider the following:

1996		2016
7%	30-Year Treasury Bond Nominal Yield	3.50%
4%	Inflation Rate	0.50%
3%	"Real Interest Rate"	3%

Over the past 20 years, as the inflation rate has dropped in the United States, nominal rates have fallen at a similar rate. However, the "real interest rate" on 30 year Treasury bonds has not changed at all - it has stayed right around 3%. What this chart implies is that nominal interest rates for Treasury bonds really have 2 components - the "real" interest rate of 3% plus that year's inflation rate.

So, as inflation rates drop, nominal rates fall in tandem, and real rates stay the same. On the other hand, if inflation heats up again, then nominal rates will rise. This will hurt the holders of conventional long-term Treasury Bonds.

With the addition of TIPS, the Treasury is really giving the investor a choice - you can buy a 3.50% conventional 30 year Treasury bond that is subject to interest rate risk; or you can buy a 3% TIPS, where each year, your return will be the 3% "real interest rate" plus an additional return equal to that year's inflation rate.

So if inflation rises to, say, 1% in 2017, the TIPS return for that year will be the 3% real rate + the 1% inflation rate for that year = 4% total return. (The 3% is received as interest, while the inflation component is added to the principal amount of the bond.)

If the inflation rate rises to 2% in 2018, then the TIPS return for that year will be the 3% real rate + the 2% inflation rate for that year = 5% total return.

If the inflation rate rises again to 3% in 2019, then the TIPS return for that year will be the 3% real rate + the 3% inflation rate for that year = 6% total return.

Thus, as inflation rises, the return rises, and the TIPS price will not fall.

Treasury Notes

Over 1-10 Years

Quoted In 32nds

Treasury Notes: Intermediate-term securities issued with maturities ranging from over 1 to 10 years. The notes are issued in minimum denominations of $100 par value and pay interest semi-annually to registered holders. Treasury notes are quoted as a percentage of par value in 32nds. Notes are non-callable.

Treasury Bills

Up To 12 Months

Yield Basis Quote

Treasury Bills: Short-term securities issued with 1, 3, 6 and 12 month maturities (this should be known as 4 weeks, 13 weeks, 26 weeks and 52 weeks as well). Treasury Bills are issued at a discount from par ($100 minimum) and mature at par. The discount earned is considered to be the interest income. They are quoted on a discount yield basis.

Cash Management Bill (CMB)

5 Days To 6 Months

Cash Management Bill: These are very short-term Treasury securities with typical maturities that can range anywhere from 5 days to 6 months. Unlike other Treasury securities that are sold at a regular scheduled auction, these are sold at auction on an "as needed" basis when the Treasury is running low on cash. Thus, they are used by the Treasury to smooth out its cash flow needs. They are sold in $100 minimum amounts and pay a slightly higher interest rate than equivalent maturity T-Bills sold on a regular auction schedule.

3c. U.S. GOVERNMENT AGENCY OBLIGATIONS

Our government believes that certain aspects of American life are sacrosanct - Motherhood, Apple Pie, Farming, and Home Ownership. Government policy promotes these aspects of American life. U.S. Government agencies have been formed to finance the last two sacred cows.

Federal Farm Credit System

Farmers can obtain low rate financing through the Federal Farm Credit System. To provide funding to farmers, such as short-term loans for planting and harvest; intermediate term loans to buy equipment; and long term loans to buy land and buildings; the Federal Farm Credit Banks Funding Corporation issues the following securities:

Discount Notes: Short-Term Obligations of 1 year or less, sold at a discount from minimum $5,000 face amount, with $1,000 increments thereafter. Because these are an agency obligation, with no "direct" U.S. Government guarantee, they yield more than equivalent maturity T-Bills.

Designated Bonds: Traditional non-callable bonds that pay interest semi-annually issued in 2-10 year maturities. These are issued in $5,000 minimum face amounts, with $1,000 increments thereafter.

Bonds: Traditional callable bonds issued with up to a 30 year maturity that pay interest semi-annually. These can either be fixed rate bonds, issued in $5,000 minimum face amounts, with $1,000 increments thereafter; or floating rate bonds issued in $100,000 minimum face amounts, with $1,000 increments thereafter.

Retail Bonds: Designed for retail investors, these are similar to the Bonds offering listed above, but are available in minimum $1,000 denominations and they have a unique estate planning feature. These bonds have a "survivor's option" which allows the bond to be redeemed at par plus accrued interest upon death. Since estate taxes (if any) are due 9 months after death, these bonds can be redeemed and used to pay that death tax liability.

Unlike Treasuries which are sold at auction, these agency obligations are offered by a selling group of dealers, mainly large commercial banks and brokerage firms. They are given the same rating as Treasuries (AAA from Moody's and Fitch's; AA from Standard and Poor's), due to the "implied" backing of the U.S. Government. However, they typically yield .25% more than equivalent maturity Treasuries, because they do not have a direct U.S. Government guarantee.

Also note that these selling dealers quote agencies on a "yield spread basis" to equivalent maturity Treasuries.

For example, if the 30 year Treasury Bond is yielding 4.50%, while the 30 year Federal Farm Credit Bond is yielding 4.75%, the dealer will quote the FFCB bond at "25 basis points over."

The U.S. Government promotes home ownership through the activities of the:

- Federal Home Loan Banks (FHLB)
- Federal National Mortgage Association ("Fannie Mae")
- Government National Mortgage Association ("Ginnie Mae")
- Federal Home Loan Mortgage Corporation ("Freddie Mac")

Secondary Market For Home Mortgages

These agencies make a secondary market in home mortgages. They purchase the mortgages from the local banks that originated the loans. This injects new funds into the local banks, allowing them to give more mortgages.

NOT Directly Backed By U.S. Government Except For GNMA

The agencies obtain the funds to buy the mortgages by selling bonds to the public. The U.S. Government does not directly back these issues with the exception of the Government National Mortgage Association. "Ginnie Maes" are directly backed by the government, whereas the other agencies are backed implicitly, not directly.

Also note that the Federal Government "takeover" of Fannie and Freddie in the fall of 2008 due to overwhelming mortgage losses still does not mean that these securities are directly government guaranteed. Fannie and Freddie are in a "conservatorship" where their management and operations are controlled by the Federal Government - but their securities are still not government "guaranteed."

The activities of the agencies are:

Federal Home Loan Bank (FHLB)

Federal Home Loan Banks: FHLB was the first mortgage agency, created in 1932 in the Great Depression to provide funds to Savings and Loans so they could give homeowners mortgages. It loans funds to Savings and Loan institutions, with the main collateral for the loans being S & L mortgages.

To finance this activity, FHLB issues:

Discount Notes

Discount Notes: Short-Term Obligations of 1 year or less, sold at a discount from minimum $100,000 face amount, with $1,000 increments thereafter. Because these are an agency obligation, with no "direct" U.S. Government guarantee, they yield more than equivalent maturity T-Bills.

Callable Bonds

Non-Callable Bullet Bonds

Bonds: Traditional callable bonds issued with up to a 30 year maturity that pay interest semi-annually. These are fixed rate bonds, issued in $10,000 minimum face amounts. Also note that FHLB issues "so-called" bullet bonds. These are non-callable bonds. The term "bullet bond" comes from the fact that these non-callable bonds are identified in dealer offering listings with a "bullet" next to the listing, indicating a non-callable bond.

As with all agency securities, these securities are offered through a selling group of dealers.

"Fannie," "Freddie," "Ginnie"

Issuers Of Mortgage-Backed Securities

The other 3 housing agencies - Fannie Mae, Freddie Mac and Ginnie Mae - are primarily the issuers of "mortgage-backed pass through certificates." They also issue other types of debt, but the vast majority of their debt issuance is in the form of "MBSs" - Mortgage Backed Securities. There is a huge amount of mortgage backed debt issued by these agencies - about $14 trillion as of the end of 2016 (as compared to $20 trillion of Treasury debt).

Before going into the specifics of each agency, let's cover MBSs, because they are completely different from conventional bonds.

Debt Securities

$25,000 Minimum Mortgage Backed Pass Through Certificates	Each agency continuously buys mortgages from originating banks. This gives the bank fresh funds to lend out on new mortgages. Once a sufficient amount of mortgages have been purchased (say $1 billion - yes, this market deals in big numbers!), they are placed into a "pool." The agency divides the pool into $25,000 mortgage backed pass through certificates and sells them to investors. (The reason why these are sold in $25,000 minimums, as opposed to $1,000 or $5,000 minimums for most other bonds, is to make them unattractive to the small investor. MBSs have an unusual risk that small investors may not understand, prepayment risk, covered following).
Monthly Mortgage Payments Passed Through To The Certificate Holder	As mortgage payments are received from the pooled mortgages, the payments are funneled to the certificate holders. Payments are made monthly, with each payment representing a portion of principal and interest (since these are mortgage payments). The certificates are self-liquidating as the mortgages are paid off.
Prepayment Risk	The length of the certificate depends on the underlying mortgages in the pool. In reality, the actual life of the certificate is shorter because mortgage prepayments occur when homes are sold or mortgages refinanced. These prepayments are passed through to the certificate holder. Because of prepayment risk, the real maturity is unknown.
	Now let's cover a bit of detail on each of the 3 agencies:
Fannie Mae **Buys VA And FHA Guaranteed Mortgages** **Buys Conventional Mortgages**	Fannie Mae: Buys government guaranteed and insured mortgages (such as Veterans Administration "VA" insured and Federal Housing Administration "FHA" guaranteed mortgages) as well as conventional mortgages from banks. It derives its income from the spread between the rate at which it borrows funds from the public and the rate it earns on purchased mortgages. It earns fees, as well, for servicing pass through certificates.
Fannie Mae Is "Privatized"	Fannie Mae was formed in 1938 in the Great Depression as a government agency to buy mortgages from banks, providing the banks with fresh funds to make new mortgages. It was "spun off" by the Federal government in 1968 as a separate profit making corporation and was NYSE-listed. In the 1990s during the Clinton Administration, Fannie Mae was mandated to buy "subprime" mortgages to make housing affordable to lower income groups. Many of these loans turned out to be bad credits, and the enormous amount of these bad loans purchased through the years forced Fannie (and Freddie Mac, covered following) into bankruptcy in 2008.
Debt Rated AAA (Moody's) Or AA (Standard + Poor's)	Due to its bankruptcy and placement in government conservatorship in 2008, its stock was delisted and now trades in the Pink Sheets for well under $1 per share. However, Fannie Mae debt obligations are implicitly backed by the Federal government and are still rated AAA by Moody's and AA by Standard and Poor's

Ginnie Mae

Ginnie Mae: The "Government National Mortgage Association" was created in 1968 - the same year that Fannie Mae was spun off by the Federal government. It is the only housing agency that is directly owned and backed by the Federal government.

It was created when the MBS was first beginning to be introduced to the marketplace. Because it was a new security at the time, it was believed that, to gain broad investor acceptance, having a government agency issue them with a direct government backing would create a robust market (which it did).

Ginnie Only Buys Government Insured Mortgages

In contrast to Fannie Mae (and Freddie Mac, covered next), Ginnie does not buy conventional mortgages. It only buys FHA, VA, and Farmer's Home Administration (FmHA) insured mortgages from banks and places them into mortgage pools, which are then securitized and sold to investors.

Federal Home Loan Mortgage Corp. (FHLMC)

"Freddie Mac"

Buys Conventional Mortgages Only

Freddie Mac: The "Federal Home Loan Mortgage Corporation" (FHLMC) was the final mortgage agency, created in 1970. It was listed as a stock company on the NYSE. Its purpose is to buy conventional mortgages that do not carry government insurance or a government guarantee. This contrasts with Ginnie Mae that only buys government guaranteed or insured mortgages; and Fannie Mae that can buy both government guaranteed and conventional mortgages.

Just like these other agencies, Freddie Mac buys these conventional mortgages from banks and places them into mortgage pools, which are then securitized and sold to investors. And just like Fannie Mae, Freddie Mac was mandated to buy subprime mortgages in the mid-1990s, and the mass defaults on these loans led to its bankruptcy in 2008.

Debt Rated AAA (Moody's) Or AA (Standard + Poor's)

Due to its bankruptcy and placement in government conservatorship in 2008, its stock was delisted and now trades in the Pink Sheets for around $2 per share. However, Freddie Mac debt obligations are implicitly backed by the Federal government and are still rated AAA by Moody's and AA by Standard and Poor's.

Sallie Mae

There are other agencies, but the only one that need be known is "Sallie Mae" - Student Loan Marketing Association. "Sallie Mae" purchases insured student loans from qualified lending institutions. Loans are purchased from colleges, universities, state agencies, and banks. Sallie Mae sells normal debentures paying interest semi-annually backed by these loans.

Sallie Mae Is "Privatized"

Sallie Mae is another "privatized" company, whose stock is listed on NASDAQ - and it is not bankrupt! It makes its profit from the spread between the interest rate charged on its loans to students versus the lower interest rate at which it can borrow funds.

Debt Securities

Sallie Mae is much smaller than the housing agencies, with about $200 billion of debt outstanding.

3d. COLLATERALIZED MORTGAGE OBLIGATIONS (CMOs)

Mortgage Characteristics

A mortgage is defined as a pledge of property to secure payment of a debt, typically real estate such as a house. Traditionally, most home mortgages have been structured similarly. These characteristics are:

Fixed rate of interest over the term of the loan;

Equal level payments are made monthly;

The loan is self amortizing - each monthly payment combines a portion of principal repayment with the interest payment due;

Standardized maturities - most fixed rate mortgages have a 30 year life, though 15 year mortgages are becoming more popular.

The only items left to negotiate on the loan are the interest rate and the term. Traditionally, most home mortgages have 30-year terms, though 15-year mortgages are becoming more popular. Due to the "standardization" of home mortgages, these debts lend themselves to "securitization" - which means they can be transformed into securities.

Fixed Rate Mortgage

Fixed Rate Mortgages: With a fixed rate mortgage, the mortgagor pays a fixed monthly amount, with each payment being a combination of principal and interest. The early payments are mostly interest, with very little principal repayment. As the payments progress, the interest component shrinks and the principal repayment component increases. The final payments are mostly principal and very little interest. This is depicted below:

Portion of Each Mortgage Payment Represented By Interest and Principal

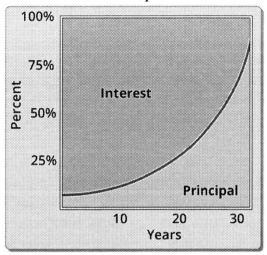

As the mortgage payments are applied to the loan balance, the principal amount due declines. Because there is very little principal repayment in the early years, the loan balance does not decline much. However, in the later years, it declines steeply due to the large principal payments being made. The diagram below shows the remaining principal balance through the years.

Remaining Principal Balance

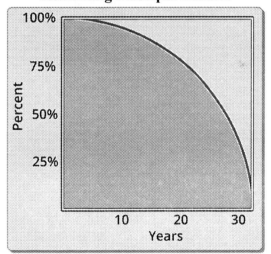

If the mortgagor **prepays** part of the mortgage, this is a direct reduction of the mortgage principal amount. If this is done, the remaining principal balance drops faster.

Securitized Mortgage

Interest Rate On GNMA Certificate Typically 50 Basis Points Lower Than Mortgage Rate

The first "securitized" mortgages were the "pass through" certificates issued by GNMA. These originated in the late 1960s. GNMA purchased mortgages from lenders with the same interest rate (say 5%) and term, and assembled them into a pool. Undivided interests in the pool were then sold to investors as "securities" - in this case, GNMA pass through certificates (yielding, say 4.50%). The 50 basis point difference is the gross profit to GNMA, out of which selling and operating expenses are paid. Each payment received by a certificate holder represents a portion of the total mortgage payments received on the pool that month.

Pass-Through Problems

Some inherent problems with pass through certificates led to the next development in the mid 1980s - CMOs - Collateralized Mortgage Obligations. The inherent problems with pass through certificates are:

Mortgage pools have a long fixed life. Most pools are either 30-year mortgages or 15-year mortgages. Investors are buying a security with a **long** life. This cuts out many investors looking for shorter term maturities.

PSA - Prepayment Speed Assumption

Furthermore, each pool of mortgages has an "average" life that is based upon the "experience" that the packagers of pass through certificates have had over long time periods. For example, based on FHA experience tables, most 30-year mortgages are paid off after 12 years. Most 15-year mortgages are paid off after 7 years. This is known as the "PSA" - Prepayment Speed Assumption.

Below is a picture of the rate of repayment that would be experienced in a 30 year mortgage pool:

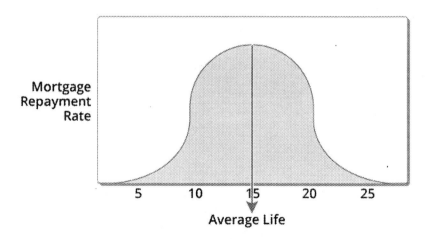

The preceding picture shows that homeowners in a 30-year mortgage pool tend to pay off their mortgages much sooner than the full 30-year term - in this case, we assume that the pool has an "average life" of 15 years. Mortgages are paid off early for either of 2 reasons:

The homeowner has sold the house and is paying off the mortgage balance; or

Interest rates have dropped and the homeowner is refinancing the mortgage at lower current interest rates.

Prepayment Risk

Similar To Call Risk

Thus, prepayment risk is greater with mortgage pools having high stated interest rates on the mortgages. When the mortgages are prepaid early, the effect is the same as a bond being called. The investor no longer gets the high interest rate and must reinvest at lower interest rates.

Principal Repaid Faster Than "PSA"

When interest rates fall by a great deal, the mortgages in the pool are paid off much earlier than expected. These principal payments come in much faster than the "PSA" (Prepayment Speed Assumption) used when the pool was created and the shape of the repayment curve "shifts" to the left as shown following:

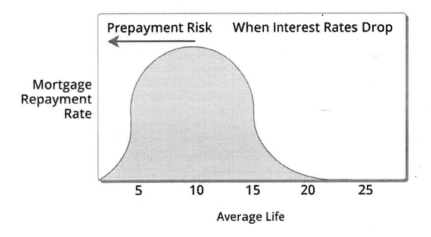

Extension Risk

Another risk is that if interest rates rise sharply, homeowners will not prepay their mortgages at the expected rate. Instead, they will hold on to their old low-rate mortgages.

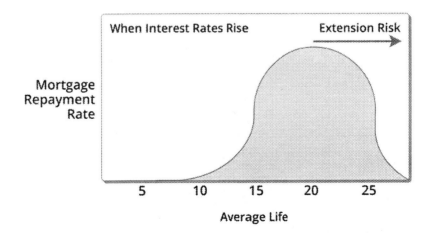

In this case, a 30-year mortgage pool would last much closer to the full 30-year life, rather than the "average" life of 15 years. Certificate holders will receive lower than market returns for a much longer time than expected. This is known as "extension risk" or "extended maturity risk." Extension risk can be visualized as a "right" shift of the repayment curve, as shown previously.

Thus, the 2 major risks for mortgage backed pass-through certificate holders are prepayment risk when interest rates drop; and extension risk when interest rates rise.

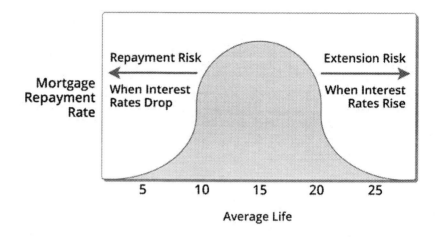

Collateralized Mortgage Obligation

Collateralized mortgage obligations (CMOs) were developed to eliminate or minimize these risks. CMOs do not view mortgage pools as a means of passing through payments to certificate holders in exactly the same form as received.

Cash Flow Basis

Tranche

Instead, the mortgage payments received are looked at on a "cash flow" basis. On the basis of expected cash flows to be received over the life of the pool, separate classes of securities called "tranches" ("slices" in French) are created. For example, a 30-year mortgage pool may be broken up into 10 tranches as listed below:

Tranche	1	1 - 3 years	4.00 %
Tranche	2	4 - 6 years	4.25 %
Tranche	3	7 - 9 years	4.50 %
Tranche	4	10 - 12 years	4.75 %
Tranche	5	13 - 15 years	5.00 %
Tranche	6	16 - 18 years	5.25 %
Tranche	7	19 - 22 years	5.50 %
Tranche	8	23 - 25 years	5.75 %
Tranche	9	26 - 28 years	6.00 %
Tranche	10	29 - 30 years	6.25 %

Each Tranche Has An Expected Life

Each tranche is said to have an "expected life," so this pool of 30-year mortgages is transformed into 10 tranches with 10 different "expected lives." This can be visualized as:

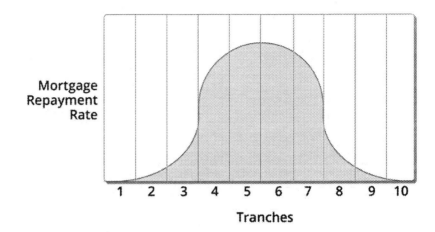

Debt Securities

Not A "Pass Through"

Yields Increase As Maturity Lengthens

Instead of passing through monthly mortgage payments to holders, a formula is used to "recut" the mortgage payments into the appropriate payments for each tranche. Note that each tranche is offered at an appropriate yield for that expected maturity, creating a variety of maturities to meet differing investor needs.

Interest Payments Applied Pro-Rata

Principal Payments Applied Sequentially

As monthly interest payments are received, the interest is distributed pro-rata to all the tranches. However, as principal is repaid, the principal repayments are first applied to Tranche 1 securities. Since repayment rates can be well estimated, the dollar size of Tranche 1 is set so that expected repayments from 1 to 3 years retire that tranche. After Tranche 1 is retired, principal repayments then are used to retire Tranche 2 starting in the 4th year, etc.

By "recutting" the cash flows received from the mortgage pool, investors can now buy a mortgage backed security with a wide range of maturities. In addition, prepayment risk is reduced, since principal payments are applied sequentially to the Tranches.

CMOs Are A Derivative Security

Plain Vanilla CMO

This is an example of a "derivative" security - the value of each tranche is derived from the method used to allocate cash flows. Older CMOs of the type just illustrated are known as "plain vanilla" CMOs, because the repayment scheme is relatively simple - as payments are received from the underlying mortgages, interest is paid pro-rata to all tranches; but principal repayments are paid sequentially to the first, then second, then third tranche, etc. Thus, the earlier tranches are retired first.

Planned Amortization Class

Companion Class

A newer version of a CMO has a more sophisticated scheme for allocating cash flows. Newer CMOs divide the tranches into PAC tranches and Companion tranches. The PAC tranche is a "Planned Amortization Class." Surrounding this tranche are 1 or 2 Companion tranches. The basic idea is that:

PACs Are Safest

The PAC tranche is given the most certain repayment date by being buffered against prepayment risk and extension risk. Because it is being relieved of these risks, it is the safest tranche and is offered at a lower yield.

Companions Are Most Risky

The Companion tranches are the "shock absorbers" that surround the PAC tranche. They absorb prepayment risk and extension risk out of the PAC. The Companion tranches have the highest risk and are offered at higher yields.

Following is a picture of a PAC tranche and its Companion tranches:

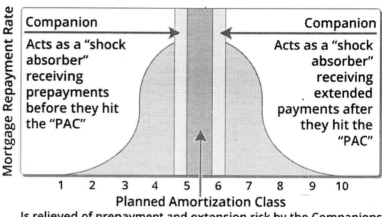

In this more sophisticated CMO structure, interest payments are still made pro-rata to all tranches, **but**:

> Principal repayments made earlier than that required to retire the PAC at its maturity are applied to the Companion class - thus, the Companions absorb any prepayment risk before the PAC is hit with the prepayments; and

> Principal repayments made later than expected are applied to the PAC maturity before payments are made to the Companion class - thus, the Companions absorb any extension risk before the PAC is hit with this risk.

PAC Is "Double Buffered" Against Both Prepayment And Extension Risk

Thus, the PAC class is given a more certain maturity date; while the Companion classes have a higher level of prepayment risk if interest rates fall; and a higher level of so-called "extension risk" - the risk that the maturity may be longer than expected, if interest rates rise.

Targeted Amortization Class

Another type of tranche is called a Targeted Amortization Class (TAC). This is a variant of a PAC. A PAC offers protection against both prepayment risk (prepayments go to the Companion class first) and extension risk (later than expected payments are applied to the PAC before payments are made to the Companion class.) From our prior picture, a PAC has 2 buffer tranches - one companion absorbs prepayment risk and 1 companion absorbs extension risk.

A TAC bond protects against prepayment risk; but does not offer the same degree of protection against extension risk. A TAC bond is designed to pay a "target" amount of principal each month. If prepayments increase, they are made to the Companion class first. However, if prepayment rates slow, the TAC absorbs the available cash flow, and goes in arrears for the balance. Thus, the average life of the TAC is extended until the arrears is paid.

TAC Is "Single Buffered" Against Prepayment Risk Only

A TAC can be visualized as a tranche that has 1 companion that only absorbs prepayment risk - there is no buffer tranche that absorbs extension risk.

Therefore, both PACs and TACs provide "call protection" against prepayments during periods of falling interest rates. TACs do not offer the same degree of protection against "extension risk" as do PACs during periods of rising interest rates - hence their prices will be more volatile during such periods.

Other types of CMO tranches can be created from the underlying mortgage cash flows. These include:

Zero (Z) Tranches

Z-Tranches are also known as accrual tranches and do not receive any payments of interest or principal until **ALL** preceding tranches are retired. This is, in essence, a zero-coupon obligation, and has the greatest price volatility of all tranches. Z-bonds are purchased by investors seeking minimum reinvestment and call risk, but they have greater interest rate risk.

Floating Rate Tranches

These are CMO PAC, TAC or companion tranches that have interest rates that are tied to a recognized index, such as LIBOR (the London Interbank Offered Rate, which is the European equivalent to the Fed Funds rate). As LIBOR moves, the interest rate on the tranche moves the same direction, subject to a maximum rate cap and a minimum rate floor. As a variable rate security, market risk is minimized with these tranches.

Principal Only (PO)

Interest Only (IO)

POs and IOs are mortgage backed securities that are created by "breaking apart" the stream of interest payments from the principal repayments generated by the underlying collateral. These can be created directly from the mortgaged backed security or can be created in the form of CMO tranches.

The "picture" of the mortgage payments from a fixed rate mortgage is shown below:

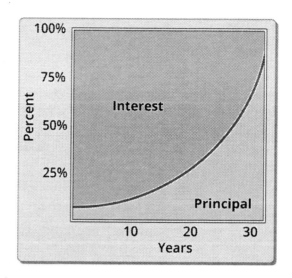

Principal Only (PO)

A Principal Only (PO) security only pays out based on the principal payments made - so it pays smaller amounts in the early years and larger amounts in the later years. Because most payments are loaded into the later years, it sells at a deep discount and exhibits great price volatility.

PO Prices Move Opposite To Market Interest Rates Like A Regular Bond

A PO's price volatility works in the same manner as a long-term bond. If market interest rates rise, prepayment speeds will decrease (extension risk) and the maturity will lengthen, so the bond's price will decrease. If market interest rates fall, prepayment speeds will increase (prepayment risk) and the maturity will shorten, so the bond's price will rise.

Interest Only (IO)

An Interest Only (IO) security only pays out based on the interest payments made - so it pays larger amounts in the early years and smaller amounts in the later years. It sells at a discount. Because most payments are loaded into the early years, it exhibits lesser price volatility.

IO Prices Move In The Same Direction As Market Interest Rates

An IO's price volatility works opposite to everything you have already learned! If market interest rates rise, prepayments speeds will decrease (extension risk) and the maturity will lengthen. Thus, the holder will be receiving interest for a greater period of time - so the price of the IO will rise as well. On the other hand, if market interest rates fall, prepayment speeds will increase (prepayment risk) and the maturity will shorten. Thus, the holder will be receiving interest for a shorter period of time - so the price of the IO will fall as well.

To summarize about PO and IO price volatility:

As market interest rates rise, PO prices fall; as market interest rates fall, PO prices rise.

As market interest rates fall, IO prices fall; as market interest rates rise, IO prices rise.

Agency CMOs

CMOs are now created directly by Ginnie Mae, Fannie Mae and Freddie Mac, using their own mortgage-backed securities (MBSs) as the underlying collateral. These are called "Agency CMOs" and because the underlying MBSs are rated AAA, the CMOs created from them are also rated AAA. This has "cut out" broker-dealers as the middleman who create CMOs that exclusively use agency MBSs as the underlying collateral.

Private Label CMOs

However, broker-dealers still package CMOs in great numbers, using both Agency MBSs and other mortgage-backed securities as collateral. Broker-dealer created CMOs are now called "Private Label" CMOs, because they contain a mix of MBSs as collateral. The broker-dealer can use Agency MBSs as a starting point, and then add MBSs created from non-conforming mortgages that Ginnie, Fannie and Freddie will not buy. These are MBSs where the underlying mortgages are too large in size, so the Agencies will not buy them (so-called "jumbo mortgages") and mortgages to do not meet the Agencies' credit standards (because they are too risky). Thus, the broker-dealer can create a CMO that ranges from very safe to very risky. With these "Private Label" CMOs, the credit rating is assigned by a ratings agency such as Moody's, based on the credit quality of the underlying collateral

Collateralized Debt Obligation (CDO)

Whereas a CMO holds underlying mortgages as collateral and then "slices and dices" the mortgage payments into cash flows to create different tranches for sale to investors, the CDO take this process to the next level. A CDO is a "special purpose entity" (SPE) that buys tranches of a CMO. CDO issuance exploded in 2006-2007 and they were indicted in the market crash of 2008-2009. CDOs would buy tranches of so-called "private label" CMOs which were created from sub-prime mortgages and not Fannie, Freddie or Ginnie backed (and therefore AAA rated) mortgages.

The ratings agencies did not understand the riskiness of the underlying sub-prime mortgage tranches (now known as the "toxic waste of the securities industry") and gave these CDOs high ratings. When the housing market collapsed, so did the sub-prime mortgage market as defaults ballooned. Correspondingly, CDO prices collapsed as well. Since then, there has been almost no issuance of CDOs, but they must be known for the exam.

$1,000 Denomination

CMOs are available in $1,000 denominations, as opposed to pass through certificates that are $25,000 denominations. This makes CMOs more accessible to small investors.

CMOs Quoted On A Yield Spread Basis To Treasuries	CMOs are quoted in 32nds, similar to Treasury issues. Very often, dealers quote CMOs on a "yield spread" basis - this means that the dealer quotes the CMO at the same yield as an equivalent maturity Treasury issue **plus** a spread. The amount of the spread depends on the liquidity of the CMO, the makeup of the pool, the coupon rate, etc. Typical spreads range from 50 to 100 basis points over Treasuries.
CMOs Are Non-Exempt Issues	Also note that while the FNMA, GNMA, and FHLMC securities held in the trust are exempt securities under the Securities Acts; CMOs are non-exempt securities. CMOs are a form of unit investment trust, a registered investment company type that is not exempt from the Securities Acts. This means that each CMO must be registered with the SEC and sold with a prospectus.

3e. TRADING OF GOVERNMENT / AGENCY DEBT

Over-The-Counter Trading	Trading of government and agency securities takes place solely in the over-the-counter market. There is no trading on any exchange floor. The participants in the market include large commercial banks, foreign banks, U.S. Government securities dealers (firms that only handle government trades whose names are not household words, such as Cantor Fitzgerald), full service brokerage firms, as well as the Federal Reserve itself.
Primary Dealers	The largest participants in the market are the "primary" U.S. Government securities dealers. There are about 20 firms which are primary dealers (e.g. Goldman Sachs, Citigroup, Nomura Securities, J. P. Morgan Chase Bank, Royal Bank of Scotland).
	The Federal Reserve designates a dealer as primary after the firm demonstrates over many years its capacity to purchase Treasury securities at the weekly auction and to make an orderly trading market in these issues (that is, the dealer is able to resell them to the public). Primary dealers are hooked up to the "Federal Reserve" wire system and deal directly with the "Fed."
Secondary Dealers	All other firms trading U.S. Government securities are termed "secondary" dealers. These firms buy and sell Treasuries in the market through the primary dealers and can also bid in the weekly auction. Most smaller banks and brokerage firms are "secondary" dealers.
Federal Reserve As Dealer **New York Fed Trading Desk**	The Federal Reserve maintains its own trading account and buys and sells large quantities of government securities in the market to manage interest rates. This activity is called "open market operations" and is discussed later in the text. The New York "Fed" has a trading floor where it trades every day with the primary government dealers.

Fed Loosening	When the Fed wishes to loosen credit, it will buy Treasury securities from the primary dealers, which places cash into the dealers (most of whom are banks). This lowers market interest rates, since banks have more cash to lend.
Fed Tightening	Conversely, when the Fed wishes to tighten credit, it will sell Treasury securities to the primary dealers, which removes cash from the dealers (most of whom are banks). This raises market interest rates, since banks have less cash to lend.
Quoted Through Computer Screens	Quotes for U.S. Government issues are placed by the primary dealers on a computer quotation system through services such as Bloomberg and Reuters.
U.S. Governments Initially Offered By Competitive Bid	The market for agency securities is dominated by the primary dealers. Whereas U.S. Government issues are initially sold by competitive bid at a weekly yield auction, (where the bidders are usually the primary dealers), agency securities are issued differently. Each agency has assembled a selling group of firms who market the agency's issues. They act as fiscal agents for the agency.
Agency Debt Initially Offered By "Fiscal Agents"	When an issue is coming to market, the firms collect customers for the issue and receive a fee of about 1% for placing the issue. The firm may also buy part of the issue for its own inventory to resell at a later date. (Note: New issue procedures are covered in detail in the "New Issues" chapter).
Agency Debt Trading Less Active Than U.S. Governments	Trading of agency securities, once they are issued, is much less active than that for U.S. Government securities. Most agency issues are bought by institutions that hold them. For example, Ginnie Mae and Fannie Mae certificates are purchased by investment companies and sold to investors as mutual fund shares, since the $25,000 minimum per certificate is more than most people can handle. Dealers distribute quotes for agency securities through computer quotation systems.
Agencies Are Quoted On A Yield Spread Basis To Equivalent Maturity Treasuries	Most agency securities are quoted by dealers on a yield spread basis against equivalent maturing Treasuries. For example, a dealer may quote a 10-year GNMA certificate at "25 basis points over the Treasury." If 10 year Treasury notes are yielding 5.00%, the dealer is pricing the GNMA to yield 5.25%. The typical "spread" over Treasuries is 25 - 50 basis points, though this can vary depending upon market conditions.

3f. SETTLEMENT AND ACCRUED INTEREST

Regular Way Settlement - Next Day For Treasuries	Trades of the U.S. Government (Treasury Bills, Notes and Bonds) settle "regular way" on the business day after trade date.

Regular Way Settlement - "Depends" For Agencies	Trades of Agency securities that pay interest semi-annually generally settle "regular way" 1 business day after trade date (though there are some exceptions). Trades of mortgage backed securities (which pay monthly) settle on pre-established dates each month. Because of the complexity of Agency settlements, these are not tested.
Cash - Same Day	Cash settlement for U.S. Government and Agency trades is the same business day, before 2:30 PM .
Trades Settle In "Fed Funds"	Trades of U.S. Government and Agency securities clear through the Federal Reserve Wire System. These trades settle in "Fed Funds" - good funds immediately payable at a Federal Reserve Branch member institution.
U.S. Government Accrued Interest (Actual/Actual)	Accrued interest on government issues that make semi-annual interest payments (T-Notes and T-Bonds) is computed on an actual day month / actual day year basis, with interest accruing up to, but not including settlement.

For example, a customer buys a 10% $1,000 par government bond at 90 in a regular way trade. The trade date is Monday, March 3rd. The bond pays interest on Jan 1 and Jul 1. How many days of accrued interest are due to the seller? How much accrued interest will be paid? It is not a leap year.

Answer: The trade date is Monday, March 3rd. Regular way settlement is next business day so settlement takes place on Tuesday, March 4th. Interest accrues up to settlement, so it accrues through March 3rd. The number of days is:

January	31 days
February	28 days
March	3 days
Total	62 days

Amount Paid = 62 days / 181 days x $50 semi-annual interest = $17.13

(Please note that actual day month / actual day year accrual is only used for T-Notes and T-Bonds. While there is no accrued interest on T-Bills (since they are an original issue discount obligation), the discount is earned over the life of the bills. To make things even more confusing, this discount is earned on a 30 day month / 360 day year basis. However, this fact is **NOT** tested on Series 7.)

Agency Accrued Interest 30 / 360	Accrued interest on agency issues is computed on a 30-day month / 360 day basis. Government and agency bonds never trade flat. If they default, a financial crisis of major proportions would occur.

3g. GOVERNMENT AND AGENCY DEBT FINANCIAL LISTINGS

Treasury Bill Quotations

U.S. Government and agency obligations are quoted in the news media daily. Information on Treasury Bills is presented in the following format:

Treasury Bonds, Notes and Bills
Bill yields in basis points (hundredths)

Treasury Bills

Date 2016	Days to Mat	Bid	Ask	Chg (Bid)	Ask Yld (YTM)
Dec 08	1	4.97	4.87	+0.26	4.94
Dec 15	8	4.87	4.77	+0.11	4.84
Dec 22	15	5.43	5.33	+0.05	5.42
Jan 05	29	5.00	4.90	+0.07	4.99
Jan 12	36	5.22	5.18	+0.11	5.28

The first and second columns give the maturity date of the Treasury Bill, with the number of days to maturity. Assuming that it is now December 7, 2016, the bill maturing Dec 8th has 1 day to maturity; Dec 15th has 8 days to maturity; Dec 22nd has 15 days to maturity, etc.

The third column gives the discount yield that government dealers are willing to buy at that day (the "bid"). The dealer is willing to buy the bills dated December 22nd priced to yield 5.43%. This yield is a discount from par value. To actually find the dollar price of the T-Bill (assuming par is $1,000) and that it is now Dec 7, the approximate formula is:

$$\frac{\text{Days to Maturity}}{\text{Days in Year}} \times \text{Interest Rate} \times \text{Par} = \text{Discount}$$

$$\frac{15 \text{ days}}{360 \text{ days}} * \times 5.43\% \times \$1{,}000 = \$2.263$$

Dollar Price = $1,000 - $2.263 discount = $997.737 Bid Price

*Note that, to make things even more confusing, the discount accrues on T-Bills on a 30/360 basis; as compared to an actual/actual basis for interest accrual on Treasury Notes and Bonds. However, this need not be known for the exam. Only the general "concept" must be understood.

The fourth column gives the discount yield that government dealers are willing to sell at that day (the "ask"). The dealer is willing to sell the bills dated December 22 priced to yield 5.33%. This yield is a discount from par value. To actually find the dollar price of the T-Bill (assuming par is $1,000 and it is now Dec 7), the approximate formula is:

$$\frac{\text{Days to Maturity}}{\text{Days in Year}} \times \text{Interest Rate} \times \text{Par} = \text{Discount}$$

$$\frac{15\ days}{360\ days} \times 5.33\% \times \$1,000 = \$2.221$$

Dollar Price = $1,000 - $2.221 discount = $997.779 Ask Price

Please note that the bid price per $1,000 bill was $997.737; the ask price was $997.779. This indicates that the "spread" that the dealer works on is $.042 per $1,000. This is small and reflects the highly competitive nature of this market. For every "round turn" trade, (a buy and sell of this particular bill), the dealer earns 4.2 cents. Narrow spreads are typical for active trading markets - and the government market is the most active in the world.

The fifth column shows how much the bid has changed from the prior day. For the Dec 22 T-Bill, the bid has increased by .05% - that is, 5 basis points. This shows that interest rates rose that day since the yield has increased. If the yield has increased, the discount is greater. Thus, the purchase price of the bill decreases. Remember, as interest rates rise, debt prices fall.

The sixth column shows the yield an investor gets holding the T-Bill to maturity (yield to maturity). This is higher than the discount yield since YTM is a compounded yield. An investor can buy the Dec 22nd T-Bill at the dealer's asking price (here it is a discount yield of 5.33% = $997.779 price). However, the true yield to maturity is 5.42%.

Treasury Note

Bond Quotations

Treasury Note and Bond quotes are presented below:

Treasury Bonds, Notes and Bills
Prices in 32nd of a point, bill yields in basis Points

Rate	Mo/Yr	Bid	Asked	Chg	Ask Yld
4 1/4	Jan18n	99:24	99:26	-1	5.43
4 1/8	Jun19n	98:21	98:23	-3	6.47
4	Jan19n	96:12	96:14	-5	7.28
7 7/8	Jan21n	100:13	100:15	-6	7.70
8	Aug21	100:13	100:17	-11	7.66
13 3/8	Aug28	128:30	129:02	-12	7.73
12 3/8	May33	129:20	129:24	-9	7.85

The first column gives the interest rate.

The second column gives the maturity. The symbols next to the maturity are: n-regular Treasury Note; no symbol-regular Treasury Bond.

The third column gives the dealer's bid price. The dealer is willing to buy the Jan '18 notes at 99:24 which is 99 and 24/32nds = 99.75 = $997.50 per $1,000 par note. The dealer is willing to buy the May '33 bonds at 129:20 which is 129 and 20/32nds = 129.625 = $1,296.25.

The fourth column is the dealer's ask price. The dealer is willing to sell the Jan '18 notes at 99:26 which is 99 and 26/32nds = 99.8125 = $998.125 per $1,000 par note. The dealer is willing to sell the May '33 bonds at 129:24 = 129 and 24/32nds = 129.75 = $1,297.50.

Note that the bid price for the Jan '18 notes was 99:24; the ask price was 99:26. This means that the "spread" the dealer works on is 2/32nds per $1,000 par note equals $.625. This is small and reflects the highly competitive nature of this market. For every "round turn" trade (a buy and sell of this particular note), the dealer earns $.625. Narrow spreads are typical for active trading markets - and the government market is the most active in the world.

The fifth column shows how much the bid has changed from the prior day. For the Jan '18 Note, the bid has dropped by 1/32nd. This indicates that interest rates have increased that day since the price has fallen.

The sixth column shows the yield to maturity on the security. The Jan '18 4 1/4% note is priced to yield 5.43% to maturity. Since the note is priced at a discount, it makes sense that the YTM is higher than the nominal yield.

Agency Bond Quotations

Agency securities are quoted in identical fashion to long-term U.S. Government securities (T-Notes and T-Bonds). No narrative is given since the format is identical to that just discussed.

3h. TAX STATUS OF GOVERNMENT AND AGENCY DEBT INTEREST

Government And "Unprivatized" Agency Debt Subject To Federal Tax And Is Exempt From State And Local Tax

The interest income from U.S. Government Notes and Bonds and "unprivatized" Agency debt making periodic interest payments is subject to federal income tax but is exempt from state and local income tax. This tax status derives from the fact that one level of government does not tax the other. Bonds and notes pay interest semi-annually, so two interest payments are included on each year's federal income tax return.

Discount On T-Bills Taxed As Interest Income In Year Received

The discount on short-term Treasury Bills and short-term "unprivatized" Agency Notes is taxed as interest income in the year the obligation matures. This interest is subject to federal income tax but is exempt from state and local tax.

Discount On STRIPS Must Be Accreted And Taxed Annually

The discount on long-term so-called "original issue discount" obligations, such as STRIPS, (zero-coupon issues) is treated as annual taxable interest income, pro-rated over the life of the bond. The annual accretion amount (the discount earned) is taxable each year, even though no interest payment has been received from the issuer. Since people don't like to pay tax on income that is not actually received, these securities are held typically in retirement plans (tax deferred envelopes), so that tax is not paid until the monies are withdrawn from the retirement plan.

TIPS - Annual Upwards Adjustment Is Taxable In That Year

Regarding TIPS - Treasury Inflation Protection Securities - if the principal amount is adjusted upwards due to inflation, the adjustment amount is treated as taxable interest income (not capital gains) for that year. Conversely, if the principal amount is adjusted downwards due to deflation, the adjustment amount is treated as deductible interest expense for that year.

"Privatized" Agency Debt Fully Taxable

The interest income from securities issued by "privatized" agencies, such as Fannie Mae and Freddie Mac, is fully taxable, similar to regular corporate obligations.

Ginnie Mae Pass-Throughs Fully Taxable

In addition, the interest income from Ginnie Mae pass through certificates is fully taxable. (This makes sense since the mortgage interest was deductible by the mortgagee on both of his or her federal and state returns.)

(Note: The tax status of the interest income received from Government, Agency, Corporate and Municipal debt instruments is summarized at the end of the Municipals section of this chapter. Also, the tax rules are summarized in the Taxation chapter.)

U.S. GOVERNMENT DEBT SECTION EXAMINATION

1.
Which of the following is an original issue discount obligation?

- a. GNMA certificate
- b. Treasury bill
- c. U.S. Government bond
- d. FNMA bond

2.
Trades of which of the following securities will settle in Fed Funds?

- I   Treasury Bills
- II   Treasury Notes
- III   Municipal Bonds
- IV   Corporate Bonds

- a. I only
- b. I and II only
- c. III and IV only
- d. I, II, III, IV

3.
All of the following trade "and interest" **EXCEPT:**

- a. Treasury Bills
- b. Treasury Notes
- c. Treasury Bonds
- d. Corporate Bonds

4.
Which of the following are **TRUE** statements regarding Treasury Bills?

- I   The maturity is 52 weeks or less
- II   Treasury Bills are callable at any time at par
- III   Treasury Bills trade at a discount to par
- IV   Payment is backed by the full faith and credit of the U.S. Government

- a. I and III only
- b. II and IV only
- c. I, III, IV
- d. II, III, IV

5.
Interest received from all of the following securities is exempt from state and local taxes **EXCEPT:**

- a. Fannie Mae Pass Through Certificates
- b. Treasury Notes
- c. Federal Farm Credit Funding Corporation Bonds
- d. Federal Home Loan Bank Bonds

6.
A government bond dealer is making good delivery to another government dealer. Payment is to be made in:

- a. 1 business day in federal funds
- b. 1 business day in clearing house funds
- c. 2 business days in federal funds
- d. 2 business days in clearing house funds

7.
Which is considered to be a direct obligation of the U.S. Government?

- a. Federal National Mortgage Association Pass Through Certificates
- b. Government National Mortgage Association Pass Through Certificates
- c. Federal National Mortgage Association Bonds
- d. Federal Home Loan Bank Bonds

8.
New issues of Treasury Notes are issued in:

   a.   book entry only form
   b.   bearer form
   c.   fully registered form
   d.   registered to principal only form

9.
A 5 year, $1,000 par, 3 1/2% Treasury Note is quoted at 101-4 - 101-8. The note pays interest on Jan 1 and Jul 1. Which statement is **TRUE?**

   a.   The spread is 4 basis points
   b.   The spread is $1.25 per $1,000
   c.   The spread is $4.00 per $1,000
   d.   The spread is $5.00 per $1,000

10.
A 5 year $1,000 par 3 1/2% Treasury Note is quoted at 101-4 - 101-8. The note pays interest on Jan 1st and Jul 1st. A customer buys 1 note at the ask price. What is the current yield, disregarding commissions?

   a.   3.26%
   b.   3.46%
   c.   3.66%
   d.   3.86%

11.
A 5 year 3 1/2% Treasury Note is quoted at 101-4 - 101-8. The note pays interest on Jan. 1st and Jul. 1st. If a customer buys 5 T-Notes on Monday, Mar. 31st in a regular way trade, how many days of accrued interest are owed to the seller? (It is not a leap year.)

   a.   89
   b.   90
   c.   95
   d.   96

12.
A 5 year 3 1/2% Treasury Note is quoted at 101-4 - 101-8. The note pays interest on Jan 1st and Jul 1st. All of the following statements are true regarding this trade of T-Notes **EXCEPT**:

   a.   interest accrues on an actual day month; actual day year basis
   b.   the yield to maturity will be higher than the current yield
   c.   the trade will settle in Fed Funds
   d.   the trade will settle next business day if performed "regular way"

13.
Which of the following are **TRUE** statements regarding Treasury Bills?

   I   T-Bills are registered in the owner's name in book entry form
   II   T-Bills are issued in bearer form in the United States
   III   T-Bills are callable at any time
   IV   T-Bills are issued at a discount

   a.   I and III
   b.   I and IV
   c.   II and III
   d.   II and IV

14.
Which statements are **TRUE** regarding Treasury STRIPS?

   I   Interest is paid semi-annually
   II   The bonds are issued at a discount
   III   Interest income is accreted and taxed annually
   IV   Interest earned is subject to reinvestment risk

   a.   I and II only
   b.   II and III only
   c.   II and IV only
   d.   I and IV only

15.

U.S. Treasury securities are considered subject to which of the following risks?

I   Credit Risk
II Purchasing Power Risk
III Marketability Risk
IV Default Risk

a.   II only
b.   I and IV only
c.   II and III only
d.   I, II, III, IV

16.

A 5 year 3 1/4% Treasury Note is quoted at 101-4 - 101-8. The note pays interest on Jan. 1st and Jul. 1st. If a customer buys 5 T-Notes on Friday, April 4th in a regular way trade, how many days of accrued interest are owed to the seller? (It is not a leap year.)

a.   94
b.   95
c.   96
d.   97

17.

Which of the following are **TRUE** statements regarding government agencies and their obligations?

I   Fannie Mae is a publicly traded company
II Ginnie Mae obligations trade at higher yields than Fannie Mae obligations
III Agency obligations have the direct backing of the U.S. Government
IV Ginnie Mae securities are listed and trade

a.   I only
b.   I and II only
c.   II and IV only
d.   I, III, IV

18.

Interest payments on Ginnie Mae pass-through certificates are made:

a.   weekly
b.   monthly
c.   semi-annually
d.   annually

19.

Which of the following designates "primary" U.S. Government securities dealers?

a.   Securities and Exchange Commission
b.   Federal Reserve
c.   Office of the Comptroller of Currency
d.   Congress

20.

All of the following are true statements about Treasury Bills **EXCEPT:**

a.   T-Bills are traded at a discount from par
b.   T-Bills are the most actively traded money market instrument
c.   T-Bills have a maximum maturity of 9 months
d.   T-Bills can be purchased directly at weekly auction

21.

If interest rates rise, which of the following U.S. Government debt instruments would show the greatest percentage drop in value?

a.   Treasury Bills
b.   Treasury Notes
c.   Treasury Bonds
d.   Savings (EE) Bonds

22.

All of the following agencies provide financing for residential housing **EXCEPT:**

    a.   Fannie Mae

    b.   Sallie Mae

    c.   Ginnie Mae

    d.   Freddie Mac

23.

Which of the following would **NOT** purchase STRIPS?

    I   Pension fund

    II   Money market fund

    III Individual seeking current income

    IV Individual wishing to avoid reinvestment risk

    a.   I and III

    b.   I and IV

    c.   II and III

    d.   II and IV

24.

Which of the following are issued with a fixed coupon rate?

    I   Treasury Bills

    II   Treasury Notes

    III Treasury Bonds

    IV Treasury STRIPS

    a.   I and IV only

    b.   II and III only

    c.   II, III, IV

    d.   I, II, III, IV

25.

All of the following statements are true about Treasury Receipts **EXCEPT:**

    a.   the full faith and credit of the U.S. Government backs the securities underlying the issue

    b.   they are "packaged" by broker-dealers

    c.   the interest coupons are sold off separately from the principal portion of the obligation

    d.   the securities are purchased at par

26.

All of the following are true statements regarding both Treasury Bills and Treasury Receipts **EXCEPT:**

    a.   interest is paid at maturity

    b.   the securities are sold at a discount

    c.   the maturity is 1 year or less

    d.   payment of interest and principal on the underlying security is guaranteed by the U.S. Government

27.

Which of the following statements are **TRUE** regarding the trading of government and agency bonds?

    I   The trading market is very active, with narrow spreads

    II   Trading is confined to the primary dealers

    III All government and agency securities are quoted in 32nds

    IV The market is regulated by the Securities and Exchange Commission

    a.   I only

    b.   I, II

    c.   II, III

    d.   I, II, III, IV

28.

Which risk is **NOT** applicable to Ginnie Mae Pass Through Certificates?

a. Purchasing power risk

b. Risk of early prepayment of mortgages if interest rates fall

c. Risk of default if homeowners do not make their mortgage payments

d. Risk of loss of principal if interest rates rise

29.

All of the following statements are true about the Government National Mortgage Association Pass-Through Certificates **EXCEPT:**

a. GNMA is empowered to borrow from the Treasury to pay interest and principal if necessary

b. interest payments are exempt from state and local tax

c. certificates are issued in minimum units of $25,000

d. the credit rating is considered the highest of any agency security

30.

Which statements are **TRUE** regarding collateralized mortgage obligations?

I CMOs are backed by agency pass-through securities held in trust

II CMOs have investment grade credit ratings

III CMOs give the holder a limited form of call protection that is not present in regular pass-through obligations

IV CMOs are issued by government agencies

a. I and II only

b. III and IV only

c. I, II, III

d. I, II, III, IV

31.

"PSA" stands for:

a. Prepayment Speed Assumption

b. Planned Securitization Algorithm

c. Predicted Standardized Amortization

d. Privatized Syndicated Asset

32.

All of the following statements are true regarding CMOs **EXCEPT:**

a. CMOs are available in $1,000 denominations

b. CMOs make payments to holders monthly

c. CMOs are subject to a higher level of prepayment risk than a pass through certificate

d. CMOs receive the same credit rating as the underlying pass-through securities held in trust

33.

Which statements are **TRUE** about prepayment experience on collateralized mortgage obligations?

I When interest rates rise, prepayment rates rise

II When interest rates rise, prepayment rates fall

III When interest rates fall, prepayment rates rise

IV When interest rates fall, prepayment rates fall

a. I and III

b. I and IV

c. II and III

d. II and IV

34.

CMO "Planned Amortization Classes" (PAC tranches):

   a. reduce prepayment risk to holders of that tranche

   b. increase prepayment risk to holders of that tranche

   c. eliminate prepayment risk to holders of that tranche

   d. have the same prepayment risk as companion classes

35.

Which statements are **TRUE** when comparing PAC CMO tranches to "plain vanilla" CMO tranches?

   I   Holders of PAC CMO tranches have lower prepayment risk

   II Holders of PAC CMO tranches have higher prepayment risk

   III Holders of "plain vanilla" CMO tranches have lower prepayment risk

   IV Holders of "plain vanilla" CMO tranches have higher prepayment risk

   a. I and III

   b. I and IV

   c. II and III

   d. II and IV

36.

Which CMO tranche is **MOST** susceptible to interest rate risk?

   a. Z-Tranche

   b. Companion Tranche

   c. PAC tranche

   d. TAC tranche

37.

A structured product that invests in tranches of private label subprime mortgages is a:

   a. CMO

   b. CDO

   c. CMB

   d. CAB

38.

Which Treasury security is **NOT** sold on a regular auction schedule?

   a. CMBs

   b. Treasury Bills

   c. STRIPS

   d. TIPS

39.

If the principal amount of a Treasury Inflation Protection Security is adjusted upwards due to inflation, the adjustment amount is:

   a. not taxable

   b. taxable in that year as interest income received

   c. taxable in that year as long term capital gains

   d. taxable at maturity

40.

Which CMO tranche is **LEAST** susceptible to interest rate risk?

   a. Z-tranche

   b. Floating rate tranche

   c. PAC tranche

   d. TAC tranche

U.S. GOVERNMENT DEBT EXAMINATION EXPLANATIONS

1. The best answer is **b**. Treasury Bills are original issue discount obligations. They are auctioned off weekly by the Federal Reserve acting as agent for the U.S. Treasury. When the bills mature, the difference between the purchase price and the redemption value at par is taxable as interest income. GNMA (Government National Mortgage Association) certificates, Treasury Bonds, and FNMA (Federal National Mortgage Association) bonds are all issued at par and make periodic interest payments.

2. The best answer is **b**. Securities that are eligible to be traded by the Federal Reserve are those backed by the guarantee of the U.S. Government as well as certain agency obligations. Both Treasury Bills and Treasury Notes are eligible securities. Trades in eligible securities settle through the Federal Reserve system, and therefore settle in "Fed Funds." Municipal bond trades and trades in corporate securities are not eligible for trading and settling through the Federal Reserve system; these securities settle in "clearing house" funds.

3. The best answer is **a**. Original issue discount obligations trade "flat" - without accrued interest. Every day the issue is held, its value increases towards the redemption price of par. This increase in value is the interest income earned on the obligation. Obligations issued at par make periodic interest payments. They trade "and interest" - with accrued interest. These include Treasury Notes, Treasury Bonds, Corporate Bonds, and Municipal Bonds.

4. The best answer is **c**. Treasury Bills are original issue discount obligations of the U.S. Government which mature in 52 weeks or less. They are not callable (as a rule, short term obligations are never callable - why would the issuer bother calling in obligations that will mature in the near future?)

5. The best answer is **a**. The interest income from direct issues of the U.S. Government and most agency obligations is subject to federal income tax but is exempt from state and local tax. An exception is the interest income received from mortgage backed pass through certificates (issued by GNMA, FNMA, FHLMC). This interest income is subject to both federal income tax and state and local tax. The logic behind this tax treatment is that the mortgage interest paid by the homeowners was fully deductible from both federal, state, and local taxes. When this interest is received by the certificate holder, both the federal and state government want to recapture this interest income and tax it.

6. The best answer is **a**. Trades of U.S. Government bonds settle through the Federal Reserve System in Fed Funds. Settlement of government securities trades takes place the business day following trade date. "Non-eligible" securities settle through national clearing houses of which broker/dealers are members. These trades settle in 2 business days in clearing house funds.

7. The best answer is **b**. GNMA certificates are backed by a pool of mortgages, the full faith and credit of GNMA, as well as the full faith and credit of the U.S. Government. GNMA is empowered to appropriate the funds necessary to pay interest and principal on its obligations from the U.S. Treasury. As such, this is considered a direct obligation of the U.S. Government. FNMA and FHLB are implicitly backed; there is no direct guarantee.

8. The best answer is **a**. The U.S. Government issues Treasury Securities in book entry form only. No physical certificates are issued.

9. The best answer is **b**. The spread between the bid and ask is 4/32nds. Remember, government and agency securities are quoted in 32nds (with the exception of T-Bills, quoted on a yield basis). 4/32nds = .125% of $1,000 par = $1.25.

10. The best answer is **b**. The customer buys the bonds at 101 and 8/32s = 101.25% of $1,000 = $1,012.50. The formula for current yield is:

$$\frac{\text{Annual Income}}{\text{Market Price}} = \text{Current Yield}$$

$$\frac{\$35}{\$1,012.50} = 3.46\%$$

11. The best answer is **b**. Interest accrues on U.S. Government securities on an actual day month/actual day year basis. Settlement is next business day, with interest accruing up to but not including, settlement date. Thus, the interest due is 31 days for Jan, 28 days for Feb, and 31 days for Mar (settlement is on Apr 1st). Total days of accrued interest are 90.

12. The best answer is **b**. Because these T-Notes are trading at a premium, the yield to maturity will be lower than the current yield. The current yield does not factor in the loss of the premium over the life of the bond, whereas yield to maturity does. Government bond trades settle next business day; accrued interest is computed on an actual month/actual year basis; and trades settle through the Federal Reserve system in "Fed Funds."

13. The best answer is **b**. T-Bills are registered in the owner's name in book entry form only; no bearer securities can currently be issued in the U.S. to individual residents. T-Bills are original issue discount obligations and are not callable, since they are short term.

14. The best answer is **b**. Treasury STRIPS are bonds "stripped" of coupons, meaning all that is left is the principal repayment portion of the bond (sometimes called the "corpus" or body). This security is a zero coupon obligation which is an original issue discount. The accretion of the discount over the bond's life represents the interest earned. Even though no payments of interest are made annually, the discount must be accreted annually and is taxable as interest income earned. This investment is not subject to reinvestment risk since no interest payments are made. The rate of return on this bond is "locked in" at purchase. Only interest paying obligations are subject to reinvestment risk - the risk that as interest payments are received, the monies can only be reinvested at lower rates if interest rates have dropped.

15. The best answer is **a**. Securities issued by the U.S. Government represent the largest securities market in the world (remember, the national debt is $20 trillion and rising) and the most actively traded. Therefore, very little marketability risk exists. Default risk and credit risk are the same - U.S. Government securities are considered to have virtually no default risk. (The government can always tax its citizens to pay the debt or can print the money to do it). All debt obligations are susceptible to purchasing power risk - the risk that inflation raises interest rates, devaluing existing obligations.

16. The best answer is **c**. Since settlement is next business day, the trade note settles on Monday, April 7th. Accrued interest is calculated for Governments on an actual day month / actual day year basis, with interest accruing from the last interest payment date of January 1st. Thus, accrued interest due is: 31 days for January, 28 days for February, 31 days for March and 6 days for April (up to but not including the settlement date of April 7th) = 96 days.

17. The best answer is **a**. Fannie Mae was "spun off" by the government as a public company listed on the NYSE (so was Freddie Mac). Its stock was listed for trading on the NYSE, but Fannie went "bust" in 2008 after purchasing too many "sub prime" mortgages and was placed into government conservatorship. Its shares were delisted from the NYSE and now trade OTC in the Pink OTC Markets.

Ginnie Mae obligations trade at lower yields than Fannie Mae obligations since Ginnie Maes are directly backed by the U.S. Government whereas Fannie Maes are only implicitly backed. Ginnie Mae has not been "spun off" by the government as a private company and cannot be spun off because of the guarantee of the U.S. Government that its securities carry.

18. The best answer is **b**. All pass through certificates pass on the monthly mortgage payments received from the pooled mortgages to the certificate holders. Thus, payments are received monthly. These represent a payment of both interest and principal on the mortgage. These certificates are self-amortizing and are completely paid off with the last mortgage payment.

19. The best answer is **b**. The Federal Reserve designates a dealer as a "primary" dealer - meaning one entitled to trade with the Federal Reserve trading desk. There are about 20 primary dealers (such as Cantor Fitzgerald, Nomura Securities, Citibank, Goldman Sachs, Royal Bank of Scotland, etc.) The rest of the government dealers are termed "secondary" dealers. They do not enjoy a special relationship with the Federal Reserve.

20. The best answer is **c**. T-Bills have a maximum maturity of 12 months, not 9 months. They are sold at a discount from par; are the most widely traded money market instrument since the bulk of the government's financing is through T-Bills; and can be purchased directly at auction by anyone who tenders a non-competitive bid.

21. The best answer is **c**. The longer the maturity, the more volatile the price movements of the bond as interest rates move. The longest maturity listed here is T-Bonds. Savings bond prices are not affected by interest rate movements. These are non-negotiable instruments that are not traded - instead they are redeemable with the government at any time.

22. The best answer is **b**. Sallie Mae is the Student Loan Marketing Association. It buys student loans from state agencies and issues bonds to finance this activity. Fannie Mae, Ginnie Mae, and Freddie Mac all buy mortgages from banks (Fannie and Ginnie Mae buy FHA and VA insured mortgages; Freddie Mac buys conventional mortgages) and packages them into pools for sale to the public as pass through certificates.

23. The best answer is **c**. Pension funds and retirement accounts are the large purchasers of STRIPS. These zero-coupon bonds are purchased at a deep discount and are held to maturity to fund future retirement liabilities. There is little credit risk, because the U.S. Treasury is a top credit. There is no current income because they don't pay until maturity. They have a huge amount of purchasing power risk as a long-term zero coupon obligation, but this is not an issue if they are held to maturity. Retirement plan managers like STRIPS because they don't have to worry about reinvestment risk - there are no semi-annual interest payments to reinvest! It is an investment that can be "tucked away" for 20 or 30 years, with no further work or worry on the part of the retirement fund manager.

24. The best answer is **b**. Treasury Notes and Bonds are issued at par with a stated interest rate. Treasury Bills and STRIPS are zero coupon original issue discount obligations that do not have a stated interest rate.

25. The best answer is **d**. Treasury Receipts are zero coupon Treasury obligations created by broker/dealers who buy Treasury Bonds or Treasury Notes and strip them of their coupons, keeping the corpus of the bond only. The bonds are put into a trust, and "units" of the trust are sold to investors. Treasury Receipts are purchased at a discount and mature at par. The discount earned over the life of the bond is the "interest income."

Once the Federal government started "stripping" bonds itself (in 1986) and selling them to investors, this market evaporated. However, 30 year T-Receipts will trade until they all mature.

26. The best answer is **c**. T-Bills mature in 52 weeks or less, while Treasury Receipts are long term bonds stripped of coupons (long term zero coupon obligations). Both are guaranteed by the U.S. Government; interest is paid at maturity; and both trade at a discount until maturity.

Once the Federal government started "stripping" bonds itself (in 1986) and selling them to investors, the market for broker-created T-Receipts evaporated. However, 30 year T-Receipts will trade until they all mature.

27. The best answer is **a**. The government obligation trading market is the deepest and most active market in the world. Trading is performed by both the primary and secondary dealers, and by the Federal Reserve trading desk. While long term government and agency securities are quoted in 32nds, T-Bills are quoted on a discount yield basis. The market is unregulated - these are exempt securities under the Securities laws, however the Federal Reserve does exert influence over the primary dealers.

28. The best answer is **c**. Ginnie Maes are guaranteed by the U.S. Government so there is no risk of default. Ginnie Mae is authorized to raid the U.S. Treasury to make up any payment shortfalls, if required. The holder of a certificate is subject to potential loss of principal if interest rates rise, and to loss of interest income if mortgages are prepaid early (these prepayments are passed on to the certificate holders).

29. The best answer is **b**. Interest received by the holder of a mortgage backed pass through security is fully taxable by both federal, state, and local government. Ginnie Mae is backed by the guarantee of the U.S. Government, making it the highest credit rated agency security. The other agencies are only implicitly backed. Certificates are issued in minimum $25,000 denominations. For most investors this is too much money to invest, so they buy shares of a Ginnie Mae mutual fund instead.

30. The best answer is **c**. The first 3 statements are true. Collateralized mortgage obligations are backed by mortgage pass-through certificates that are held in trust. The underlying mortgage backed pass-through certificates are issued by agencies such as FNMA, GNMA and FHLMC, all of whom have an "AAA" (Moody's or Fitch's) or "AA" (Standard and Poor's) credit rating. The CMO takes on the credit rating of the underlying collateral.

CMOs take the payment flow from the underlying pass-through certificates and allocate them to so-called "tranches." A CMO backed by 30 year mortgages might be divided into 15-30 separate tranches. As payments are received from the underlying mortgages, interest is paid pro-rata to all tranches; but principal repayments are paid sequentially to the first, then second, then third tranche, etc. Thus, the earlier tranches are retired first.

The CMO purchaser buys a specific tranche. Because of the sequencing of principal repayments from the underlying mortgages, the holder has a more definite maturity date on the issue, as compared to actually buying a mortgage backed pass-through certificate. This is true because prepayments on pass-through certificates are allocated pro-rata. During periods of falling rates, all certificate holders receive their share of those repayments pro-rata. The holder of a specific tranche of a CMO will only receive prepayments after all earlier tranche holders are repaid. Thus, CMOs give holders a form of "call protection" not available in regular pass-through certificates.

CMOs are not issued by government agencies; the agency issues the underlying pass-through certificates. CMOs are packaged and issued by broker-dealers.

31. The best answer is **a**. Mortgage backed pass-through certificates are "paid off" in a shorter time frame than the full life of the underlying mortgages. For example, 30 year mortgages are now typically paid off in 10 years - because people move. This "prepayment speed assumption" is used to "guesstimate" the expected life of a mortgage backed pass-through certificate. Note, however, that the "PSA" can change over time. If interest rates fall rapidly after the mortgage is issued, prepayment rates speed up; if they rise rapidly after issuance, prepayment rates fall.

32. The best answer is **c**. CMOs are available in $1,000 denominations, as opposed to pass-through certificates that are $25,000 denominations. This makes CMOs more accessible to small investors. Most CMOs make payments to holders monthly. CMOs are subject to a lower degree of prepayment risk than the underlying pass-through certificates. During periods of falling interest rates, prepayments of mortgages in a pool are applied pro-rata to all holders of pass-through certificates. CMOs divide the cash flows into "tranches" of varying maturities; and apply prepayments sequentially to the tranches in order of maturity. Thus, prepayments are applied to earlier tranches first, so the actual date of repayment of the tranche is known with more certainty. CMOs receive the same credit rating (AAA or AA) as the underlying mortgage backed pass-through certificates held in trust.

33. The best answer is **c**. Homeowners will prepay mortgages when interest rates fall, so they can refinance at more attractive lower current rates. They tend not to prepay mortgages when interest rates rise, since there is no benefit to a refinancing. The main reason for prepayments when interest rates have risen is that the homeowner has moved, and the house was sold.

34. The best answer is **a**. Older CMOs are known as "plain vanilla" CMOs, because the repayment scheme is relatively simple - as payments are received from the underlying mortgages, interest is paid pro-rata to all tranches; but principal repayments are paid sequentially to the first, then second, then third tranche, etc. Thus, the earlier tranches are retired first.

A newer version of a CMO has a more sophisticated scheme for allocating cash flows. Newer CMOs divide the tranches into PAC tranches and Companion tranches. The PAC tranche is a "Planned Amortization Class." Surrounding this tranche are 1 or 2 Companion tranches. Interest payments are still made pro-rata to all tranches, but principal repayments made earlier than that required to retire the PAC at its maturity are applied to the Companion class; while principal repayments made later than expected are applied to the PAC maturity before payments are made to the Companion class. Thus, the PAC class is given a more certain maturity date; while the Companion class has a higher level of prepayment risk if interest rates fall; and a higher level of so-called "extension risk" - the risk that the maturity may be longer than expected, if interest rates rise.

35. The best answer is **b**. Older CMOs are known as "plain vanilla" CMOs, because the repayment scheme is relatively simple - as payments are received from the underlying mortgages, interest is paid pro-rata to all

tranches; but principal repayments are paid sequentially to the first, then second, then third tranche, etc. Thus, the earlier tranches are retired first.

A newer version of a CMO has a more sophisticated scheme for allocating cash flows. Newer CMOs divide the tranches into PAC tranches and Companion tranches. The PAC tranche is a "Planned Amortization Class." Surrounding this tranche are 1 or 2 Companion tranches. Interest payments are still made pro-rata to all tranches, but principal repayments made earlier than that required to retire the PAC at its maturity are applied to the Companion class; while principal repayments made later than expected are applied to the PAC maturity before payments are made to the Companion class. Thus, the PAC class is given a more certain maturity date; while the Companion class has a higher level of prepayment risk if interest rates fall; and a higher level of so-called "extension risk" - the risk that the maturity may be longer than expected, if interest rates rise.

36. The best answer is **a**. A Z-tranche is a "Zero" tranche. It gets no payments until all prior tranches are retired. Then it is paid off at par. It acts like a long-term zero-coupon bond, so it is most susceptible to interest rate risk. The other tranches receive payments earlier in their life, so they are less susceptible to interest rate risk.

37. The best answer is **b**. CDOs - Collateralized Debt Obligations - are structured products that invest in CMO tranches (and they can also invest in other debt obligations that provide cash flows). They are used to create tranches with different risk/return characteristics - so a CDO will have higher risk tranches holding lower quality collateral and lower risk tranches holding higher quality collateral.

The housing bubble that ended badly in 2008 with a market crash was fueled by massive issuance of sub-prime mortgages to unqualified home buyers, that were then packaged into CDOs and sold to unwitting institutional investors who relied on the credit rating assigned by S&P or Moodys. These credit ratings agencies really did not understand the complex structure of CDOs and how risky their collateral was (sub-prime mortgage loans that were often "no documentation liar loans"). The CDO market collapsed with the housing crash in 2008-2009 and has still not recovered (as of 2017).

38. The best answer is **a**. CMBs are Cash Management Bills. They are sold at auction by the Treasury on an "as needed" basis to meet unexpected cash shortfalls, so they are not part of the regular auction cycle. They are the shortest-term U.S. government security, often with maturities as short as 5 days. They are sold in $100 minimums at a discount to par value, just like Treasury Bills.

39. The best answer is **b**. If the principal amount of a Treasury Inflation Protection Security is adjusted upwards due to inflation, the adjustment amount is taxable in that year as ordinary interest income. Conversely, if the principal amount of a Treasury Inflation Protection Security is adjusted downwards due to deflation, the adjustment is tax deductible in that year against ordinary interest income.

(TIPS are usually purchased in tax qualified retirement plans that are tax-deferred. This avoids having to pay tax each year on the upwards principal adjustment.)

40. The best answer is **b**. A floating rate CMO tranche has an interest rate that varies, tied to the movements of a recognized interest rate index, like LIBOR. Therefore, an interest rates move up, the interest rate paid on the tranche goes up as well; and when interest rates drop, the interest rate paid on the tranche goes down as well. There is usually a cap on how high the rate can go and a floor on how low the rate can drop. Because the interest rate moves with the market, the price stays close to par - as is the case with any variable rate security.

SECTION 4: MUNICIPAL DEBT

4a. MUNICIPAL DEBT CHARACTERISTICS

Municipal Bonds

Interest Exempt From Federal Income Tax

Municipal bonds are debt issues of state and local governments, territories, and political subdivisions (such as special districts, agencies or authorities). A principal feature of municipal bonds is the tax status of the interest income. Generally, it is exempt from Federal income tax, but subject to state and local tax (unless purchased by a resident of that state - this is covered at the end of this section).

New Issues Are Book Entry

Older Bonds Are Fully Registered Or Bearer

Currently, virtually all new municipal debt is issued in book-entry form. However, older bonds that have not matured still trade and come in fully registered form or bearer form (at least until all bearer bonds mature in the upcoming years). These bond forms were covered in Section 2 of this chapter.

Legal Opinion

Bond Counsel

All municipal issues also have a legal opinion printed on the face of the bond. Before a bond can be issued, the municipality retains a bond counsel. The bond counsel examines the issue to make sure that it is legally binding on the issuer, is valid, and that the interest is exempt from Federal tax under current law.

Unqualified Opinion

Qualified Opinion

The bond counsel prepares all the legal documentation necessary for the issue and renders an opinion. Issuers desire an "unqualified legal opinion." Here, the bond counsel says everything is "OK" - there are no problems. If the counsel does find a problem, he "qualifies" the opinion, stating that there is a legal uncertainty of which any purchaser should be aware. For example, new Federal tax rulings may make the interest taxable.

Serial Bonds

Municipalities issue long term debt and short-term notes. Most long term issues are "serial maturities" - with the maturities spread over a sequence of years. These bonds are issued at par and pay interest semi-annually. Short-term notes are issued at a discount from par and mature at par value.

Level Debt Service

Note that with a serial structure, generally part of the issue is maturing each year, thus both interest on all outstanding bonds, and the principal repayment scheduled for that year, are due. If the issue is structured so that the combined annual payments of interest and principal equal the same total amount each year, then the issue is said to have "level debt service." (This is the same type of structure as a mortgage payment schedule for a homeowner.)

Municipalities like level debt service bond issues because it allows them to budget the same annual dollar amount to pay debt service requirements. As long as they pay the level debt service amount yearly, the bond issue will be completely retired at maturity.

Municipal issues are broadly categorized into general obligation bonds, revenue bonds, special types of bonds, and short-term notes.

4b. GENERAL OBLIGATION BONDS

General Obligation Bonds

Unlimited Ad Valorem Tax Backing For "Local" Issues

A general obligation bond is backed by the full faith, credit and taxing power of the issuer. The type of taxes which back general obligation bonds depends on the issuing entity. Local governments have the ability to collect property taxes, known as "ad valorem" taxes. It is unusual that local governments (towns and cities) collect income taxes, although New York City has an income tax. Therefore, local governmental issues are usually backed by "unlimited" ad valorem taxes. This means that the issuer promises to raise taxes without any limit in order to pay off the bondholders.

Limited Tax Bonds

In some cases, local issuers will sell bonds backed by "limited" taxing power. This means that there is a limit placed on the rate that the issuer uses to assess taxes. If the issuer is not collecting enough taxes to pay the bondholders and is at the maximum millage rate (defined below), then the bondholders are at risk. Obviously, limited tax bonds have more credit risk than unlimited tax bonds and sell at higher interest rates.

Mill Rate

Ad valorem taxes back local G.O. bond issues. These taxes are assessed based on "millage."

One mill = $1/10^{th}$ of 1 percent or .001

$1 Tax Due For Every $1,000 Of Assessed Value

If a municipality has a tax rate of 6 mills, a property with an assessed valuation of $100,000 would pay taxes of .006 x $100,000 = $600. This is the same as $1 of tax for every $1,000 of assessed value.

State Issues Backed By Income And Sales Taxes

State issues are backed by a different source of taxing power. Most states do not assess property taxes; instead the revenue sources are income and sales taxes.

Constitutional Debt Limit

Because local issues are backed by property taxes, and property owners are very unhappy when mill rates are raised, most municipalities have imposed a debt limit on the dollar amount of G.O. bonds that can be outstanding at any one time. This is either a statutory or constitutional limit which is expressed as a percentage of assessed valuation. If a municipality is at its limit, it cannot issue additional G.O. bonds. The only way to change the limit is through majority approval in a public referendum.

Debt limits are also imposed by state constitutions on G.O. debt issued by each state, similar to the Federal debt limit.

Capital Appreciation Bond	A Capital Appreciation Bond (CAB) is a municipal zero coupon bond with a "legal" twist to it. A conventional zero coupon G.O. bond is counted against an issuer's debt limit at par value because the discount is treated as "principal." If a new issue discount bond is legally crafted as a CAB, then the principal counted against the issuer's debt limit is the discounted principal amount and the discount earned is considered to be interest income.
G.O. Holders Have Legal Right To Compel Tax Levy	In the event of a default, G.O. bondholders have the right to compel a tax levy or legislative appropriation to make payment on the debt. Because of this, G.O. bonds are generally considered the safest type of municipal credit. Of course, the actual rating of each issuer can vary and is provided by the ratings services.

4c. REVENUE BONDS

Revenue Bond **Not Backed By Taxing Power**	A revenue bond is one backed by a specific source of revenue to which the full faith and credit of the issuer is not pledged. Such bonds do not allow bondholders to compel taxation or legislative appropriation for payment, as is true of G.O. bonds. Since only the specified revenues back a revenue bond, this is said to be a self-supporting debt. The types of revenue that back these bonds are revenues from the operation of the project, user fees, rents, grants, excise and other non-ad valorem taxes.
Self-Supporting	Revenue bond issues are self-supporting. To ensure that a proposed project makes economic sense, the issuance of revenue bonds is dependent on the completion of a "feasibility study."
	For example, a town proposes to build a new hospital to be financed by a revenue bond issue. A report will be prepared showing the need for the facility, the projected costs of running and financing the facility, the expected revenues from the facility, an engineer's report on the costs of building the facility, the effect of competing hospitals, etc. If the report shows that the project is economically feasible, then the town will go ahead with the issue.
Feasibility Study	The feasibility study is usually prepared by outside consultants, who do not have a vested interest in seeing the facility built.
Trust Indenture	Because revenue bonds are backed by a single source of funds, they have greater credit risk than G.O. bonds. As such, they trade at higher yields. Investors in revenue bonds demand greater protections than G.O. bond purchasers since there is no ability to collect if the project fails. Because of this, most revenue bonds are issued under a "Trust Indenture." A trust indenture is a legal requirement for corporate issues under the Trust Indenture Act of 1939, but municipal issues are exempt from this act. The use of a "Trust Indenture" is optional, but revenue issues are hard to sell without one.

Bond Contract	All bonds are issued under a "bond contract" prepared by the bond counsel. The "contract" consists of various pieces, depending on the type of issue. Every bond contract has an "authorizing resolution" (bond resolution) which allows the sale of the securities. Each contract has a "security agreement" pledging an income source to back the issue, such as full faith, credit, and taxing power for a G.O. bond or specified revenues for a revenue bond. And most revenue bond contracts have a "Trust Indenture" - a contract between the issuer and a trustee for the benefit of the bondholders.
Trust Indenture Protective Covenants	The trustee's job is to monitor the issuer's compliance with the bond contract and, more specifically, compliance with "protective covenants" specified in the contract. If the issuer is not living up to the contract, the trustee has legal power to enforce the contract on behalf of the bondholders by initiating court proceedings. The types of covenants which are found in the trust indenture are:
Maintenance Covenant	Maintenance Covenant: A promise by the issuer to maintain the facility in good repair
Rate Covenant	Rate Covenant: A promise by the issuer to maintain fees for using the facility at a high enough level to cover debt service. If fees are not sufficient, the issuer is obligated to raise rates.
Segregation Of Funds Covenant	Segregation of Funds: A promise by the issuer to keep the revenues collected from and monies expended on running the facility separate from other municipal accounts.
Books And Records Covenant	Maintenance of Books and Records: A promise to maintain proper record keeping of accounts. Generally, there is an annual audit requirement as well.
No Sale Covenant	No Sale or Encumbrance: A promise by the issuer not to sell the facility or to allow liens to be placed on the facility (e.g. obtain a mortgage which would jeopardize the bondholders' position in a liquidation).
Additional Bonds Covenant	Additional Bonds: A promise not to issue additional bonds against the facility unless specified "earnings tests" are met. If earnings are high enough, additional bonds of equal status (called "parity bonds") can be issued. This test is called an "additional bonds test." This is true if the bond contract has an "open end lien" - that is, more bonds can be issued. If the contract is "closed end lien," no additional bonds may be sold until the existing bonds are redeemed.
Insurance Covenant	Insurance: A promise to insure the facility in an amount sufficient to pay off the bondholders if the facility is destroyed or inoperable.

Catastrophe (Calamity) Call Covenant	Catastrophe Call: A promise to call in the bonds if the facility is destroyed. Since the facility can no longer generate revenues, the bondholders should be happy to get their money back. The funds to call the bonds would come from the insurance proceeds.
Revenue Pledge	Under the security agreement included in the bond contract, the issuer pledges the revenues of the facility to pay the debt service. The "revenue pledge" outlines exactly how the issuer will apply collected revenues. To understand what happens, we must look at the "flow of funds" stated in the contract.
Flow Of Funds	The "flow of funds" states the priority of collecting and disbursing pledged revenues. The normal flow of funds (from first to last) is: • Revenue fund; • Operation and maintenance fund; • Sinking fund; • Debt service reserve fund; • Reserve maintenance fund; • Renewal and replacement fund; • Surplus fund.
Revenue Fund	Revenue Fund: All gross revenues from the facility are placed in this fund and all monies to be disbursed are taken from this fund.
Operation And Maintenance Fund	Operation and Maintenance Fund: Monies to run the facility are deposited in this fund from the Revenue Fund.
Net Revenue Pledge **Gross Revenue Pledge**	Most revenue bonds are issued under a "Net Revenue Pledge." The bondholders do not have claim to the "gross revenues," but rather the "net revenues" from the facility. Net revenues are gross revenues less operation and maintenance. After operation and maintenance are paid, then the bondholders are paid. Very few "gross lien" revenue bonds are issued where the bondholders are paid before operation and maintenance.
Sinking Fund	Sinking Fund: Monies to meet debt service requirements are deposited to the sinking fund. The bondholders are paid from this fund.
Debt Service Reserve	Debt Service Reserve Fund: A fund of "extra" monies (usually one year's worth) to pay bondholders if revenues are insufficient at any one time. If it is depleted, it must be refunded as soon as sufficient revenues are available.
Reserve Maintenance	Reserve Maintenance Fund: Monies to pay extraordinary maintenance or replacement costs.
Renewal And Replacement	Renewal and Replacement Fund: Monies to pay for regularly scheduled major repairs and replacement.

Debt Securities

Surplus

Surplus Fund: Monies "left over" after all other uses are exhausted. It can be used in any legal way by the issuer.

To understand the "Flow of Funds," below is a sample Revenue Bond Financial Statement:

New Jersey Turnpike Authority Statement of Revenues and Expenses Year Ending 12/31/20XX	
Collected Tolls:	$100,000,000
Interest on Reserve Funds:	$10,000,000
Gross Revenues:	$110,000,000
Operation and Maintenance:	$75,000,000
Net Revenues:	$35,000,000
Debt Service:	$20,000,000
Addition to Reserves:	$15,000,000

Net Revenue Pledge

If this revenue bond issue included a "Net Revenue Pledge" in the Trust Indenture, then the $35,000,000 of Net Revenues (**after** Operation and Maintenance expenses have been paid) is the amount pledged to the bondholders.

Gross Revenue Pledge

If this revenue bond issue included a "Gross Revenue Pledge" in the Trust Indenture, then the $110,000,000 of Gross Revenues (**before** Operation and Maintenance expenses have been paid) is the amount pledged to the bondholders.

4d. SPECIAL TYPES OF MUNICIPAL DEBT

The two largest types of municipal offerings, by far, are G.O. bonds and revenue bonds. Revenue bond financing accounts for about 45% of municipal issues, while G.O. bonds account for another 45%. The rest of the municipal market is composed of "special" types of bonds. These are:

Special Tax

Special Tax Bonds: An issue secured by a tax other than an ad valorem tax, usually excise taxes such as cigarette, liquor, gasoline taxes. The tax source does not have to relate to the type of project.

Special Assessment

Special Assessment Bonds: To fund an improvement which does not benefit the general public, but rather a small portion of the community, a municipality will float a bond issue backed by a "special assessment" of increased taxes designed to pay for the improvement. For example, new street lights may be put in one area, and only that area is assessed higher taxes to pay for the improvement.

Moral Obligation

Ultimate Payment By Legislative Apportionment

Moral Obligation Bond: Assume an issuer is at or above its statutory debt limit and cannot legally issue more debt backed by taxing power. Also assume that the issuer needs more financing, mainly to have the funds to "roll over" existing debt or it will default. This is the situation that New York City faced in 1975. The solution: issue a bond backed by the "promise" to pay, but not the legal obligation to pay. In New York City's case, the State assumed the moral obligation to pay if the city could not, with the State legislature authorized, but not obligated, to apportion the funds needed to service the debt, if necessary. This "moral obligation" bond is only issued in times of distress and has a higher level of credit risk.

Recent Moral Obligation Bond Issues Are Revenue Bonds

Recent moral obligation bond issues have been revenue bonds that are being used to build ever-more costly ball stadiums. The projected revenues from these super-expensive projects may not cover the debt service, so a state agency or authority secures the bond with a non-binding covenant that any deficiency in pledged revenues will be included in the budget recommendation made to the state legislature, which may appropriate the funds to make up the shortfall (but is not obligated to do so).

Double-Barreled

Double-Barreled Bond: An issue backed by a revenue source other than ad valorem taxes but also backed by the faith, credit and taxing power of a municipal issuer. For example, a housing bond (revenue) may be backed as well by the issuer's ad valorem taxing power to improve its credit rating. This type of bond is treated as a G.O. bond since the ultimate source of payment is taxing power. Also note that the term "double-barreled" bond is sometimes, though erroneously, used in reference to bonds secured by any two sources of revenue. Do not do this on the exam!

Certificate Of Participation (COP)

Certificate Of Participation: As municipalities reached their debt limits with G.O. bond issuance, they found it hard to get voter approval to increase the limits so that more bonds could be issued. To get around this, the "COP" - Certificate of Participation - was invented by creative municipal bond attorneys. These allow state entities to issue a tax-exempt security that pledges the revenue (lease payments received) from a project, such as a university dormitory, prison, municipal office building, etc. These lease payment is made based on the governing body making an annual appropriation from tax collections. The governing body is not "legally" obligated to make the annual appropriation, so it is not legally a G.O. bond (however, the annual appropriation will be made, otherwise the issuer's credit rating would be destroyed).

Lease Rental

Lease Rental Bond: An issue used to finance office construction where the user is a state or city agency. The rents paid by the user are the revenue source and the user is generally obligated to appropriate the funds for the lease payments from general tax revenues.

Industrial Development Bond	Industrial Development Bond: Bonds issued by a state, city, or local agency to build an industrial facility that is leased to a private company. The lease payments of the company are the revenue source. IDBs are also guaranteed by the private user, take on its credit rating, and are considered the user's liability - not the issuer's.
BABs - Build America Bonds	In April 2009, Congress passed the "American Recovery and Reinvestment Act" which included a number of economic stimulus provisions to help the economy rebound after the market meltdown and "great recession" of 2008.
Build America Bonds Are Taxable But Issuer Gets 35% Interest Rate Credit	To help with an economic recovery, municipalities could issue "Build America Bonds," which are taxable bond issues. However, these bonds get a 35% interest rate credit from the Federal Government.
Federal Tax Credit On Interest Paid	Thus, if a municipality issues a 10% BAB, it will get a payment from the Federal Government equal to 3.5%, so the issuer's net interest cost is 6.50%.
Municipalities Can Sell Bonds In The Broader "Taxable" Bond Market	The "idea" is that the municipality would now be able to sell bonds to the larger investor base for taxable investments, including international investors that have no reason to buy "tax-free" municipal issues. With a larger pool of potential buyers, municipalities should be able to raise much needed funds during a recessionary period where falling tax revenues and other receipts have sharply limited their ability to finance new projects.
BABs Could Only Be Used For Capital Projects That Would Be Funded With Tax-Free Bonds	The program ran through the end of 2010 and only permitted bond issues to be sold where the proceeds would be used for infrastructure improvements. Capital projects that could be funded with BABs included public buildings, courthouses, schools, roads, public housing, transportation infrastructure, government hospitals, public safety facilities, water and sewer projects, environmental projects, and public utilities. Essentially, the bonds could be used for any capital project that would normally be financed with a tax-free bond issue.
	This was a pure and simple economic stimulus program to encourage capital investment in 2009 and 2010, and thus, create jobs and growth. At the end of 2010, Congress chose not to extend the "BAB" program when it extended the lower "Bush-Era" income tax rates, but these bonds trade in the market.

4e. SHORT TERM MUNICIPAL NOTES

Usually Under 1 Year Maturity	Municipalities issue short term notes, usually with less than 12-month maturities, although it is not uncommon for notes to be issued with maturities as short as 3 months and for as long as 3 years.

Notes are issued for 2 general purposes:

- For temporary financing of capital improvements
- To even out cash flows

Usually Issued At Par With A Stated Interest Rate

These notes usually are sold at par with a stated rate of interest and are redeemed at par plus accrued interest. However, some are sold at a discount and mature at par.

Short-term notes can be categorized in types. The first type is used to obtain short-term financing for a building project, to be replaced by permanent financing at the completion of the project. These are:

BANs

Secured By General Obligation Pledge

Bond Anticipation Notes (BANs): Issued to start capital projects; the note is paid off by the placement of the final long term bond issue. BANs are used because the ultimate final cost of the project is unknown during the construction period. Once all the costs are tallied, a long-term bond financing is floated to pay off the BAN issue. Most BANs are secured by the general obligation pledge of the issuer.

CLNs

Take-Out Financing

Construction Loan Notes (CLNs): Issued to start the building of multifamily housing projects; the note is paid off by the placement of a final long-term bond issue. The final long-term bond issue is known as the "take-out" loan, since it replaces the CLN issue. The permanent financing plan is typically arranged for at the time of the CLN issuance, usually with GNMA.

2-3 Year Length

CLNs are typically issued for periods of 2-3 years. Such notes are typically issued during periods when interest rates are high; the borrower is hoping that interest rates will have dropped by the time the take-out loan is issued.

The second type of municipal short term note is used to "pull forward" an income source and use the monies before they are actually collected.

For example, tax revenues come in on April 15th. On March 1st of that year, an issuer may sell Tax Anticipation Notes maturing on April 30th. The notes are paid off by the collected taxes, but the issuer has had use of the funds since March 1st.

These are:

TANs

Backed By G.O. Pledge

Tax Anticipation Notes (TANs): Issued in anticipation of future property (ad valorem) tax receipts; paid off from those receipts. TANs are secured by the general obligation pledge of the issuer.

Debt Securities

RANs **Backed By G.O. Pledge**	Revenue Anticipation Notes (RANs): Issued in anticipation of future revenue collections and tax collections other than ad valorem taxes. An example of an income source is intergovernmental capital construction grants such as Federal Highway Funds. The notes are paid off from those collections. Most RANs are also backed by the general obligation pledge of the issuer, making them very marketable.
TRANs	Tax and Revenue Anticipation Notes (TRANs): Issued in anticipation of both future tax collections **and** revenue collections. This is really a combination of a TAN and RAN offering.
GANs	Grant Anticipation Notes (GANs): Issued in expectation of receiving grant monies, usually from the federal government for mass transit, energy conservation, and pollution control programs.
Tax-Exempt Commercial Paper - Backed By Bank Line Of Credit	There are two unusual forms of short term municipal financing. Some issuers have sold "tax-exempt commercial paper" with very short maturities (under 30 days). To make these marketable, they are sold backed by a bank line of credit. Thus, if the municipal issuer cannot pay, the bank is obligated to pay.
Variable Rate Demand Notes **Long-Term Debt Issued At Short-Term Rates**	Finally, some issuers have sold "variable rate" demand notes. The issuer resets the interest rate daily or weekly based on a given index. At the reset point, the note holder has the option of redeeming the note at par or holding it for the next period (1 day or 1 week) at the new interest rate. This was the first attempt by issuers to sell long-term bonds (because there is no stated maturity date) at short-term interest rates (because the holder can redeem at each reset date).
Step-Up / Step-Down Notes	Because the interest rate can either be "stepped-up" or "stepped-down" at the reset date, these are sometimes referred to as "step-up" or "step-down" notes (or bonds).
Variable Rate Notes Have Almost No Market Risk	Unlike bonds with fixed interest rates, such "reset" bonds will show very little price fluctuation in response to market interest rate movements, since the interest rate is being reset to the prevailing market rate daily or weekly. Thus, the price tends to stay at, or close to, par.

4f. DEBT RETIREMENT PROVISIONS

Municipal debt may be redeemed at maturity, or if call provisions are included in the bond contract, it may be retired prior to maturity. Municipal call features differ somewhat from those of corporate bonds. The call may be at par or may be at a premium, similar to corporate bonds. The call may be optional or mandatory. These are:

Optional Redemption	Optional Redemption: The issuer has the right to call bonds after a certain date, usually at a premium, but has no obligation to do so.

Mandatory Redemption

Mandatory Redemption: The issuer is required to call bonds on a schedule included in the bond contract. The contract specifies the dollar amount of bonds to be called but does not specify the particular bonds. These are drawn randomly on the redemption dates. The issuer is often allowed to buy the bonds in the open market if the price is better than the call price. The point is that as parts of the issue are called, the remaining bonds become more valuable, as the issuer demonstrates its creditworthiness.

Unusual circumstances can also cause early redemption. These early redemption provisions are:

Extraordinary Optional Redemption

Extraordinary Optional Redemption: The issuer has the option of calling the bonds if an unusual event specified in the contract occurs. An example is a bond issue used to fund local housing by giving mortgages. If the mortgages are prepaid, the revenue source for the bond issue is reduced. The issuer can have the right to call in bonds by using the mortgage prepayments.

Extraordinary Mandatory Redemption

Extraordinary Mandatory Redemption: The issuer must call the bonds if unusual events specified in the contract occur. For example, the issuer does not use the bond issue proceeds because the project is canceled; or the facility is destroyed in a disaster. This is also known as a "catastrophe call" covenant.

Refunding

An issuer may issue new bonds and use the proceeds to retire old maturing bonds. This is a refunding, which was covered in Corporate Debt.

Advance Refunding

Municipal issuers may also "advance refund" debt. Assume that a G.O. bond issuer believes that interest rates have bottomed and wants to sell long-term debt now, while rates are low. Also assume that the issuer believes that the sale of additional debt may reduce its credit rating at this time. The issuer can buy U.S. Government bonds and deposit them with a trustee. The interest payments from these bonds are earmarked to service the issuer's old debt. At maturity, the issuer uses the principal repayment to retire the old bonds. Since the source of revenues backing the issuer's old bonds is no longer taxing power, but rather the interest and principal from the U.S. Government bonds held in trust, the G.O. bonds are no longer considered a debt of the issuer. The issuer is free to issue new bonds at the current low interest rates.

Debt Securities

Defeasance **Escrowed To Maturity** **Acceptable Securities For Escrow**	The technical term for the issuer's elimination of the G.O. debt as its liability is defeasance. The issuer has defeased its debt; the obligation rests with someone else (the U.S. Government bonds held in escrow). Defeased debt is also called "ETM"- escrowed to maturity - or advance refunded debt. Escrowed bonds are rated AAA and trade at low yields. Municipal issuers are typically permitted to defease their debt with U.S. Government bonds, agency bonds, and sometimes, bank certificates of deposit. Each of these represents security of the highest quality, satisfying the requirements of the existing bondholders and also yields a higher nominal amount than "tax-free" municipal debt, giving the municipality "extra" income.
IRS Arbitrage Regulations	The excess of interest earned on these "taxable" investments, over and above interest owed on the issuer's outstanding "tax free" municipal debt is limited under IRS regulations that govern arbitrage on such transactions. Municipalities would not defease their debt with lower credit rated issues (corporates) or with lower yielding investments (i.e., other municipal bonds).
Pre-Refunding	Assume the issuer has 20-year bonds outstanding, callable in 10 years. The issuer defeases the debt by escrowing 10-year Treasury Notes. Once this occurs, the bondholders know that the issue will be called. The bonds are said to be pre-refunded. They will not be paid at maturity, but rather will be called early.
Tender (Put) Option **Tender Offer**	Municipal issues may also be sold with a tender option, allowing the purchaser to "put" the bonds to the issuer after a certain date. This was covered in Section 1. An issuer may also retire debt prior to maturity by making a tender offer for the bonds. Interested bondholders can "tender" their bonds for a stated cash price, but are under no obligation to do so. An issuer would only use this method if the bonds are non-callable.

4g. ANALYZING MUNICIPAL DEBT

To analyze G.O. debt, one would look at the debt statement of the municipality. This will outline the issuer's total bonded debt, which is the total obligation outstanding at that time.

Debt Statement	Bonded Debt, also called Overall Net Debt, is computed in two steps:
Step 1	Net Direct Debt = Gross Direct Debt - Sinking Fund Deposits and Self Supporting Debt
Step 2	Overall Net Debt = Net Direct Debt + Overlapping Debt

The components of Overall Net Debt are:

Gross Direct Debt	Gross Direct Debt: All indebtedness of the issuer

Sinking Fund Deposits and Self-Supporting Debt: Monies held on deposit in a sinking fund reduce the issuer's obligation, since these funds are earmarked to retire debt. Self-supporting debt (meaning debt other than G.O. bonds) is also deducted to arrive at the true amount of debt supported by taxpayers.

Net Direct Debt

Net Direct Debt: The amount of debt of the issuer that is ultimately the responsibility of the taxpayers.

Overlapping Debt

Overlapping Debt: The issuer's share of debt of other governmental bodies which are wholly or partly within the same geographic boundaries. For example, a school district may consist of three separate towns. Debt issued in the name of the school district would be shared by the three towns. This is an "overlapping debt."

Total Net Direct And Overlapping Debt

Net Direct and Overlapping Debt: The true debt liability of the issuer to be paid from taxing power.

Once Total Net Direct and Overlapping debt has been computed, ratio tests are performed to evaluate the issuer.

$$\text{Debt per Capita} = \frac{\text{Overall Net Debt}}{\text{Population}}$$

$$\text{Debt to Assessed Valuation} = \frac{\text{Overall Net Debt}}{\text{Assessed Property Value}}$$

Debt Per Capita Is Used Widely

Debt Per Capita is the most common measure used to evaluate the relative debt burden of one municipality as compared to another. It is used because its components are computed consistently from one municipality to the next.

Debt To Assessed Valuation Is Not Used Widely

Debt To Assessed Valuation is not as widely used because each municipality assesses property value based on differing methods. Because there is no consistency, this measure is not used as widely.

To illustrate how the ratios are computed, following is the debt statement of the City of Kenosha, Wisconsin, a city with a population of 80,889 at the time this statement was issued.

Debt Statement – Kenosha, Wisconsin			
Year Ending 12/31/20XX ($000)			
Bonded Debt Outstanding:			$ 27,120
Unfunded Debt - Notes:			$ 400
Gross Direct Debt:			$ 27,520
Less: Water and Sewer Rev. Bds			$ 6,165
Gateway Tech Instit.			$ 635
Direct Net Debt:			$ 20,720
Overlapping Debt	Amt	%	
Kenosha County	$10,088	54.1	$ 5,458
Kenosha U.S.D.*	$12,534	74.2	$ 9,295
(* - Unified School District)			
Overall Net Debt:			$ 35,473

In looking at the Debt Statement of Kenosha, we find that the city has Gross Direct Debt of $27,520,000. This consists of **ALL** debt issued by Kenosha. To arrive at the net burden to be borne by property taxpayers, "self-supporting debts" are subtracted. In this case, these include water and sewer revenue bonds and revenue bonds of a city-sponsored school / technology complex (Gateway). In addition, if this city had any escrowed bonds, these would be deducted as a self-supporting debt.

To arrive at Overall Net Debt, we must add any "overlapping debts" of other issuers for which Kenosha residents are partly (or wholly) responsible. These debts consist of $10,088,000 of Kenosha County bonds, which overlap the City of Kenosha by 54.1%, and Kenosha Unified School District Bonds totaling $12,534,000, which overlap the city of Kenosha by 74%. Including these proportionate amounts gives an Overall Net Debt of $35,473.000. Thus, Overall Net Debt of a municipality is:

$$\text{Overall Net Debt} = \text{Net Direct} + \text{Overlapping Debt}$$

$$\text{Debt per Capita} = \frac{\text{Overall Net Debt}}{\text{Population}} = \frac{\$35,473,000}{80,889} = \$439$$

As a comparison, the average overall debt per capita for cities comparable to Kenosha's size is $460, so Kenosha is somewhat better than average.

General Factors To Consider About G.O. Bonds

To evaluate a G.O. bond issuer, other factors also must be considered. These include the community's attitude towards its debt (if times are tough, will they do everything possible to pay off the debt or would they file for bankruptcy?); its tax base; the diversification of the local economy; its financial condition (including unfunded pension liabilities - a potentially large liability); population trends in the area; and tax collection ability as measured by its collection ratio.

$$\text{Collection Ratio} = \frac{\text{Taxes Collected}}{\text{Taxes Assessed}}$$

The collection ratio should be well above 90% - any lower ratio indicates that the municipality is not able to collect its taxes and is experiencing a high level of delinquencies.

Also to be evaluated are the issuer's debt trend (is it going up?); its ratio of debt service to annual revenues; its future debt service requirements; and the anticipated life of any improvements (which should not be less than the bond issue life).

Revenue Bond Analysis

Analysis of Revenue Bonds is totally different from that for G.O. Bonds. Revenue bonds are self-supporting and must be economically justified. There must be a need for the facility and little current or potential competition. For example, a new hospital should not be built if three other hospitals are going up nearby.

The feasibility study and engineering reports would be examined, as would the protective covenants in the trust indenture. For example, is there a rate covenant? Is there an insurance covenant? Is there a net revenue pledge or a gross revenue pledge? Is the trust indenture open ended or closed end? (Thus, no new bonds can be issued against the facility's revenues).

Debt Service Coverage Ratio

A test that would be used to evaluate safety is the Debt Service Coverage Ratio.

$$\text{Debt Service Coverage} = \frac{\text{Pledged Revenues}}{\text{Debt Service Requirement}}$$

Ideally, this ratio should be comfortably above 1, indicating there are sufficient revenues to meet debt service requirements. Using the Statement of Revenues and Expenses presented earlier in this section, the Debt Service Coverage Ratio, assuming a Net Revenue Pledge would be:

$$\text{Debt Service Coverage} = \frac{\$35,000,000}{\$20,000,000} = 1.75 \text{ to } 1$$

Given a choice, every municipal issuer would like to see Moody's and Standard and Poor's rate the issue AAA. The agencies perform an analysis of the bonds, considering all the items just discussed. Issuers can get an AAA rating if the bonds are insured. Municipal bond insurers are:

- **AMBAC**: American Municipal Bond Assurance Corp.
- **MBIA**: Municipal Bond Insurance Association Corp.
- **FGIC**: Financial Guaranty Insurance Corporation
- **FSA**: Financial Security Assurance Corp.

Debt Securities

| **Rated "AAA"** | These are private companies (e.g. MBIA is listed on the New York Stock Exchange) that insure both the timely payment of interest and the repayment of principal on a given issue, for which a fee (similar to an insurance premium) is paid by the issuer. Due to the better credit rating, as well as the cost of the insurance, insured issues typically yield about 1/2 percent less than similar uninsured issues. |

4h. TRADING OF MUNICIPAL DEBT

Municipals Trade Over-The-Counter	Trading in the municipal bond market is very limited. All trades take place over-the-counter. The cause of this is the fact that, in addition to the federal tax exemption that municipal interest enjoys, if a bond is purchased by the resident of a state, most states will also exempt the issue from state and local tax (a "triple" exempt issue - Federal, State and Local).
Intrastate Issues Triple Exempt	
Thin Market	Generally, this confines investor interest in municipal issues to residents of the state of issuance. In effect, the municipal market is a state by state market. People in Maine buy Maine bonds, not New York bonds; people in New York buy New York bonds, not Maine bonds, etc.
No Short Sales	Another factor that limits municipal trading is that most issues are "serial" maturities. Within a bond offering are multiple maturities, with each maturity having a relatively small principal amount. The small amount of each maturity available limits trading. For example, if a customer wants to buy a Chicago bond maturing in 2020, you can't give him a 2021 bond. This also limits short sales of municipal bonds. When a security is sold short, it is borrowed and sold on the condition that it be replaced later by purchasing the issue in the market. If one borrows and sells a 2020 bond, one must buy back the same 2020 bond (not a 2019 or 2021).
Municipal Market Participants	Firms that trade in the municipal market include banks (such as J. P. Morgan Chase), full service brokerage firms (such as Raymond James), and firms that deal only in municipal bonds whose names are not as familiar (such as J. J. Kenny Drake or Stoever Glass and Co.).
Bloomberg For Quotes	Dealer offerings of municipal bonds are published by diversified quote providers like Bloomberg that electronically post government, corporate and municipal bond offerings; and also by the larger bond dealers who post their own bond offerings directly on their own websites.
	In Bloomberg, serial bonds are quoted on a yield basis while term bonds are quoted on a percentage of par basis. This is a wholesale listing of bonds offered dealer to dealer. If a public customer wants to buy a bond that the firm does not have, the firm uses Bloomberg to find the dealer offering the bond and calls to obtain a firm price. (Quotes in Bloomberg, while firm at the time of publication, can be changed at any time in response to market conditions). The dealer then buys the bond for the customer and charges him a commission for this service.

All Offers Made In Dealer Publications Must Be "Bona-Fide"	Note that all offers of municipal securities made in dealer publications must be "bona-fide" - that is, the dealer must have been willing to sell those securities at the indicated prices at the time that the offer was made. Note that it is not required that the dealer actually own the securities at the time that the bona-fide offer is made - the only requirement is that the dealer must know where such securities can be obtained if the offer is accepted.
Municipal Broker's Broker	Another participant in the municipal market is the "municipal broker's broker." There are very few of these firms (12 at last count) which perform a specialized service, usually for large institutions. Assume that Citibank wants to sell a very large block of New York City G.O. bonds. If it listed the offering in Bloomberg, everyone would know that it wants to sell a large amount and pressure would be put on Citibank to drop the price.
Does Not Carry Inventory **Acts As Agent**	Instead, Citibank can use a "broker's broker" to obtain bids for the bonds. The broker's broker will call up other dealers and offer small portions of the issue, keeping Citibank anonymous in the transaction. In this manner, the issue can be sold evenly into the market. Municipal broker's brokers do not deal with the public and do not carry an inventory of bonds. They handle large transactions for institutions.
Bid **Firm Bid** **Nominal Bid**	Municipal trading terminology is a bit unusual, to accommodate the fact that the market is quite illiquid and not actively traded. A dealer bidding for a bond is willing to buy at the stated price or yield. A "firm" quote means the dealer will honor that price. If the quote is "nominal," the dealer is giving an idea of the price, but not an actual price. Dealers can qualify their bids. A typical qualification is that the legal opinion must be printed on the bond (some older bonds have them on a separate piece of paper) or that delivery be made by a stated date.
	Assume the following scenario: A customer in California is moving to New York, and wants to buy some New York bonds prior to moving. He contacts a local dealer in California to buy the bonds. The dealer in California is familiar with California issues, but not those of New York. The dealer in California must call dealers in New York, shopping around for the "best offer."
Firm Offer	The first dealer contacted in New York gives a firm price for the desired bonds. However, the California dealer is reluctant to make the purchase without further "shopping around" to see if this quote **is** the best price. The California dealer says "I can't buy yet because I want to get some other quotes." Upon hearing this, the dealer in New York states "I'll offer the bonds to you firm for 1/2 hour with a 5 minute recall."

Debt Securities

Firm Offer With A Recall

By giving the bonds "firm" for 1/2 hour, the New York dealer is allowing the California dealer to shop around for 1/2 hour, and will not change the stated price during that time period. This allows the California dealer to look for a better price, knowing that the New York dealer will not change his quote during that 1/2 hour. However, the New York dealer, by adding a 5 minute recall, is protecting himself in the following way. If someone else comes along during that 1/2 hour to the New York dealer, wishing to buy that same bond, the New York dealer will call the California dealer, and demand that a purchase decision be made within the next 5 minutes (the "5 minute recall"). If the California dealer does not accept within 5 minutes, the offer is null and void.

Assume the following scenario: A customer from New York has moved to California. After moving, he realizes that he has some New York bonds that he wishes to sell. He contacts a dealer in California to sell the bonds. The dealer in California is familiar with local California issues, but not those of New York. The dealer in California must call dealers in New York, shopping around for the "best bid."

Workable - Likely Bid

The first dealer contacted in New York does not give a firm price (bid) for the bonds - instead the dealer says "I think I might buy them at about par." The New York dealer has not given a firm bid; he has given a "municipal workable," which is a likely price at which he might buy the bonds. The California dealer will contact a number of New York firms, getting "workables" from each, and then will go back to the firm that gave the best "workable" to nail down a firm bid.

These methods of bidding (workables) and offering (firm offers with recalls) are needed because the trading market is thin and many different firms may have to be contacted to finally make a trade at the best price. Remember, there are no automated trading systems for municipals as there are for stocks, nor are there real-time trade reports.

What happens when a customer calls up and states he wants to buy or sell a bond, but wants an idea of the price first? You can't get a quote from a computer system; there is none. You might get a quote from Bloomberg for a similar bond, but that is yesterday's quote. What you do is call other municipal dealers and solicit price indications, finally homing-in on the best price in the market. This is done by getting municipal "workables" when customers wish to sell; and getting "firm offers with recalls" when customers wish to buy.

Round Lot

A round lot of municipal bonds is usually considered to be $100,000 face amount. (For corporate bonds, a round lot is $5,000 face amount).

Secondary Market Joint Accounts **Similar To New Issue Syndicates**	To handle very large municipal transactions in the secondary market, a number of firms can join together into a "joint account." Municipal joint accounts are used to either purchase or distribute large blocks of bonds. The joint account is established under a written "joint account agreement," with a manager appointed to manage the account and make all decisions for the account. This is similar to a new issue "Syndicate Agreement" (covered in the New Issues chapter). The manager establishes the procedures for accepting orders for the bonds; establishes an "order period" (a short time period where orders are to be accepted for the benefit of the entire account; thereafter each order is credited wholly to the member placing that order); and the concessions (similar to commissions) to be earned by members that place orders.
Account May Only Publish One Quote	When such an account publishes quotes, only 1 quote is allowed - the members of the account are prohibited from publishing multiple quotes. This makes sense, since the account is acting as one trading entity.
Municipal Bond Trade Reports **RTRS**	In 2005, the MSRB started requiring its members to report municipal bond trades on a real-time basis (via the "RTRS" - Real time Trade Reporting System). Trades must be reported within 15 minutes of execution. This gives the municipal bond market a level of price transparency that did not exist before.
EMMA - Electronic Municipal Market Access	The RTRS trade reports are fed into a website maintained by the MSRB called "EMMA" - Electronic Municipal Market Access. EMMA is designed for the retail investor, and includes new issue information and trading market information. Regarding the trading market, RTRS trade reports are shown on EMMA, as well as details of each municipal issue outstanding and general market statistics.

4i. SETTLEMENT AND ACCRUED INTEREST

	Settlement terms (Regular Way, Cash, Seller's Option, When Issued) are essentially the same for municipal bonds as for corporate bonds as discussed previously.
Interest On L.T. Bonds Accrues On 30 / 360 Basis	Accrued interest for municipal bonds is computed in the same manner as for corporate bonds (30/360, accrues up to but not including settlement).
Interest On Notes Accrues On Actual / Actual Basis	Please note that accrued interest for short-term municipal notes differs from that for municipal bonds. Interest on short-term notes accrues on an actual day month / actual day year basis. This is the usual arrangement for any "money market" (under 1 year maturity) instrument.

4j. MUNICIPAL DEBT FINANCIAL LISTINGS

Alphabetical Listing By State

Municipal bonds are not regularly quoted in public media such as newspapers or the internet because the market is so thin. Sources for dealer quotes are services such as Bloomberg and J.J. Kenny Drake. Dealer municipal bond offerings are arranged in alphabetical order by State (Alabama first; Wyoming last).

Separate Listings

In addition, dealer offerings segregate and list separately:

Special Tax Status

Bonds with special tax status:

- Taxable Municipal Bonds;
- Bank Qualified Bonds;
- Bonds Subject To The Alternative Minimum Tax.
  (Note: These are covered at the end of the section.)

Enhanced Credit

Bonds with enhanced credit:

- Pre-Refunded Bonds
- Insured Bonds

Zero Coupon Issues

Bonds with unusual interest payments:

- Zero Coupon Bonds

Corporate And Agency Issues

Non-Municipal issues that dealers have in inventory:

- Government Agency Bonds
- Corporate Bonds

These last 2 listings are usually very small and are not a primary source for dealer quotes in these securities, but must be known for the exam.

List of Current Municipal Offerings

AMT M.	Security	Rate	Maturity	Yield or Price	Offered By
25	ALABAMA	4.75	7/1/18	100	CITIBANK
100	ALABAMA	4.90	7/1/19	5.40	RAYJAMES
20	ALABAMA (P/R@103)	5.20	1/1/18	5.60	WELLSFARGO
25	ALABAMA	5.50	1/1/19	6.00	FBC
250	ALABAMA HIGHWAY AUTH	6.75	3/1/23	5.75	BANKOFAM
100	ALABAMA HIGHWAY AUTH	7.00	3/1/25	6.50	GOLDMAN

Starting with the regular bond listings, the first offering is 25M = $25,000 of Alabama G.O. bonds (if there is no identifier such as **Auth**ority, **Fac**ility - it is a G.O. issue) with a stated interest rate of 4.75%, 2018 maturity, offered at par. (Note: "M" is Latin for $1,000 so 25M = $25,000 face amount of bonds.)

The second offering is $100,000 of Alabama 4.90% G.O. bonds maturing 2019 offered by Raymond James priced to yield 5.40%.

The third offering is $20,000 of Alabama 5.20% bonds maturing in 2018 which have been pre-refunded at 103 (a call premium). The bonds are priced to yield 5.60%.

The fourth offering is $25,000 of Alabama 5.50% G.O. bonds maturing on 1/1/19, priced to yield 6.00%.

The fifth and sixth offerings are Alabama Highway Authority bonds - these are revenue bonds.

Note that for most of these bonds, the price is shown on a yield basis - known as a basis quote. To find the actual dollar price for such a bond, an advanced calculator must be used - and this is not tested on the exam. However, the following basic relationships must be known:

> If the basis quote is the same as the coupon rate, the bond is being offered at par;

> If the basis quote is higher than the coupon rate, the bond is being offered at a discount; and

> If the basis quote is lower than the coupon rate, the bond is being offered at a premium.

For example, the quote for the fourth offering is a 5.50% G.O. bond maturing on 1/1/19, priced to yield 6.00%. The bond was issued with a fixed coupon rate of 5.50% of par. Once the bond is trading in the market, this rate is fixed. The only way for the yield to be raised above the stated coupon rate is for the dealer to drop the bond's price below par. Using a bond calculator, assuming that the bond has 9 years to maturity, the price comes out to:

> 96.56% of par or .9656 times $25,000 = $24,140.00.

To Approximate Price Of Long Term Bond, Divide Coupon By The Basis

(General note: A quick way to "approximate" the price of a bond quoted on a yield basis is to divide the Coupon by the Basis. This only works for long-term bonds. For example, a long term 5.50% bond quoted on a 6.00% basis has an "approximate" price of 5.50/6.00 = 91.66% of par. So we know the bond is trading at a discount.)

List of Current Municipal Offerings

AMT M.	Security	Rate	Maturity	Yield or Price	Offered By
	PRE-FUNDED BONDS				
50	UTAH (CAP.IMP) ETM	6.20	6/1/20	4.20	FBC
30	MASSACHUSETTS (P/R @ 104)	8.00	3/1/17 M'29	4.80	JPMORGAN
	NOTES				
500	BROWARD, FL 5/1/17 TAN	5.90	5/12/17	5.50	SOUTHFE
900	ERIE CO. NY 5/2/17 RAN	6.62	5/20/17	6.20	GOLDSACHS

Pre-Refunded Bonds

The pre-refunded bond listing shows escrowed bonds listed in order of redemption. The Utah Capital Improvement bonds are "ETM"- escrowed to maturity by U.S. Governments. The Massachusetts bonds are pre-refunded at 104 and will be redeemed in 2017 even though the maturity is 2029 (M'29). The bonds will be called at a price of 104 in 2017.

The Broward County, Florida "tax anticipation notes" will mature in 2017 and are priced to yield 5.50%. Erie County, New York "revenue anticipation notes" will mature in 2017 and are priced to yield 6.20%.

Other Info. Sources

Other information sources for the secondary market are:

Munifacts

Munifacts: A newswire service distributed by the Daily Bond Buyer (covered in the New Issues Chapter), that mainly announces new issue offerings, **but** also includes general news items affecting the secondary market.

4k. TAX STATUS OF MUNICIPAL DEBT INTEREST

Interest Exempt From Federal Income Tax - Subject To State Tax

Municipal bond interest income is exempt from Federal income tax, but is subject to state and local tax. The Federal tax emption arises from the fact that one level of government cannot tax another's obligations under the U.S. Constitution.

If Purchased By State Resident - Triple Tax Exempt

For most issues, if the purchaser is a resident of the state of issuance, state and local governments exempt the issue from taxation. In this case, the issue becomes triple tax exempt.

Territory And Possession Issues - Triple Exempt

Issues of territories or possessions of the U.S. (such as Puerto Rico, Guam, or the Virgin Islands) are always triple tax exempt, no matter where the purchaser resides.

To compare the tax status of the interest income received from all securities covered so far in this chapter, please review the following table:

Type of Debt	Tax Status of Interest Rec'd	
	Federal Tax	State Tax
U.S. Govt	Subject	Exempt
Gov't Agency	Subject	Exempt
Privatized Gov't Agency	Subject	Subject
Corporate	Subject	Subject
Municipal	Exempt	Subject*

*But, if the bond is purchased by a State resident, then it typically is exempt

The interest income received from U.S. Government and Agency Issues is subject to Federal income tax, but is exempt from State and Local tax. Compare this to the tax status of municipal interest income, which is exempt from Federal income tax, but is subject to State and Local tax.

This is the result of the constitutional relationship between Federal and State governments - one level of government cannot tax the other.

Also note that the interest income received from corporate issues is taxable at the Federal, State, and Local level. Interest income received from the privatized agency issuers - such as FNMA (Fannie Mae) and FHLMC (Freddie Mac) is taxed the same way. Finally, even though GNMA (Ginnie Mae) is not privatized, it is taxed in the same manner as FNMA and FHLMC (this was covered in the previous section of the text).

Subject To Capital Gains Tax

The special Federal tax status of the interest income from municipal issues does not apply to capital gains. Capital gains on municipals are taxable; capital losses are deductible. The rules for capital gains and losses are covered in the Taxation Chapter.

Since municipal bond interest income is not taxable by the Federal government, municipal yields are lower than corporate yields (which are taxable). To have a valid comparison of municipal and corporate yields, 2 formulas are needed:

$$\text{Equivalent Taxable Yield} = \frac{\text{Tax Free Yield}}{100\% - \text{Tax Bracket \%}}$$

$$\text{Equivalent Tax Free Yield} = \text{Taxable Yield} \times (100\% - \text{Tax Bracket \%})$$

For example, a customer in the 20% tax bracket is considering buying a 10% corporate bond or a 7% municipal bond. Which gives a higher effective yield?

The equivalent taxable yield on the municipal bond is:

$$\frac{7\%}{100\% - 20\%} = \frac{7\%}{.8} = 8.75\%$$

Since the corporate bond yields 10%, it gives a higher taxable yield.

For example, a customer owns a 10% corporate bond and is in the 25% tax bracket. The customer is considering buying municipal bonds. What is the equivalent tax-free yield?

Tax Free Yield = 10% (100% - 25%) = .10 x (.75) = 7.5%

The tax code was revised in 1986 to provide for different tax treatment of varying types of municipal bonds. The Tax Reform Act of 1986 provides for 3 classes of bonds:

Public Purpose Bond Issue

Tax-Free Interest

Public Purpose Bonds: Bonds issued by governmental units and agencies to meet essential government functions, such as school financings and road improvements. The interest income on these bonds is free from Federal Income Tax.

Qualified Private Activity Bond Issue

Non-Governmental Public Use Bonds

Interest Exempt From Regular Income Tax But Is Subject To AMT

Qualified Private Activity Bonds: Bonds issued where the proceeds are used to finance activities of persons not associated with the issuing government, and whose proceeds are used to provide a public benefit. These include bond issues for individual housing, student loans, pollution control facilities, water and sewer systems, redevelopment, etc. The interest income is tax free for Regular Income Tax purposes, **but** the income is included as a tax preference item for those persons subject to the Alternative Minimum Tax (AMT). The AMT is discussed in the Taxation chapter. These are known as "AMT" bonds.

Non-Essential Use, Private Activity Bond Issue

Interest Income Subject To AMT Or Regular Tax

Non-Essential Use, Private Purpose Bonds: Bonds issued where the proceeds are used to finance activities of persons not associated with the issuing government, and whose proceeds do not benefit the public. These are bonds issued for non-qualifying private purposes. Examples are convention center, sports stadium, and industrial development bond issues. If the issue is limited in size (the dollar amounts vary by State), the interest income is subject to the AMT. If the issue exceeds the dollar "cap," then the interest income on these bonds is taxable under the Regular Income Tax - the same treatment given to corporate obligations.

Taxation Of Interest Income From Industrial Development Bonds

The interest income earned from Industrial Development Bond Issues that were issued prior to 1986 was generally tax-exempt. The Tax Reform Act of 1986 made this "private use" interest income taxable. An issue arises regarding older "tax-free" industrial revenue bond issues. Essentially, the lease payments made by the corporation are used to fund the interest payments made on the outstanding debt.

These lease payments are tax deductible to the corporate lessee. If the corporation were to buy the outstanding bond issue, it would receive interest payments on the bonds that are tax-free. Effectively, the corporation has taken a tax deduction for the lease payments; and has converted these payments into tax-free interest income.

If Purchaser Of Older Industrial Revenue Bonds Is Substantial User Of Facility; Interest Income Is Taxable

The IRS does not allow this. If the purchaser of the bonds is a "substantial user" of the facility being leased, then the interest income received becomes taxable to the corporate lessee. This is only fair, since the lease payments used to fund the payment of that interest income were tax deductible to the corporation.

Bank Qualified Municipal Issues

Certain smaller issues of General Obligation bonds (not Revenue bonds), limited in size to a maximum of $10,000,000, are "bank qualified" municipal bonds under the tax code.

Bank May Deduct 80% Of Interest Expense Yet Receives Tax Free Income

When such issues are purchased by banks only, as an investment, the bank gets a substantial tax benefit. On bank qualified issues, the bank is allowed to deduct 80% of the interest carrying cost of the deposits acquired by the bank used to fund the purchase of the bonds. The bank can do this, even though the interest income from the issue is not taxable to the bank!

For example, assume a bank gets $10,000,000 of deposits, on which it is paying 10% interest. Also assume that the bank uses these funds to buy 9% Bank Qualified bonds.

The bank is permitted to deduct 80% of the 10% interest cost (.80 x 10% = 8% deduction) against its income. The bank receives the entire 9% interest on the bank qualified bonds free of Federal tax.

Positive Carry

Regarding the term "carrying cost" as it relates to bond investments, if the interest rate on the monies borrowed to buy bonds (interest expense paid) is less than the interest rate earned on those bonds, then the bonds are said to have a "positive carry" - translated, this means that the investor is making money on the interest rate "spread" (difference between the interest rate at which the funds are borrowed versus the interest rate earned on the bonds).

Negative Carry

Conversely, if the interest rate on the monies borrowed to buy bonds (interest expense paid) is more than the interest rate earned on those bonds, then the bonds are said to have a "negative carry" - translated, this means that the investor is losing money on the interest rate "spread" (difference between the interest rate at which the funds are borrowed versus the interest rate earned on the bonds).

MUNICIPAL DEBT
SECTION EXAMINATION

1.

Which of the following statements are **TRUE** regarding a municipal bond issue that is advance refunded?

I The security that backs the advance refunded bonds will change after the issue is refinanced

II The bondholder's lien on pledged revenues will be defeased in accordance with the terms of the bond contract

III The marketability of the advance refunded bonds will increase

IV The funds to pay the debt service requirements on the advance refunded bonds are set aside in escrow

a. II only
b. III and IV only
c. I, II, IV
d. I, II, III, IV

2.

Short sales of municipal bonds rarely occur because:

a. Rule 10b-5 of the Securities Exchange Act of 1934 prohibits the short sale of municipal bonds for most traders

b. round lot trades ($100,000 face value) are too expensive to carry

c. the trading market is thin, making short covering difficult

d. only municipal broker's brokers are allowed to take short positions

3.

A double barreled revenue bond is one which offers investors:

a. double the normal interest rate due to the high risk factor

b. both a high rate of interest and a high level of creditworthiness

c. the choice of both term and serial maturities

d. general obligation backing in addition to a revenue pledge

4.

The amount by which the par value of a municipal bond exceeds the purchase price of the bond is termed the:

a. spread
b. discount
c. premium
d. takedown

5.

Which of the following are **TRUE** statements regarding the tax equivalent yield of a municipal bond?

I The tax equivalent yield is disclosed on the customer confirmation

II The yield will vary depending on the tax bracket of the customer

III The tax equivalent yield will change as the market price of the bond varies

IV The tax equivalent yield is the complement of the current yield

a. I and IV
b. III and IV
c. II and III
d. II, III, IV

6.

Municipal bond traders execute transactions:

   I   on the floor of recognized exchanges

   II   with bank dealers in the over-the-counter market

   III with brokerage wire houses in the over-the-counter market

   IV with municipal broker's brokers

   a.   I only

   b.   IV only

   c.   II, III, IV

   d.   I, II, III, IV

7.

Significant investment features for the purchaser of municipal bonds include all of the following **EXCEPT**:

   a.   interest is currently federal tax exempt

   b.   maturities and issues may be diversified

   c.   interest is currently state and local tax exempt

   d.   insured issues are available for customers wishing minimum credit risk

8.

Which of the following insure municipal bonds?

   I   MBIA

   II   AMBAC

   III SIPC

   IV FDIC

   a.   I and II

   b.   III and IV

   c.   I and IV

   d.   II and III

9.

A municipal dealer offers bonds to another dealer "firm for one-half hour with a five minute recall." This means that the:

   I   selling dealer cannot change the price for one-half hour

   II   selling dealer cannot change the price for the next five minutes

   III selling dealer has the right to contact the other dealer during the half hour to change the quote if a transaction does not take place in the next five minutes

   IV buying dealer must call back the selling dealer in five minutes if it wishes to purchase the bonds

   a.   I and III

   b.   I and IV

   c.   II and III

   d.   II and IV

10.

Municipal bonds are offered out "firm" by one dealer to another. All of the following are true regarding this **EXCEPT** the:

   a.   buying dealer has control over the bonds for a specified time period

   b.   buying dealer is able to renegotiate the price

   c.   buying dealer can sell the bonds before actually purchasing them

   d.   selling dealer will not change the price for a specified time period

11.

A customer purchases 5M of New York 3% G.O.'s, maturing in 2042 at 90. The interest payment dates are Jan 1st and Jul 1st. The trade took place on Tuesday, Feb 1st. How much will the customer pay for the bonds, excluding commissions and accrued interest?

   a. $850

   b. $1,000

   c. $4,500

   d. $5,000

12.
A customer purchases 5M of New York 8% G.O. bonds, maturing in 2042 at 90. The interest payment dates are Jan. 1st and Jul. 1st. The trade took place on Wednesday, February 2nd. How much accrued interest will the customer be required to pay the seller?

   a. $16.16
   b. $33.33
   c. $36.67
   d. $66.67

13.
In order to construct a diversified municipal bond portfolio, which of the following would be considered?

   I   The geographic location of the issuers
   II   The credit rating of each issue
   III   The denominations available of each issue
   IV   The revenue source backing each issue

   a.   I, III
   b.   II, IV
   c.   I, II, IV
   d.   I, II, III, IV

14.
A municipality has issued a general obligation bond. Which of the following are sources of income available for debt service?

   I   Ad valorem taxes
   II   License fees
   III   Fines
   IV   Assessments

   a.   I and IV
   b.   II and III
   c.   I, III, IV
   d.   I, II, III, IV

15.
Which of the following municipal bonds would **MOST** likely be refunded by the issuer?

   a.   5% G.O., M '37, callable in 2017 at par
   b.   6% G.O., M '37, callable in 2017 at 102
   c.   7% G.O., M '37, callable in 2017 at 102
   d.   8% G.O., M '37, callable in 2017 at par

16.
BABs are:

   I   subject to Federal income tax
   II   exempt from Federal income tax
   III   issued in the taxable bond market
   IV   issued in the tax-exempt bond market

   a.   I and III
   b.   I and IV
   c.   II and III
   d.   II and IV

17.
A municipal issuer would call an issue for all of the following reasons **EXCEPT:**

   a.   substantial funds have accumulated in the issuer's surplus account
   b.   interest rates have risen sharply since the issuance of the bonds
   c.   the facility built with the proceeds of the issue has been destroyed in a flood
   d.   the proceeds of the issue were never expended due to legal obstacles

18.
All of the following are necessary to calculate the total purchase price for a municipal bond traded on a yield basis in the secondary market **EXCEPT:**

   a.   coupon rate
   b.   yield to maturity
   c.   dated date
   d.   trade date

19.

Under a municipal revenue bond rate covenant, charges for the use of a facility must be set at a level sufficient to cover:

I   Operation and maintenance of the facility
II   Debt service and mandatory deposits to the debt service reserve fund
III Optional sinking fund deposits
IV   Deposits to the reserve maintenance fund

a.   I only
b.   I and II
c.   III and IV
d.   II and III

20.

Which of the following would be used to evaluate a general obligation bond issue?

I   The trend of assessed property valuation
II   The collection ratio of the issuer
III The debt ratios of the issuer
IV   The mill rate trend of the issuer

a.   I and IV only
b.   II and III only
c.   I and III only
d.   I, II, III, IV

21.

A customer in the 28% tax bracket is considering the purchase of a municipal bond yielding 8% or a corporate bond yielding 11%. Both bonds have similar maturities and credit ratings. Which statement is **TRUE?**

a.   The effective yield on the municipal bond is higher
b.   The effective yield on the corporate bond is higher
c.   Both effective yields are equivalent
d.   The coupon rates for each bond are necessary to determine the effective yield

22.

A municipal revenue bond trust indenture includes an "additional bonds test" covenant. This means that:

a.   an earnings test must be satisfied before additional bonds can be issued against the same revenue source
b.   additional bonds can only be issued if they have a subordinated lien on pledged revenues
c.   additional bonds can only be issued after the original issue is called or advance refunded
d.   additional bond issues having a lien on the same revenue source are prohibited

23.

Types of funds used to back revenue bond issues include all of the following **EXCEPT:**

a.   excise taxes
b.   lease rentals
c.   ad valorem taxes
d.   enterprise activity income

24.

Mandatory redemption provisions of a municipal bond contract may be met by:

I   making periodic deposits to a segregated account (sinking fund)
II   advance refunding the issue
III making a tender offer for outstanding bonds

a.   I only
b.   I and III
c.   II and III
d.   I, II, III

25.

If an issuer defaults on a moral obligation bond, payment can only be made by:

a. legislative apportionment
b. judicial edict
c. legal authorization
d. municipal injunction

26.

Below is a listing of municipal bonds with the same credit ratings and maturities. Arrange the bonds in order of highest yield to lowest yield:

I   General Obligation Bond
II   Public Purpose Revenue Bond
III Non-Essential Use Private Purpose Revenue Bond

a. I, II, III
b. II, III, I
c. III, II, I
d. III, I, II

27.

Regarding the flow of funds set forth in a municipal bond contract, collected monies would **FIRST** be deposited to the:

a. Operations and Maintenance Fund
b. Debt Service Reserve Fund
c. Revenue Fund
d. Reserve Maintenance Fund

28.

A bond counsel would render a qualified legal opinion in which of the following circumstances?

I   After examining the city property records, it appears that clear title cannot be given to land on which a proposed facility is to be built
II   The issue has not been registered with the Securities and Exchange Commission and is being offered without a prospectus
III The feasibility study projects revenues for a new dormitory without taking into account the impact of competing facilities nearing completion
IV   The interest on the bonds may be taxable based on preliminary IRS regulations

a. I and II only
b. II and III only
c. I and IV only
d. I, II, III, IV

29.

A facility built with a revenue bond issue has been condemned. Which of the protective covenants found in the trust indenture would be activated?

a. defeasance covenant
b. catastrophe call covenant
c. maintenance covenant
d. sinking fund covenant

30.

Which of the following would **NOT** be considered when evaluating the credit risk of a municipal revenue bond?

a. Coverage ratios
b. Legislative actions
c. Competing facilities
d. Management experience

31.
Which municipal bond is **MOST** likely to have a mandatory sinking fund provision in the Trust Indenture?

    a.   Tax Anticipation Notes
    b.   Water District Bonds
    c.   Dormitory Revenue Bonds
    d.   School District Bonds

32.
All of the following are true statements regarding revenue bonds **EXCEPT**:

    a.   issuance of the bonds is dependent on earnings requirements
    b.   the bonds may be double barreled with backing by ad valorem taxes
    c.   revenue bonds are only suitable for investors willing to assume a high level of risk
    d.   yields for revenue bond issues are generally higher than yields for comparable G.O. issues

33.
The best measure of a municipality's ability to collect the taxes necessary to service general obligation debt is the ratio of:

    a.   debt per capita
    b.   pledged revenues to debt service
    c.   taxes collected to taxes assessed
    d.   debt to assessed valuation

34.
The ratio of pledged revenues to debt service requirements would be used to analyze which of the following municipal issues?

    a.   School District Bonds
    b.   Hospital Revenue Bonds
    c.   Special Tax Bonds
    d.   General Obligation Bonds

35.
The flow of funds stated in the trust indenture has payments being made to a sinking fund after the operations and maintenance fund is paid. The sinking fund is where monies:

    a.   to meet debt service requirements are deposited
    b.   to pay extraordinary maintenance or replacement costs are deposited
    c.   to pay for regularly scheduled repairs and replacements are deposited
    d.   "left-over" after all other uses are exhausted are deposited

36.
The final responsibility for the debt service on industrial revenue bonds rests with the:

    a.   issuing municipality
    b.   corporate lessee of the facility
    c.   bond trustee
    d.   bond underwriter

37.
Which of the following municipal securities would be considered a "double barreled" issue?

    a.   Revenue Bond backed by two sources of revenue
    b.   Hospital Revenue Bond backed by Ad Valorem taxing power
    c.   Moral Obligation Bond
    d.   Bond Anticipation Note

Debt Securities

38.

Which of the following statements are **TRUE** regarding callable municipal issues?

   I   Bonds are usually called when interest rates have declined

   II   Callable bond yields are higher than non-callable bond yields

   III   As interest rates fall, callable bonds trading at a premium will rise in value at a greater rate than non-callable issues

   IV   Call premiums usually fully compensate the bondholder for any lost income arising from the bonds being called

   a.   I and II

   b.   II and IV

   c.   I and III

   d.   III and IV

39.

A workable quotation given by a municipal dealer represents a(n):

   a.   firm bid

   b.   likely bid

   c.   approximate market value, with no bid or offer

   d.   bid or offer for 100 bonds

40.

An investor is seeking a municipal bond issue offering call protection. An issue having which features would **NOT** be an appropriate investment?

   I   Low stated interest rates

   II   High stated interest rates

   III   Low stated call premiums

   IV   High stated call premiums

   a.   I and III

   b.   I and IV

   c.   II and III

   d.   II and IV

MUNICIPAL DEBT EXAMINATION EXPLANATIONS

1. The best answer is **d**. All of the statements are true regarding advance refunding of a municipal bond issue. In an advance refunding, the issuer floats a new bond issue and uses the proceeds to "retire" outstanding bonds that have not yet matured. These funds are deposited to an escrow account and are used to buy U.S. Government securities. The escrowed Government securities become the pledged revenue source backing the refunded bonds. These bonds no longer have claim to the original revenue source. Since there is a new source of backing for the bonds (and an extremely safe one!), the credit rating on the pre-refunded bonds increases, as does their marketability. The pre-refunded bonds no longer have any claim to the original pledged revenues - and thus have been "defeased" - that is, removed as a liability of the issuer.

2. The best answer is **c**. Municipal bonds are usually not sold short because the trading market is very limited. Unlike corporate securities and government securities which receive no special tax status, municipal bonds are typically exempt from state and local tax if purchased by a resident of that state (in addition to the federal tax exemption). Thus, trading of municipal issues is typically confined to the state in which it was issued: there is no national trading market.

Shorting a security requires the trader to buy back (and therefore replace) the exact security that was sold. This is difficult to do if there are few bonds trading at any one time. Another important reason why muni's are not shorted is because most issues are serial bonds. Serial bonds mature over a sequence of years. Thus, if a bond maturing in the year 2030 is shorted, it must be replaced with a 2030 bond. Out of the total issue, there may have been very few 2030 bonds, further limiting the potential trading market.

3. The best answer is **d**. A "double barreled" bond is one backed by a specified source of revenue as well as the full faith and credit of an issuer with ad valorem taxing power. Revenue bonds are "double barreled" to increase the credit rating of the issue and hence reduce interest cost and increase marketability.

4. The best answer is **b**. If par value is higher than the purchase price, then the bond is selling for less than par. This is the bond's discount.

5. The best answer is **c**. The tax equivalent yield of a municipal bond varies with the customer's tax bracket. Remember, the formula for tax equivalent yield is:

$$\frac{\text{Tax Free Yield}}{100\% - \text{Tax Bracket}} = \text{Equivalent Taxable Yield}$$

As the customer's tax bracket increases, so does the tax equivalent yield. In addition, as the market price of the bond moves, its yield changes. This also changes the tax equivalent yield.

There is no requirement to disclose the tax equivalent yield on a customer's confirmation. The last choice (IV) is irrelevant.

6. The best answer is **c**. Municipal bonds are traded in the over-the-counter market. They are not traded on national stock exchanges. Remember, there is no national trading market in municipals - a requirement for listing - so municipal markets are generally confined to the state of issuance. Bonds can be traded in the OTC market with bank dealers, other brokers, as well as with municipal broker's brokers. These are wholesale firms (of which only 12 exist in the U.S.) that only trade with retail municipal brokers. These firms do not take inventory positions. They act as an agent, usually helping the retail firm with large institutional trades.

7. The best answer is **c**. Interest income derived from municipal bonds is currently exempt from federal income tax; however it is subject to state and local tax unless the state exempts the issue from taxation. Most states allow this only for issues that are purchased by residents of that state.

8. The best answer is **a**. MBIA (Municipal Bond Insurance Association) and AMBAC (American Municipal Bond Assurance Corporation) are private insurers of municipal issues. Currently, insured issues are rated AAA. The issuer pays the insurance premium to MBIA or AMBAC. If the bond defaults, the insurer will pay. SIPC (Securities Investor Protection Corporation) insures brokerage accounts, while FDIC (Federal Deposit Insurance Corporation) insures bank accounts.

9. The best answer is **a**. The selling dealer offering the bonds "firm" means that for a stated time period the price will not be changed. These bonds are offered firm for one-half hour; during this time period the buying dealer can try and round up a customer for the bonds before actually purchasing them. The selling dealer also specifies a "five minute recall." This means that during the half hour, the selling dealer can recontact the buying dealer to tell him that he has five minutes to buy the bonds at the offered price or else the quote will be changed.

10. The best answer is **b**. Since the quote is "firm," the price will not be changed for the time period specified. During this time period, the buying dealer has control over the bonds (since he has a firm price that will be honored) and can actually "sell" the bonds before buying them.

11. The best answer is **c**. These bonds are quoted at 90 meaning 90% of par value. "5M" means that $5,000 face amount of bonds are being purchased (M is Latin for $1,000). Municipal bonds that are quoted this way are called dollar bonds and are usually term issues. Serial bonds are quoted on a yield to maturity basis.

$$90\% \text{ of } \$5,000 \text{ par} = \$4,500$$

12. The best answer is **c**. Interest accrues on municipal bonds on a 30 day month/ 360 day year basis, with interest accruing up to, but not including settlement date. The trade took place on Wednesday, Feb. 2nd. Settlement occurs 2 business days after trade date. Therefore, settlement takes place on Friday, Feb. 4th. The last interest payment was made on January 1st, so the buyer owes the seller 30 days of interest for January and 3 days for February (up to, but not including the settlement date of February 4th).

$$\frac{33 \text{ days interest x } \$80 \text{ x 5 bonds}}{360} = \$36.67$$

Note that "5M" stands for $5,000 face amount of bonds (M is Latin for $1,000).

13. The best answer is **c**. When constructing a diversified municipal bond portfolio, one is trying to diversify away as much risk as possible. It would be logical to make sure that the portfolio is geographically diversified since having too great a concentration in one state or region is unwise if the local economy goes bad. A mix of credit ratings also helps to diversify the portfolio. Lower credit rated bonds give higher yields and make sense in a large portfolio, as long as the concentration is not too great. A mix of revenue sources also helps diversify away risk. The denominations of the bonds in the portfolio have no bearing on the risks inherent in those bonds.

14. The best answer is **d**. General obligation bonds are backed by the full faith, credit, and taxing power of the issuer. Ad valorem taxes, fines collected for paying taxes late, assessments of additional taxes, as well as

fees collected that are not a specified income source for revenue bonds, are all sources of income backing G.O. issues.

15.   The best answer is **d**.   In a refunding, an issuer refinances an outstanding debt by issuing new bonds. The proceeds of the new issue are used to retire the old debt; or are placed in escrow to "pre-refund" an older issue that cannot be immediately repaid. This is either done to reduce interest cost or to remove an onerous restrictive covenant. The bonds most likely to be refunded are those with the highest interest rates (to be replaced by lower interest rate bonds) and low call premiums (so it will not be too expensive to the issuer to call in the debt for refunding).

16.   The best answer is **a**.   "BABs" are Build America Bonds. Build America Bonds were issued by municipalities in 2009 and 2010. They are taxable municipal bonds that get a 35% Federal interest rate subsidy and the bond proceeds must be used for capital improvements (this is part of the economic stimulus program after the 2008-2009 "great recession"). These bonds were meant to create jobs and make to it easier for municipalities to access the debt market for needed capital projects.

17.   The best answer is **b**.   If substantial funds have accumulated in the surplus account, the issuer would use the monies to retire debt and reduce the annual interest cost. If a facility is destroyed by a flood, a catastrophe call covenant would be activated, requiring the issuer to call in the bonds. This is done since the facility can no longer generate the revenues to service the debt. If a bond issue is floated and the monies collected are never used for their intended purpose, most bond contracts require that the issuer refund the money to the bondholders. This would be accomplished by calling in the bonds.

An issuer would only call in bonds when interest rates have fallen, since the debt could be replaced with lower interest rate financing. An issuer would never refund its debt if interest rates have risen. (Would you go out and refinance your mortgage at a higher interest rate?)

18.   The best answer is **c**.   The dated date has no bearing on the calculation of the purchase price of a municipal bond. It is the date of issuance of the bonds, from which time interest will be paid. In order to calculate the bond's price, a bond calculator would be used. To do the calculation requires the coupon rate, yield to maturity, and years to maturity. The trade date is necessary to compute the amount of accrued interest that is due.

19.   The best answer is **b**.   When a revenue bond is issued under a "Net Revenue Pledge," there is usually a rate covenant that accompanies the pledge. In a Net Revenue Pledge, the issuer pledges its "net revenues" (gross revenues net of operation and maintenance costs) to the bondholders. A rate covenant is a promise to set rates for the use of a facility at a sufficient level to cover both of these items - operation and maintenance, as well as required debt service payments. There is no requirement to cover "optional" sinking fund deposits or reserve fund deposits.

20.   The best answer is **d**.   In order to evaluate a general obligation bond issue, all of the factors listed would be evaluated. One would look for a trend of increasing assessed property valuation; a consistently high collection ratio - meaning that most of the taxes assessed are actually being collected; a low ratio of debt to assessed valuation and low ratio of debt per capita; as well as a consistent mill rate - meaning that property tax rates are not being raised too quickly, causing people to flee from the area.

21.   The best answer is **a**.   In order to compare the tax free municipal yield to the taxable corporate yield, the two must be equalized.

$$\boxed{\frac{\text{Tax Free Yield}}{100\% - \text{Tax Bracket}} = \text{Equivalent Taxable Yield}}$$

$$\frac{8\%}{(100\% - 28\%)} = 11.11\%$$

Since the corporate bond is yielding 11%, the equivalent municipal yield is higher.

22. The best answer is **a**. An "additional bonds test" means that the issuer is prohibited from issuing new bonds against the revenues of a facility, unless the facility's revenues are sufficient. Typically, the debt service on the old bonds is added to that of the new bonds. The revenues of the facility must cover, by an adequate margin, the combined debt service before additional bonds can be sold.

23. The best answer is **c**. Ad valorem taxes back general obligation bonds. Revenue bonds can be backed by any source of revenue other than ad valorem taxes. These sources include revenue from facility operations, grants, excise taxes, or other non-ad valorem taxes, like sales and income taxes.

24. The best answer is **a**. Mandatory redemption provisions can only be met by depositing the required funds to the sinking fund. Once these monies are deposited, the issuer must use them to retire bonds as specified in the bond contract. The bonds may be retired by calling in bonds or by purchasing bonds in the open market. The issuer will buy the bonds in the open market if the price is lower than the call price including any premiums.

Advance refunding an issue or making a tender offer do not satisfy mandatory redemption provisions.

25. The best answer is **a**. Moral obligation bonds are backed by pledged revenues and also by a non-binding pledge to report any revenue deficiencies to the state legislature. The legislature is authorized to apportion the funds necessary to service the debt, but is under no obligation to do so.

26. The best answer is **c**. The "non-essential" use private purpose revenue bond would have the highest yield because the interest income is subject to the AMT - Alternative Minimum Tax. A public purpose revenue bond would have a lower yield because its interest income is not subject to the AMT. The G.O. bond would have the lowest yield because it is backed by ad valorem taxing power (considered the safest income source) and is not subject to the AMT.

27. The best answer is **c**. The trust indenture of a revenue bond issue includes a "flow of funds" - meaning how revenues will be applied by the issuer. As revenues are collected, they are deposited to a revenue fund, also called a general collection account. The monies are then applied, in sequence, to the operation and maintenance account; sinking fund; debt service reserve fund; reserve maintenance fund; renewal and replacement fund; and finally to the surplus fund.

28. The best answer is **c**. A municipal bond counsel examines the legal and tax aspects of a proposed bond issue and renders an opinion as to whether the issue is valid and binding on the issuer and also gives an opinion on the tax status of the interest income. A qualified opinion is one where the bond counsel has some reservations about the issue, so instead of giving a "clean" opinion, the counsel renders one that has some "qualifications." Clearly, if a facility will be built on land where there is no clear title, the counsel would qualify the opinion, stating the reason why. Thus, anyone buying the bonds who reads the opinion knows that this "problem" exists which has potential consequences (such as a person proving that he owns the land and

wants the facility moved). Because municipals are exempt securities, there is no requirement to register them and sell them with a prospectus, making Choice II incorrect. The bond counsel does not give economic opinions, (only legal and tax opinions), so the bond counsel will not be concerned with the feasibility study, making Choice III incorrect. Finally, since the opinion covers tax issues, the bond counsel will qualify an opinion if there are potential problems with the tax free status of the bonds.

29.   The best answer is **b**. If a facility is condemned, it can no longer generate revenues. Though the question is not clear as to why it was condemned, the best choice is that a catastrophe call provision would be activated. This requires the issuer to call in the bonds, repaying the bondholders if a disaster occurs. Of the other choices, sinking fund covenants and defeasance covenants have no bearing. A maintenance covenant requires the issuer to maintain the facility in good repair. This covenant is not "activated" by a condemnation, as is a catastrophe call covenant.

30.   The best answer is **b**. Credit risk is the risk that a bond will default. To evaluate this risk for a revenue bond issue, one would examine coverage ratios; the effect of competing facilities; and the management of the facility. Legislative actions have no bearing on credit risk. Potential effects of adverse legislative actions would be evaluated as legislative risk.

31.   The best answer is **c**. A mandatory sinking fund requirement would be used for a risky bond issue, where a purchaser needs additional assurance that the funds will be available to service the debt. Of the issues listed, a Dormitory Revenue Bond is the most risky, since the revenue depends on students renting out the dorm. School district bonds are backed by ad valorem taxes and are therefore safer. Water district bonds are backed by water charges - we all drink water so this issue is safe. Tax Anticipation Notes are short term notes issued in advance of incoming tax collections (property taxes are typically collected twice a year) and are paid off by these collections - very safe securities.

32.   The best answer is **c**. In order to issue revenue bonds, a feasibility study must be prepared and it must show adequate net revenues ("earnings") to service the debt before the bonds can be floated. A revenue bond can be double barreled to improve its safety by additionally backing the issue with the ad valorem taxing power of the issuer. Yields on revenue bonds are higher than that of comparable G.O. bonds because of generally higher risk. Revenue bonds are suitable for investors willing to take on low, medium or high risk. To evaluate credit risk on these issues, look at Moody's or Standard and Poor's ratings.

33.   The best answer is **c**. The collection ratio of a municipality is:

$$\text{Collection Ratio} = \frac{\text{Taxes Collected}}{\text{Taxes Assessed}}$$

One looks for a very high ratio (better than 95%), meaning that the municipality is truly collecting the taxes it is assessing.

34.   The best answer is **b**. The ratio of pledged revenues to debt service requirements applies to revenue bonds. Pledged revenues are those pledged to pay debt service and any other requirements set in the bond contract. The bondholder has a lien on these revenues. The higher this ratio, the safer a revenue bond, since there is a greater ratio of revenues to cover debt service.

School district bonds are G.O. issues, paid by unlimited ad valorem taxing power; applicable ratio tests would be debt per capita (How much debt is each citizen of the town responsible for?); debt to assessed valuation (How much debt is there outstanding against the real properties that are assessed taxes to pay for the interest expense on that debt?); and the collection ratio (Of the taxes assessed by the municipality, what percentage is actually collected?)

35. The best answer is **a**. The sinking fund is where monies to meet debt service requirements are deposited. Choice **B** is the Reserve Maintenance Fund; Choice **C** is the Renewal and Replacement Fund; and Choice **D** is the Surplus Fund.

36. The best answer is **b**. Industrial development bonds are backed by the rental revenues paid by the corporate lessee as well as by the guarantee of the corporate lessee. These bonds, therefore, take on the credit rating of the corporation leasing the facility.

37. The best answer is **b**. A "double barreled" bond is a revenue issue that is also backed by a municipal issuer's taxing power. A revenue bond backed by two sources of revenue is known as a parity bond since the bondholders have equal claim to both sources of revenue backing the bond issue.

38. The best answer is **a**. Bonds are typically called when interest rates have fallen, allowing the issuer to refinance at a lower interest cost. Because of "call risk" - the risk that a high yielding issue can be called away if interest rates drop - callable bonds have higher yields than similar non-callable issues. As interest rates fall, premium bonds will rise further in value. The issuer has the incentive to call in the bonds (if the call premium isn't too large) and refinance at lower current interest rates. The risk of this happening is thus greater for premium callable issues as compared to non callable bonds and suppresses upward price movement as interest rates fall. The call premium is usually not sufficient to compensate for the interest income that would be lost if the bonds are called (assuming reinvestment at the prevailing lower interest rate).

39. The best answer is **b**. A workable quote is one where the dealer indicates a willingness to buy at a stated price. The dealer who solicits the "workable" is usually acting for a customer who wants to sell the bonds. Since there is no active trading market, the customer has no idea what price he can get for the bonds. The selling broker gets the customer a "workable" quote, that is, a likely price at which a dealer will buy, and the customer can then decide whether he wants to sell at that price.

40. The best answer is **c**. An investor seeking call protection does not want the bonds to be called away. Most likely to be called are bonds with low call premiums and high interest rates. After calling the bonds, the issuer can refund the issue at lower rates, given that interest rates have fallen.

SECTION 5: MONEY MARKET DEBT / STRUCTURED PRODUCTS

5a. CHARACTERISTICS OF MONEY MARKET INSTRUMENTS

Money Market - 1 Year Or Less

Capital Market - Over 1 Year

A money market instrument is a debt obligation which matures in one year or less. Because of the short maturity, it will be turned into "money" very rapidly, hence the name. Longer term obligations are called "capital market" instruments because they are a source of long term capital for the issuer. All of the long term bond types discussed previously in this chapter were capital market instruments.

Institutional Market

Typically, money market obligations are traded in large units ($1,000,000 or $5,000,000 minimum) between institutions. They are issued at a discount to par value, maturing at par, with the gain being the "interest income." Some instruments are issued at par and mature "with accrued interest."

Role Of Federal Reserve

Open Market Operations

"Eligible" Securities For Fed Training

A critical player in the "Money Market" is the Federal Reserve. The Fed attempts to control the amount of credit available through "open market operations" - which is the buying and selling of money market instruments with bank dealers. When the Fed buys money market instruments, it puts cash into the banks, increasing credit availability. When the Fed sells money market instruments, it drains cash from the banks, decreasing credit availability. Not all money market instruments are traded by the Fed - only the safest are eligible for Fed trading. Those that are eligible are the most actively traded and liquid instruments.

5b. TYPES OF MONEY MARKET INSTRUMENTS

Treasury Bills

Unbeknownst to you, you have already learned about the largest money market instrument - T-Bills, which obviously are an eligible security for Fed trading. Remember that Treasury Bills are available in initial 1 month, 3 month, 6 month and 12 month maturities.

Any Treasury Security Maturing Within 1 Year

In addition, any Treasury security that has 1 year or less to maturity is also considered to be a "money market" instrument. For example, a Treasury Note that was originally issued with a 10-year maturity, but which will mature within the next year, is defined as a money market instrument.

Commercial Paper

Maximum Maturity 270 Days

Commercial paper is the corporate money market instrument, also covered previously in detail in the Corporate Debt section. Note that the maximum maturity on commercial paper is 270 days for the securities to be exempt from the provisions of the Securities Acts. If commercial paper were issued with a longer maturity than 270 days (which does not happen), registration with the SEC and sale with a prospectus would be required, making it very costly for issuers to sell such securities. Commercial paper is not eligible for Fed trading.

The other money market instruments are:

Banker's Acceptance

Time Draft

Banker's Acceptance: This instrument is used to finance imports and exports. Before a foreign exporter will ship goods to the U.S., he wants assurance that the funds are ready for payment when the goods arrive. The exporter will demand a draft, let us say for $100,000, on a bank payable at a future date, which is guaranteed by the bank.

Prime BA

The bank is now obligated to pay on that date. BAs are bearer securities, and can be held to maturity or can be traded (though most BAs are simply held to maturity - the trading market for these securities is illiquid). The maturity is 9 months or less and the security trades at a discount to face value. Only the highest quality BAs are eligible for Fed trading, known as "prime BA's."

Negotiable Certificate Of Deposit (CD)

Negotiable Certificates of Deposit: These are "jumbo CDs" with a minimum face amount of $100,000 (however, many banks now issue these in minimums of $1,000,000). The issuer promises to pay par plus accrued interest at maturity (usually less than 1 year with most being 1-3 months). Unlike conventional bank CDs, which can only be redeemed with the issuing bank, these CDs are negotiable, so they can be traded. If one holds a 3-month CD and wants to cash out after 2 months, one can sell it in the secondary market. The price received depends on interest rate movements. Negotiable CDs are not eligible securities for Fed trading.

(Also note that even though FDIC insurance coverage on bank deposits was permanently increased from $100,000 to $250,000 in mid-2010, the "definition" of a jumbo CD (a negotiable CD) has not changed. This also means that "jumbo CDs" of up to $250,000 now receive FDIC coverage as long as they are titled in the customer's name.)

Repurchase Agreement

Repurchase Agreements: Dealers in government securities carry a large inventory at any given time. In order to improve liquidity (get cash), a dealer will "sell" some of those securities to another dealer with an agreement to buy them back at a later date at a price to give a fixed yield. In effect, a security is created, collateralized by underlying U.S. Governments and any other eligible security. Therefore, "repos" are eligible securities.

Repos By The Federal Reserve Loosen Credit	The biggest player in the "repo" market is the Federal Reserve. To inject cash into the money supply, it will enter into repurchase agreements with dealers (the large banks), where the Fed buys the "paper" from the dealer backed by eligible securities. The bank then gets cash which can be lent out.
Reverse Repos - Tightens Credit **Matched Sale**	To tighten the money supply, the Fed enters into "reverse repurchase agreements," selling the "paper" to government dealers. The dealers are temporarily drained of cash, tightening the money supply. This is also called a "matched sale," since the sale is matched to a later buy-back of the security.
Repurchase Agreement Interest Rates Track The Federal Funds Rate	Repurchase agreements can have a fixed maturity or can be payable "on demand." The interest rate is negotiated between buyer and seller and is not published. Interest rates on repurchase agreements track the "Federal Funds Rate" - the rate for overnight loans of reserves from bank to bank (covered next). Since repurchase agreements are secured, whereas loans of Federal Funds are unsecured, the interest rate on repurchase agreements is **lower** than for loans of "Fed Funds."
Overnight Repurchase Agreement	The duration of repurchase agreements can range from "overnight" to many weeks. Overnight repurchase agreements are common for transactions between banks and the Federal Reserve. In such agreements, the seller loses control of the underlying government securities in exchange for the cash. The buyer gets the government securities covered under the agreement as collateral.
No Liquidity Risk	Due to the fact that the agreement is fully collateralized and the short duration (overnight), there is virtually no liquidity risk.
Does Have Purchasing Power Risk	However, such agreements do have purchasing power risk. Even though the agreement covers a time period of 1 day, the underlying collateral consists of longer maturity government securities. If, during the 1 day period of the agreement, interest rates rise, then on the next day, the collateral is returned to the seller at the pre-agreed price. However, this collateral may be substantially devalued due to the rise in interest rates!
Federal Funds **Effective Fed Funds Rate**	Federal Funds: This is the shortest term money market instrument, available only to member institutions of the Federal Reserve System. Reserves held on deposit by member banks are called "Federal Funds." A bank with excess reserves can lend them to a bank that is deficient, at the Federal Funds Rate. These loans are overnight and the interest rate is quite volatile, changing as the demand for reserves changes. The "effective" Federal Funds Rate gives an indication of the daily demand for reserves and is a daily average of many banks' rates.

Debt Securities (side tab)

Eurodollars **LIBOR**	Eurodollars: Deposits denominated in dollars held in a bank branch outside the U.S. These are large dollar deposits, typically made by corporations, with a fixed term from 1 day to 5 years. Foreign banks trade these deposits similar to the domestic trading of Fed Funds. Domestic banks with a reserve deficiency can borrow "Euros" as a substitute for Fed Funds. The difference is that Fed Funds are loaned "overnight" - "Euros" can be loaned for longer periods. The interest rate charged on Eurodollar loans between major international banks is "LIBOR" - the London Interbank Offered Rate. "LIBOR" is the average offered rate for Eurodollar loans of 5 major banks centered in London.

5c. LONG TERM CERTIFICATES OF DEPOSIT

Long Term CDs	While most conventional CDs have lives of 1 year or less, banks have increased their offerings of CDs that have a longer maturity than 1 year. We already know that the longer the maturity on a debt instrument, the greater the security's price movements in response to market interest rate changes. Retail customers who buy long term certificate of deposits often believe that because these are issued by banks, that these securities do not have market risk - which is absolutely wrong.
"Brokered CDs"	Long term CDs are often called "brokered" CDs, and differ in key respects from conventional CDs issued by banks. The most common way that they are issued is that the brokerage firm buys a large (say $10,000,000) CD from a bank, and then chops it up into units, say $10,000, to be sold to its customers.
Risk Disclosures For Long Term CDs	When a retail customer wishes to buy a long term certificate of deposit sold through a broker, the following is required:
CDs Subject To Market Risk	These CDs are not redeemable prior to maturity, but they may be resold in the secondary market. The customer must be informed that sale of the instrument prior to maturity is subject to market price fluctuations by then-prevailing market interest rates;
Pre-Maturity Sale Price May Be Less Than Purchase Price	Disclosure must be made to the customer that pre-maturity sale price of a long term CD may be less than the original purchase price (if market interest rates have risen);
Limited Secondary Market	The customer must be informed that the secondary market for this instrument may be limited;
Callable CD Subject To Reinvestment Risk	If the CD is callable (yes, these exist), the customer must be informed that if the CD is called (which the issuer will do if market interest rates fall), and the customer reinvests the proceeds, reinvestment will occur at the lower current market interest rate;

Step-Up/Step-Down CD Yield May Not Reflect Current Market Rate	If the CD is a "step-up" or "step-down" instrument, the customer must be informed that the initial rate may not reflect the current market interest rate (it might be set higher by the issuing bank to attract a new customer - a so-called "teaser rate" - and would then "step-down" to the current market or a slightly lower-than-market rate, at a pre-set date), nor does it reflect the security's yield to maturity; and
FDIC Insured Only If Titled In The Customer's Name	The customer must be informed that the ownership title of the CD determines whether FDIC insurance covers the instrument. If the CD is titled in the customer's name, then FDIC insurance covers the instrument; if the title is held in the name of the broker-dealer solely, then the instrument is **NOT** FDIC insured to the customer.
CDs Priced At Market Value On Customer Account Statements	Additionally, on customer account statements, long term CDs must be shown priced at current market value; not at face value (this is true for all marketable securities, but in the past, many firms showed CDs at face value since they can be difficult to price as the secondary market can be very limited for these).
No Prepayment Penalty	Also note that unlike conventional CDs, which can have penalties imposed for early withdrawal of funds, there is no prepayment penalty for early redemption because there is no early redemption of these instruments by the holder. The only way for a holder to "cash out" prior to maturity is to sell the instrument in the secondary market.

5d. INDEX-LINKED STRUCTURED PRODUCTS

Structured Products - Derivative Security	Structured products are securities based on, or derived from, a basket of securities, an index, or other securities, commodities, or currencies. There are many types of structured products, but generally they consist of a "bond" portion, which pays interest based on the performance of a well-known index such as the S&P 500 Index. In addition, they have a derivative component (an embedded option) that allows the holder to sell the security back to the issuer (at par) at maturity. These are often marketed as debt instruments, but that is not really the case. Structured products are created by many different brokerage firms and each firm's version is somewhat different.
Market Index Linked CD Return Tied To S&P 500 Index	A "structured product" variation of the CD is a "Market Index Linked CD." Market Index Linked Certificates of Deposit tie their investment return to an equity index, usually the Standard and Poor's 500 Index. At first glance, it appears that this is a hybrid product that gives the advantages of a bank certificate of deposit (FDIC insurance up to $250,000; no risk of loss of principal) along with a "stock market" rate of return. Alas, first glances usually don't tell the whole story.
	FINRA has seen increased sales of market index linked certificates of deposit and worries that investors are not being informed of the differences between traditional CDs and these hybrid products.

In particular, customers need to know that:

Market Risk

There is Market Risk: Redemption of a traditional CD prior to maturity might involve a loss of interest; but there is no loss of principal. In contrast, there can be penalties imposed for redeeming a market index linked CD prior to maturity (most have a minimum 3 year maturity) that result in a loss of principal (e.g., a 3-5% principal penalty for early withdrawal has been fairly common). Thus, market index linked CDs can have market risk if there is an early redemption. (This penalty is imposed because to "structure" the product, the issuer had to buy a put option at par for the maturity date. This cost the issuer a premium, which the penalty recovers.)

Liquidity Risk

There is Liquidity Risk: Most market index linked CDs only allow redemption on pre-set quarterly dates. During the rest of the year, these cannot be redeemed. Thus, there is liquidity risk because they cannot be redeemed on demand.

Credit Risk

There is Credit Risk: These securities are backed by the faith and credit of the issuing bank. There may not be an underlying pool of securities that can be claimed if the issuer goes bankrupt. Essentially, the bank is promising to pay a return tied to an equity index, and this evaporates if the issuer goes bust (just ask anyone who purchased Lehman Brothers structured products!).

Cap On Investment Return

Floor On Investment Return

The Return May Have a Limit: Some market index linked CDs place a cap on the amount that can be earned. For example, in a year when the S&P Index, rises by 15%, there might be a cap limiting earnings on the product to, say 10%. Also note that in return for this, the product typically has a minimum "floor" return - say of 1% per year. So in a year when the index drops by 10%, the product will still give a minimum 1% return.

Participation Rate

Participation Rate: The product will only credit interest at a stated percentage of the growth in the reference index. For example, if the structured product has an 80% participation rate, then in a year when the index rises by 10%, the product will only get an 8% interest payment - again, subject to the cap and floor.

Tax Issues: Even though the return is linked to an equity index, returns are taxed as "interest" at a maximum rate of 39.6%, as opposed to the maximum tax rate on dividends and long term gains of 15% (or 20% for very high earners).

Most customers are attracted to CDs for their safety and known rate of return. This hybrid product offers less safety since there is some market risk and a potentially higher rate of return (subject to limits).

Structured Product "Reasonable Basis" Suitability

Because of the complexity of these products, FINRA requires that the member firm perform a "reasonable basis" suitability determination to evaluate the product's potential rewards and risks (relative to other similar structured products offered by other firms).

Structured Product "Customer Specific" Suitability

Once a reasonable basis suitability determination has been completed, then the member firm can offer the structured product only to its customers that are suitable for that investment. This is "customer specific" suitability. Because of the embedded option in the product, FINRA strongly encourages member firms to use the same suitability and approval standards as it uses for options accounts when recommending structured products.

ETN - Exchange Traded Note

A variation on a "structured product," first introduced in 2006, was created to eliminate the liquidity risk of the security. This is the "ETN" - Exchanged Traded Note. An ETN gives a return linked to a market index, has a set maturity date, and is backed by the credit rating of the issuing bank. They are listed on an exchange and trade, so an investor can "get out" at any time at the current market price. ETNs have been given catchy acronyms by their issuers, such as EAGLEs, ASTROS and CYCLEs.

The ETN is a debt instrument, but it does not make periodic interest payments. The value "grows" based on the performance of the underlying index, and the difference between the purchase price and the sale price (or redemption price at maturity) is taxable. A major tax benefit of the ETN is that under current IRS rules for this type of synthetic structured product, the gain is treated as taxable capital gain, taxed at preferential rates (15% or 20% for very high earners maximum, instead of 39.6% maximum).

Credit Risk

The Major problem with ETNs, just like structured products, is that they have credit risk - if the issuing bank fails, the purchaser is left with nothing.

ETN Has Tax Advantage As Compared To Other Debt Instruments

The main advantage of an ETN as compared to a structured product are:

No Liquidity Risk; and

Tax Efficiency.

ETN Investors Can Get Access To Exotic Investment Strategies

A variety of ETNs have been created by banks to give investors access to returns tied to "more exotic" indexes. For example, ETNs have been created that give returns tied to commodity indexes based on the performance of stocks in Third World countries (e.g., an India Index or a Brazil Index.)

ETN Has No Relation To An ETF

Do not confuse an ETN with an ETF - an Exchange Traded Fund. An ETF is an investment company product (covered in a later chapter) where the shareholder owns a piece of the underlying portfolio. An ETN has no underlying portfolio - the issuer is promising to give a return tied to the index, but the investments in that index may, or may not, be owned by the issuer. The ETN is really only backed by the credit rating of the issuing bank.

Reverse Convertible Note **At Maturity, If Reference Price Is Above The "Knock-In" Price, Holder Gets Par; If Below, The Holder Gets Shares Of Stock**	Another type of "structured product" is a reverse convertible note. These were created for customers looking for enhanced yield in a low interest rate environment. Of course, any enhanced yield comes with higher risk. The note is linked to the price movements of an underlying stock (or vary rarely, an underlying index). At maturity, the holder will receive par value, as long as the price of the reference stock is above the "knock-in" price (typically 70-80% of the initial reference price). On the other hand, if, at maturity, the reference stock falls below the "knock-in" price, then the holder will receive the shares of stock.
Maximum Gain Is Coupon Rate **Maximum Loss Is Value Of Reference Stock Offset By Coupon Received**	Thus, the maximum gain potential for the holder is earning the coupon rate and getting 100% of principal back at maturity. On the other hand, the maximum risk is getting the reference stock at maturity, and that stock has become worthless. Investors accept this risk because they get a higher coupon rate and believe that this adequately compensates them for the risk of principal loss if the stock price declines. Basically, the buyer of a reverse convertible note is neutral or slightly bullish on the reference equity security, and is seeking a fixed coupon security that offers a higher level of income.
Takes On Credit Rating Of Issuing Bank	Note that, as a structured product, these are an obligation of the issuing bank - not the reference company. Like other structured products, these are only as good as the credit of the issuing bank.

5e. AUCTION RATE SECURITIES

Auction Rate Security - Long Term Bond With Interest Rate Reset By Weekly Auction	An Auction Rate Security (ARS) is another "derivative" that is a debt instrument with a long term nominal maturity, but the interest rate on the security is reset, usually weekly, via a Dutch auction. In this Dutch auction, the bids are in terms of interest rate. Here is the marketing concept behind an ARS. The issuer is able to sell debt at short term interest rates, yet it does not have to repay the debt, so it gets long term funding at short term rates. The purchaser of an ARS gets a choice at the weekly auction - it can be renewed for the next week at the interest rate set by the auction; or it can be sold to someone else at the auction. Thus, the purchaser never gets repaid by the issuer.
Dutch Auction	The mechanics of the Dutch Auction work as follows: Each bid and order size is ranked from lowest to highest minimum bid rate. The amount of bonds for sale are auctioned from lowest interest rate bid on up, until the whole amount of the sale is filled.
"Clearing Rate"	All winning bids are filled at the highest interest rate that completed the sale (this is called the "clearing rate").

Thus, the clearing rate is the lowest rate at which there are purchasers willing to buy all of the auction rate securities offered for sale in the auction. Any interest rate bids that are higher than the clearing rate will not be filled.

If the clearing rate is set at 4.00% and customer has bid an interest rate of 3.80%, that bid will be filled at the auction and the customer will be paid a 4.00% interest rate for the next period.

On the other hand, if the clearing rate is set at 4.00% and a customer bids an interest rate of 4.20% (meaning that customer wishes to earn a minimum of 4.20%), then the bid will not be filled.

Only Suitable For Sophisticated Investors

$25,000 Minimums

Auction Rate Securities give issuers the benefit of typically lower short term interest rates (since the interest rate is based on a 1-week maturity, though some issuers hold the auction monthly) on what is really a long term security. They are available for both corporate and municipal bonds. There are many variations on these instruments, and because of their complexity, they are available in $25,000 minimums or greater to make them unattractive to small unsophisticated investors.

Failed Auctions

ARSs are typically sold as short term securities, comparable to money market instruments. However, the auctions started to fail in early 2008 because of a lack of orders to buy these securities (the credit markets were starting to freeze at that point - the beginning of the collapse of securities markets and banks that occurred through 2008). Customers who bought these as short term instruments found that there was no market to sell them.

The reasons for an auction failure are simple - either:

there are more sellers than buyers (bidders) for those securities that week at the auction - so there is an excess supply available without willing buyers at the auction; or

the interest rates set forth in the bids are too high.

Most Auction Rate Securities establish a maximum interest rate that can be bid. This process protects issuers from having to pay exorbitant interest rates during periods when market conditions are unsettled. If all bids received are above the maximum rate, or if there are not enough bidders, the auction "fails" and the sellers (holders) will receive the maximum rate for that week.

Thus, if the auction fails, the existing holders hold their positions at a maximum interest rate set in the securities offering document until the next auction occurs where there are sufficient bidders to establish a clearing rate.

Marketability Risk	Registered representatives that sell ARSs to customers must disclose that these products have marketability risk - the customer may not be able to sell at the weekly auction. As a result of the failed auctions, the future of this market is in doubt. Also a note that the examination covers why these auctions have failed.

5f. CREDIT DEFAULT SWAPS

CDS - Credit Default Swap	A Credit Default Swap (CDS) is a financial agreement that originated to allow a lender (creditor) to reduce its potential loss in the event that a loan that it made defaults. Assume that Bank A makes a loan of $20 million to ACME Corp. To Reduce its loss exposure if ACME Corp. defaults, Bank A, in essence, buys insurance from a seller, which might be another bank or institutional investor.
In The Event Of A Default, The Seller Pays The Buyer The Face Amount Of The Loan	Bank A (the buyer) enters into an agreement where the seller agrees that if the loan defaults, the seller takes possession of the defaulted loan and pays the buyer the face amount of the loan. In essence, the seller insures the buyer against the default of the reference loan. Thus, Bank A has the peace of mind knowing that it is protected if ACME Corp. defaults on the loan. Note that the borrower (ACME Corp.) has no idea that the loan is the subject of the CDS.
The Buyer Pays An Annual Premium To The Seller	The seller of the Credit Default Swap takes on the risk of default because the buyer (in our example, Bank A that made the loan to ACME Corp.) pays the seller regular (usually quarterly) premium payments over the life of the CDS - which typically last anywhere from 1 to 10 years. The annual premium paid is expressed as "the spread."
CDS Spread	For example, if the CDS spread for ACME Corp. debt is 50 basis points on a $20 million loan, then the annual premium paid from buyer to seller is .50% of $20 million = $100,000.
Naked CDS	Also note that buyers that have not made loans can buy CDSs without actually owning the loan of the reference corporation. These "naked" CDSs are done purely for speculative purposes and are now the largest portion of the CDS market.
Unregulated OTC Market	Note that Credit Default Swaps trade over-the-counter in an unregulated market, with the biggest participants being large commercial banks and insurance companies. When times are good and default rates are low, banks and insurance companies that sell CDSs collect premiums as additional income and have little risk. However, when times are bad, sellers experience default rates that greatly outstrip collected premiums.

The key points to know about a CDS are:

CDS Buyer

The buyer of the CDS is either hedging an existing loan; or in the case of a "naked" CDS, is betting that the loan will default.

The buyer pays an annual premium for the contract.

If the loan defaults, the buyer receives a cash payment from the seller equal to the face amount of the loan.

CDS Seller

The seller of the CDS receives the annual premium and is betting that the loan will **NOT** default. If this is the case, the seller earns the premium with no further obligation.

If the loan defaults, the seller must pay the face amount of the loan to the buyer, and the seller takes title to the underlying defaulted loan.

MONEY MARKET DEBT / STRUCTURED PRODUCTS SECTION EXAMINATION

1.
A customer buys a Brokered CD for $100,000. Upon receipt of his next account statement, the customer sees that the market value of the CD is shown as $99,800. This would occur because:

a. interest rates have risen
b. interest rates have fallen
c. the broker's commission for selling the CD has been subtracted out
d. the bank that issued the CD has charged an up-front handling fee

2.
Which securities will trade with accrued interest?

a. Negotiable Certificates of Deposit
b. Treasury Bills
c. Banker's Acceptances
d. Treasury Receipts

3.
The effective Fed Funds Rate is the:

a. rate charged by the largest members of the Federal Reserve System
b. averaged rate of member banks throughout the United States
c. highest rate charged by member banks, calculated on Wednesdays
d. lowest rate charged by member banks, calculated on Wednesdays

4.
When the Federal Reserve enters into a repurchase agreement, it:

a. tightens credit
b. loosens credit
c. increases the discount rate
d. decreases the discount rate

5.
A Prime Banker's Acceptance is one:

a. rated AAA by Moody's
b. rated P-1 by Moody's
c. eligible for trading with the Federal Reserve
d. eligible for trading with commercial banks

6.
Which debt instrument is used to finance imports and exports?

a. Eurodollar Bonds
b. Banker's Acceptances
c. American Depositary Receipts
d. Commercial Paper

7.
The money market instrument with the shortest maturity is:

a. Federal Funds
b. Eurodollar Certificates of Deposit
c. Commercial Paper
d. Treasury Bills

8.
All of the following are money market instruments **EXCEPT:**

a. BAs
b. REPOs
c. CDs
d. ADRs

9.
Which of the following securities is **NOT** eligible for Fed trading?

a. Treasury Bonds
b. Treasury Bills
c. Commercial Paper
d. Prime Banker's Acceptances

10.

Which of the following actions by the Federal Reserve will tighten credit?

I   Repurchase Agreement
II   Reverse Repurchase Agreement
III Matched Sale

a. I only
b. II only
c. II and III
d. I, II, III

11.

The longest initial maturity available for new issues of Treasury Bills is:

a. 4 weeks
b. 8 weeks
c. 26 weeks
d. 52 weeks

12.

On customer account statements, long-term negotiable certificates of deposit must be shown at:

a. market value
b. market value plus accrued interest
c. face value
d. face value plus accrued interest

13.

LIBOR stands for:

a. London Interbank Offered Rate
b. Leading Interest Borrowing Rate
c. Lagging Interest Borrowing Rate
d. Lowest Interbank Offered Rate

14.

Which of the following disclosures must be made to customers who wish to purchase long-term negotiable certificates of deposit?

I   Sale prior to maturity can result in a price that is lower than the original purchase amount
II   Trading in the secondary market is limited
III Step-Down CD yields may not reflect the actual market interest rate
IV Callable CDs are subject to reinvestment risk

a. I and II only
b. III and IV only
c. I, II, III
d. I, II, III, IV

15.

The shortest initial maturity available for Treasury Bills is:

a. 4 weeks
b. 13 weeks
c. 26 weeks
d. 52 weeks

16.

Long-term negotiable certificates of deposit are subject to which of the following risks?

I   Interest rate risk
II   Call risk
III Reinvestment risk
IV Marketability risk

a. I and II only
b. III and IV only
c. I, II, III
d. I, II, III, IV

Debt Securities

17.

In order to determine whether a Brokered CD being recommended to a customer will qualify for FDIC insurance, the registered representative must know all of the following **EXCEPT:**

- a. name of the bank issuing the CD
- b. ownership title of the CD
- c. face amount of the CD
- d. call dates of the CD

18.

Trades of all of the following securities will settle in Fed Funds **EXCEPT:**

- a. Treasury Bills
- b. Treasury Notes
- c. Municipal Bonds
- d. Agency Bonds

19.

Auction Rate Securities:

- I have the interest rate reset weekly via Dutch auction
- II have a fixed interest rate for the life of the issue set by competitive bid auction
- III have an embedded put option
- IV do not have an embedded put option

- a. I and III
- b. I and IV
- c. II and III
- d. II and IV

20.

The interest rate paid on Eurodollar deposits is:

- a. Prime rate
- b. LIBOR
- c. Fed Funds Rate
- d. Discount rate

21.

Which of the following statements are **TRUE** regarding Federal Funds?

- I Federal funds are overnight loans between member institutions of the Federal Reserve System
- II Federal funds are overnight loans of reserves from the Federal Reserve Bank to a member institution
- III The interest rate charged on Federal Funds is the Federal Funds Rate
- IV The interest rate charged on Federal Funds is the Discount Rate

- a. I and III
- b. I and IV
- c. II and III
- d. II and IV

22.

Which statements are **TRUE** regarding structured products?

- I Structured products are standardized
- II Structured products are not standardized
- III Structured products have a fixed maturity date (similar to a debt security)
- IV Structured products do not have a maturity date (similar to an equity security)

- a. I and III
- b. I and IV
- c. II and III
- d. II and IV

23.
Under FINRA rules, if a member firm wishes to offer a structured product to its customers, all of the following statements are true **EXCEPT** the member:

a. has an obligation to perform a reasonable basis suitability determination before recommending the product to any of its customers

b. must use its expertise to determine if the potential yield of the structured product is an appropriate rate of return in relation to the volatility of the reference asset

c. must determine that its recommendation to purchase a structured product is suitable for that particular investor

d. must determine that an investment in the reference asset is suitable for that particular investor

24.
Which statement about Auction Rate Securities is **FALSE**?

a. Auction Rate Securities are long-term instruments

b. The interest rate on an Auction Rate Security is reset weekly or monthly

c. Auction Rate Securities can be put back to the issuer at the reset date

d. Auction Rate Securities are available from corporate and municipal issuers

25.
The "essential" difference between an ARS and a VRDO is:

a. weekly reset of interest rate

b. long-term security with short-term interest rate

c. embedded put option

d. money market instrument similarity

26.
An ETN offers an investor all of the following benefits **EXCEPT:**

a. lack of liquidity risk

b. lack of credit risk

c. tax-efficiency

d. access to returns of foreign investments

27.
When comparing an ETN to a structured product, which statements are **TRUE**?

I ETNs can be traded at any time while structured products cannot

II Structured products can be traded at any time while ETNs cannot

III ETN income is taxable at lower rates than income from structured products

IV Structured product income is taxable at lower rates than income from ETNs

a. I and III

b. I and IV

c. II and III

d. II and IV

28.
A repurchase agreement is effected between two U.S. Government securities dealers. The interest charged under the agreement is the:

a. coupon rate of the underlying U.S. Government securities, paid directly from the issuer to the securities' original buyer

b. coupon rate of the underlying U.S. Government securities, paid directly from the issuer to the securities' original seller

c. "repo" rate, paid by the buyer of the securities to the seller

d. "repo" rate, paid by the seller of the securities to the buyer

29.

All of the following statements are true about ETNs **EXCEPT:**

a. ETNs can be traded in the market like any other stock

b. ETNs offer an investment return tied to a benchmark index

c. ETNs are an equity security

d. ETNs are tax-advantaged

30.

Which statements are **TRUE** about ETNs?

I ETNs are a structured product

II ETNs are an investment company product

III ETNs are suitable for investors seeking income

IV ETNs are suitable for investors seeking long-term capital gains

a. I and III

b. I and IV

c. II and III

d. II and IV

MONEY MARKET DEBT / STRUCTURED PRODUCTS EXAMINATION EXPLANATIONS

1. The best answer is **a**. If interest rates rise after issuance, the value of the CD in the secondary market will fall. Since the interest rate on the instrument is fixed at issuance, if market interest rates rise, then the price of this instrument must fall to bring its yield up to current market levels.

2. The best answer is **a**. Negotiable CDs that mature in 1 year or less are issued at par and mature with accrued interest. Those issued for longer periods pay interest semi-annually and trade with accrued interest. The other choices are all original issue discount obligations, which trade flat.

3. The best answer is **b**. The effective Federal Funds Rate is the average daily rate charged by member banks for overnight loans of reserves.

4. The best answer is **b**. In a repurchase agreement, the Fed buys government securities from a dealer (giving the dealer cash) and will sell them back at a later date. This injects cash into the banking system, loosening credit.

5. The best answer is **c**. A Prime BA is of sufficient quality to be an eligible for Fed trading.

6. The best answer is **b**. Banker's Acceptances are a money market instrument used to finance imports and exports with "Third World" countries.

7. The best answer is **a**. Federal Funds are overnight loans of reserves from bank to bank. This is the shortest maturity for a debt obligation.

8. The best answer is **d**. American Depositary Receipts (ADRs) evidence that shares of a foreign company are being held in an overseas branch of an American bank. This is the ownership form by which foreign securities trade in the U.S. ADRs are equity, not short term debt, and hence are not a money market instrument.

9. The best answer is **c**. Commercial paper, which is issued by corporations, is not eligible for Fed trading. The eligible securities are U.S. Government debt, Government Agency debt, and prime Banker's Acceptances. These are the securities that the Fed trades with the primary U.S. Government dealers (the major commercial banks and brokerage firms) to control credit availability in the economy.

10. The best answer is **c**. To tighten credit, the Federal Reserve will sell government securities to bank dealers (draining the dealers of cash that could be lent out) with an agreement to buy them back at a later date. The sale is being "matched" to a future purchase and is used to temporarily drain cash from the credit markets. This is called a reverse repo or matched sale.

11. The best answer is **d**. Treasury Bills are issued in initial 4 week (1 month); 13 week (3 month); 26 week (6 month); and 52 week (12 month) maturities.

12. The best answer is **a**. All securities positions on customer account statements must be shown at market value - not face value. The amount of accrued interest earned on a debt instrument as of the statement date is not disclosed.

13. The best answer is **a**. "LIBOR" stands for London Interbank Offered Rate.

14. The best answer is **d**. Customers who wish to buy long-term negotiable certificates of deposit must be informed that sale prior to maturity can result in a loss on the security (if market interest rates have risen in the interim); that while a secondary market exists for these securities, it is limited; that CDs with Step-Up or Step-Down yields may not give an interest rate that is reflective of the market (since many issuers entice buyers with higher than market initial interest rates that then step-down over time to the current market rate); and that long term CDs, if they are callable, subject the customer to reinvestment risk.

15. The best answer is **a**. Treasury Bills are issued in initial 4 week (1 month); 13 week (3 month); 26 week (6 month); and 52 week (12 month) maturities.

16. The best answer is **d**. Long-term negotiable Certificates of Deposit (over 1 year maturity) are subject to interest rate risk, as is any fixed rate debt instrument. If market rates go up, the market value of the CD will decline. Long-term CDs can be callable, so they are subject to call risk in a declining interest rate environment. Interest is paid semi-annually and, again in a declining interest rate environment, if these payments are reinvested in new CDs, the rate of return on reinvested monies will decline - thus they have reinvestment risk. Finally, the secondary market for these securities is limited - so they can have marketability risk.

17. The best answer is **d**. Brokered CDs are sold by brokerage firms that are representing issuing banks. FDIC insurance of $250,000 maximum covers bank deposits - but only if the deposit is titled in the customer's name. If the CD is titled in the brokerage firm's name, then the insurance coverage would not apply! For example, if a customer wishes to buy a $75,000 CD, as long as the customer does not have deposits at the issuing bank in excess of $175,000 (thus not exceeding the $250,000 maximum FDIC coverage) and the CD is titled in the customer's name, then the CD would be FDIC insured. Therefore, the bank name must be known because the customer gets only one coverage at that bank. The CD must be titled in the customer's name for the FDIC coverage to apply. Since coverage is a maximum of $250,000 per customer at each bank, the amount of the CD must be aggregated with any other customer deposits held at the bank to determine if the FDIC limit is exceeded. Call features are irrelevant to FDIC coverage.

18. The best answer is **c**. Securities that are eligible to be traded by the Federal Reserve are those backed by the guarantee of the U.S. Government as well as certain agency obligations. Both Treasury Bills and Treasury Notes are eligible securities. Trades in eligible securities settle through the Federal Reserve system, and therefore settle in "Fed Funds." Municipal bond trades and trades in corporate securities are not eligible for trading and settling through the Federal Reserve system; these securities settle in "clearing house" funds.

19. The best answer is **b**. Auction Rate Securities are long-term debt issues where the interest rate is reset weekly (or monthly) via Dutch auction. This gives the issuer the advantage of paying a short-term market interest rate on a long-term security. However, unlike a variable rate demand note (VRDO), they have no embedded put option - meaning that the issuer is not obligated to buy them back at the reset date. The failure of the weekly auctions in 2008 created a situation where holders could not sell these securities to get out of them.

20. The best answer is **b**. Eurodollar deposits are U.S. currency held in banks in foreign countries, mainly in Europe. The Eurodollar market is centered in London - and the interest rate paid on these deposits is "LIBOR" = London Interbank Offered Rate.

21. The best answer is **a**. Federal Funds are overnight loans of reserves from Fed member bank to Fed member bank. The interest rate charged on Fed Funds is the Federal Funds Rate. When the Federal Reserve Bank lends directly to a member bank, it does so at the discount rate.

22. The best answer is **c**. Structured products are securities based on, or derived from, a basket of securities, an index, or other securities, commodities or currencies. There are many types of structured products, but generally they consist of a "bond" portion, which pays interest based on the performance of a well known index such as the S&P 500 Index. In addition, they have a derivative component (an embedded option) that allows the holder to sell the security back to the issuer (at par) at maturity. These are often marketed as debt instruments, but that is not really the case. Structured products are created by many different brokerage firms and each firm's version is somewhat different.

23. The best answer is **d**. Because of the complexity of structured products, which is typically a zero-coupon "synthetic bond" that gives a return tied to a market index such as the NASDAQ 100 Index or the Standard and Poor's 500 Index; and which has a maturity based on an embedded option; FINRA requires that the member firm perform a "reasonable basis" suitability determination to evaluate the product's potential rewards and risks (relative to other similar structured products offered by other firms). Once a "reasonable basis" suitability determination has been completed, then the member firm can offer the structured product only to its customers that are suitable for that investment. This is "customer specific" suitability. There is no requirement to determine whether an investment in the reference asset (say a NASDAQ 100 Exchange Traded Fund) is suitable for the investor.

24. The best answer is **c**. Auction Rate Securities are long-term debt issues where the interest rate is reset weekly (or monthly) via Dutch auction. This gives the issuer the advantage of paying a short-term market interest rate on a long-term security. However, unlike a variable rate demand note (VRDO), they have no embedded put option - meaning that the issuer is not obligated to buy them back at the reset date. ARSs are available from both corporate and municipal issuers. The failure of the weekly auctions in 2008 created a situation where holders could not sell these securities to get out of them.

25. The best answer is **c**. Auction Rate Securities are long-term debt issues where the interest rate is reset weekly (or monthly) via Dutch auction. This gives the issuer the advantage of paying a short-term market interest rate on a long-term security. However, unlike a variable rate demand note (VRDO), they have no embedded put option - meaning that the issuer is not obligated to buy them back at the reset date.

26. The best answer is **b**. An ETN is an Exchange Traded Note. It is a type of structured product offered by banks that gives a return tied to a benchmark index. The note is a debt of the bank, and is backed by the faith and credit of the issuing bank. Thus, if the bank's credit rating is lowered, the value of the ETN will fall as well - so it has credit risk. ETNs are listed on an exchange and trade, so they have minimal liquidity risk. Their return can be based on "exotic" indexes, such as a Brazil or India index, so they can give investors access to the returns of foreign markets. Finally, ETNs make no interest or dividend payments. Their value grows as they are held based on the growth of the benchmark index, with any gain at sale or redemption currently taxed at capital gains rates. Thus, they are tax-advantaged as compared to conventional debt instruments.

27. The best answer is **a**. An ETN is an Exchange Traded Note. It is a type of structured product offered by banks that gives a return tied to a benchmark index. The note is a debt of the bank, and is backed by the faith and credit of the issuing bank. ETNs are listed on an exchange and trade, so they have minimal liquidity risk. In comparison, a regular structured product is non-negotiable and, if redeemed prior to maturity, imposes an early-redemption penalty. ETNs make no interest or dividend payments. Their value grows as they are held

based on the growth of the benchmark index, with any gain at sale or redemption currently taxed at capital gains rates. Thus, they are tax-advantaged as compared to other structured debt products.

28. The best answer is **d**. In a repurchase agreement between 2 government dealers, a government securities dealer "sells" securities to another dealer, with an agreement to buy them back at a later date. The selling dealer obtains cash, and for this, agrees to pay interest to the buying dealer. The interest rate charged is known as the "repo" rate - the repurchase agreement interest rate. The rate fluctuates with, and parallels, the Federal Funds rate.

29. The best answer is **c**. An ETN is an Exchange Traded Note. It is a type of structured product offered by banks that gives a return tied to a benchmark index. The note is a debt of the bank, and is backed by the faith and credit of the issuing bank. They are not an equity security - they are a debt instrument. ETNs are listed on an exchange and trade, so they have minimal liquidity risk. Finally, ETNs make no interest or dividend payments. Their value grows as they are held based on the growth of the benchmark index, with any gain at sale or redemption currently taxed at capital gains rates. Thus, they are tax-advantaged as compared to conventional debt instruments.

30. The best answer is **b**. An ETN is an Exchange Traded Note. It is a type of structured product offered by banks that gives a return tied to a benchmark index. The note is a debt of the bank, and is backed by the faith and credit of the issuing bank. ETNs make no interest or dividend payments, so they are not suitable for an investor seeking income. Their value grows as they are held based on the growth of the benchmark index, with any gain at sale or redemption currently taxed at capital gains rates. Thus, they are tax-advantaged as compared to conventional debt instruments.

SECTION 6: EURODOLLAR DEBT

6a. EURODOLLAR DEBT CHARACTERISTICS

Eurodollar Bonds

The Eurobond market currently is larger than the U.S. Corporate bond market. This market is centered in London, with trading taking place "across the globe." Bonds in the Euromarket are either denominated in dollars or in foreign currencies such as the British Pound or the Euro. Many Eurobonds are "Eurodollar" bonds. Eurodollar bonds are:

- Denominated in U.S. dollars;
- Underwritten by an international syndicate;
- Issued outside the U.S.

Foreign investors have shown a preference for Eurodollar bonds over U.S. Government bonds (which also pay in dollars) and over corporate bonds of that country.

Bearer Form

Some foreign investors prefer Eurodollar issues because the maturities typically range from 5-10 years, which is shorter than normal, and call protection is longer than average. The bonds are also not subject to withholding taxes and are issued in bearer form - which is a necessity when selling bonds in Europe. (In the U.S., new bearer issues are illegal. In Europe, virtually all bond issues are bearer form, since investors are concerned about political instability and want to be able to pack up their assets and take them to a safe haven, if necessary).

Advantages Of Eurodollar Bonds For U.S. Based Issuers

Because of this preference, foreign investors bid up the prices of Eurodollar bonds, often reducing yields below that offered by U.S. This makes the market particularly attractive to U.S. issuers who can float debt at lower interest rates than those found in the U.S. In addition, corporate issuers in the U.S. must register the securities with the SEC, which takes time and is expensive. This cost is avoided with Eurodollar bonds. Finally, Eurodollar bonds pay interest once a year, instead of the normal twice a year schedule found in the U.S.

The issuers of Eurodollar bonds include:

- U.S. Corporations
- U.S. State and Local Governments
- Foreign Corporations
- Sovereign Governments
- Supranational Agencies

Not Issued By U.S. Government

(Note: The U.S. Government does not issue Eurodollar bonds.)

Domestic corporations use the Eurodollar bond market to issue bonds in foreign markets at lower cost than can be accomplished in the U.S. The bonds are payable in dollars, and not the currency of the country in which they are sold. Thus, if the foreign currency appreciates, it has no effect on the issuer, who is obligated to pay in dollars - not the more expensive foreign currency.

U.S. corporations find the Eurodollar bond market attractive for three reasons:

No Currency Exchange Risk For U.S. Issuers

The first is that foreign currency exchange risk is eliminated since the bonds are payable in dollars.

Lower Interest Rates

The second is that interest rates in the Euromarket have tended to be lower than domestic interest rates in recent years.

Lower Issuance Expenses

The third is that the issue does not have to be registered with the SEC, since it is being sold outside the U.S., saving on the expenses of making the initial offer of the securities.

State and local governments in the U.S. have used the Eurodollar market to float issues at lower interest cost than could be achieved in the U.S. This has occurred when interest rates in the U.S. for municipals have been higher than Eurodollar rates.

Foreign corporations owned by U.S. companies are also big users of the Eurodollar bond market (for example, IBM of Europe, a wholly-owned subsidiary of IBM, can issue Eurodollar bonds).

Foreign governments, aside from selling domestic issues, can float Eurodollar bond issues to attract investors from outside that country who want payment in the "international currency" - which is American dollars. And international agencies can raise funding in the Eurodollar market - such as the consortium that financed the building of the English Channel Tunnel.

Once the bonds are issued, trading is centered in the London market. These bonds can not trade in the United States, since they have not been registered with the SEC.

This leaves us with a big question - why are Eurodollar bonds included on this exam, which covers the U.S. securities markets, when they cannot be traded in the U.S?

EURODOLLAR DEBT SECTION EXAMINATION

1.

All of the following issue Eurodollar bonds **EXCEPT:**

    a.   U.S. Corporations

    b.   Foreign Corporations

    c.   U.S. Government

    d.   Foreign Governments

2.

Which of the following statements are **TRUE** about Eurodollar bonds?

    I   The bonds are issued in the U.S.

    II   The bonds are issued outside the U.S.

    III The purchasers are U.S. residents

    IV The purchasers are foreign residents

    a.   I and III

    b.   I and IV

    c.   II and III

    d.   II and IV

3.

Payments on Eurodollar bonds are made:

    a.   only in U.S. dollars

    b.   only in designated foreign currencies

    c.   in either U.S. dollars or designated foreign currencies

    d.   in Special Drawing Rights (SDRs)

4.

Interest on Eurodollar bonds is paid:

    a.   annually

    b.   semi-annually

    c.   quarterly

    d.   monthly

5.

Which statements are **TRUE** about Eurodollar bonds?

    I   The bonds are issued in bearer form

    II   U.S. corporate issuers are not subject to foreign currency risk

    III Foreign corporate issuers are not subject to foreign currency risk

    IV Trading is centered in the European market

    a.   I and II only

    b.   II and III only

    c.   I, II, IV

    d.   I, II, III, IV

EURODOLLAR DEBT EXAMINATION EXPLANATIONS

1. The best answer is **c**.   The U.S. Government does not issue Eurodollar bonds. U.S. corporations and foreign subsidiaries of U.S. corporations issue the bonds to gain access to lower cost foreign capital markets. Foreign governments and international agencies issue the bonds to broaden the available market for their bonds beyond the country of issuance (since they are dollar denominated).

2. The best answer is **d**.   Eurodollar bonds are issued outside the U.S. and are purchased by foreigners. These bonds are denominated in, and make payment in, U.S. dollars. The bonds are not registered for sale in the U.S.

3. The best answer is **a**.   Payments on Eurodollar bonds are made only in U.S. dollars.

4. The best answer is **a**.   Unlike normal interest bearing obligations in the U.S. which pay interest semi-annually, Eurodollar bonds pay interest once a year.

5. The best answer is **c**.   Eurodollar bonds are issued in bearer form outside the U.S. Trading is centered in London. Because the bonds are payable only in dollars, U.S. based issuers do not run any foreign currency risk. If foreign currency values rise, it has no effect on the issuer who pays in dollars. On the other hand, foreign issuers of Eurodollar bonds are subject to foreign currency risk. For example, if a British corporation issues Eurodollar bonds, and the British Pound declines in value relative to the dollar, then it will cost the British company more (in Pounds) to pay the debt service on the bonds.

OPTIONS

OPTIONS

OPTIONS

Options

OPTIONS

SECTION 1: OPTION BASICS

1a. DEFINITION OF AN OPTION

Option Contract

An option is a contract entered into between two parties. The buyer of the contract is called the option **holder**. The seller of the contract is called the option **writer**.

Holder Or Writer

Long Or Short

Other terminology is used as well to describe the holder and writer of a contract. The holder is said to be the buyer of the contract and is "long" the contract. The writer is said to be the seller of the contract and is "short" the contract.

> **Contract Holder = Contract Buyer = Long Position**
> **Contract Writer = Contract Seller = Short Position**

Call Contract

Two types of contracts exist. The first type of contract allows the holder **to buy** a security from the writer at a fixed price at any time during the life of the option. This type of option allows the holder to "call away" the security from the writer and hence is termed a "**call**" option. If the writer is "called," the contract obligates the writer to deliver the securities to the holder at the fixed price.

Put Contract

The second type of contract allows the holder **to sell** a security to the writer at a fixed price at any time during the life of the option. This type of option allows the holder to "put" the security to the writer and hence is termed a "**put**" option. If the securities are "put" to the writer, the contract obligates the writer to buy the securities at the fixed price.

Strike Price

Expiration Date

The fixed price specified in the contract at which the holder can either "call away" the security or "put" the security is called the strike price or exercise price. The life of the contract is specified by the expiration date of the contract. The amount of the underlying security covered by the contract (termed the "multiplier") differs depending on the underlying security.

Multiplier Is 100

If the underlying instrument is stock, the contract covers 100 shares. Options are also available for other underlying instruments, including stock indexes; interest rate indexes; and foreign currencies. The multiplier for stock and interest rate indexes is 100. For foreign currencies, the multiplier is also standardized at "100" – but this has been manipulated to make currency options just like other options. This is covered in the last section of this chapter.

For example, a customer buys 1 XXX Jan 120 Call.

The customer has the right to buy 100 shares of XXX stock at $120 share until the contract expires in January, no matter what happens to XXX's market price.

For example, a customer buys 1 XXX Jan 120 Put.

The customer has the right to sell 100 shares of XXX stock at $120 a share until the contract expires in January, no matter what happens to XXX's market price.

Premium

In order to secure the contract, the holder will pay a **"premium"** to the writer. The premium is really the price of the contract. Do not confuse the premium with the strike price of the underlying security. If a customer buys 1 XXX Jan 120 Call @ $5, he is paying a premium of $5 per share ($500 for the contract).

The holder of a contract has 3 choices regarding the contract - it can be exercised, it can be left to expire, or it can be traded.

Contract Exercised

If a call contract is exercised, the holder buys the underlying security at the strike price from the contract writer. Thus, the writer is obligated to sell the underlying security upon exercise.

If a put contract is exercised, the holder sells the underlying security at the strike price to the contract writer. Thus, the writer is obligated to buy the underlying security upon exercise.

Contract Expires

If the holder of a contract allows the contract to expire, he loses the premium paid. Conversely, the writer earns the premium received.

Contract Traded

If a holder trades his contract, he sells it to someone else prior to expiration. He will profit if the premium received exceeds that which he originally paid for the contract.

1b. TRADING OF OPTIONS AND THE PREMIUM

Trading Of Options On Exchanges

Option contracts are traded on exchanges. The exchange where the option trades is usually different from the exchange where the underlying security trades. For example, IBM stock is listed on the New York Stock Exchange, but IBM option contracts trade on the Chicago Board Options Exchange (CBOE).

Also, please note that until mid-1999, each major option contract was only traded on 1 exchange. For example, IBM options were traded on the CBOE only; they were not traded on the AMEX, PHLX or PAC exchanges. However, in response to a Justice Department inquiry on anti-competitive practices in listing options contracts, this "exclusive" listing arrangement was abandoned. All of the options exchanges now compete and options contracts are multiple listed. (Note: The NYSE owns the AMEX and has renamed the AMEX equities market as "NYSE-MKT" but it continues to use the AMEX name for the AMEX options market.)

Premium Is Market Price Of Option

Just as the market price of IBM stock is continuously determined on the floor of the NYSE, the market price of IBM Calls and Puts is determined on the floor of the CBOE. The market price of an option is called the "**premium.**" To buy a contract, the holder pays the premium. Conversely, the writer of a contract receives the premium.

Longer "Time" Increases Premium

The premium or "price" of a contract is influenced by a number of factors. First, the longer the contract has until expiration, the greater the chance that the underlying security's price will move in the desired direction. This will increase the option premium.

Greater Volatility Increases Premium

Second, the more volatile the underlying security, the greater the chance that the underlying security's price will move in the desired direction. This will also increase the option premium.

"Intrinsic Value" Increases Premium

Third, at the time of the trade, the contract may have "intrinsic value." If the contract has intrinsic value, this amount is included in the premium. The higher the intrinsic value, the higher the premium.

1c. INTRINSIC VALUE - "IN THE MONEY" AND "OUT THE MONEY"

The strike price of an option contract is set in a standardized fashion that makes the contracts easy to trade. When a new contract is issued, it would seem to make sense that the current market price of the stock would be the strike price of the contract. Doing this would make options very difficult to trade. For every point a stock rises, there would be 100 different contracts issued with prices in increments of cents. If a stock rose 5 points, there would be 500 different contracts trading. With trading spread among so many contracts, the market would become very thin for each contract and marketability risk would increase.

Standardized Option

Instead, options strike prices are standardized. For most stocks, the interval is set at 2 1/2 points. Therefore, if a stock is at $21, contracts cannot be issued at a $21 strike price, but they could be issued at strike prices of $17.50, $20.00, $22.50, etc. For each stock trading at $20 or less, strike prices can be issued up to 100% higher or lower. For stocks over $20, the range is +/- 50%. So if a stock is trading at, say, $50, options can now be issued with strike prices ranging from $25 to $75.

Strike Price Is Fixed; Premium Varies

Once the contract is issued, the strike price is fixed. As the market price of the stock now moves, the contract premium or "price" moves to reflect the changing value.

"In The Money"

Time Premium

Assume that a customer wants to buy 1 ABC Jan 50 Call when the market price of ABC is $52 per share. This contract has "intrinsic value" of $2 per share since the holder has the right to buy stock at $50 when the stock is worth $52. The call contract is said to be "in the money" by $2. The $2 of intrinsic value represents the minimum premium for the contract. Assume that the writer of the ABC Jan 50 Call is willing to sell the contract for a premium of $5 per share. Of the total $5 premium, $2 represents the "in the money" amount, while the remaining $3 is called the "time" premium. This is the amount above intrinsic value that the buyer pays for the remaining time to expiration of the contract.

"At The Money"

Assume a customer wants to buy 1 ABC Jan 50 Call at a $3 premium when the market price of ABC stock is $50 per share. This contract has **no** intrinsic value (the holder can buy stock at $50 which is worth $50). The total premium of $3 is all time value. This contract is said to be "at the money."

"Out The Money"

Assume a customer wants to buy 1 ABC Jan 50 Call at a $1 premium when the market price is $47 per share. This contract has no intrinsic value. As a matter of fact, this contract won't be worth very much at all since the holder has the right to buy stock at $50 which is currently worth $47. This contract is "out the money" by $3. Because the contract is "out the money," the premium is quite low ($1) and really represents the time value of the contract reduced in the market by the out the money amount. The total premium of an out the money contract is considered to be "time" premium.

For example, a customer buys 1 ABC Jan 50 Call @ 4 when the market price of ABC is $51. How much of the premium is time value?

Answer: Since the contract is in the money by $1 per share (the holder can buy stock for $50 when it is worth $51), the remaining $3 per share is the time premium.

For example, a customer buys 1 ABC Jan 50 Call @ 2 when the market price of ABC is $49. How much of the premium is time value?

Answer: Since the contract is out the money by $1 per share (the holder can buy stock for $50 when it is worth $49), the entire $2 premium is time value.

As Contract Goes "In The Money" - Premium Increases

As a contract moves "in the money," the premium increases in the market to reflect the increased value. As a contract moves "out the money," the premium falls in the market to reflect the decreased value.

As Contract Goes "Out The Money" - Premium Decreases

"In the money" and "out the money" amounts are always looked at from the holder's perspective. An in the money contract is one which can be exercised to the profit of the holder. An out the money contract is one which would not be exercised so that the writer keeps the entire premium.

"In" And "Out" Always Holder's Perspective

Thus, holders are happy when contracts go "in the money"; writers are unhappy about this. Conversely, holders are unhappy when contracts go "out the money"; writers are happy about this.

To summarize for call contracts:

- Calls are "in the money" when the market price is HIGHER than the strike price.

- Calls are "at the money" when the market price is the SAME as the strike price.

- Calls are "out the money" when the market price is LOWER than the strike price.

The situation is reversed for put contracts.

To summarize for put contracts:

- Puts are "in the money" when the market price is LOWER than the strike price.

- Puts are "at the money" when the market price is the SAME as the strike price.

- Puts are "out the money" when the market price is HIGHER than the strike price.

Examples of "in" and "out" for put contracts are shown below:

A customer buys 1 ABC Jan 50 Put @ $5 when the market price of ABC stock is $48. Since the holder has the right to sell stock for $50 when it is worth $48 in the market, the contract has intrinsic value of $2 per share. The put is "in the money" by $2. Since the total premium is $5, the $3 excess premium above intrinsic value is the "time premium."

A customer buys 1 ABC Jan 50 Put @ $3 when the market price of ABC stock is $50. The holder can sell stock for $50 which is worth $50 in the market. This contract is "at the money" and has no intrinsic value. The entire premium is "time premium."

A customer buys 1 ABC Jan 50 Put @ $1 when the market price of ABC stock is $52. The holder can sell stock for $50 which is currently worth $52. This contract is "out the money" by $2 per share. The low premium of $1 reflects this and is all "time premium."

Parity

Another term that must be known for options contracts is "parity." When the market premium exactly equals the intrinsic value of the option, the contract is said to be trading at parity. For example, an ABC Jul 50 Call @ $3 is at "parity" when the market price of ABC stock is at $53. An ABC Jul 50 Put @ $3 is at "parity" when the market price of ABC stock is at $47.

1d. FURTHER DISCUSSION OF PREMIUMS

In addition to the factors already discussed that influence the options premium, there are other items to be considered. We already know that the greater the time to expiration, the greater the premium; and the greater a contract's "intrinsic value," the greater the premium. We also know that the greater the volatility of the underlying instrument, the greater the premium.

The other factors that influence premiums are:

Higher Dividend Rate; Lower Call Premiums

The Dividend Rate: If the dividend rate on a security is high, it becomes more attractive to take the physical security position than to buy call options on that security (since the call holder does not earn dividends). For call options, as the dividend rate on the stock increases, the options premium will fall.

Higher Dividend Rate; Higher Put Premiums

Conversely, if the dividend rate on a security is high, it becomes more expensive to take a "short position" in that security - since the short seller must pay the dividends to the lender of the stock. Thus, the higher the dividend rate, the less attractive it is to take a "short position" - and that makes it more attractive to buy puts on that security. Therefore, the higher the dividend rate on a security, the greater the demand will be for put contracts on that security, raising the premium.

Higher Interest Rates; Higher Call Premiums

Short-Term Interest Rates: This is a minor factor in pricing of options premiums, and must be known for the exam only as something that influences the options premium. As market interest rates rise, it becomes more attractive to buy call options instead of buying the underlying stock on margin (at high current market interest rates). This tends to push the price of calls up as market interest rates rise.

Higher Interest Rates; Lower Put Premiums

As market interest rates rise, it is more attractive to actually sell stock positions and get the cash out of them that can be reinvested at higher current market interest rates than to buy a put option that allows the later sale of the stock upon exercise. Thus, there is less demand for put options as market interest rates rise and put premiums fall.

1e. OPENING AND CLOSING POSITIONS

OCC Keeps Record Of All Listed Options Contracts

The Options Clearing Corporation receives a report of each options trade that occurs on an exchange and keeps the record of all contracts that have been created through "opening" trades; and all contracts that have been extinguished with "closing" trades.

When the OCC receives a trade report, it needs to know how to reflect it on its record of options contracts. Therefore, each order for a new position taken by either a holder or a writer must be marked on the order "opening" so the OCC will record the new contract on its books. Any order that will close out an existing position must be marked "closing" so that the OCC will remove the position from its books.

Opening Purchase

We have already stated that there are two parties to an option contract, the holder and the writer. To establish the contract, the holder is said to make an "opening purchase" of the contract.

Closing Sale

The holder can choose to exercise the contract, resulting in a stock transaction, can let the contract expire, or can trade the contract. If the holder trades the contract to someone else, he closes his position with a "closing sale."

Opening Sale

The writer of that contract makes an "opening sale" of the contract. The term "opening" is used because a new short position is being created. (Please note that when any security is traded, one does not have to buy first and then sell second. One can also sell first (a "short sale") and buy back second.)

Closing Purchase

The writer is passive in that he cannot choose to exercise the contract - that is decided by the holder. But, the writer can trade the contract to someone else. If the writer trades the contract to someone else, he closes the position with a "closing purchase."

Open Interest

The number of open contracts is termed the "open interest."

If both the holder and writer "open" a position at the same time, this means that, on the books of the OCC, a new buyer has been matched to a new seller, creating 1 new contract. The open interest in that contract has been increased by 1 contract;

If both the holder and the writer "close" a position at the same time, this means that, on the books of the OCC, that contract has been extinguished. The open interest in that contract has been decreased by 1 contract;

If a holder "opens" a position against a writer who is "closing" or vice-versa, there is no change in open interest. In essence, the person who is opening a position is assuming the existing contract of the person who is closing that position, so there is no change in the number of contracts outstanding.

As contracts get close to expiration, closing transactions increase, reducing the "open interest." At expiration, the open interest is zero since all remaining open contracts are void.

The larger the "open interest" in a specific option, the greater the number of existing contracts available to trade. Thus, professional traders are more likely to trade contracts with a large "open interest," since their market is more liquid, than those less-liquid contracts with a small "open interest."

Options

OPTION BASICS
SECTION EXAMINATION

1.

Which of the following influence the premium of a listed option?

   I   Length of time until expiration of the contract

   II   Volatility of underlying security

   III   Market price of underlying security

  a. I only

  b. II only

  c. III only

  d. I, II, III

2.

"Intrinsic value" is defined as the:

  a. excess of premium over the underlying security's market price

  b. excess of time premium over the "in the money" amount

  c. difference between the strike price and market price of the underlying security, if exercise is profitable to the holder

  d. maximum potential gain on a contract

3.

Which statements are **TRUE** about option contracts?

   I   Long puts go "in the money" when the market price rises above the strike price

   II   Long puts go "in the money" when the market price falls below the strike price

   III   Short puts go "in the money" when the market price rises above the strike price

   IV   Short puts go "in the money" when the market price falls below the strike price

  a. I and III

  b. I and IV

  c. II and III

  d. II and IV

4.

What is the "time premium" of the following contract?

    1 ABC Jan 55 Put @ $9
    ABC Market Price = $49

  a. $0

  b. $3

  c. $6

  d. $9

5.

Which of the following contracts has the greatest intrinsic value?

  a. ABC Jan 50 Call when the market price of ABC stock is $55

  b. ABC Jan 50 Call when the market price of ABC stock is $50

  c. ABC Jan 50 Put when the market price of ABC stock is $40

  d. ABC Jan 50 Put when the market price of ABC stock is $60

6.

To establish a short call position, an order ticket must be marked:

  a. opening purchase

  b. opening sale

  c. closing purchase

  d. closing sale

7.

To liquidate a long put position, the order ticket must be marked:

  a. opening purchase

  b. opening sale

  c. closing purchase

  d. closing sale

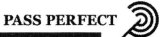

8.

A customer buys 1 ABC Feb 50 Put @ $7 when the market price of ABC is $49. If the stock goes to $41 and just prior to expiration, the customer closes out the position with a closing sale at intrinsic value, the gain or loss is:

a. $200 gain

b. $500 loss

c. $700 gain

d. $900 loss

9.

Which of the following will decrease "open interest"?

I   Opening Purchase

II   Opening Sale

III Closing Purchase

IV   Closing Sale

a. I and II

b. III and IV

c. I and IV

d. II and III

10.

Which contract will likely have the highest premium when ABC closes at $38?

a. ABC Jan 35 Call

b. ABC Jan 35 Put

c. ABC Jan 40 Call

d. ABC Jan 30 Put

OPTION BASICS EXAMINATION EXPLANATIONS

1. The best answer is **d**. The longer the life of the option, the higher the premium; the greater the volatility of the underlying security, the higher the premium; the higher the market price of the stock, the higher the premium on a call contract (since it goes further "in the money"). The lower the market price of the stock, the higher the premium on a put contract (since it goes further "in the money"). Therefore, all 3 choices influence the premium.

2. The best answer is **c**. Intrinsic value is the amount by which an option contract is "in the money." It is the difference between the strike price and market price, if exercise is profitable to the holder.

3. The best answer is **d**. An "in the money" contract is one, that if exercised, would result in a profitable stock trade to the holder. Puts go "in the money" when the market price falls below the strike price - it makes no difference if the contract is "long" or "short." Being "in the money" is good for the contract holder and bad for the contract writer. The put holder will exercise and sell the stock at a strike price that is higher than the current market. Calls go "in the money" when the market price rises above the strike price. The call holder will exercise and buy stock at the strike price that is lower than the current market price.

4. The best answer is **b**. Time premium is any premium paid above the intrinsic value of the contract. In this case, the holder of the put can sell the stock at the strike price of $55 when the market price is $49, for a $6 profit to the holder. This is the "intrinsic value" of the contract. Since the total premium paid is $9, the time premium is $3.

5. The best answer is **c**. Calls go "in the money" when the market price rises above the strike price. Puts go "in the money" when the market price falls below the strike price. Of the contracts listed, Choice **A** and Choice **C** are "in the money." A 50 Call when the market is at $55 is 5 points "in the money." And a 50 Put when the market price is $40 is "in the money" by 10 points.

6. The best answer is **b**. To establish a short option position, the order ticket must be marked "opening sale." To liquidate this position, the order ticket is marked "closing purchase."

7. The best answer is **d**. To establish a long option position, the order ticket is marked "opening purchase." When this order is executed, a contract has been purchased for a holder. To liquidate this position, the order ticket is marked "closing sale." When this order is executed, the contract is sold to someone else.

8. The best answer is **a**. The customer established the long put position with an opening purchase at $7. He closes the position with a closing sale at $9 (intrinsic value when the put strike price is $50 and the market price is $41). The net profit is $9 - $7 = $2 per share or $200 for the contract.

9. The best answer is **b**. Open Interest is the number of option contracts (both calls and puts) outstanding. Opening purchases and opening sales increase open interest; closing sales and closing purchases decrease open interest. The greater the open interest, the greater the likely trading volume in the issue.

10. The best answer is **a**. The contract with the highest premium is likely to be the one that is the most "in the money." With the market price at 38, the 35 call is "in the money" by 3 points. The 35 put is "out the money" by 3 points. The 40 call is "out the money" by 2 points. The 30 put is "out the money" by 8 points.

SECTION 2: SPECULATIVE STRATEGIES

2a. SPECULATIVE STRATEGIES OVERVIEW

Bull And Bear Strategies

A speculative option strategy is one which attempts to profit if the market price of the underlying security rises or falls. Strategies which profit from a rising market are "bull" strategies. Strategies which profit from falling markets are "bear" strategies.

There are four speculative strategies. They are:

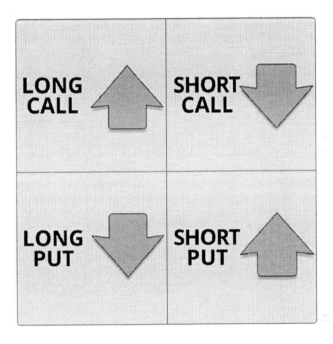

The purchase of a call (long call) or the sale of a put (short put) will give the speculator a profit in a rising market. These are the bull strategies.

The purchase of a put (long put) or the sale of a call (short call) will give the speculator a profit in a falling market. These are the bear strategies.

2b. LONG CALL STRATEGY

Holder Has "Right To Buy" Underlying Security

Assume that a customer buys 1 ABC Jan 50 Call @ $5 when the market price of ABC stock is at $51. The customer has the right to buy ABC stock at $50 during the life of the option, and he pays a premium of $5 per share for this right.

Unlimited Upside Gain Potential

If the market rises, the customer can exercise the option and buy the stock for $50. He could then sell the stock in the market for its true value. Since the stock can rise an unlimited amount, he has theoretically unlimited gain potential as the contract goes further and further "in the money."

**Call Holder Gains
When Market
Rises**

**Maximum Loss Premium
Paid**

On the other hand, if the market drops below $50, it would not make sense to exercise the option since the contract is now "out the money." The customer would let the contract expire and would lose the premium paid. This represents the maximum potential loss.

**Breakeven = Strike Price +
Premium**

To breakeven, the customer has to recover the $5 premium paid. He will do this when the market price rises to $55. At this point, the contract is "in the money" by $5, yielding a profit on the stock that exactly offsets the premium paid.

The best way to calculate maximum potential gain, maximum potential loss, breakeven, as well as any true gain or loss on an option contract is by setting up the problem on a "T" diagram. If this is done properly, all of these facts stand out.

For example, a customer buys 1 ABC Jul 60 Call @ $5 when the market price of ABC is $51. What is the maximum potential loss? What is the maximum potential gain? What is the breakeven point?

To handle this problem, we set up the "T."

OPTION	STOCK
Buy -$5	

The customer pays a $5 per share premium. This amount is put on the "option" side of the "T" as a negative number. If nothing else happens and the contract expires, he loses the $5 premium for a $500 total loss.

The next step to find both maximum potential gain and breakeven is to assume that the option has been "exercised." If this occurs, the customer buys the stock at the strike price. The "T" now shows:

OPTION		STOCK		
Buy	-$5	Buy	-$60	Breakeven = $65

If the customer exercises, he has paid $60 for the stock in addition to the $5 for a total of $65. To breakeven, he must recover the $65 paid when he liquidates the stock position.

Since the stock can rise an unlimited amount, the gain potential is unlimited as well. Assume that the customer is able to sell the stock in the market for $75. What is his net gain or loss?

OPTION		STOCK		
Buy	-$5	Buy	-$60	Breakeven = $65
		Sell	+$75	
	-$5		+$15	Net Gain = $10

For the stock, the customer makes $15 per share profit, offset by the $5 premium paid. The net gain is $10 per share or $1,000 on the hundred shares covered by the call contract.

Instead of exercising, the customer could have simply traded the call contract to someone else. In doing so, he closes out his interest in the contract prior to expiration. Assume that the customer sells this contract in a closing sale transaction to someone else for a $9 premium. What is his net gain or loss? The "T" should show:

OPTION		STOCK
Buy	-$5	
Sell	+$9	
	+$4	

Because the contract was never exercised, there is no transaction in the underlying security (the stock). The option was simply closed out by trading the contract, resulting in a net gain of $4 per share or $400 for the contract.

To summarize the characteristics of buying a call:

LONG CALL		Bullish market direction
Maximum Gain	=	Unlimited
Maximum Loss	=	Premium paid
Breakeven Point	=	Strike price + Premium

2c. SHORT CALL STRATEGY

Writer Has Obligation To Deliver (Sell) At The Strike Price

Assume that a customer sells 1 ABC Jan 50 Call @ $5 when the market price of ABC stock is at $51. The customer is obligated to deliver (sell) ABC stock at $50 during the life of the option, and he receives a premium of $5 per share for this obligation.

Maximum Potential Loss – Unlimited

Naked Call Writer

If the market rises, the customer will be exercised and must deliver the stock for $50. He would then have to buy the stock in the market for its true value to be able to deliver on the sale. Since the stock can rise an unlimited amount, he has theoretically unlimited loss potential as the contract goes further and further "in the money." Because of the exposure to unlimited risk, this call writer is termed "naked" - exposed to substantial risk.

Maximum Potential Gain = Premium Received

On the other hand, if the market drops below $50, it would not make sense to exercise the option since the contract is now "out the money." The contract would expire and the writer would keep the premium received. This represents the maximum potential gain.

Call Writer Gains When Market Falls

Breakeven = Strike Price + Premium

To breakeven, the customer has to lose the $5 premium received. He will do this when the market price rises to $55. At this point, the contract is "in the money" by $5, yielding a loss on the stock that exactly offsets the premium received.

For example, a customer sells 1 ABC Jul 60 Call @ $5 when the market price of ABC is $51. What is the maximum potential gain? What is the maximum potential loss? What is the breakeven point?

To handle this problem, we set up the "T."

OPTION		STOCK	
Sell	+$5		

The writer receives a $5 per share premium, so this is placed on the "option" side of the "T." If nothing else happens, meaning the contract expires, he gains the $5 premium for a $500 total gain.

The next step to find both maximum potential loss and breakeven is to assume that the option has been "exercised." If this occurs, the customer sells the stock at the strike price. The "T" now shows:

OPTION		STOCK		
Sell	+$5	Sell	+$60	Breakeven = $65

If the writer is exercised, he has received $60 for selling the stock in addition to the $5 premium for a total of $65. To breakeven, he must lose the $65 received when he purchases the stock position for delivery on the sale. Since the stock can rise an unlimited amount, the loss potential is unlimited as well. Assume that the writer is able to buy the stock in the market for $75. What is his net gain or loss?

OPTION		STOCK		
Sell	+$5	Sell	+$60	Breakeven = $65
		Buy	-$75	
	+$5		-$15	Net Loss = $10

On the stock, the writer loses $15 per share, offset by the $5 premium received. The net loss is $10 per share or $1,000 on the hundred shares covered by the call contract.

Instead of waiting to be exercised, the writer could have simply traded the call contract to someone else. In doing so, he closes out his interest in the contract prior to expiration. Assume that the customer buys this contract back in a closing purchase transaction from someone else for a $9 premium. What is his net gain or loss? The "T" should show:

OPTION		STOCK
Sell	+$5	
Buy	-$9	
	-$4	

Because the contract was never exercised, there is no transaction in the underlying security (the stock). The option was simply closed out by trading the contract, resulting in a net loss of $4 per share or $400 for the contract.

To summarize the characteristics of selling a call:

SHORT NAKED CALL		Bearish market direction
Maximum Gain	=	Premium received
Maximum Loss	=	Unlimited
Breakeven Point	=	Strike price + Premium

2d. LONG PUT STRATEGY

Holder Has "Right To Sell" At The Strike Price

Assume that a customer buys 1 ABC Jan 50 Put @ $5 when the market price of ABC stock is at $49. The holder has the right to sell ABC stock at $50 during the life of the option, and he pays a premium of $5 per share for this right.

Potential Gain Increases As Market Falls - Maximum Is Strike Price - Premium

If the market falls, the holder can exercise the option and sell the stock for $50. He could then buy the stock in the market for its true value to deliver on the sale. Since the stock can fall to a value of "0," he has increasing gain as the contract goes further and further "in the money."

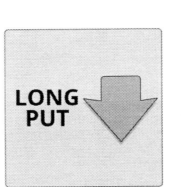

Put holder gains when market falls

Maximum Potential Loss = Premium Paid

On the other hand, if the market rises above $50, it would not make sense to exercise the option since the contract is now "out the money." The customer would let the contract expire and would lose the premium paid. This represents the maximum potential loss.

Breakeven = Strike Price - Premium

To breakeven, the customer has to recover the $5 premium paid. He will do this when the market price falls to $45. At this point, the contract is "in the money" by $5, yielding a profit on the stock that exactly offsets the premium paid.

For example, a customer buys 1 ABC Jul 60 Put @ $5 when the market price of ABC is $59. What is the maximum potential loss? What is the maximum potential gain? What is the breakeven point?

To handle this problem, we set up the "T."

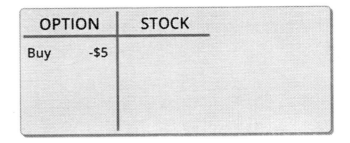

OPTION	STOCK
Buy -$5	

The customer pays a $5 per share premium, so this is shown on the "option" side of the "T." If nothing else happens and the contract expires, he loses the $5 premium for a $500 total loss.

The next step to find both maximum potential gain and breakeven is to assume that the option has been "exercised." If this occurs, the customer sells the stock at the strike price. The "T" now shows:

OPTION		STOCK		
Buy	-$5	Sell	+$60	Breakeven = $55

If the customer exercises, he has received $60 for selling the stock, offset by the premium paid of $5, for a net price of $55. To breakeven, he must pay the same $55 to buy the stock position for delivery on the sale. Since the stock can fall to zero, the maximum gain occurs at this point. At a value of "0," the gain as shown on the "T" is:

OPTION		STOCK		
Buy	-$5	Sell	+$60	Breakeven = $55
		Buy	-$0	
	-$5		+$60	Net Gain = $55

The maximum gain is $55 per share or $5,500 for the contract. This assumes the customer can buy the stock for "nothing" to deliver on the sale.

Assume that the stock has fallen to $45 and is bought to make delivery on the sale. The customer's position now shows:

OPTION		STOCK		
Buy	-$5	Sell	+$60	Breakeven = $55
		Buy	-$45	
	-$5		+$15	Net Gain = $10

On the stock, the customer makes $15 per share, offset by the $5 premium paid. The net gain is $10 per share or $1,000 on the hundred shares covered by the put contract.

Instead of exercising, the holder could have simply traded the put contract to someone else. In doing so, he closes out his interest in the contract prior to expiration. Assume that the holder sells this contract to someone else in a closing sale transaction for a $9 premium. What is his net gain or loss? The "T" should show:

OPTION		STOCK
Buy	-$5	
Sell	+$9	
	+$4	

Because the contract was never exercised, there is no transaction in the underlying security (the stock). The option was simply closed out by trading the contract, resulting in a net gain of $4 per share or $400 for the contract.

To summarize the characteristics of buying a put:

LONG PUT		Bearish market direction
Maximum Gain	=	When stock price falls to zero and equals Strike price - Premium
Maximum Loss	=	Premium paid
Breakeven Point	=	Strike price - Premium

2e. SHORT PUT STRATEGY

Writer Has Obligation To Buy At The Strike Price

Assume that a customer sells 1 ABC Jan 50 Put @ $5 when the market price of ABC stock is at $49. The customer has the obligation to buy ABC stock at $50 during the life of the option, and he receives a premium of $5 per share for this obligation.

Loss Increases As Market Falls With Max. Loss = Strike Price - Premium

If the market falls, the contract will be exercised and the customer will buy the stock for $50. He could then sell the stock in the market for its true value. Since the stock can fall to a value of "0," he has increasing loss as the contract goes further and further "in the money."

Maximum Potential Gain = Premium Received

On the other hand, if the market rises above $50, the contract would not be exercised since it is now "out the money." The contract would expire and the writer will earn the premium received. This represents the maximum potential gain.

Options

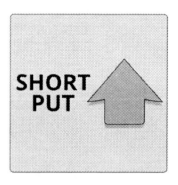

SHORT PUT

Put writer gains when market rises

Breakeven = Strike Price - Premium

To breakeven, the customer has to lose the $5 premium received. He will do this when the market price falls to $45. At this point, the contract is "in the money" by $5, yielding a loss on the stock that exactly offsets the premium received.

For example, a customer sells 1 ABC Jul 60 Put @ $5 when the market price of ABC is $59. What is the maximum potential gain? What is the maximum potential loss? What is the breakeven point?

To handle this problem, we set up the "T."

OPTION	STOCK
Sell +$5	

The customer receives a $5 per share premium, so this is placed on the "option" side of the "T." If nothing else happens, the contract expires, and he earns the $5 premium for a $500 maximum gain.

The next step to find both maximum potential loss and breakeven is to assume that the option has been "exercised." If this occurs, the customer buys the stock at the strike price. The "T" now shows:

OPTION	STOCK	
Sell +$5	Buy -$60	Breakeven = $55

If the customer is exercised, he pays $60 to buy the stock, offset by the premium received of $5. To breakeven, he must sell the stock for $55 in the market. Since the stock can fall to zero, the maximum loss occurs at this point. At a value of "0," the loss as shown on the "T" is:

OPTION		STOCK		
Sell	+$5	Buy	-$60	Breakeven = $55
		Sell	+$0	
	+$5		-$60	Net Loss = $55

The maximum loss is $55 per share or $5,500 for the contract. This assumes the customer sells the stock for "nothing" in the market. Because the writer is exposed to substantial risk, he is termed a "naked" put writer.

Assume that the stock has fallen to $45 and is sold in the market. The customer's position now shows:

OPTION		STOCK		
Sell	+$5	Buy	-$60	Breakeven = $55
		Sell	+$45	
	+$5		-$15	Net Loss = $10

On the stock, the customer loses $15 per share, offset by the $5 premium received. The net loss is $10 per share or $1,000 on the hundred shares covered by the put contract.

Instead of being exercised, the customer could have simply traded the put contract to someone else. In doing so, he closes out his interest in the contract prior to expiration. Assume that the customer buys in this contract in a closing purchase transaction for a $9 premium. What is his net gain or loss? The "T" should show:

OPTION		STOCK
Sell	+$5	
Buy	-$9	
	-$4	

Because the contract was never exercised, there is no transaction in the underlying security (the stock). The option was simply closed out by trading the contract, resulting in a net loss of $4 per share or $400 for the contract.

To summarize the characteristics of selling a put:

SHORT NAKED PUT		Bullish market direction
Maximum Gain	=	Premium
Maximum Loss	=	When stock price falls to zero and equals Strike price - Premium
Breakeven Point	=	Strike price - Premium

Below is a chart that summarizes the 4 "Speculative" Options Strategies. This chart must be memorized for the exam. We recommend that when you go into the test, you write this chart on the paper or small whiteboard provided, so you have it for reference during the test. Also note that we will be adding more content to the chart throughout this chapter.

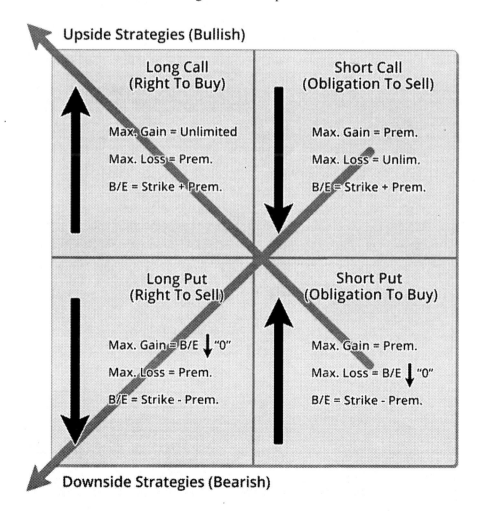

Upside Strategies (Bullish)

Long Call (Right To Buy)
Max. Gain = Unlimited
Max. Loss = Prem.
B/E = Strike + Prem.

Short Call (Obligation To Sell)
Max. Gain = Prem.
Max. Loss = Unlim.
B/E = Strike + Prem.

Long Put (Right To Sell)
Max. Gain = B/E ↓ "0"
Max. Loss = Prem.
B/E = Strike - Prem.

Short Put (Obligation To Buy)
Max. Gain = Prem.
Max. Loss = B/E ↓ "0"
B/E = Strike - Prem.

Downside Strategies (Bearish)

SPECULATIVE STRATEGIES
SECTION EXAMINATION

1.

A customer buys 1 ABC Jan 35 Call @ $3 when the market price of ABC is at $34. ABC goes to $42 and the customer exercises the call and sells the stock at the market. The customer has a:

   a. $200 gain
   b. $300 gain
   c. $400 gain
   d. $700 gain

2.

The purchase of a call is a:

   a.   bull strategy
   b.   bear strategy
   c.   neutral strategy
   d.   bear/neutral strategy

3.

In November, a customer buys 1 ABC Jan 70 Call @ $4 when the market price of ABC is 71. If ABC falls to $67 and stays there through January, the customer will:

   a.   gain $400
   b.   lose $400
   c.   gain $6,700
   d.   lose $6,700

4.

In November, a customer buys 1 ABC Jan 70 Call @ $4 when the market price of ABC is $71. The breakeven point for the position is:

   a. $66
   b. $67
   c. $74
   d. $75

5.

In November, a customer buys 1 ABC Jan 70 Call @ $4 when the market price of ABC is 71. The customer's maximum potential gain is:

   a. $400
   b. $6,600
   c. $7,400
   d.   unlimited

6.

In November, a customer buys 1 ABC Jan 70 Call @ $4 when the market price of ABC is $71. If the customer closes out the position prior to expiration by selling the call at $10, the gain or loss is?

   a. $400 gain
   b. $400 loss
   c. $600 gain
   d. $1,000 gain

7.

A customer sells 1 ABC Feb 50 Call @ $7 when the market price of ABC is $52. If the market value of ABC falls to $48 and stays there through February, the customer will:

   a.   gain $700
   b.   lose $700
   c.   gain $4,300
   d.   lose $4,300

8.

A customer sells 1 ABC Feb 50 Call @ $7 when the market price of ABC is $52. The customer's breakeven point is:

   a. $43
   b. $45
   c. $57
   d. $59

Options

9.

A customer sells 1 ABC Feb 50 Call @ $7 when the market price of ABC is 52. The customer's maximum potential loss is:

   a. $700
   b. $4,300
   c. $5,700
   d.   unlimited

10.

A customer sells 1 ABC Feb 50 Call @ $7 when the market price of ABC is $52. The stock moves to $80 and the customer is assigned. The stock is bought in the market for delivery. The gain or loss to the writer is:

   a. $700 gain
   b. $700 loss
   c. $2,300 loss
   d. $3,000 loss

11.

A customer sells 2 ABC Jan 60 Puts @ $4 when the market price of ABC is $59. If ABC stock rises to $62 and the customer closes the positions at $1, the gain or loss is:

   a. $600 gain
   b. $600 loss
   c. $700 gain
   d. $1,000 loss

12.

A customer buys 2 ABC Jan 60 Puts @ $4 when the market price of ABC is $59. The maximum potential loss for the customer is:

   a. $400
   b. $800
   c. $11,200
   d. $12,000

13.

A customer buys 2 ABC Jan 60 Puts @ $4 when the market price of ABC is $59. The breakeven point is:

   a. $52
   b. $56
   c. $64
   d. $68

14.

A customer buys 2 ABC Jan 60 Puts @ $4 when the market price of ABC is $59. ABC stock falls to $40 and the customer buys the stock in the market and exercises the puts. The gain is:

   a. $800
   b. $1,600
   c. $3,200
   d. $4,000

15.

A customer buys 2 ABC Jan 60 Puts @ $4 when the market price of ABC is $59. If ABC stock rises to $62 and the customer closes the positions at $1, the gain or loss is:

   a. $300 loss
   b. $600 loss
   c. $700 gain
   d. $1,000 loss

16.

A customer sells 1 ABC Jul 40 Put at $6 when the market price of ABC is $38. ABC stock rises to $60 and stays there through July. The customer:

   a.   gains $600
   b.   loses $600
   c.   gains $1,400
   d.   loses $1,400

17.

A customer sells 1 ABC Jul 40 Put at $6 when the market price of ABC is $38. The customer's maximum potential gain is:

a. $600
b. $3,400
c. $4,000
d. unlimited

18.

A customer sells 1 ABC Jul 40 Put at $6 when the market price of ABC is $38. The breakeven point is:

a. $32
b. $34
c. $44
d. $46

19.

A customer sells 1 ABC Jul 40 Put at $6 when the market price of ABC is $38. The market falls to $25 and the customer is assigned. The customer then sells the stock in the market. The loss is:

a. $600
b. $900
c. $1,500
d. $2,500

20.

A customer sells 1 ABC Jul 40 Put at $6 when the market price of ABC is $38. The maximum potential loss to the writer is:

a. $600
b. $3,400
c. $4,000
d. unlimited

SPECULATIVE STRATEGIES EXAMINATION EXPLANATIONS

1. The best answer is **c**. The customer buys the stock at $35 through the exercise of the call; and sells position in the market at $42 for a $7 point gain per share. However, since $3 per share was paid in premiums, the net gain is $4 per share, or $400 for the contract covering 100 shares.

2. The best answer is **a**. The buyer of a call has the right to buy stock at a fixed price in a rising market. The buyer has unlimited gain potential as the market rises, so this is a bull market strategy.

3. The best answer is **b**. The holder of a call pays the premium for the contract. This is the maximum loss if the contract expires "out the money."

4. The best answer is **c**. The holder of a call breaks even if the market price rises by enough to recover the premium paid. The holder paid $4 for the right to buy stock at $70. The effective cost if he exercises is $74. He must be able to sell the stock for $74 to breakeven. To summarize, the formula for breakeven on a long call is:

> **Long Call Breakeven = Strike Price + Premium**

5. The best answer is **d**. The holder of a call has unlimited gain potential. He or she has the right to buy stock at a fixed price - and the stock can rise an unlimited amount.

6. The best answer is **c**. The customer bought the call (opening purchase) for a $4 premium and then closed with a sale of the contract at $10 for a $600 profit (6 points).

7. The best answer is **a**. If the market falls to $48, the 50 call expires "out the money" and the writer keeps the $700 premium.

8. The best answer is **c**. The writer received $7 and obligated him- or herself to deliver stock he or she does not own for $50 per share. If exercised, the writer receives $50 for selling + the writer already received the $7 premium for a total of $57 collected. If the writer buys the stock for delivery at this price, the writer breaks even. To summarize, the formula for breakeven on a short call is:

> **Short Call Breakeven = Strike Price + Premium**

9. The best answer is **d**. The writer of a naked call is obligated to deliver stock that he does not own. If exercised, the stock must be bought in the market for delivery. Since the market price can rise an unlimited amount, the maximum potential loss is unlimited as well.

10. The best answer is **c**. A call writer, when exercised, is obligated to deliver stock at $50 per share. He must buy the stock at $80 in the market losing 30 points. Since $700 (7 points) was collected in premiums, the net loss is 23 points or $2,300.

11. The best answer is **a**. The puts were sold in an opening sale at $4 and bought in a closing purchase at $1 for a gain of 3 points ($300 per contract). Since 2 contracts are involved, the net gain is $600.

12. The best answer is **b**. The holder of a put buys the right to sell at a fixed price. If the contract expires "out the money," the maximum loss is the premium paid. $400 was paid per contract ($800 for 2 contracts), so $800 is the maximum potential loss. This occurs if the market price rises above the strike price.

13. The best answer is **b**. The holder of the put paid a $4 premium per share for the right to sell ABC stock at $60. The customer's net sale proceeds upon exercise equals $56 per share. To breakeven, the customer must buy the stock in the market at this price. To summarize, the formula for breakeven on a long put is:

Long Put Breakeven = Strike Price - Premium

14. The best answer is **c**. The customer buys the stock for $40, and exercises the put to sell at $60 for a 20 point profit. Since 4 points were paid in premiums, the net profit per contract is 16 points or $1,600. The profit on 2 contracts is $3,200.

15. The best answer is **b**. Each put was bought in an opening purchase at $4 and sold in a closing sale at $1 for a loss of 3 points ($300 per contract). Since 2 contracts are involved, the net loss is $600.

16. The best answer is **a**. If the market rises to $60, the put expires "out the money" (since the strike price is $40). The writer keeps the $600 collected in premiums.

17. The best answer is **a**. The maximum gain for the writer of a naked call or put is the premium collected. This happens if the contract expires "out the money."

18. The best answer is **b**. The writer collected $6 in premiums by obligating him- or herself to buy the stock at $40. If exercised, the customer's net outlay is $34 for the stock. To breakeven, he or she must be able to sell the position for $34. To summarize, the formula for breakeven on a short put is:

Short Put Breakeven = Strike Price - Premium

19. The best answer is **b**. When exercised, the writer must buy the stock for $40. He then sells the stock at $25 for a 15 point loss. Since 6 points was collected as premiums, the net loss is 9 points or $900.

20. The best answer is **b**. The worst case for the writer of a put is being exercised and being forced to buy worthless stock at the strike price. In this case, the put writer agrees to buy the stock at $40, but collected $6 of premiums, for a net outlay of $34. If the stock is worthless, this is the maximum loss per share ($3,400 for the contract).

This page intentionally left blank

SECTION 3: HEDGING STRATEGIES

3a. HEDGING OVERVIEW

Protect A Long Stock Position By Buying A Put

Option contracts can be used to hedge a stock position taken by a customer. If a customer owns stock (has a long stock position), he will lose if the market drops. To hedge against this, he can buy some insurance by purchasing a put option on the stock. If the stock declines, he can exercise the put and sell the stock at the strike price, eliminating the risk of falling stock prices (known as "market risk").

Protect A Short Stock Position By Buying A Call

Conversely, if a customer has taken a short position in a security, he will lose if the market rises. The potential loss is unlimited. To hedge against this, he can buy some insurance by purchasing a call option on the stock. If the stock rises, he can exercise the call and buy the stock at the strike price (to cover the short stock position), eliminating the risk of rising stock prices.

3b. LONG PUT TO HEDGE LONG STOCK POSITION

To Protect A Long Stock Position From A Falling Market

Assume that a customer buys 100 shares of ABC stock at $60 per share. She believes that the stock is a good investment and wishes to hold on to the position. However, she is worried that the market may drop, dragging the stock's price down, and she wants to hedge against this possibility.

If Market Drops, Can Sell Stock At Strike Price

The customer buys 1 ABC Jul 60 Put @ $5 as a hedge. If the stock drops, the customer can always exercise the put and sell the stock for $60, no matter how far the market price falls.

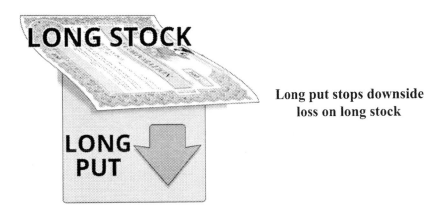

Long put stops downside loss on long stock

If the stock's price rises, she lets the put expire "out the money" and sells the stock in the market at the higher price.

To calculate maximum potential gain, breakeven, and maximum potential loss for this position, again we use the "T." The customer has taken the following positions:

Buy 100 shares of ABC stock @ $60
Buy 1 ABC Jul 60 Put @ $5

The positions are entered into the "T":

OPTION		STOCK	
Buy	-$5	Buy	-$60

Breakeven = Cost Of Stock + Premium Paid

The customer has bought the stock and has bought the put contract. Once the top line of the "T" is completed, we also have found the breakeven point. The customer has paid a total of $65 for both positions. To breakeven, the stock position must now be liquidated for $65. This shows on the "T" as:

OPTION		STOCK		
Buy	-$5	Buy	-$60	Breakeven = $65

Maximum Loss = Premium Paid (Net Of Any Difference Between Stock Cost And Strike Price)

If the market price of the stock falls, the customer is hedged. She will simply exercise the put and sell the stock at the strike price. If she does this, her loss is limited to $500. Assume that the stock's price falls to zero in the market. The customer exercises the put. The "T" now shows:

OPTION		STOCK		
Buy	-$5	Buy	-$60	Breakeven = $65
		Sell	+$60	
	-$5		$0	Net Loss = $5

Because the customer owned the Jul 60 Put, she sold the stock position for $60. She is not exposed to any market loss on the stock during the life of the contract. She did lose her "insurance" premium of $500, however.

If the market price of the stock rises, the put will expire out the money. The customer will sell the stock at the higher market price. Assume that the price of the stock rises to $75 and the customer lets the put expire and sells the stock in the market. The "T" now shows:

OPTION		STOCK		
Buy	-$5	Buy	-$60	Breakeven = $65
		Sell	+$75	
	-$5		+$15	Net Gain = $10

Maximum Potential Gain = Unlimited

The customer makes $15 on the stock offset by the $5 premium paid. The net gain is $10 per share. In a rising market, the customer's potential gain is unlimited. The put would expire worthless and the customer would sell the stock at whatever price the market dictated.

To summarize the characteristics of using a long put to hedge a long stock position:

LONG STOCK / LONG PUT		Hedge to protect stock in falling market
Maximum Gain	=	Unlimited
Maximum Loss	=	Premium (offset by difference between Stock cost and Put strike price)
Breakeven Point	=	Stock cost + Premium

3c. LONG CALL TO HEDGE SHORT STOCK POSITION

To Protect A Short Stock Position From A Rising Market

Assume that a customer sells short 100 shares of ABC stock at $60 per share. She believes that the stock will fall and is speculating by taking this position. However, she is concerned that the market may rise, forcing her to cover (buy in) at a large loss and she wants to hedge against this possibility.

If Market Rises, Can Buy Stock At Strike Price To Cover

The customer buys 1 ABC Jul 60 Call @ $5 as a hedge. If the stock rises, the customer can always exercise the call and buy the stock for $60, no matter how far the market price rises.

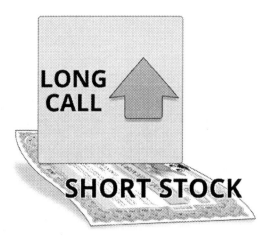

Long call stops upside loss on short stock

If the stock's price falls, she lets the call expire "out the money" and buys the stock in the market at the lower price to cover the short stock position at a profit.

To calculate maximum potential loss, breakeven, and maximum potential gain for this position, again we use the "T." The customer has taken the following positions:

Sell short 100 shares of ABC stock @ $60
Buy 1 ABC Jul 60 Call @ $5

The positions are entered into the "T" as follows:

OPTION		STOCK	
Buy	-$5	Sell	+$60

Breakeven = Sale Price Of Stock - Premium Paid

The customer has sold short the stock and has bought the call contract. Once the top line of the "T" is completed, we also have found the breakeven point. The customer has received a net amount of $55 for both positions. To breakeven, the stock position must now be bought in for $55. This shows on the "T" as:

OPTION		STOCK		
Buy	-$5	Sell	+$60	Breakeven = $55

Maximum Loss = Premium (Net Of Any Difference Between The Short Sale Price And The Call Strike Price)

If the market price of the stock rises, the customer is hedged. She will simply exercise the call and buy the stock at the strike price to cover the short stock position. If she does this, her loss is limited to $500. Assume that the stock's price rises to $100 in the market. The customer exercises the call. The "T" now shows

OPTION		STOCK		
Buy	-$5	Sell	+$60	Breakeven = $55
		Buy	-$60	
	-$5		$0	Net Loss = $5

Because the customer owned the Jul 60 Call, she bought the stock position for $60. She is not exposed to any market loss on the stock during the life of the contract. She did lose her "insurance" premium of $500, however.

If the market price of the stock falls, the call will expire out the money. The customer will buy the stock at the lower market price. Assume that the price of the stock falls to zero and the customer lets the call expire and buys the stock in the market. The "T" now shows:

OPTION		STOCK		
Buy	-$5	Sell	+$60	Breakeven = $55
		Buy	$0	
	-$5		+60	Net Gain = $55

Maximum Gain = Short Sale Price - Premium

The customer makes $60 on the stock offset by the $5 premium paid. The net gain is $55 per share. This is the customer's maximum potential gain.

To summarize the characteristics of using a long call to hedge a short stock position:

Options

SHORT STOCK / LONG CALL		Hedge to protect stock in rising market
Maximum Gain	=	Short sale price - Premium paid
Maximum Loss	=	Premium (offset by difference between Short sale price and Call strike price)
Breakeven Point	=	Stock sale price - Premium paid

3d. ADVANCED UNDERSTANDING

(Note: This section is not critical for passing the options portion of the exam, but many students find that once they understand this, options questions on hedging strategies are much easier to answer.)

When a customer buys stock and buys a put on that stock, the customer has created a position that has the following characteristics:

Unlimited Upside Gain Potential (from the stock);

Limited Downside Loss (since the stock can be sold at the put strike price).

These characteristics are no different than simply buying a call, which gives unlimited upside gain potential, and gives limited loss (equal to the premium paid) if the market should fall.

Long Stock / Long Put Is Really The Same As A Long Call

For example, if one:

Buys 100 shares of ABC stock at $50; and
Buys 1 ABC Jan 50 Put @ $5; or

Buys 1 ABC Jan 50 Call @ $5;

they both have the same gain potential (unlimited) and the same loss potential ($500). Thus, an equivalent strategy to buying stock and buying a protective put on that stock is to simply buy a call! From the standpoint of the "T" account:

Long Call Exercised		Long Stock / Long Put	
OPTION	STOCK	OPTION	STOCK
—	—	—	—
"Minus" because call premium was paid	*"Minus"* because stock is purchased on exercise	*"Minus"* because put premium was paid	*"Minus"* because stock was purchased

These strategies, from a math standpoint, are "Minus - Minus" strategies.

When a customer shorts stock and buys a call on that stock position, the customer creates a position that has the following characteristics:

Downside Gain Potential To "0" (from the stock);

Limited Upside Loss (since the stock can be purchased at the call strike price).

These characteristics are no different than simply buying a put, which gives gain potential all the way down to "0" and gives limited loss (equal to the premium paid) if the market should rise.

Short Stock / Long Call Is Really The Same As A Long Put

For example, if one:

Sells short 100 shares of ABC stock at $50; and
Buys 1 ABC Jan 50 Call @ $5; or

Buys 1 ABC Jan 50 Put @ $5;

they both have the same gain potential ($4,500) and the same loss potential ($500). Thus, an equivalent strategy to shorting stock and buying a protective call on that stock is to buy a put! From the standpoint of the "T" account:

Long Put Exercised		Short Stock / Long Call	
OPTION	STOCK	OPTION	STOCK
—	+	—	+
"Minus" because put premium was paid	*"Plus"* because stock is sold on exercise	*"Minus"* because call premium was paid	*"Plus"* because stock was sold

These strategies, from a math standpoint, are "Minus - Plus" strategies. Now let's add these to our options chart:

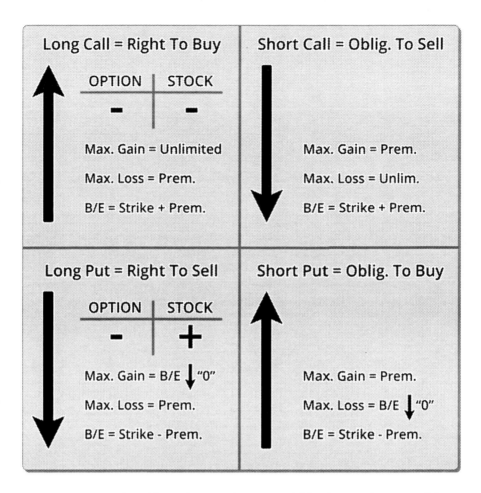

Now, if you have written down this chart at the start of the exam, here is how it is useful.

Sample Question: A customer buys 100 shares of ABC stock at $50 and buys 1 ABC Jan 50 Put @ $5 on the same day. What is the maximum potential gain?

Because the customer paid the premium and paid for the stock, this is a "Minus-Minus" strategy.

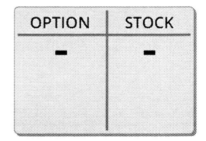

It makes no difference how a "Minus-Minus" strategy is created. You can do it by buying the stock and buying a put on that stock; or you can simply buy a call. From the options chart, you know that any "Minus-Minus" strategy has unlimited gain potential. This is the answer.

Sample Question: A customer sells short 100 shares of ABC stock at $50 and buys 1 ABC Jan 50 Call @ $5 on the same day. What is the maximum potential gain?

Because the customer paid the premium and sold for the stock, this is a "Minus-Plus" strategy.

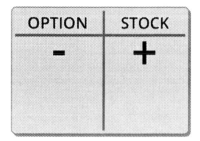

It makes no difference how a "Minus-Plus" strategy is created. You can do it by shorting the stock and buying a call on that stock; or you can simply buy a put. From the options chart, you know that any "Minus-Plus" strategy has a maximum gain of Breakeven down to "0." Because the customer sold the stock short at $50, it must drop to $45 (the amount of premium paid) to give 5 point offsetting gain. This is the breakeven. If the stock continues to drop, the customer gains all the way from $45 down to "0" - so the maximum gain is $4,500.

Sample Question: A customer buys 100 shares of ABC stock at $50 and buys 1 ABC Jan 50 Put @ $5 on the same day. What is the maximum potential loss?

Because the customer paid the premium and paid for the stock, this is a "Minus-Minus" strategy.

OPTION	STOCK
-	-

It makes no difference how a "Minus-Minus" strategy is created. You can do it by buying the stock and buying a put on that stock; or you can simply buy a call. From the options chart, you know that any "Minus-Minus" strategy has maximum loss potential equal to the premium paid = $500. This is the answer. The customer bought the stock at $50; and has the right to sell it at $50 (in a falling market). There is no loss on the stock, however, the premium paid of $500 is lost.

(Note: The only time the chart does not work exactly is if the stock cost and the exercise price are different. If this is the case, the maximum loss will be the premium, offset by any gain or loss on the sale of the stock. This same logic applies to all combinations of stock with an option that are shown in this section and the following section.)

The bottom line is that if you write down the chart at the beginning of the exam (and there is more to come about the chart in the upcoming sections), you have a reference sheet that lays out the basic answers to many potential test questions. In the "stress" of an exam, rather than having to think about each option question without having any frame of reference, the chart provides the information to take you to the correct answer!

HEDGING STRATEGIES SECTION EXAMINATION

1.
Buying a put on a stock position held long is a suitable strategy when the market is expected to:

I   rise sharply
II   fall sharply
III   be stable
IV   be volatile

a.   I and III
b.   I and IV
c.   II and III
d.   II and IV

2.
A customer buys 100 shares of ABC stock at $40 and buys 1 ABC Oct 40 Put @ $4. ABC stock falls to $36 and just prior to expiration, the customer exercises the put, delivering the stock position. The customer:

a.   breaks even
b.   lost $400
c.   gained $400
d.   lost $3600

3.
A customer buys 100 shares of ABC stock at $40 and buys 1 ABC Oct 40 Put @ $4. The breakeven point is:

a. $36
b. $40
c. $44
d. $48

4.
A customer buys 100 shares of XYZ at $49 and buys 1 XYZ Jan 50 Put @ $5. The stock falls to $32 and the customer exercises the put, delivering the long stock position. The customer's gain or loss is:

a. $100 gain
b. $400 loss
c. $500 loss
d. $5,000 gain

5.
A customer buys 100 shares of XYZ at $49 and buys 1 XYZ Jan 50 Put @ $5. The breakeven point is:

a. $44
b. $45
c. $54
d. $55

6.
A customer buys 100 shares of XYZ at $49 and buys 1 XYZ Jan 50 Put @ $5. The maximum potential gain is:

a. $500
b. $4,400
c. $5,500
d.   unlimited

7.
A customer buys 100 shares of XYZ at $49 and buys 1 XYZ Jan 50 Put @ $5. The maximum potential loss is:

a. $400
b. $500
c. $4,400
d.   unlimited

Options

8.
A customer buys 100 shares of XYZ at 49 and buys 1 XYZ Jan 50 Put @ $5. Just prior to expiration, the stock is trading at $49. The customer closes the option position at a premium of $2. One week later, the stock moves to $55 and the customer sells the stock position in the market. The net gain or loss on all transactions is:

a. $300 loss
b. $300 gain
c. $600 loss
d. $600 gain

9.
Which of the following option positions is used to hedge a short stock position?

a. long call
b. short call
c. long put
d. short put

10.
Which of the following option positions is used to hedge a long stock position?

a. long call
b. short call
c. long put
d. short put

11.
A customer sells short 100 shares of ABC stock at 40 and buys 1 ABC Mar 40 Call @ $5. The stock rises to $80 and the customer exercises the call. The gain or loss is:

a. $500 gain
b. $500 loss
c. $3,500 gain
d. $3,500 loss

12.
A customer sells short 100 shares of ABC stock at $40 and buys 1 ABC Mar 40 Call @ $5. The maximum potential loss is:

a. $500
b. $3,500
c. $4,500
d. unlimited

13.
A customer sells short 100 shares of ABC stock at $40 and buys 1 ABC Mar 40 Call @ $5. The maximum potential gain is:

a. $500
b. $3,500
c. $4,500
d. unlimited

14.
A customer sells short 100 shares of ABC stock at $40 and buys 1 ABC Mar 40 Call @ $5. The breakeven point is:

a. $35
b. $40
c. $45
d. $50

15.
On the same day, a customer buys 100 shares of ABC at $40 and sells short 100 shares of XYZ at $50. The customer then buys 1 ABC Jan 40 Put @ $4 and 1 XYZ Jan 50 Call @ $5. XYZ rises to $60 and the customer exercises the call. ABC falls to $25 and the customer exercises the put. The net gain or loss on all transactions is:

a. $500 loss
b. $900 gain
c. $900 loss
d. breakeven

16.

On the same day, a customer buys 100 shares of ABC at $40 and sells short 100 shares of XYZ at $50. The customer then buys 1 ABC Jan 40 Put @ $4 and 1 XYZ Jan 50 Call @ $5. The breakeven points are:

   a.   ABC: $36 / XYZ: $45

   b.   ABC: $44 / XYZ: $45

   c.   ABC: $36 / XYZ: $55

   d.   ABC: $44 / XYZ: $55

17.

A customer sells short 100 shares of PDQ at $58 and buys 1 PDQ Jul 60 Call @ $3. The customer's maximum potential loss is:

   a. $200

   b. $300

   c. $500

   d.   unlimited

18.

A customer sells short 100 shares of PDQ at $58 and buys 1 PDQ Jul 60 Call @ $3. The breakeven point is:

   a. $55

   b. $57

   c. $61

   d. $64

19.

A customer buys 100 shares of XYZ stock at $72.25 and buys 1 XYZ Oct 70 Put @ $.50 on the same day in a cash account. The stock rises to $75.38. The put expires and the customer sells the stock in the market at the current price. The customer has a:

   a. $50 loss

   b. $175 loss

   c. $263 gain

   d. $313 gain

20.

A customer buys 100 shares of ABC at $30 and buys 1 ABC Jan 30 Put @ $5. At which market price is the position profitable?

   a. $25

   b. $30

   c. $35

   d. $40

Options

HEDGING STRATEGIES EXAMINATION EXPLANATIONS

1. The best answer is **d**. Buying a put allows the holder to sell a security at a fixed price. Thus, it protects the owner of the underlying stock position in a falling market.

2. The best answer is **b**. The customer bought the stock at $40 and sold at $40 by exercising the put. There is no gain or loss on the stock position. However, the customer did lose the $400 premium paid.

3. The best answer is **c**. The customer paid $4 for the put and $40 for the stock, for a total of $44. To breakeven, she must sell the stock at $44. To summarize, the formula for breakeven for a long stock / long put position is:

> **Long Stock / Long Put Breakeven = Stock Cost + Premium**

4. The best answer is **b**. The customer bought the stock at $49 and sold at $50 by exercising the long put, for a 1 point gain. Since 5 points were paid in premiums, the customer lost 4 points or $400.

5. The best answer is **c**. The customer paid $5 for the put and $49 for the stock, for a total outlay of $54. To breakeven, she must be able to sell the stock at $54. To summarize, the formula for breakeven for a long stock / long put position is:

> **Long Stock / Long Put Breakeven = Stock Cost + Premium**

6. The best answer is **d**. Since the customer has a long stock position, his potential gain is unlimited. If the market moves up, he or she lets the put expire "out the money" and sells the stock in the market at the higher price.

7. The best answer is **a**. The long put gives the stock owner the right to sell at $50. Since he bought the stock at $49, exercising results in a 1 point stock profit. However, the premiums paid of $5 are lost, for a net loss of 4 points or $400 maximum.

8. The best answer is **b**. The put contract was purchased at $5 and closed (sold) at $2 for a net loss of $3. The stock was purchased at $49 and sold at $55 for a net gain of $6. The net of all transactions is a 3 point or $300 gain.

9. The best answer is **a**. When one has a short stock position, borrowed shares have been sold with the agreement that the customer will buy back the position at a later date. If the market rises, the loss potential is unlimited. The purchase of a call allows the stock to be bought in at a fixed price, limiting upside risk.

10. The best answer is **c**. Buying a put allows the owner of stock to sell it a fixed price (strike price) if the market falls. This limits downside risk on the long stock position.

11. The best answer is **b**. If the market rises, the customer can exercise the call and buy the stock at $40. These shares can be used to replace the "borrowed" shares sold short at $40. On the stock, there is no gain or loss. However, the customer loses the $500 paid in premiums.

12. The best answer is **a**. The long call limits loss on the short stock position in a rising market. The stock was sold for $40 and can be bought back at $40 by exercising the call. The only loss to the customer is the premium paid of 5 points or $500.

13. The best answer is **b**. If the stock falls, the customer gains on the short stock position. The customer sold the stock for $40. If it falls to "0," the customer can buy the shares for "nothing" to replace the borrowed shares sold and make 40 points. The customer lets the call expire "out the money" losing 5 points, so the maximum potential gain is 35 points = $3,500.

14. The best answer is **a**. The customer sold the stock at $40 and paid $5 for the call, receiving a net amount of $35 per share. To breakeven, he must be able to buy the stock at $35 per share (to cover the short stock position). To summarize, the formula for breakeven for a short stock / long call position is:

> **Short Stock / Long Call Breakeven = Short Sale Price - Premium**

15. The best answer is **c**. When XYZ rises, the customer exercises the long call to buy XYZ at $50. This stock is used to cover the short sale of XYZ stock at $50. There is no gain or loss on the stock but the premiums paid of $500 for the call are lost. When ABC falls, the customer exercises the long put to sell ABC at $40. Since the customer bought the stock at $40, there is no gain or loss on the stock. However, the customer does lose the $400 paid in premiums for the put. The total loss is $900.

16. The best answer is **b**. The customer paid $4 for the ABC put and $40 for ABC stock, for a total of $44. This is the breakeven on ABC stock. The customer sold XYZ stock short for $50, but paid $5 for the XYZ call, for a net receipt of $45. He or she must buy back XYZ at this price to break even. To summarize, the breakeven formulas for long stock / long put and short stock / long call positions are:

> **Long Stock / Long Put Breakeven = Stock Cost + Premium**

> **Short Stock / Long Call Breakeven = Short Sale Price - Premium**

17. The best answer is **c**. The long call allows the customer to buy in the stock position at $60. Since the stock was sold at $58, exercise results in a net loss of $2 on the stock. The customer paid $3 for the call, so the total loss is $500.

18. The best answer is **a**. The customer sold the stock for $58 and paid $3 in premiums for the long call, for a net receipt of $55. To breakeven, the customer must buy back the stock position at this price. To summarize, the formula for breakeven for a short stock / long call position is:

> **Short Stock / Long Call Breakeven = Short Sale Price - Premium**

19. The best answer is **c**. The customer buys the put for .50 and buys the stock at $72.25 for a total outlay of $72.75 per share. The put has been purchased as protection if the stock price should fall. In this case, the stock price rises to $75.38, so the customer lets the put expire "out the money" and sells the stock in the market at the current price. The net gain is $75.38 - $72.75 = $2.63 or $263 on 100 shares.

20. The best answer is **d**. To breakeven, the customer must recover the $5 paid in premiums and the $30 paid for the stock (total of $35). He must sell the stock in the market above $35 to have a profit. The only choice

above $35 is Choice **D**, which is $40. To summarize, the formula for breakeven for a long stock / long put position is:

> **Long Stock / Long Put Breakeven = Stock Cost + Premium**

SECTION 4: INCOME STRATEGIES

4a. INCOME STRATEGIES OVERVIEW

Sell Contracts To Earn Premiums

"Covered Writer" Has The Underlying Security Position

Income strategies involve selling (writing) option positions against an established stock position. The premium received from selling the option enhances the yield from the underlying security. If the option is exercised, the existing stock position is used to satisfy the exercise notice. Because the writer is not exposed to the risk of going to the market to satisfy an exercise notice, the writer is covered against market risk on the short option contracts. Hence, these are called "covered" writing strategies.

The overriding factor needed to understand income strategies is that the stock position comes first and foremost. While writing the option gives extra income from the stock position, any gain or loss is also derived from the stock position.

Suitable In Stable Markets

Income strategies are used during periods when the market is expected to be stable. They are not suitable in a rising market; nor are they suitable in a falling market.

Long Stock

Short Call

The first income strategy is to sell a call option against a long stock position. Assume a customer owns 100 shares of ABC stock purchased at $50 and he writes 1 ABC Jan 50 Call @ $5. If the market stays at $50, the call expires "at the money" and the $5 premium is earned with no loss in value of the stock.

Write calls against long stock for income

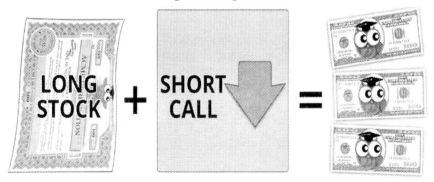

If the market rises, however, he will be exercised and will have to deliver the stock at $50. He does not enjoy the market appreciation of the stock since he "sells" at the same price he paid for the stock ($50). He only earns the premium of $5 per share. Conversely, if the market falls, the call expires and he keeps the stock position. In a falling market, he can lose all of the stock's value.

Short Stock

Short Put

The second income strategy is to sell a put option against a short stock position. Assume a customer has sold short 100 shares of ABC stock at $50 and he writes 1 ABC Jan 50 Put @ $5. If the market stays at $50, the put will expire "at the money" and he earns the $5 premium with no loss from the stock position.

Write puts against short stock for income

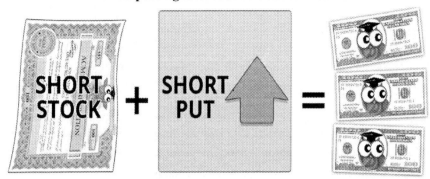

If the market falls, however, he will be exercised and will have to buy the stock at $50. He does not enjoy the gain on the short stock position since he "buys" at the same price he sold the stock for ($50). He only earns the premium of $5 per share. Conversely, if the market rises, the put expires and he keeps the stock position. In a rising market, he can lose a theoretically infinite amount.

These two income strategies are now covered more completely.

4b. WRITING CALLS AGAINST LONG STOCK POSITIONS

Assume that a customer buys 100 shares of XXX stock at $70 because it is a solid corporation paying a high dividend rate (let us say $5 per year). The customer expects that, over the long term, the stock will appreciate. But for the short term he expects the price to be stable. In order to enhance his return, he writes 1 XXX Jul 70 Call @ $5.

The customer's position now is:

> Long 100 shares of XXX stock @ $70
> Short 1 XXX Jul 70 Call @ $5

If the stock rises, the call will be exercised and he will deliver the stock for the $70 strike price, keeping the $5 premium. If the stock falls, the call expires and he keeps the stock position, losing money every step of the way as the stock drops.

To find the maximum potential gain, breakeven, and maximum potential loss, we use the "T." We start off by inserting the existing positions into the "T":

OPTION	STOCK
Sell +$5	Buy -$70

Breakeven = Cost Of Stock - Premium Received

The short call position and long stock position now show. The customer has paid out a net amount of $65 for the stock. If he liquidates the stock position for this price, he breaks even. (We also know that the first line of the "T" always gives the breakeven point.)

OPTION	STOCK	
Sell +$5	Buy -$70	Breakeven = $65

If the market rises, the call will be exercised and the customer is obligated to deliver 100 shares of XXX for $70 per share. Assume that the market rises to $100 and the customer is exercised. The "T" shows:

OPTION	STOCK	
Sell +$5	Buy -$70	Breakeven = $65
	Sell +$70	
+$5	+$0	Net Gain = $5

Maximum Gain = Premium Received (Net Of Difference Between Stock Cost And Strike Price)

There is no gain on the stock. The customer agreed to sell the stock for $70 if he was exercised. He gave up all potential gain on the stock for the $5 premium. This represents his maximum potential gain while he has both the stock and short call positions.

On the other hand, if the market falls, the call will expire "out the money." The customer will be free to sell his stock in the market. Assume that XXX goes bankrupt and the stock falls to zero. The customer's loss is:

OPTION		STOCK		
Sell	+$5	Buy	-$70	Breakeven = $65
		Sell	+$0	
	+$5		-$70	Net Loss = $65

Maximum Potential Loss = Cost Of Stock - Premium Received

The customer loses the full value of the stock net of the premium collected. The maximum loss for the customer is $65 per share or $6,500. Obviously, this is not an appropriate strategy in a falling market. Simply sell the stock!

Sale Of "Out The Money" Covered Calls Is Used In A Rising Market

The prior example shows how the sale of covered calls against long stock positions is profitable in a stable market. This strategy can also be employed in a slightly different fashion, if an individual believes that the market will rise. In this case, the individual can sell "out of the money contracts" against the long stock position. If the market rises, as long as the increase in price is not too steep, the contracts will remain "out the money" and will expire, earning the premium for the writer.

> For example, a customer owns 100 shares of XXX stock, valued at $70. She believes that the market price will rise, but does not expect the price to increase beyond $80 per share. The customer sells 1 XXX Jul 80 Call @ $2. Note that this contract is 10 points "out the money."

> If the market rises, XXX's price must increase above $80 for the call to be exercised. If the price increases to $79 at expiration, the call would expire and the customer earns the premium income.

Lower Premiums Earned; Lower Risk Of Exercise

Please note that premiums earned with this version of the strategy are lower, since the contracts are "out the money" when they are written. Conversely, the risk of exercise is also reduced, since the market price must rise sharply for the call contracts to move "in the money."

To summarize the characteristics of covered call writing:

LONG STOCK / SHORT CALL		Income strategy in a flat market; Income strategy in a rising market if out the money contracts are sold
Maximum Gain	=	Premium offset by difference between Stock purchase price and Call strike price
Maximum Loss	=	Occurs if the market price of the stock falls to zero and equals the Stock cost - Premium
Breakeven Point	=	Stock cost - Premium

4c. WRITING PUTS AGAINST SHORT STOCK POSITIONS

This income strategy is not very popular for reasons that will become obvious as we work through an example. Assume that a customer believes that the price of XXX stock will decline over the longer term, and has sold short 100 shares of XXX at $70 to profit from this expectation.

However, for the next few months, he does not expect the price to drop. To generate some income during this interim period, he sells 1 XXX Jul 70 Put @ $5. If the price stays at $70 over the next few months, as expected, the put will expire and the customer can buy back the stock at $70 to cover the short position. He earns the $5 premium as extra income.

The customer's original position is:

Sell Short 100 Shares of XXX @ $70
Sell 1 XXX Jul 70 Put @ $5

If the stock rises, the put expires "out the money" and the customer loses all the way up on the short stock position. Conversely, if the market falls, the put is exercised and the customer must buy the stock for $70. Since he sold the stock for $70, his gain is limited to the premium collected.

To find the maximum potential gain, breakeven, and maximum potential loss, we again use the "T."

OPTION		STOCK	
Sell	+$5	Sell	+$70

Breakeven = Sale Price Of Stock + Premium

The "T" shows the short put position as well as the short stock position. The customer has received a total of $75. In order to breakeven, he would have to buy in the stock position at $75. This shows on the "T" as:

OPTION		STOCK		
Sell	+$5	Sell	+$70	Breakeven = $75

If the market falls, the put will be exercised since it is "in the money" and the customer will be obligated to buy the stock at $70. These shares are used to cover the short stock position. The "T" now shows:

OPTION		STOCK		
Sell	+$5	Sell	+$70	Breakeven = $75
		Buy	-$70	
	+$5		+$0	Net Gain = $5

Maximum Gain = Premium Received (Net Of Difference Between Stock Sale Price And Cost)

The customer only gains the $5 premium. All potential profit on the short stock position was "sold off" for the premium collected by selling the put. This is the maximum potential gain while the customer has both the short put and short stock position.

Maximum Potential Loss - Unlimited On The Short Stock Position

If the market rises, the put will expire "out the money." The customer is left with a short stock position in a rising market. Since he has to buy back the stock to cover this position, his potential loss is unlimited. Assume that the stock rises to $100 and the customer closes out the short stock position by buying the stock. The "T" shows:

OPTION		STOCK		
Sell	+$5	Sell	+$70	Breakeven = $75
		Buy	-$100	
	+$5		-$30	Net Loss = $25

The loss of $30 on the stock position is partially offset by the $5 premium received. From this example it becomes clear why this strategy is not popular - one gets unlimited risk on the upside and the gain is limited to the premium on the downside. The put writer is covered against risk on the option, but he has unlimited risk on the stock position.

To summarize the characteristics of a covered put writer:

SHORT STOCK / SHORT PUT		Income strategy in a flat market; Income strategy in a falling market if out the money contracts are sold
Maximum Gain	=	Premium offset by difference between Stock sale price and Put strike price
Maximum Loss	=	Occurs if the market price of the stock rises and is therefore Unlimited
Breakeven Point	=	Stock sale price + Premium

4d. ADVANCED UNDERSTANDING

(Note: This section is not critical for passing the options portion of the exam, but many students find that once they understand this, options questions on income strategies are much easier to answer.)

When a customer buys stock and sells a call on that stock position, the customer creates a position that has the following characteristics:

> Limited Upside Gain Potential (if the market rises, the stock is called away and only the premium is earned);

> Downside Loss Potential To "0" (from the stock);

Long Stock / Short Call Is Really The Same As A Short Put

These characteristics are no different than simply selling a put, which gives limited upside gain potential equal to the premium received, and gives downside loss all the way to "0" (because, if the short put is exercised, the stock is purchased at the strike price and it could be worthless).

For example if one:

> Buys 100 shares of ABC stock at $50;

> Sells 1 ABC Jan 50 Call @ $5; or

> Sells 1 ABC Jan 50 Put @ $5;

> they both have the same gain potential ($500) and the same loss potential ($4,500).

Thus, an equivalent strategy to buying stock and selling a call on that stock is to simply sell a put! From the standpoint of the "T" account:

Short Put Exercised		Long Stock / Short Call	
OPTION	STOCK	OPTION	STOCK
+	**–**	**+**	**–**
"Plus" because put premium was received	*"Minus"* because stock is purchased on exercise	*"Plus"* because call premium was received	*"Minus"* because stock was purchased

These strategies, from a math standpoint, are "Plus - Minus" strategies.

When a customer shorts stock and sells a put on that stock position, the customer creates a position that has the following characteristics:

Limited Downside Gain Potential To "0" (if the market falls, short put is exercised, forcing the customer to buy the stock - and this long stock is used to cover the short stock position. Only the premium is earned);

Unlimited Upside Loss (if the market rises, the short put expires, leaving the customer with a short stock position).

Short Stock / Short Put Is Really The Same As A Short Call

These characteristics are no different than simply selling a call, which gives gain potential equal to the collected premium in a falling market and gives unlimited loss if the market should rise. For example, if one:

Sells short 100 shares of ABC stock at $50; and

Sells 1 ABC Jan 50 Put @ $5; or

Sells 1 ABC Jan 50 Call @ $5;

they both have the same gain potential ($500) and the same loss potential (unlimited).

Thus, an equivalent strategy to shorting stock and selling a put on that stock is to simply sell a call! From the standpoint of the "T" account:

Short Call Exercised		Short Stock / Short Put	
OPTION	STOCK	OPTION	STOCK
+	**+**	**+**	**+**
"Plus" because call premium was received	*"Plus"* because stock is sold on exercise	*"Plus"* because put premium was received	*"Plus"* because stock was sold

These strategies, from a math standpoint, are "Plus - Plus" strategies.

Now let's add these to our options chart:

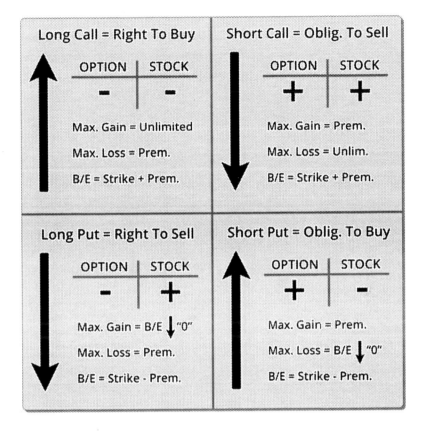

Now, if you have written down this chart at the start of the exam, here is how it is useful.

Sample Question: A customer buys 100 shares of ABC stock at $50 and sells 1 ABC Jan 50 Call @ $5 on the same day. What is the maximum potential gain?

Because the customer received the premium and paid for the stock, this is a "Plus-Minus" strategy.

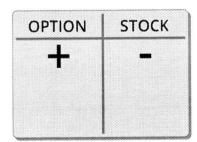

It makes no difference how a "Plus-Minus" strategy is created. You can do it by buying the stock and selling a call on that stock; or you can simply sell a put. From the options chart, you know that any "Plus-Minus" strategy has a maximum gain equal to the premium. This is the answer. The customer bought the stock at $50; and is obligated to sell it at $50 (in a rising market). There is no gain or loss on the stock, however, the premium received of $500 is earned.

(Note: The only time the chart does not work exactly is if the stock cost and the exercise price are different. If this is the case, the maximum gain will be the premium, offset by any gain or loss on the sale of the stock. This same logic applies to all combinations of stock with an option. As long as you know that whenever the chart tells you that the "premium" is the answer - watch out and account for any difference in stock cost and exercise price.)

Sample Question: A customer sells short 100 shares of ABC stock at $50 and sells 1 ABC Jan 50 Put @ $5 on the same day. What is the maximum potential loss?

Because the customer received the premium and sold the stock, this is a "Plus-Plus" strategy.

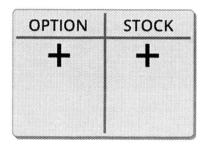

It makes no difference how a "Plus-Plus" strategy is created. You can do it by shorting the stock and shorting a put on that stock; or you can simply sell a call. From the options chart, you know that any "Plus-Plus" strategy has unlimited loss potential.

Sample Question: A customer shorts 100 shares of ABC stock at $61 and sells 1 ABC Jan 60 Put @ $4 on the same day. What is the maximum potential gain?

Because the customer received the premium and sold the stock, this is a "Plus-Plus" strategy.

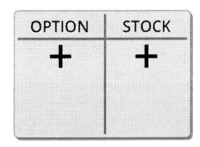

It makes no difference how a "Plus-Plus" strategy is created. You can do it by shorting the stock and selling a put on that stock; or you can simply short a call. From the options chart, you know that any "Plus-Plus" strategy has gain potential equal to the premium received = $400. However, watch out, because the stock was sold at $61, and the exercise of the put obligates the customer to buy that stock at $60, so another $1 is gained on the exercise. Thus, the actual gain is approximately the premium ($400 premium + $100 stock gain) = $500. Notice that it makes no difference how low the stock price drops - gain is capped at approximately the premium (which is what the chart says!).

4e. PLACING A COLLAR ON A STOCK POSITION

Collar On The Price Of A Security

An option strategy can be used to maintain the price of a security within a desired range, known as placing a "collar" on a position. This can be achieved at minimal cost, and is popular when a security position has appreciated substantially so that near term upside future appreciation is not likely.

Collar = Long Out The Money Put And Short Out The Money Call

For example, assume that a customer has bought 100 shares of ABC stock at $40 that is now trading at $60. The customer does not wish to lose the gain and wishes to sell if the price of the stock falls below $55 per share, so the customer buys 1 ABC Jan 55 Put (out of the money by 5 points) at a low premium, say $1. The customer does not believe that the stock will appreciate much between now and January (but is long term bullish). The customer sells 1 ABC Jan 65 Call (out of the money by 5 points) and receives a low premium, say $1. The net cost to the customer of the "collar" is "0."

If the stock falls to $55, the put will be exercised, and the customer still has a 15 point gain on the stock ($40 cost vs. $55 sell). Since the cost of the "collar" is zero, this does not reduce the gain. If the stock rises above $65 (which is not anticipated during the life of the call contract), the short call will be exercised, and the stock will be delivered at $65 (gain of $25 above the $40 cost per share).

Essentially, this strategy is a combination of both a hedge (buy a put) and income strategy (sell a call) against the stock position to lock in a sales price for the stock within a desired range at minimal cost.

The options chart helps in visualizing collars.

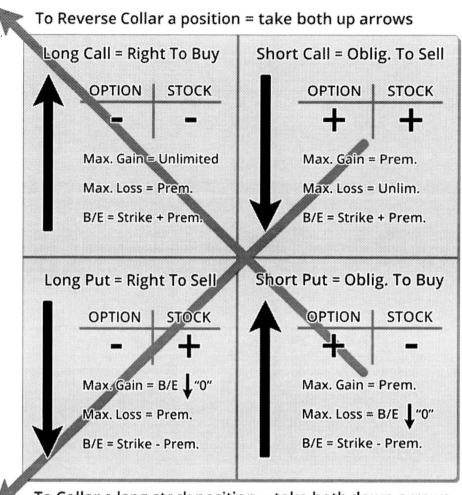

To Reverse Collar a position = take both up arrows

Long Call = Right To Buy

OPTION	STOCK
-	-

Max. Gain = Unlimited

Max. Loss = Prem.

B/E = Strike + Prem.

Short Call = Oblig. To Sell

OPTION	STOCK
+	+

Max. Gain = Prem.

Max. Loss = Unlim.

B/E = Strike + Prem.

Long Put = Right To Sell

OPTION	STOCK
-	+

Max. Gain = B/E ↓ "0"

Max. Loss = Prem.

B/E = Strike - Prem.

Short Put = Oblig. To Buy

OPTION	STOCK
+	-

Max. Gain = Prem.

Max. Loss = B/E ↓ "0"

B/E = Strike - Prem.

To Collar a long stock position = take both down arrows

(Note that the chart includes a long stock collar (already covered) and a short stock collar, included to be complete, but this is not tested.)

Collars Are Used To Create Structured Products

A "real world" use of collars is in "structured products" such as equity-indexed CDs and equity-indexed annuities. These products give a return tied to the Standard and Poor's 500 Index, but they give a minimum guaranteed rate of return. To ensure that in a bear market they give the guaranteed minimum rate of return, index puts are bought (index options are covered in a later section). To reduce the cost of the "put" protection, out of the money calls are sold. This places a "cap" on the maximum return that the products give in a bull market.

INCOME STRATEGIES
SECTION EXAMINATION

1.

Covered call writing is an appropriate strategy in a:

  a. declining market
  b. rising market
  c. stable market
  d. fluctuating market

2.

The sale of covered calls is used to:

  a. hedge a long stock position in a falling market
  b. protect a short stock position in a falling market
  c. generate additional income in a stable market
  d. profit if the market drops

3.

A customer buys 100 shares of ABC stock at $49 and sells 1 ABC Jan 50 Call @ $4. The market rises to $55 and the call is exercised. The customer has a:

  a. $100 profit
  b. $400 profit
  c. $500 profit
  d. $900 profit

4.

A customer buys 100 shares of ABC stock at $49 and sells 1 ABC Jan 50 Call @ $4. The breakeven point is:

  a. $45
  b. $46
  c. $53
  d. $54

5.

A customer buys 100 shares of ABC stock at $49 and sells 1 ABC Jan 50 Call @ $4. The maximum potential loss is:

  a. $400
  b. $4,500
  c. $4,900
  d. unlimited

6.

A customer buys 100 shares of ABC stock at $49 and sells 1 ABC Jan 50 Call @ $4. Prior to expiration, the customer closes the short call position at $1. The customer retains the long stock position. The gain or loss on the option is:

  a. $100 loss
  b. $300 gain
  c. $400 gain
  d. $500 loss

7.

A customer buys 200 shares of GE at $72 and sells 2 GE 70 Calls @ $6. The market rises to $80 and the calls are exercised. The customer has a(n):

  a. $400 gain
  b. $800 gain
  c. $1,200 gain
  d. $2,800 gain

8.

A customer buys 200 shares of GE at $72 and sells 2 GE Feb 70 Calls @ $6. The breakeven point is:

  a. $58
  b. $60
  c. $64
  d. $66

9.

A customer buys 200 shares of GE at $72 and sells 2 GE Mar 70 Calls @ $6. The maximum potential loss is: ·

    a. $6,400

    b. $12,800

    c. $13,200

    d. $14,400

10.

A customer buys 200 shares of GE at 72 and sells 2 GE Jun 70 Calls @ $6. The maximum potential gain is:

    a. $800

    b. $1,200

    c. $7,000

    d.   unlimited

11.

Which of the following strategies has unlimited loss potential?

    a.   long stock / short call

    b.   long stock / long put ·

    c.   short stock / long call

    d.   short stock / short put

12.

A customer sells short 100 shares of ABC at $50 and sells 1 ABC Jan 50 Put @ $5. This position results in a profit when the market:

    I   rises

    II   falls

    III   is stable

    a.   I only

    b.   II only

    c.   I and III

    d.   II and III

13.

A customer sells short 100 shares of ABC stock at $60 and sells 1 ABC Oct 60 Put @ $6. The maximum potential loss is:

    a. $600

    b. $5,400

    c. $6,000

    d.   unlimited

14.

A customer sells short 100 shares of ABC stock at $60 and sells 1 ABC Oct 60 Put @ $6. The breakeven point is:

    a. $54

    b. $60

    c. $66

    d. $70

15.

A customer sells short 100 shares of ABC stock at $60 and sells 1 ABC Oct 60 Put @ $6. The maximum potential gain while both positions are in place is:

    a. $600

    b. $4,400

    c. $5,000

    d.   unlimited

16.

A customer sells short 100 shares of PDQ at $49 and sells 1 PDQ Sep 50 Put @ $6. The customer will have a loss at which of the following market prices for PDQ?

    a. $42

    b. $43

    c. $55

    d. $56

17.

A customer owns ABC stock, purchased at $50 per share, and believes that the market can decline to $45 per share. The customer wishes to generate extra income from the stock position, but also wishes to protect the position from a large downside movement. The customer should:

a. Sell an ABC 50 Call and buy an ABC 45 Put

b. Buy an ABC 45 Put

c. Buy an ABC 50 Call and buy an ABC 45 Put

d. Sell an ABC 45 Call

18.

A customer sells short 100 shares of ABC stock at $80 per share. The stock falls to $70, at which point the customer writes 1 ABC Sept 70 Put at $4. The stock falls to $62 and the put is exercised. The customer has a gain per share of:

a. 14 points

b. 16 points

c. 18 points

d. 24 points

19.

A customer sells short 100 shares of DEF stock at $63 and sells 1 DEF Oct 60 Put @ $6. The market rises to $68 and the put expires. The customer buys the stock in the market covering her short stock position. The gain or loss is:

a. $100 gain

b. $100 loss

c. $300 gain

d. $300 loss

20.

18 months ago, a customer purchased 100 shares of ABC stock at $32 in a cash account. It is now January and the stock is now trading at $50. The customer believes that the stock will continue to appreciate in the next 6 months to $55 per share, at which point no further appreciation is expected. The customer wishes to maximize the return on this stock with the smallest capital commitment. If the customer sells 1 ABC Jul 55 Call @ $3, the breakeven point will be:

a. $29 per share

b. $47 per share

c. $53 per share

d. $57 per share

Options

INCOME STRATEGIES EXAMINATION EXPLANATIONS

1. The best answer is **c**. A covered call writer owns the underlying stock position. The customer sells the call contract to generate extra income from the stock during periods when the market is expected to be stable. If the customer expects the market to rise, he or she would not write the call against the stock position because the stock will be "called away" in a rising market. If the customer expects the market to fall, he or she would sell the stock or buy a put as a hedge.

2. The best answer is **c**. Covered call writing is used to generate extra income from a long stock position in a stable market.

3. The best answer is **c**. If the market rises to $55, the short call is "in the money" and is exercised. The stock which was bought for $49 must be delivered for $50 per share (short call strike price) for a $100 profit. The writer also earns the $4 ($400) premium collected. The total gain is $500.

4. The best answer is **a**. The customer paid $49 for the stock and received a $4 premium from the sale of the call, for a net cost of $45. To breakeven, the stock must be sold for this amount. To summarize, the formula for breakeven for a long stock / short call position is:

> **Long Stock / Short Call Breakeven = Stock Cost - Premium**

5. The best answer is **b**. The worst case is the stock becoming worthless. The customer loses the full value of the stock ($4,900) net of the $400 in collected premiums, for a net loss of $4,500.

6. The best answer is **b**. The short call was opened at $4 and closed with a purchase at $1 for a net gain of 3 points or $300 for the contract.

7. The best answer is **b**. If the calls are exercised, the stock (which cost $72 per share) must be sold at the $70 strike price for a $200 loss per contract. Since $600 was collected in premiums per contract, the net gain per contract is $400. The gain for 2 contracts = $800.

8. The best answer is **d**. The customer paid $72 per share for the stock and collected $6 per share in premiums for selling the call, resulting in a net cost of $66 per share. To breakeven, the stock must be sold for that amount. Note that breakeven is always computed on a per share basis - the fact that there are 2 contracts has no effect on the computation. To summarize, the formula for breakeven for a long stock / short call position is:

> **Long Stock / Short Call Breakeven = Stock Cost - Premium**

9. The best answer is **c**. The worst case is that the stock becomes worthless. The customer paid $72 per share, reduced by $6 in collected premiums, for a net cost of $66. As the market drops, the calls will expire "out the money." The customer can lose all $66 per share x 200 shares = $13,200.

10. The best answer is **a**. If the market rises, the calls are exercised. The stock (which cost $72) must be delivered at $70 for a loss of $2 per share. Since $6 was collected in premiums for selling the call, the net gain, if exercised, is 4 points or $400 per contract x 2 contracts = $800.

11.   The best answer is **d**.   With a long stock position, the maximum loss is the value of the stock. With a short stock position, the potential loss is unlimited. If a long call is purchased against a short stock position, the upside loss is limited. If a short put is sold against a short stock position the upside loss is still unlimited since in a rising market the short put will expire "out the money." The short stock position must be covered by purchasing the stock at the higher market price - and the price can rise an infinite amount.

12.   The best answer is **d**.   If the market remains stable, the put expires "at the money" and the customer earns the $500 premium. The stock which was sold at $50 can be bought for $50, so there is no further effect on the customer. If the market falls, the short put is exercised and the customer must buy the stock at 50. Since he sold the stock at $50, there is no further effect on the customer. He does earn the $500 of premiums from the sale of the put. If the market rises, the short put expires "out the money." The customer must cover the short sale at $50 by purchasing the stock in the market. His loss potential is unlimited on this short stock position.

13.   The best answer is **d**.   If the market rises, the short put expires and the short stock position must be covered by making a purchase in the market. The loss potential is unlimited.

14.   The best answer is **c**.   The stock was "sold" at $60 and $6 was collected in premiums for selling the put, for a total of $66 collected per share. To breakeven, the stock must be purchased at this price. To summarize, the formula for breakeven for a short stock / short put position is:

> **Short Stock / Short Put Breakeven = Short Sale Price + Premium**

15.   The best answer is **a**.   If the market drops, the short put is exercised and the customer must buy the stock at $60. Since the stock was sold at $60, the customer has no gain or loss on the stock - but he or she does keep the $600 of collected premiums. This is the maximum potential gain. Conversely, if the market rises, the short put expires, leaving a short stock position that has potentially unlimited loss.

16.   The best answer is **d**.   A customer with a short stock / short put position loses if the market rises. The customer sold the stock at $49 and collected $6 in premiums, for a total of $55. To break even, the stock must be bought for this amount. If the stock is bought for more than $55, the customer loses. Therefore, a loss is experienced at $56. To summarize, the formula for breakeven for a short stock / short put position is:

> **Short Stock / Short Put Breakeven = Short Sale Price + Premium**

17.   The best answer is **a**.   This customer has a stock position from which he wishes to generate income - therefore the sale of a covered call is appropriate. In addition, he wishes to protect against the possibility of a sharp downward price movement giving him a loss on the stock. For this, the purchase of a put option is appropriate, allowing the customer to "put" the stock if the market price should decline sharply. The customer has placed a "collar" on the stock position.

18.   The best answer is **a**.   The customer sold the stock short at $80 per share (sale proceeds). Later, the customer sold a Sept 70 Put @ $4 on this stock. If the short put is exercised, the customer is obligated to buy the stock at $70 per share. Since the customer received $4 in premium when the put was sold, the net cost to the customer is $66 per share for the stock (this is the cost basis in the stock for tax purposes). The stock that has been purchased is delivered to cover the short sale, closing the transaction. The customer's gain is: $80 sale proceeds - $66 cost basis = 14 points.

19.   The best answer is **a**.   If the market rises, the short put expires. Here, the customer buys the stock at $68 to cover her short stock position that was originally sold at $63. There is a 5 point or $500 loss, that is offset by the $600 in premiums received. Thus, there is a net gain of $100.

20.   The best answer is **a**.   This customer bought the stock at $32 per share. The customer sold an ABC Jul 55 Call, receiving a premium of $3 per share. This reduces the customer's cost per share to $32 - $3 = $29. This is the breakeven point. The fact that the stock has appreciated has no effect on the breakeven computation.

SECTION 5: STRADDLES

5a. OVERVIEW OF STRADDLES AND COMBINATIONS

So far, all of the strategies that have been covered are suitable only when the market is moving in one direction (either up or down) or are suitable when the market is expected to be stable. Consider this scenario: A customer believes that the market is going to move sharply from its present point, but he also believes that the move has an equal chance of being on the upside or on the downside. What do you do? You recommend that the customer buy a straddle! By straddling the market, the customer will profit if the market moves up or if it moves down. On the other hand, if the market stays flat, he will lose.

Long Straddle = Long Call + Long Put

Profit If Price Moves Up Or Down By More Than Total Premiums

When a customer **buys** a straddle, he purchases a call and a put on the **same** stock having the **same** strike price and expiration. If the market moves up, he gains on the call and the put expires. If the market moves down, he gains on the put and the call expires. If the market stays the same, both the put and call expire "at the money" and he loses the double premiums paid. Thus, the customer is betting that the market will be volatile.

Short Straddle = Short Call + Short Put

Profit If Price Stays The Same

Conversely, a customer can **sell** a straddle - selling a call and a put on the **same** stock having the **same** strike price and expiration. He does this if he absolutely believes that the market will stay flat. If this happens, both the call and the put expire "at the money" and he earns the double premiums. If the market rises, the call goes "in the money" and will be exercised while the put will expire "out the money." He is obligated to deliver stock that he doesn't have and has unlimited loss potential on the upside. If the market falls, the put goes "in the money" and will be exercised while the call will expire "out the money." He is obligated to buy stock that is worth less in the current market and he continues to lose as the market price of that stock drops towards zero.

By selling a straddle, the customer takes on double the risk (upside and downside) to earn a double premium. Because of the high risk of this strategy, it is not very popular.

To help remember what comprises a straddle, following is the diagram of speculative options positions seen previously:

Options

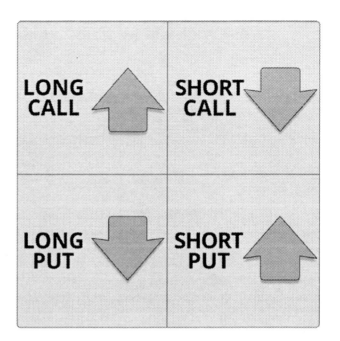

We know that buying a call gives potentially unlimited upside market gain while buying a put gives increasing gain as the market falls to zero. To profit if the market either rises **or** falls, buy both and the picture becomes:

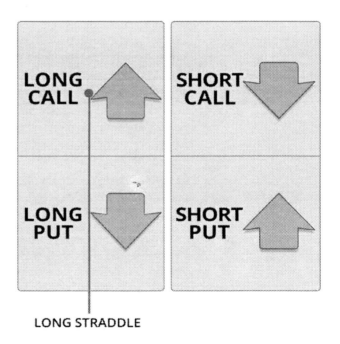

LONG STRADDLE

On the other hand, we know that selling a call allows the writer to earn the premium if the market stays flat or falls while selling a put allows the writer to earn the premium if the market stays flat or rises. By selling both a call and a put, he earns double premiums if the market stays flat. If it moves, he loses on the call on the way up or loses on the put on the way down. To complete the diagram:

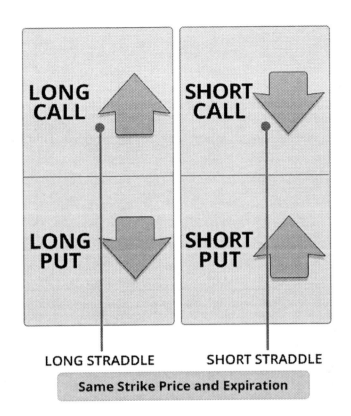

LONG STRADDLE   **SHORT STRADDLE**

Same Strike Price and Expiration

A long straddle or short straddle requires that the security, strike price, and expiration all be the **same**. If the customer buys a call and put on the same security with either **different** strike prices and/or expirations, it is termed a long combination. If he sells a call and put on the same security with either different strike prices and/or expirations, it is termed a short combination.

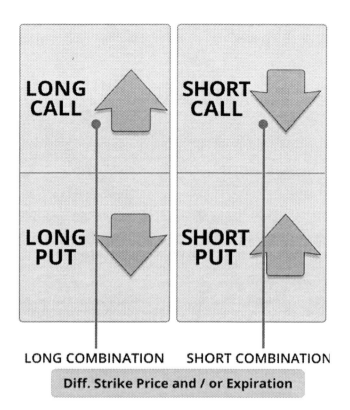

LONG COMBINATION   SHORT COMBINATION

Diff. Strike Price and / or Expiration

Combinations have essentially the same characteristics as straddles and one should be able to identify them.

Another Name For A Combination Is A "Strangle"

Also note that another name for a combination is a "strangle" - which is actually a more descriptive name. For example, a "long strangle" is purchase of an "out the money" call (so its strike price is higher than the current market) and the purchase of an "out the money" put (so its strike price is lower than the current market). Because they are "out the money," the premiums paid are lower. However, the market must move more sharply, either up or down, to be profitable, as compared to the purchase of a long straddle.

5b. LONG STRADDLES

A customer believes that the market will move sharply but is uncertain as to the direction. You recommend that he buy a straddle on ABC stock to profit from this. The customer takes the following positions:

> Buy 1 ABC Jan 50 Call @ $5
> Buy 1 ABC Jan 50 Put @ $4
>
> ABC Current Market Price = $51

This is a long straddle since the security, strike price and expiration are the **same**. If the market moves up, the call is exercised and the put expires. If the market moves down, the put is exercised and the call expires.

To find the maximum potential gain, breakeven points, and maximum potential loss, we can use the "T" but it is actually simpler not to, because there is a breakeven point for **both** the call side of the straddle and for the put side of the straddle. The steps to solving problems having more than one option position are:

Step 1: Stack the positions one atop the other with the call position on top.

Step 2: Total the premiums.

Step 3: If the customer is buying, the total premiums result in a "debit."

Step 4: The debit is the amount the customer pays for the long straddle and is his maximum loss.

Step 5: To breakeven the debit must be recovered. Add the debit to the call strike price for the upside breakeven point. Subtract the debit from the put strike price for the downside breakeven.

Step 6: Maximum potential gain is unlimited since the customer owns a call.

To solve this problem, first we stack the positions and total the premiums.

Buy 1 ABC Jan 50 Call @ $5
Buy 1 ABC Jan 50 Put @ $4
$9 **Debit**

Maximum Loss = Total Premium Paid (Debit)

The customer must pay $9 in premiums or $900 total for the long straddle. This is his maximum potential loss if the market stays at $50 and both contracts expire at the money.

Upside Breakeven = Call Strike Price + Debit

If the market rises above $50, the call will go in the money and the put expires out the money. To breakeven on the upside, the entire $9 debit must be recovered from the long call. The upside breakeven is:

50 + 9 = 59 Breakeven
Buy 1 ABC Jan 50 Call @ $5
Buy 1 ABC Jan 50 Put @ $4
$9 Debit

Downside Breakeven = Put Strike Price - Debit

If the market drops below $50, the put will go in the money and the call expires out the money. To breakeven on the downside, the entire $9 debit must be recovered from the long put. The downside breakeven is:

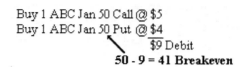

Buy 1 ABC Jan 50 Call @ $5
Buy 1 ABC Jan 50 Put @ $4
$9 Debit
50 - 9 = 41 Breakeven

Maximum Potential Gain = Unlimited

The customer's maximum potential gain is unlimited because he owns a long call option.

To summarize the characteristics of buying a straddle:

LONG STRADDLE		Speculative strategy that is both bullish and bearish
Maximum Potential Gain	=	Unlimited (on Call side)
		Strike price - Combined Premium (on Put side)
Maximum Potential Loss	=	Combined Premium
Breakeven Points	=	Call strike price + Combined Premium
		Put strike price - Combined Premium

5c. SHORT STRADDLE

A customer believes that the market will stay the same and is willing to assume a high level of risk. You recommend that he sell a straddle on ABC stock to profit from this. The customer takes the following position:

Sell 1 ABC Jan 50 Call @ $5
Sell 1 ABC Jan 50 Put @ $4

ABC Current Market Price = $51

This is a short straddle since the security, strike price and expiration are the **same**. If the market stays at $50, both the call and put will expire and he will earn double premiums. But if the market moves up, the call will be exercised and the put expires. He will lose on the short call position. If the market moves down, the put will be exercised and the call expires. He will lose from the short put position.

To find the maximum potential gain, breakeven points, and maximum potential loss for more than one option, we use the steps outlined previously with slight modifications:

Step 1: Stack the positions one atop the other with the call position on top.

Step 2: Total the premiums.

Step 3: If the customer is selling, the total premiums result in a "credit."

Step 4: The credit is the amount the customer received for the short straddle and is his maximum potential gain.

Step 5: To breakeven the credit must be lost. Add the credit to the call strike price for the upside breakeven point. Subtract the credit from the put strike price for the downside breakeven.

Step 6: Maximum potential loss is unlimited since the customer has a naked short call position.

To solve this problem, first we stack the positions and total the premiums.

Sell 1 ABC Jan 50 Call @ $5
Sell 1 ABC Jan 50 Put @ $4
$9 Credit

Maximum Potential Gain = Combined Premiums (Credit)

The customer received $9 in premiums or $900 total for the short straddle. This is his maximum potential gain if the market stays at $50 and both contracts expire at the money.

Upside Breakeven = Call Strike Price + Credit

If the market rises above $50, the call will go in the money and the put expires out the money. To breakeven on the upside, the entire $9 credit must be lost from the short call. The upside breakeven is:

50 + 9 = 59 Breakeven
Sell 1 ABC Jan 50 Call @ $5
Sell 1 ABC Jan 50 Put @ $4
$9 Credit

Downside Breakeven = Put Strike Price - Credit

If the market drops below $50, the put will go in the money and the call expires out the money. To breakeven on the downside, the entire $9 credit must be lost from the short put. The downside breakeven is:

Sell 1 ABC Jan 50 Call @ $5
Sell 1 ABC Jan 50 Put @ $4
$9 Credit
50 - 9 = 41 Breakeven

Maximum Potential Loss = Unlimited

The customer's maximum potential loss is unlimited because he has a short call position which is naked.

To summarize the characteristics of selling a straddle:

Options

SHORT STRADDLE		Speculative strategy that is suitable in flat markets
Maximum Potential Gain	=	Combined premium
Maximum Potential Loss	=	Unlimited (on Call side)
		Strike price - Combined Premium (on Put side)
Breakeven Points	=	Call strike price + Combined Premium
		Put strike price - Combined Premium

STRADDLES
SECTION EXAMINATION

1.

Which of the following create a straddle?

    I   Long 1 ABC Jan 50 Call
         Long 1 ABC Jan 50 Put
    II   Long 1 ABC Jan 50 Call
         Short 1 ABC Jan 60 Put
    III Short 1 ABC Jan 50 Call
         Short 1 ABC Jan 50 Put
    IV   Short 1 ABC Jan 50 Call
         Short 1 ABC Jan 60 Put

    a.   I and II
    b.   I and III
    c.   II and IV
    d.   III and IV

2.

A customer who is long 1 ABC Jan 50 Call wishes to create a "long straddle." The second option position that the customer must take is?

    a.   Long 1 ABC Jan 50 Call
    b.   Long 1 ABC Jan 50 Put
    c.   Short 1 ABC Jan 50 Call
    d.   Short 1 ABC Jan 50 Put

3.

A long straddle is profitable in a:

    I   rising market
    II   falling market
    III stable market

    a.   I only
    b.   II only
    c.   III only
    d.   I and II

4.

A customer buys 1 ABC Jan 50 Call @ $4 and buys 1 ABC Jan 50 Put @ $3 when the market price of ABC = $51. The market rises to $70 and the call is exercised. The stock is sold in the market. The put expires. The customer's gain is:

    a. $700
    b. $1,300
    c. $2,000
    d. $2,700

5.

A customer buys 1 ABC Jan 50 Call @ $4 and buys 1 ABC Jan 50 Put @ $3 when the market price of ABC = $51. The breakeven points are:

    a. $46 and $53
    b. $47 and $54
    c. $43 and $57
    d. $45 and $55

6.

A customer buys 1 ABC Jan 50 Call @ $4 and buys 1 ABC Jan 50 Put @ $3 when the market price of ABC = $51. The maximum potential gain is:

    a. $700
    b. $4,300
    c. $5,700
    d.   unlimited

7.

A customer buys 1 ABC Jan 50 Call @ $4 and buys 1 ABC Jan 50 Put @ $3 when the market price of ABC = $51. The maximum potential loss is:

    a. $700
    b. $4,300
    c. $5,700
    d.   unlimited

8.

A customer sells 1 ABC Jul 30 Call @ $1 and sells 1 ABC Jul 30 Put @ $3.50 when the market price of ABC is $29. The maximum potential loss is:

   a. $450

   b. $2,550

   c. $3,450

   d.   unlimited

9.

A customer sells 1 ABC Jul 30 Call @ $1 and sells 1 ABC Jul 30 Put @ $3.50 when the market price of ABC is $29. The maximum potential gain is:

   a. $450

   b. $2,550

   c. $3,450

   d.   unlimited

10.

A customer sells 1 ABC Jul 30 Call @ $1 and sells 1 ABC Jul 30 Put @ $3.50 when the market price of ABC is $29. The breakeven points are:

   a. $26.50 and $31.00

   b. $25.50 and $34.50

   c. $27.50 and $33.50

   d. $29.00 and $35.00

STRADDLES EXAMINATION EXPLANATIONS

1. The best answer is **b**.   A straddle is the purchase of a call and a put; or the sale of a call and a put; on the same underlying security with the same strike price and expiration.

2. The best answer is **b**.   A long straddle consists of a long call and a long put on the same stock, with both contracts having the same strike price and expiration. With a long straddle, the customer is hoping that the market moves either up or down; he loses if the market stays the same. If the market rises, the customer gains on the call and the put expires. If the market falls, the customer gains on the put and the call expires. If the market stays the same, both contracts expire "at the money" and the customer loses both premiums paid.

3. The best answer is **d**.   A long straddle is the purchase of a call and the purchase of a put on the same stock at the same strike price and expiration. If the market moves up, the call is profitable. If the market moves down, the put is profitable.

4. The best answer is **b**.   The customer created a long straddle.

> Buy 1 ABC Jan 50 Call@ $4
> Buy 1 ABC Jan 50 Put @ $3
> $7 Debit

If the market rises to $70, the call is exercised, while the put expires "out the money." There is a 20 point profit on the call offset by $7 paid in premiums for a net profit of 13 points or $1,300.

5. The best answer is **c**.   Long straddles are profitable if the market either moves up or down. To breakeven, the total premium paid must be recovered by the market moving either up or down. To breakeven, the $7 Debit paid for the straddle must be recovered. This happens at 50 + 7 = $57 on the call side of the straddle and 50 - 7 = $43 on the put side of the straddle. To summarize, the breakeven formulas for a long straddle are:

> **Upside Breakeven = Call Strike Price + Combined Premium**

> **Downside Breakeven = Put Strike Price - Combined Premium**

6. The best answer is **d**.   The customer created a long straddle, which is the purchase of a call and a put on the same stock, with the same strike price and expiration. Since one side of the straddle is a long call, there is unlimited upside gain potential. On the put side of the straddle, the maximum potential gain occurs if the stock drops to zero.

7. The best answer is **a**.   If the market stays at $50, both contracts expire "at the money." The customer loses the $700 paid in premiums. This is the maximum potential loss.

8. The best answer is **d**.   Since one side of a short straddle is a short naked call, if the market rises there is unlimited risk.

9. The best answer is **a**. The customer created a short straddle.

    Sell 1 ABC Jul 30 Call @ $1.00
    Sell 1 ABC Jul 30 Put @ $3.50

                    $4.50 Credit

If the market stays at $30, both contracts expire "at the money" and the writer earns the credit of $450. This is the maximum gain.

10. The best answer is **b**. A short straddle is the sale of a call and a put on the same stock, with the same strike price and expiration. To breakeven, the writer must lose the 4.50 point credit received for selling the straddle. If the market rises, the call side will be exercised at a loss to the writer. The call breakeven is $30 + $4.50 = $34.50. If the market falls, the put side will be exercised at a loss to the writer. The put breakeven is $30 - $4.50 = $25.50. To summarize, the breakeven formulas for a short straddle are:

> **Upside Breakeven = Call Strike Price + Combined Premium**

> **Downside Breakeven = Put Strike Price - Combined Premium**

SECTION 6: SPREADS

6a. SPREADING OVERVIEW

A spread position is the **purchase and sale of a call**, or the **purchase and sale of a put** at:

- **different** strike prices, or
- **different** expirations, or
- both the strike price and expiration being **different**.

Spread positions can be visualized using the options diagram as:

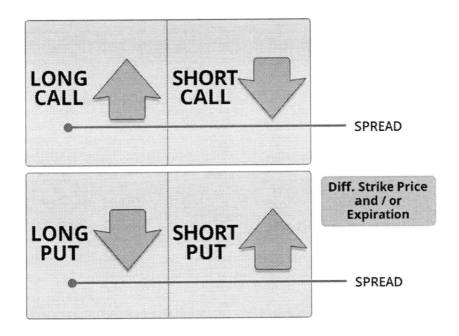

Hedged Option

Limits Risk And Gain

The theory behind spreading is that instead of taking a "pure" one-sided position on the direction of the market (such as buying a call because one is sure the market will go up), one takes a second position as a partial hedge (such as selling a call at a different strike price or expiration). By taking the second position as a partial offset, one limits potential gain and limits potential risk as well.

Price Or Vertical Spread

In essence, spreads are hedged option positions. Hedges where the strike prices are different are called price spreads or "vertical" spreads. An example of a price spread is:

Buy 1 ABC Jan 50 Call @ $7
Sell 1 ABC Jan 60 Call @ $3

Notice how the strike prices are stacked "vertically" one above the other. There are 4 types of price spreads, which substitute for taking the pure option position.

Long Call Spread - Debit Spread

Instead of buying a call, one can "buy a call spread." This is a **"long" call spread**, where the long call premium is higher. For example:

> Buy 1 ABC Jan 50 Call @ $7
> Sell 1 ABC Jan 60 Call @ $3
> $4 Debit

The spread is a "long spread" because it results in a net debit of $4 (one must pay $4 so one is a "net buyer" of the spread position). In a long call spread one buys the lower strike price (which has a higher premium) and sells the higher strike price - always!

Short Call Spread - Credit Spread

Instead of selling a call, one can "sell a call spread." This is a **"short" call spread**, where the short call premium is higher. For example:

> Sell 1 ABC Jan 50 Call @ $7
> Buy 1 ABC Jan 60 Call @ $3
> $4 Credit

The spread is a "short spread" because it results in a net credit of $4 (one receives $4 so one is a "net seller" of the spread position). In a short call spread one sells the lower strike price (which has the higher premium) and buys the higher strike price - always!

Long Put Spread - Debit Spread

Instead of buying a put, one can "buy a put spread." This is a **"long" put spread**, where the long put premium is higher. For example:

> Buy 1 ABC Jan 60 Put @ $7
> Sell 1 ABC Jan 50 Put @ $3
> $4 Debit

The spread is a "long spread" because it results in a net debit of $4 (one must pay $4 so one is a "net buyer" of the spread position). In a long put spread one buys the higher strike price (which has the higher premium) and sells the lower strike price - always!

Short Put Spread - Credit Spread

Instead of selling a put, one can "sell a put spread." This is a **"short" put spread**, where the short put premium is higher. For example:

> Sell 1 ABC Jan 60 Put @ $7
> Buy 1 ABC Jan 50 Put @ $3
> $4 Credit

The spread is a "short spread" because it results in a net credit of $4 (one receives $4 so one is a "net seller" of the spread position). In a short put spread, one sells the higher strike price option (which has the higher premium) and buys the lower strike price option - always!

These 4 spread positions do not have the same gain potential as taking the pure single option position, but they also do not carry the same risk. They are used when one is not completely sure of the direction the market will take; rather one is "moderately" sure of the market direction.

Each of the 4 price spreads will be discussed separately.

The diagram to envision price spread is:

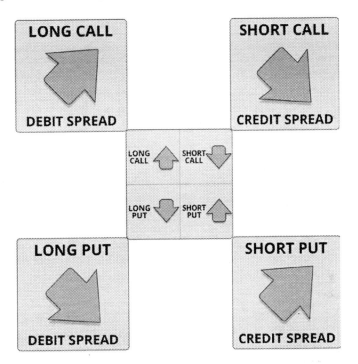

After the sections on the 4 price ("vertical") spreads, time spreads ("horizontal" spreads) will be discussed. A time spread has different expirations, not different strike prices. A spread can also consist of contracts with **both** different strike price and expirations - this is termed a "diagonal" spread.

6b. LONG CALL SPREAD (BULL SPREAD)

Assume that a customer believes that XXX stock will rise in the near future, but he knows that the stock is not very volatile and doesn't expect the stock to rise by more than 10 points. The customer could simply buy 1 XXX Jul 70 Call @ $5 (assume the market price is $71) and enjoy unlimited gain potential in return for the 5 point premium paid.

Being a cautious person, he decides to do the following:

Buy 1 XXX Jul 70 Call @ $5
Sell 1 XXX Jul 80 Call @ $1

(Market Price = $71)

Short Call Is Covered By Long Call

If XXX does not move above $80 per share, the short call will expire. The premium earned on the short call of $1 reduces his money outlay from $5 to $4. In return for the reduced cash outlay, his gain potential is reduced. If the market rises above $80, the short call will be exercised, requiring him to deliver 100 shares of stock at the $80 strike price. The short call is covered by the long call position, because he can always exercise the long call and buy the stock at $70 for delivery. He does not have to go to the market to get the stock. On the upside, his gain is limited to 10 points (Buy at $70, Sell at $80).

Moderately Bullish

Also Used When Time Premiums Are High

Buying a call spread is used when one is moderately bullish. The long spread costs less than taking the simple long call position, but gives lower potential gain. If time premiums are very high, persons may choose long call spreads rather than simple long call positions. This is done as a way of reducing the premium outlay. The diagram for the long call spread is:

Using the spread position shown above, the steps to find maximum potential loss, breakeven, and maximum potential gain are:

Step 1: Stack the positions with the higher premium position on top and determine if this is a net debit or net credit.

Buy 1 XXX Jul 70 Call @ $5
Sell 1 XXX Jul 80 Call @ $1
$4 **Debit**

Note that the call spread stacking order is low strike price over high strike price, since the low strike price call (right to buy at a lower price) is more valuable.

Step 2: If it is a net debit, it is a long spread. Since this is a spread with calls, this is a: **Long Call Spread** (Bullish)

Step 3: The debit is the deposit and is the maximum potential loss if the market drops and both calls expire out the money.

Deposit = $400 debit = Maximum potential loss

Step 4: If the market rises above $70, the long call will be exercised and the customer will buy the stock at $70. If the market continues to rise, above $80, the short call is exercised. The maximum gain is 10 points on the stock (the difference in the strike prices) net of $400 paid in premiums = $600.

Maximum gain = difference between strike prices net of debit = $1,000 - $400 = $600

Step 5: To breakeven, the customer must recover the $400 (4 points) paid in premiums. He makes money from the long call (remember, this is a long call spread) so the breakeven is 70 + 4 = 74.

Breakeven = Long Strike Price + Net Debit = 70 + 4 = 74

6c. SHORT CALL SPREAD (BEAR SPREAD)

Assume that a customer believes that XXX stock will fall in the near future, but he knows that the stock is not very volatile and doesn't expect the stock to fall by more than 10 points. The customer could simply sell 1 XXX Jul 70 Call @ $5 (assume the market price is $71) and if XXX falls below $70 and stays there, he earns $500 of premiums. But if XXX rises, he is exposed to unlimited upside risk. He wishes to limit this risk, so he takes the following position:

Sell 1 XXX Jul 70 Call @ $5
Buy 1 XXX Jul 80 Call @ $1

(Market Price = $71)

Short Call Is Only Partially Covered By Long Call

If XXX moves below $70 and stays there, both options will expire. The premium earned on the short call of $5 is reduced by the long call premium of $1. In return for the reduced cash received, his loss potential is reduced. If the market rises above $70, the short call will be exercised, requiring him to deliver 100 shares of stock at the $70 strike price. The short call is partially covered by the long call position, because he can always exercise the long call and buy the stock at $80 for delivery. He does not have to go to the market to get the stock. On the upside, his loss is limited to 10 points (Buy at $80, Sell at $70), less premiums received.

Moderately Bearish

Selling a call spread is used when one is moderately bearish. The short spread earns less than taking the simple short call position if the contract goes out the money, but it limits potential risk. The diagram for the short call spread is:

Using the spread position created above, the steps to find maximum potential loss, breakeven, and maximum potential gain are:

Step 1: Stack the positions with the higher premium position on top and determine if this is a net debit or net credit

Sell 1 XXX Jul 70 Call @ $5
Buy 1 XXX Jul 80 Call @ $1
$4 Credit

Note that the call spread stacking order is low strike price over high strike price, since the low strike price call (right to buy at a lower price) is more valuable.

Step 2: If it is a net credit, it is a short spread. Since this is a spread with calls, this is a **Short Call Spread** (Bearish)

Step 3: The credit is the maximum potential gain if the market drops and both calls expire out the money.

Maximum Potential Gain = Net Credit = $400

Step 4: If the market rises above $70, the short call will be exercised and the customer must deliver the stock at $70. If the market continues to rise, above $80, the long call is exercised to get the stock for delivery. The maximum loss is 10 points on the stock (the difference in the strike prices) net of $400 received in premiums = $600. Since $600 is the most that can be lost, this is the deposit amount for the short spread position

Maximum Loss = Difference between strike prices net of credit = $1,000 - $400 = $600 = Deposit

Step 5: To breakeven, the customer must lose the $400 (4 points) received in premiums. He loses money from the short call (remember, this is a short call spread) so the breakeven in 70 + 4 = 74.

Breakeven = Short Strike Price + Net Credit = 70 + 4 = 74

6d. LONG PUT SPREAD (BEAR SPREAD)

Assume that a customer believes that XXX stock will fall in the near future, but he knows that the stock is not very volatile and doesn't expect the stock to fall by more than 10 points. The customer could simply buy 1 XXX Jul 80 Put @ $5 (assume the market price is $79) and enjoy increasing gain as the stock drops in return for the 5 point premium paid.

Being a cautious person, he decides to do the following:

Buy 1 XXX Jul 80 Put @ $5
Sell 1 XXX Jul 70 Put @ $1

(Market Price = $79)

Short Put Is Covered By Long Put

If XXX does not move below $70 per share, the short put will expire. The premium earned on the short put of $1 reduces his money outlay from $5 to $4. In return for the reduced cash outlay, his gain potential is reduced. If the market falls below $70, the short put will be exercised, requiring him to buy 100 shares of stock at the $70 strike price. The short put is covered by the long put position, because he can always exercise the long put and sell the stock at $80. He does not have to go to the market to get the stock. On the downside, his gain is limited to 10 points (Buy at $70, Sell at $80).

Moderately Bearish

Buying a put spread is used when one is moderately bearish. The long spread costs less than taking the simple long put position, but gives lower potential gain. The diagram for the long put spread is:

LONG PUT

DEBIT SPREAD

Using the spread position created above, the steps to find maximum potential loss, breakeven, and maximum potential gain are:

Step 1: Stack the positions with the higher premium position on top and determine if this is a net debit or net credit

$$\begin{array}{l} \text{Buy 1 XXX Jul 80 Put} \quad @ \ \$5 \\ \text{Sell 1 XXX Jul 70 Put} \quad @ \ \underline{\$1} \\ \hspace{3.5cm} \textbf{\$4 Debit} \end{array}$$

Note that the put spread stacking order is high strike price over low strike price, since the high strike price put (right to sell at a higher price) is more valuable.

Step 2: If it is a net debit, it is a long spread. Since this is a spread with puts, this is a **Long Put Spread** (Bearish)

Step 3: The debit is the deposit and is the maximum potential loss if the market rises and both puts expire out the money.
Deposit = $400 debit = Maximum Potential Loss

Step 4: If the market falls below $80, the long put will be exercised and the customer will sell the stock at $80. If the market continues to fall, below $70, the short put is exercised, and the customer buys the stock for $70. The maximum gain is 10 points on the stock (the difference in the strike prices) net of $400 paid in premiums = $600.

Maximum Gain = Difference between strike prices net of debit = $1,000 - $400 = $600

Step 5: To breakeven, the customer must recover the $400 (4 points) paid in premiums. He makes money from the long put (remember, this is a long put spread) so the breakeven is 80 - 4 = 76.

Breakeven = Long Strike Price - Net Debit = 80 - 4 = 76

6e. SHORT PUT SPREAD (BULL SPREAD)

Assume that a customer believes that XXX stock will rise in the near future, but he knows that the stock is not very volatile and doesn't expect the stock to rise by more than 10 points. The customer could simply sell 1 XXX Jul 80 Put @ $5 (assume the market price is $79) and if XXX rises above $80 and stays there, he earns $500 of premiums. But if XXX falls, he is exposed to increasing downside risk as the market drops. To limit this risk, he takes the following positions:

Sell 1 XXX Jul 80 Put @ $5
Buy 1 XXX Jul 70 Put @ $1

(Market Price = $79)

Short Put Is Only Partially Covered By Long Put

If XXX moves above $80 and stays there, both options will expire. The premium earned on the short put of $5 is reduced by the long put premium of $1. In return for the reduced cash received, his loss potential is reduced. If the market falls below $80, the short put will be exercised, requiring him to buy 100 shares of stock at the $80 strike price. The short put is partially covered by the long put position, because he can always exercise the long put and sell the stock at $70. He does not have to go to the market to sell the stock. On the downside, his loss is limited to 10 points (Buy at $80, Sell at $70).

Moderately Bullish

Selling a put spread is used when one is somewhat bullish:

The short spread earns less than taking the simple short put position if the contract goes out the money, but limits potential risk.

Using the spread position created above, the steps to find maximum potential loss, breakeven, and maximum potential gain are:

Step 1: Stack the positions with the higher premium position on top and determine if this is a net debit or net credit

Sell 1 XXX Jul 80 Put @ $5
Buy 1 XXX Jul 70 Put @ $1
$4 Credit

Note that the put spread stacking order is high strike price over low strike price, since the high strike price put (right to sell at a higher price) is more valuable.

Step 2: If it is a net credit, it is a short spread. Since this is a spread with puts, this is a **Short Put Spread** (Bullish)

Step 3: The credit is the maximum potential gain if the market rises and both puts expire out the money.

Maximum Potential Gain = Net Credit = $400

Step 4: If the market falls below $80, the short put will be exercised and the customer must buy the stock at $80. If the market continues to fall, below $70, the long put is exercised and the stock is sold for $70. The maximum loss is 10 points on the stock (the difference in the strike prices) net of $400 received in premiums = $600. Since $600 is the most that can be lost, this is the deposit amount for the short spread position.

Maximum Loss = Difference between strike prices net of credit = $1,000 - $400 = $600 = Deposit

Step 5: To breakeven, the customer must lose the $400 (4 points) received in premiums. He loses money from the short put (remember, this is a short put spread) so the breakeven is 80 - 4 = 76

Breakeven = Short Strike Price - Net Credit = 80 - 4 = 76

6f. CALENDAR SPREADS (HORIZONTAL)

The strategy behind a calendar spread is completely different from that for price spreads. In a price spread, the customer is taking a direction in the market (either up or down). A calendar spread tries to take advantage of human nature to make a profit! To explain calendar spreads, we will use XXX stock as the underlying security. Most stock options have a maximum "technical" life of 9 months (explained in the next section).

Assume that the market price of XXX is $70 and we are looking at XXX 70 Call contracts. These contracts are "at the money," so the entire premium is time value - there is no intrinsic value. Since time erodes at an even rate, as we get closer to expiration, the premium should fall evenly.

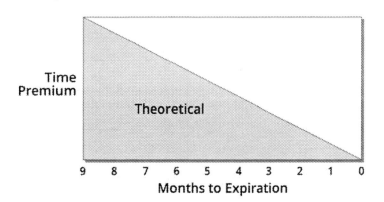

The time value graph above shows this. But, people tend to be shortsighted. The reality is shown following:

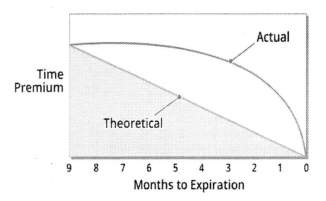

The premium stays artificially high until it is realized that expiration is fast approaching, and that the option will soon be worthless. Then, the time premium falls off rapidly, as shown in the prior exhibit. Here's how one can profit from this phenomenon. Assume that it is now December and XXX stock is trading at 70. The calls currently available are:

Expiration	Jan	Apr	Jul
XXX 70 Call	4	6	8

Since it is now December, the Jan Call has 1 month to expiration, the Apr has 4 months and the Jul has 7 months. If XXX stays at $70, we know that people will soon push down the value of the Jan Call since it is close to expiration. However, the Apr and Jul will not fall as rapidly because they have more time left.

If one is brave, one could simply:

Sell 1 XXX Jan 70 Call @ $4

Calendar Spread - Same Strike

Different Expiration

If XXX stays at $70, we know that the call will lose value rapidly and can be held to expiration for a $4 profit or bought back in the market for a low premium before expiration. But what happens if XXX rises? There is unlimited loss potential. To hedge against this one would:

Sell 1 XXX Jan 70 Call @ $4
Buy 1 XXX Apr 70 Call @ $6
$2 Debit

If the short Jan 70 call is exercised, one can always turn around and buy the stock at $70 through the long Apr 70 call. The long call covers the short call. This is charted as:

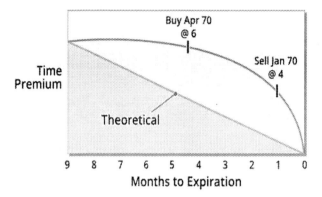

Assume it is 4 weeks later and the stock is still at $70. The Jan call is almost expired and is trading for "0." The Apr call still has 3 months to expiration and is trading at 5. The graph now shows:

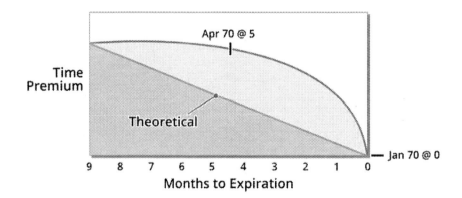

The spread was established by:

Sell 1 XXX Jan 70 Call @ $4
Buy 1 XXX Apr 70 Call @ $6
$2 Debit

The spread is now closed out by reversing the trades at the current premiums:

Buy 1 XXX Jan 70 Call @ $0
Sell 1 XXX Apr 70 Call @ $5
$5 Credit

Since the spread was established by paying $2 and closed by receiving $5, there is a $3 difference or $300 profit (100 shares x $3 profit).

Also Called "Time" Or "Horizontal" Spreads

These spreads are called time spreads or calendar spreads or "horizontal" spreads. Be able to identify and have a basic understanding of time spreads.

Diagonal Spread

A final note - a spread where both the price (vertical) and time (horizontal) are different is called diagonal spread (combining a horizontal and vertical gives a diagonal).

6g. FINAL NOTES ON SPREADS

Most Spreads Are Closed By Trading Out The Positions

We know that a spread is established either with a debit ("buying a long spread") or a credit ("selling a short spread"). Instead of exercising or waiting for positions to expire, most spreads are closed by trading out the positions as in the "time spread" example done in the Calendar Spreads section above.

Exercise Generally Does Not Occur Due To High Commission Costs

Most spreads are "closed out" by trading, rather than having both sides exercised, because of the high commission costs involved with actually buying and selling the underlying stock positions. By trading out the positions, the commissions are much lower.

If one "buys" a spread (creating a debit), the closing transaction is **always** a "sale," meaning a credit to the account. In the time spread example, the spread was created at a $2 debit and closed at $5 credit, for a $3 profit.

Debit Spread Is Profitable If Spread Between Premiums Widens

For a debit spread to be profitable, it must be closed at a larger credit. Hence, for a debit spread to be profitable, the spread between the premiums must **widen**. In our example, the spread between the premiums widened from $2 to $5, resulting in a $3 profit.

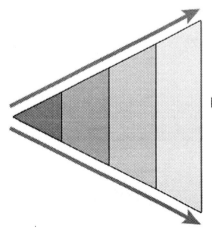

Debit spread is profitable when the spread between the premiums **WIDENS**

For example, assume that a customer establishes the following long call spread on ABC stock, when ABC's market price is $52 per share.

Buy 1 ABC Jan 50 Call @ $6
Sell 1 ABC Jan 60 Call @ $2
$4 Debit

This customer expects that the market price will rise. Now assume that ABC's market price rises to $59 the very next day. If this occurs, the 50 Call is now 9 points "in the money" and the premium will have increased in the market to at least $9 per share (the "in the money" amount). The 60 Call is still 1 point "out the money" and its premium will not have increased as much. Assume that the new premiums are:

ABC Jan 50 Call @ $12
ABC Jan 60 Call @ $ 3

Instead of exercising the "in the money" long call, the customer "closes" the positions as follows:

Sell 1 ABC Jan 50 Call @ $12
Buy 1 ABC Jan 60 Call @ $ 3
$ 9 Credit

The customer has a net profit of 5 points or $500, because the positions were established at a $4 debit and closed at a $9 credit. This customer profited on this debit spread because the spread between the premiums widened by 5 points.

Credit Spread Is Profitable If Spread Between Premiums Narrows

Conversely, if one "sells" a spread (creating a credit), the closing transaction is **always** a "purchase," meaning a debit to the account. For a credit spread to be profitable, the original credit must be larger than the closing debit. Hence, the spread between the premiums must **narrow**.

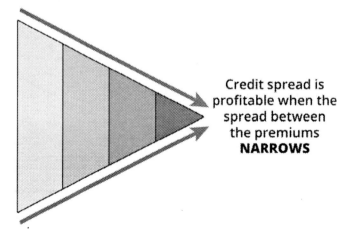

Credit spread is profitable when the spread between the premiums **NARROWS**

For example, assume that a customer establishes the following short call spread on ABC stock, when ABC's market price is $58 per share.

Sell 1 ABC Jan 50 Call @ $10
Buy 1 ABC Jan 60 Call @ $ 2
$ 8 Credit

Market Price = $58

This customer expects that the market price will fall. Now assume that ABC's market price falls to $51 the very next day. If this occurs, the 50 Call is now only 1 point "in the money" (from 8 points "in the money" the preceding day) and the premium will have decreased sharply in the market. The 60 Call is now 9 points "out the money" and its premium will also decline by a bit. Assume that the new premiums are:

ABC Jan 50 Call @ $3
ABC Jan 60 Call @ $1

Market price = $51

The customer "closes" the positions as follows:

Buy 1 ABC Jan 50 Call @ $3
Sell 1 ABC Jan 60 Call @ $1
$2 Debit

The customer has a net profit of 6 points or $600, because the positions were established at an $8 credit and closed at a $2 debit. This customer profited on this credit spread because the spread between the premiums narrowed by 6 points.

To summarize this discussion, a way of thinking about this is that one always wants to pay less (debit) than what one sells for (credit). One wants little debits and large credits!

If one starts with a debit, one knows that the position will always be closed with a credit, which one wants to be larger (widen).

If one starts with a credit, one knows that the position will always be closed with a debit, which one wants to be smaller (narrow).

SPREADS
SECTION EXAMINATION

1.

Which **TWO** choices would create a "spread"?

    I   Long 1 ABC Jan 50 Call; Short 1 ABC Jan
         60 Call
    II   Long 1 ABC Jan 60 Put; Short 1 ABC Jan
         50 Put
    III Long 1 ABC Jan 50 Call; Long 1 ABC Jan
         60 Put
    IV   Short 1 ABC Jan 60 Call; Short 1 ABC Jan
         50 Put

    a.   I and II
    b.   III and IV
    c.   I and IV
    d.   II and III

2.

Which of the following are vertical spreads?

    I   Long 1 ABC Jan 50 Call
         Short 1 ABC Jan 50 Call
    II   Long 1 ABC Jan 50 Call
         Short 1 ABC Jan 60 Call
    III Long 1 ABC Jan 50 Call
         Short 1 ABC Apr 50 Call
    IV   Long 1 ABC Jan 50 Call
         Short 1 ABC Apr 60 Call

    a.   I only
    b.   II only
    c.   I and III
    d.   II and IV

3.

A customer who is long 1 ABC Jan 40 Call wishes
to create a "bull call spread." The second option
position that the customer must take is:

    a.   Long 1 ABC Jan 50 Call
    b.   Long 1 ABC Jan 50 Put
    c.   Short 1 ABC Jan 50 Call
    d.   Short 1 ABC Jan 50 Put

4.

On the same day a customer buys 1 ABC Feb 70
Call @ $4 and sells 1 ABC Feb 80 Call @ $1
when the market price of ABC is $70.50. The
maximum potential loss is:

    a. $300
    b. $400
    c. $7,400
    d. $7,700

5.

On the same day a customer buys 1 ABC Feb 70
Call @ $4 and sells 1 ABC Feb 80 Call @ $1
when the market price of ABC is $70.50. The
breakeven point is:

    a. $73
    b. $74
    c. $76
    d. $77

6.

On the same day a customer buys 1 ABC Feb 70
Call @ $4 and sells 1 ABC Feb 80 Call @ $1
when the market price of ABC is $70.50. The
maximum potential gain is:

    a. $300
    b. $400
    c. $700
    d.   unlimited

7.

On the same day in a margin account, a customer buys 1 ABC Feb 70 Call @ $4 and sells 1 ABC Feb 80 Call @ $1 when the market price of ABC is $70.50. The position will be profitable if:

I   both contracts expire
II   both contracts are exercised
III the spread between the premiums widens above 3
IV   the spread between the premiums narrows below 3

a.   I and III
b.   I and IV
c.   II and III
d.   II and IV

8.

On the same day a customer buys 1 ABC Jan 50 Call @ $2 and sells 1 ABC Jan 35 Call @ $8 when the market price of ABC is $41. The maximum potential gain is:

a. $600
b. $800
c. $4,800
d.   unlimited

9.

On the same day a customer buys 1 ABC Jan 50 Call @ $2 and sells 1 ABC Jan 35 Call @ $8 when the market price of ABC is $41. The maximum potential loss is:

a. $600
b. $800
c. $900
d.   unlimited

10.

On the same day a customer buys 1 ABC Jan 50 Call @ $2 and sells 1 ABC Jan 35 Call @ $8 when the market price of ABC is $41. The breakeven point is:

a. $37
b. $41
c. $44
d. $48

11.

On the same day, a customer buys 1 ABC Jan 50 Call @ $5 and sells 1 ABC Jan 60 Call @ $2. Above which of the following prices will every dollar gained on the long call be exactly offset by a dollar lost on the short call?

a. $50
b. $53
c. $58
d. $60

12.

A customer who sells a "put spread" believes that the market will:

a.   rise
b.   fall
c.   remain neutral
d.   be volatile

13.

A customer buys 1 ABC Jan 50 Put @ $7 and sells 1 ABC Jan 40 Put @ $1 when the market price of ABC is $47. The maximum potential loss is:

a. $600
b. $700
c. $3,900
d. $4,300

14.

A customer buys 1 ABC Jan 50 Put @ $7 and sells 1 ABC Jan 40 Put @ $1 when the market price of ABC is $47. The breakeven point is:

a. $43
b. $44
c. $47
d. $49

15.

A customer buys 1 ABC Jan 50 Put @ $7 and sells 1 ABC Jan 40 Put @ $1 when the market price of ABC is $47. The maximum potential gain is:

a. $100
b. $400
c. $600
d. $1,000

16.

A customer buys 1 ABC Jan 50 Put @ $7 and sells 1 ABC Jan 40 Put @ $1 when the market price of ABC is $47. The position will be profitable if:

I   both contracts expire
II   both contracts are exercised
III the spread widens
IV   the spread narrows

a. I and III
b. I and IV
c. II and III
d. II and IV

17.

A customer who is long 1 ABC Jan 75 Put wishes to create a "bull put spread." The second option position that the customer must take is:

a. Short 1 ABC 65 Put
b. Short 1 ABC 85 Put
c. Short 1 ABC 65 Call
d. Short 1 ABC 85 Call

18.

A customer buys 1 ABC Jan 70 Put @ $5 and sells 1 ABC Jan 90 Put @ $19 when the market price of ABC is $75. The maximum potential gain is:

a. $1,400
b. $1,900
c. $7,100
d. $8,000

19.

A customer buys 1 ABC Jan 70 Put @ $5 and sells 1 ABC Jan 90 Put @ $19 when the market price of ABC is $75. The breakeven point is:

a. $71
b. $76
c. $85
d. $89

20.

A customer buys 1 ABC Jan 70 Put @ $5 and sells 1 ABC Jan 90 Put @ $19 when the market price of ABC is $75. The maximum potential loss is:

a. $600
b. $1,400
c. $1,900
d. $2,000

21.

A customer buys 1 ABC Jan 70 Put @ $5 and sells 1 ABC Jan 90 Put @ $19 when the market price of ABC is $75. The position will be profitable if:

I   both contracts expire
II   both contracts are exercised
III the spread widens
IV   the spread narrows

a. I and III
b. I and IV
c. II and III
d. II and IV

22.

A customer buys 1 ABC Jan 50 Call and sells 1 ABC Apr 60 Call. This is a:

a. horizontal spread

b. vertical spread

c. diagonal spread

d. butterfly spread

23.

To create a debit calendar spread:

a. Buy the near expiration / Sell the far expiration

b. Buy the far expiration / Sell the near expiration

c. Buy the near expiration / Buy the far expiration

d. Sell the near expiration / Sell the far expiration

24.

A customer buys 1 ABC Jan 50 Call and sells 1 ABC Nov 50 Call. This is a:

a. calendar debit spread

b. calendar credit spread

c. vertical debit spread

d. vertical credit spread

25.

On the same day a customer sells 1 ABC Feb 70 Call @ $4 and buys 1 ABC Feb 80 Call @ $1 when the market price of ABC is $70.50. This position is a:

I   short call spread

II   long call spread

III bullish strategy

IV   bearish strategy

a. I and III

b. I and IV

c. II and III

d. II and IV

SPREADS EXAMINATION EXPLANATIONS

1. The best answer is **a**. A "spread" is the purchase and sale of either 2 calls or 2 puts with differing strike prices and/or differing expirations. Spreads are gain limiting and risk limiting positions.

2. The best answer is **b**. A vertical spread (also called a "price" spread) is the purchase and sale of a call; or the purchase and sale of a put; at different strike prices. A horizontal spread is the purchase and sale of a call; or the purchase and sale of a put; at different expirations. A diagonal spread is the purchase and sale of a call; or the purchase and sale of a put; with both different expirations and different strike prices.

3. The best answer is **c**. A spread consists of the purchase and sale of the same type of option (calls in this case) with different strike prices and/or expirations. In a bull call spread, the customer hopes that the market will rise, but does not believe that the market will rise by a large amount. If a customer is long an ABC Jan 40 Call, he or she will gain if the market rises above $40. If the customer believes that the market will not go above $50, he or she can sell an ABC Jan 50 Call. The premium collected on the sale of the 50 call reduces the cost of the 40 call. However, the reduced cost also reduces the potential gain for this customer. If the market rises sharply, the customer can only make 10 points on the positions. This occurs because both calls would be exercised, and the stock that is purchased at $40, would be delivered at $50, for a 10 point gain.

4. The best answer is **a**. The customer has created a long call spread. The contracts are stacked high premium over low premium - the same as stacking them from low to high call strike prices.

> Buy 1 ABC Feb 70 Call @ $4
> Sell 1 ABC Feb 80 Call @ $1
> $3 Debit

The debit of $300 is the maximum potential loss occurring if both contracts expire worthless. This occurs if the market falls below $70 per share.

5. The best answer is **a**. The purchaser of a long call spread profits from the long call position. (The short call establishes a limit on the profit potential). To recover the $3 Debit, the market price must rise to $73 ($70 Long Strike + $3 Debit). To summarize, the breakeven formula for a long call spread is:

> **Long Call Spread Breakeven = Long Strike Price + Debit**

6. The best answer is **c**. If the market rises, the long call is exercised and the stock is bought at $70. If it continues to rise, the short call is exercised and the stock is sold at $80 for a 10 point profit. Since 3 points were paid in net premiums, the maximum potential gain is $700.

7. The best answer is **c**. If both contracts are exercised, the long spread results in a $700 profit ($10 profit from the exercise of the contracts, net of the $3 debit paid). If both expire, the long spread results in a $300 loss (the debit). To be profitable, this long spread must be closed out at a larger credit - so the spread between the premiums must widen.

8. The best answer is **a**. The customer has created a short call spread.

   Sell 1 ABC Jan 35 Call@ $8
   Buy 1 ABC Jan 50 Call@ $2
                 $6 Credit

The credit of $600 is the maximum potential gain, occurring if both contracts expire. This occurs if the market falls below $35.

9. The best answer is **c**. If the market rises, the short call will be exercised, requiring the customer to deliver the stock for $35 a share. The customer can always exercise the long call to buy the stock at $50, for a 15 point loss. Since 6 points were collected in premiums, the net loss is 9 points or $900.

10. The best answer is **b**. To breakeven, the customer must lose the $600 (6 points) collected in premiums. Any loss comes from the short call position (remember this is a short call spread) so breakeven occurs at $35 + $6 = $41. To summarize, the breakeven formula for a short call spread is:

> **Short Call Spread Breakeven = Short Strike Price + Credit**

11. The best answer is **d**. The breakeven point is $53 per share. As the market rises above $53, the customer gains 1 point on the long 50 call for every $1 rise in the price of ABC stock. Once the market goes above $60, the short call will be "in the money," and a dollar will be lost on the short call for every dollar gained on the long call. Thus, above 60, there is no further gain. The maximum gain potential is 7 points or $700.

12. The best answer is **a**. A sale of a "put spread" is similar to simply selling a put. In a rising market, the puts expire "out the money" and the profit is the premium received. The difference is that a short put gives ever increasing downside loss potential - all the way to "0" - in return for the premium received. A short put spread gives limited downside loss potential in return for a lower premium received.

13. The best answer is **a**. The customer has created a long put spread.

   Buy 1 ABC Jan 50 Put@ $7
   Sell 1 ABC Jan 40 Put@ $1
                $6 Debit

The debit of $600 is the maximum potential loss, occurring if both contracts expire. This occurs if the market rises above $50 per share.

14. The best answer is **b**. To breakeven, the customer must recover the $600 (6 points) paid in premiums. Any gain comes from the long put position (remember this is a long put spread), therefore the breakeven point is $50 - $6 = $44. To summarize, the breakeven formula for a long put spread is:

> **Long Put Spread Breakeven = Long Strike Price - Debit**

15. The best answer is **b**. The customer profits in a long put spread as the market drops. In a falling market, he will exercise the long put and sell the stock for $50. As the market continues to drop, the short put will be exercised and he is obligated to buy the stock at $40 for a gain of 10 points. Since $6 was paid in premiums, the maximum potential gain is 4 points or $400.

16. The best answer is **c**. If both puts are exercised, the customer makes $400. If both expire, the debit of $600 is lost. Since this is a debit spread, it must be closed out with a credit. To be profitable, the closing credit must be larger, so the spread between the premiums must widen.

17. The best answer is **b**. A spread consists of the purchase and sale of the same type of option with a different strike price and/or expiration - therefore Choices **C** and **D** are incorrect. In a bull put spread, the customer purchases the lower strike price (lower premium since the contract allows the holder to sell at a lower price) and sells the one with the higher strike (higher premium, since the contract allows the holder to sell at a higher price). The spread results in a credit received, which the customer wants to keep. If the market rises, then the contracts expire "out the money" and the net premium received is kept. This is the maximum gain. If the market falls, in this case below $75, then both contracts are exercised at a loss to the customer. If the market falls below $75, then the customer is obligated to buy stock at $85; that he sells at $75; for a 10 point loss (net of any premium credit received). This is the maximum potential loss.

18. The best answer is **a**. This is a short put spread. If the market rises, both puts will expire "out the money" and the writer will keep the net credit of $1,400. This is the maximum potential gain.

Sell 1 ABC Jan 90 Put @ $19
Buy 1 ABC Jan 70 Put @ $ 5
$14 Credit

19. The best answer is **b**. To breakeven, the writer must lose the $1,400 credit (14 points) collected in premiums. Since this is a short put spread, any loss occurs from the short put position. Breakeven is at the short strike price of $90 - $14 = $76. To summarize, the breakeven formula for a short put spread is:

Short Put Spread Breakeven = Short Strike Price - Credit

20. The best answer is **a**. If the market drops, both puts go "in the money" and are exercised, obligating the customer to buy the stock at $90. The customer can then "put it" at $70, for a 20 point loss. Since 14 points were collected in premiums, the maximum loss is 6 points or $600.

21. The best answer is **b**. If the market drops, both puts are exercised and the customer loses $600. If the market rises, both puts expire and the customer earns $1,400. Since this is a credit spread, it must be closed at a debit. To be profitable, the debit must be smaller, so the spread must narrow.

22. The best answer is **c**. A diagonal spread is the purchase and sale of a call or put with different strike prices (vertical spread) AND expirations (horizontal spread). For example:

Buy 1 ABC Jan 50 Call
Sell 1 ABC Apr 60 Call

The combination of a vertical and a horizontal gives a "diagonal."

23. The best answer is **b**. In a calendar spread, the expiration months are different but the strike prices are the same. The nearer expiration will be cheaper than the farther expiration since it has less "time." To create a debit spread, the more expensive option must be bought (the far expiration) and the cheaper option must be sold (the near expiration).

24. The best answer is **a**.   This is a horizontal or calendar spread, where the positions have the same strike price, but different expirations. Since the maximum life of a regular stock option is 9 months, the November contract must be closer to expiration than the January - that is, if it is now November, the January contract is 2 months farther out. The January option cannot be the closer expiration, since the following November is 10 months away. Since Nov expires before Jan, it will be cheaper. The customer is selling the Nov 50 Call (cheaper) and buying the more expensive Jan 50 Call, so this is a debit spread.

25. The best answer is **b**.   The customer sold the 70 call for $4 and bought the 80 call for $1, giving him a $3 credit. Since he is a net seller, this is a short call spread. Since he doesn't want to lose the credit, he wants the contracts to expire. The contracts will only expire if the market remains at $70 or below, so this is a bearish strategy.

This page intentionally left blank

SECTION 7: RATIO STRATEGIES / OPTIONS STRATEGIES SUMMARY

7a. RATIO WRITING OF CALL CONTRACTS

(Note: This is an advanced options strategy that represents only 1 or 2 questions on the Series 7 exam.)

To generate "extra" income, instead of selling call contracts against an equal underlying position, a greater number of calls can be sold. This is termed a "ratio write." For example, consider the following positions:

> Buy 100 shares of ABC stock @ 50
> Sell 2 ABC Jan 50 Calls @ $5

Selling More Call Contracts Than Long Position

This customer is selling 2 call contracts against 100 shares of stock. Thus, he is writing calls against the stock at a 2:1 ratio. In essence, he has created 1 covered call and 1 short naked call. These are shown below:

> **Covered position:** Sell 1 ABC Jan 50 Call @ $5
> **Naked position:** Sell 1 ABC Jan 50 Call @ $5

Neutral Market Strategy

Similar to simple covered call writing strategies, the customer is hoping that the market price of ABC stays at $50. If the price stays the same, both short calls expire "at the money" and the customer earns $10 in collected premiums ($5 per call contract). Effectively, this reduces the customer's cost of the long stock position to $40.

Declining Market Breakeven = Cost Of Stock - All Collected Premiums (On A Per Share Basis)

If the market price falls, both calls expire "out the money." The customer keeps the premiums, but begins to lose on the long stock position. Since $10 was collected in premiums, the acquisition cost of the stock has been reduced to $40. If the market continues to fall, the customer keeps losing on the long stock position, losing a maximum of $4,000 if the stock becomes worthless.

Rising Market Breakeven = Strike Price + ALL Collected Premiums (On A Per Share Basis)

Maximum Potential Loss = Unlimited

If the market price rises, both calls go "in the money" and will be exercised. The customer bought 100 shares of stock at $50, and must deliver those shares at $50, for no further gain or loss on that position. He is left with 1 short naked call. Since he collected $10 in premiums from selling both short calls, he can afford to lose this amount as the market rises and still will "breakeven." Therefore, if the market rises to $60, he again will breakeven. Above $60, the customer continues to lose on the short naked call - and has unlimited risk potential on this position.

Greater The "Ratio" Greater The Risk

If a customer wishes to further increase income from a stock position, he could write calls at a 3:1 ratio or a 4:1 ratio. As the ratio increases, the size of the short naked call position increases, substantially increasing upside risk potential.

To summarize, ratio call writing generates extra income, but also entails a much higher risk level than simple covered call writing.

7b. LONG STOCK / SHORT STRADDLE AKA COVERED STRADDLE

Neutral Strategy

Another means of generating "extra" income from a stock position in a neutral market is to buy the stock and sell an "at the money" straddle against the stock position. If the market does not move, both sides of the straddle expire "at the money," and the customer retains doubled premiums (effectively reducing the stock's cost). For example, assume a customer takes the following positions:

> Long 100 shares of ABC stock @ $50
>
> Short 1 ABC Jan 50 Call @ $4
> Short 1 ABC Jan 50 Put @ $3
> $7 Credit

If the market stays exactly at $50, both options expire and the customer retains the $7 credit. Since he paid $50 per share for the stock, the net cost of the stock is $43.

Upside Gain = Credit Received

If the market rises, the short call goes "in the money" and will be exercised. The customer's stock, purchased at $50, will be delivered for $50, at no gain or loss. The short put "expires" out the money. The net result is the customer earns the credit of $7 = $700 maximum gain potential.

Downside Breakeven = Cost Of Stock Less Credit Received (Per Share Basis)

If the market drops, the customer gets "nailed." The short call will expire "out the money." The short put will be exercised, forcing the customer to buy another 100 shares of the stock at $50. Since the customer collected $700 in credits, and will own 200 shares of stock if the market drops below $50, he can afford to lose $350 per 100 shares (3 1/2 per share) and still breakeven. Thus, the downside breakeven is 50 - 3 1/2 = 46 1/2.

Maximum Loss = Stock Becomes Worthless

If the market continues to drop, the customer loses on both the original stock position and the stock acquired through the exercise of the short put. He can lose a maximum of 46 1/2 per share on 200 shares = $9,300. This is the same as buying 200 shares at $50 ($10,000 of stock), less the credit of $700.

Covered Straddle

For the exam, note that this strategy is termed a "covered straddle," but in reality this is **not** a covered strategy. Only the short call is covered; the short put is not covered.

RATIO STRATEGIES / OPTIONS STRATEGIES SUMMARY SECTION EXAMINATION

1.

A customer buys 100 shares of ABC stock at $50 and sells 2 ABC Jan 50 Calls @ $5. This is a:

a. short straddle
b. ratio call write
c. covered call write
d. ratio call spread

2.

A customer owns 100 shares of ABC stock in a margin account, valued at $39 per share. The customer sells 4 ABC Jul 40 Calls @ $4. The stock moves to $52 and the calls are exercised. The customer has a:

a. $300 gain
b. $1,900 loss
c. $3,600 loss
d. $4,800 loss

3.

A customer owns 100 shares of ABC stock in a margin account, valued at $40 per share. The customer sells 2 ABC Jul 40 Calls @ $4. The maximum potential loss is:

a. $800
b. $3,200
c. $4,000
d. unlimited

4.

Which of the following positions is a Ratio Spread?

a. Buy 1 ABC Jan 50 Call; Buy 1 ABC Jan 50 Put
b. Buy 100 shares of ABC stock; Sell 2 ABC Jan 50 Calls
c. Buy 1 ABC Jan 50 Call; Sell 2 ABC Jan 60 Calls
d. Buy 1 ABC Jan 50 Call; Sell 1 ABC Jan 60 Call

5.

On the same day in a margin account, a customer buys 5 ABC January 40 Calls @ $6 and sells 10 ABC January 50 Calls @ $1 when the market price of ABC is at $43. The maximum potential profit is:

a. $2,000
b. $3,000
c. $5,500
d. unlimited

6.

In which of the following choices are both the stock and options positions on the same side of the market?

I   Long Call / Long Stock
II   Short Call / Long Stock
III   Long Put / Short Stock
IV   Short Put / Short Stock

a. I and II
b. III and IV
c. II and III
d. I and III

7.

On the same day a customer buys 100 shares of ABC stock at $30 and sells 1 ABC Jan 30 Call @ $3 and sells 1 ABC Jan 30 Put @ $2. This strategy is known as a:

    a.   covered straddle

    b.   covered call writer

    c.   ratio write

    d.   butterfly spread

8.

On the same day a customer buys 100 shares of ABC stock at $30 and sells 1 ABC Jan 30 Call @ $3 and sells 1 ABC Jan 30 Put @ $2.

The maximum potential gain is:

    a. $500

    b. $2,500

    c. $5,500

    d.   Unlimited

9.

On the same day a customer buys 100 shares of ABC stock at $30 and sells 1 ABC Jan 30 Call @ $3 and sells 1 ABC Jan 30 Put @ $2.

The maximum potential loss is:

    a. $500

    b. $2,500

    c. $5,500

    d.   Unlimited

10.

On the same day in a margin account, a customer buys 5 ABC January 40 Calls @ $6 and sells 10 ABC January 50 Calls @ $1 when the market price of ABC is at $43. The maximum potential loss is:

    a. $2,000

    b. $3,000

    c. $5,500

    d.   unlimited

RATIO STRATEGIES / OPTIONS STRATEGIES SUMMARY
EXAMINATION EXPLANATIONS

1. The best answer is **b**. If a customer who is long stock sells call contracts against the stock position, then as long as the contract amount does not exceed the long stock position, the call writer is "covered." This means that if the short call is exercised, the customer already has the stock for delivery. Hence the customer is covered against the risk of having to go to the market to buy the stock at a sky high price to make delivery. If a customer sells more call contracts than the stock position owned, this is a "ratio" call write. In this example, the customer is selling calls against the stock position at a 2:1 ratio.

2. The best answer is **b**. If the stock moves to $52, all 4 calls will be exercised. Since one of the calls is covered, 100 shares of the stock that was bought at $39 will be delivered at $40, for a 1 point or $100 gain. Since the stock is now at $52, this is the price that is paid to buy the stock to deliver at $40 on the remaining 3 naked calls, equals a 12 point loss x 300 shares = $3,600 loss. But don't forget the premiums received of 4 x $400 = $1,600 gain. The net gain or loss is: + $100 - $3,600 + $1,600 = -$1,900 loss.

3. The best answer is **d**. One of the short calls is covered by the long stock position, while the other short call is naked. The loss potential on a short naked call is unlimited.

4. The best answer is **c**. Choice **A** is a straddle. Choice **B** is a ratio call write strategy where the customer is selling more call contracts than his long position. Choice **D** is a simple vertical or price spread. Choice **C** is a ratio spread because there is more than 1 short call contract (in this case there are 2) written against the 1 long call contract.

5. The best answer is **b**. The maximum potential profit must occur at $50 per share. At this price, the customer would profit on the long call spreads, without losing anything on the 5 short calls - which would expire "at the money." At a $50 price, each long call spread results in a profit of 10 points (Buy the stock at $40 by exercising the long call and sell it at $50 in the market), net of $5 paid (net debit) in premiums per spread = $500 profit per spread x 5 spreads = $2,500 profit. The short naked 50 calls expire resulting in a $100 profit per contract ($1 credit) x 5 contracts = $500. The total profit is $2,500 + $500 = $3,000.

6. The best answer is **d**. Long calls are profitable in bull markets as are long stock positions. These are on the same side of the market (the upside). Short calls are profitable if the market drops, while long stock positions are profitable if the market rises - these are on opposite sides of the market. Long puts are profitable if the market drops and short stock positions are profitable if the market drops - these are on the same side of the market. Short puts are profitable if the market rises while short stock positions are profitable if the market falls - these are on opposite sides of the market.

7. The best answer is **a**. The customer has created a long stock/short straddle position. This is termed a "covered straddle," however this name is not really accurate. The short call is covered by the long stock position, however the short put is naked.

8. The best answer is **a**. The customer has created a long stock/short straddle position. This is shown below:

Buy 100 Shares of ABC at $30
Sell 1 ABC Jan 30 Call @$3
Sell 1 ABC Jan 30 Put @ $2
$5 Credit

The credit of $500 is the maximum potential gain occurring if both contracts expire "at the money."

If the market rises above $30, the short call is exercised, while the short put expires "out the money." The stock that was purchased at $30 is delivered for $30 - there is no further gain or loss on this position. Thus, in a rising market, the maximum gain is $500.

If the market falls below $30, the short put is exercised (requiring the customer to buy **another** 100 shares at $30), while the short call expires "out the money" As the market falls, the customer now owns 200 shares purchased at $30. Since $500 was collected in premiums, he can afford to lose 2.5 points per share and will still breakeven. Thus, the breakeven occurs at $30 - $2.50 = $27.50. If the market continues to drop to zero, the customer will lose the full value of the 200 shares purchased at $30, net of $500 collected in premiums, for a net loss of $5,500 ($27.50 per share).

9. The best answer is **c**. The customer has created a long stock/short straddle position. This is shown below:

Buy 100 Shares of ABC at $30
Sell 1 ABC Jan 30 Call @$3
Sell 1 ABC Jan 30 Put @ $2
$5 Credit

The credit of $500 is the maximum potential gain occurring if both contracts expire "at the money."

If the market rises above $30, the short call is exercised, while the short put expires "out the money." The stock that was purchased at $30 is delivered for $30 - there is no further gain or loss on this position. Thus, in a rising market, the maximum gain is $500.

If the market falls below $30, the short put is exercised (requiring the customer to buy **another** 100 shares at $30), while the short call expires "out the money" As the market falls, the customer now owns 200 shares purchased at $30. Since $500 was collected in premiums, he can afford to lose 2.5 points per share and will still breakeven. Thus, the breakeven occurs at $30 - $2.50 = $27.50. If the market continues to drop to zero, the customer will lose the full value of the 200 shares purchased at $30, net of $500 collected in premiums, for a net loss of $5,500 ($27.50 per share).

10. The best answer is **d**. This is a very difficult question. The customer is taking the following positions:

Buy 5 ABC Jan 40 Calls@ $6
Sell 5 ABC Jan 50 Calls @ $1
$5 Debit

Sell 5 ABC Jan 50 Calls @ $1 Credit

The customer is creating 5 "long call spreads" and has 5 naked calls. In effect, he is writing 2 times the number of short calls needed to create the spread. Therefore he is "writing at a 2:1 ratio." This is termed a ratio spread. Long call spreads are used when a customer is moderately bullish (in this case, the customer believes that the stock will rise no higher than 50), and wishes to reduce the cost of the long position by selling an equal number of "out the money" calls. This limits upside gain potential, but also reduces the cost of the positions. By writing twice the number of calls, the customer further reduces the cost of the positions, but also assumes unlimited upside risk on the 5 naked calls that are left.

Options

This page intentionally left blank

SECTION 8: EQUITY (STOCK) OPTIONS

8a. CONTRACT SPECIFICATIONS

While most stock options are traded on the Chicago Board Options Exchange, trading of options contracts on listed equity securities takes place on the following exchanges:

- **Chicago Board Options Exchange**
- **American Stock Exchange**
- **Pacific (ARCA) Stock Exchange**
- **Philadelphia Stock Exchange**

The largest options market is the CBOE. The AMEX is also quite large. The Pacific (ARCA) and PHLX are smaller options markets. Also note that NYSE Euronext now owns the AMEX and Pacific (ARCA) options exchanges and runs them as separate subsidiaries while NASDAQ OMX now owns the PHLX Exchange and also runs it as a separate subsidiary.

Options Clearing Corporation

Contracts traded on the options exchanges are standardized under rules set by the Options Clearing Corporation (O.C.C.), a subsidiary of the CBOE. The O.C.C. issues the contracts, guarantees the contracts, and acts as clearing house for all listed options trades.

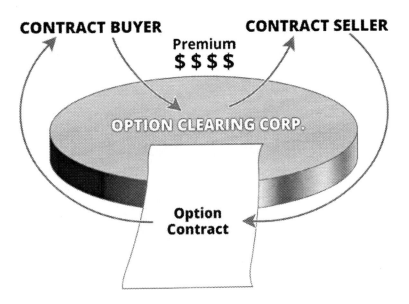

O.C.C. Contract Specifications

O.C.C. rules are designed to make options easier to trade. Because of the standardization procedure, the only thing left to the market is to determine the premium. Options are not traded on all equity securities, only larger capitalization issues that are actively traded.

Contract Size

Every contract on an equity option covers **100** shares.

Strike Price

New contracts are issued at prices that are based on the existing market price. For most stocks, the interval is set at 2 1/2 points. Therefore, if a stock is at $21, contracts cannot be issued at a $21 strike price, but they could be issued at strike prices of $17.50, $20.00, $22.50, etc.

For each stock trading at $20 or less, strike prices can be issued up to 100% higher or lower. For stocks over $20, the range is 50%. So if a stock is trading at, say, $50, options can now be issued with strike prices ranging from $25 to $75.

Premium Increments:

Premiums are quoted in "pennies," in minimum increments of 5 cents for contracts trading below $3; and 10 cents for contracts trading at $3 or more.

However, in 2007 the CBOE and the other options exchanges have been rolling out "penny pilot program" that permits trading of the more active contracts in "penny" ($.01) increments.

Expiration Date:

Contracts expire on the third Friday of each month. The actual time of expiration is 11:59 PM Eastern Time.

Expiration:

Once a contract is issued, it trades until its expiration date.

Spot

Next Month

For each equity security, an option contract can always be issued for the current trading month ("spot") and for the "next month." For example, if it is now May 1, contracts can be issued for May ("spot") and June ("next month").

Expiration Cycle

In addition, each equity security is assigned to an expiration "cycle." There are 3 cycles:

Cycle 1	Jan	Apr	Jul	Oct
Cycle 2	Feb	May	Aug	Nov
Cycle 3	Mar	Jun	Sept	Dec

For example, Mobil is on Cycle 2 - the only Mobil contracts that can be issued, other than "spot" and "next" month, are Feb, May, Aug, and Nov.

For example, General Motors is assigned to Cycle 3. The only GM contracts that can be issued, other than "spot" and "next" month, are for Mar, Jun, Sept, and Dec.

Next 2 Expiration Months

Aside from the "spot" and "next month" contracts, all of the regular expiration dates within each cycle **do not** trade at the same time. Based upon the current date, only the **next two** available expiration months within the cycle trade.

Based upon a current date of May 1st, the GM (Cycle 3) contracts that are permitted to trade are:

May	(spot)
June	(next month)
September	(the first upcoming regular cycle month in Cycle 3)
December	(the next upcoming regular cycle month in Cycle 3)

Once the May contracts expire, say on May 20th, the contracts that would be trading for GM are:

June	(spot)
July	(next month)
September	(the first upcoming regular cycle month in Cycle 3)
December	(the next upcoming regular cycle month in Cycle 3)

Once the June GM contracts expire, say on June 20th, the contracts that will be trading for GM are:

July	(spot)
August	(next month)
September	(the first upcoming regular cycle month in Cycle 3)
December	(the next upcoming regular cycle month in Cycle 3)

Once the July GM contracts expire, the contracts that will be trading for GM are:

August	(spot)
September	(next month)
December	(the first upcoming regular cycle month in Cycle 3)
March	(the next upcoming regular cycle month in Cycle 3)

Actual Maximum Contract Life - 8 Months

Note that the March contracts may start trading as soon as the July contracts expired. This occurs 8 months from the July expiration date. Thus, the actual maximum life of an equity options contract is 8 months.

Technical Maximum Contract Life - 9 Months

However, the Options Exchanges are permitted to issue contracts with a given expiration month that is 9 months in the future. As an example, for a Cycle 1 company, once January contracts expire, October contracts can be opened. Though this is not the current practice, it must be known for the examination.

Trading Hours:	Normal trading hours for listed options are 9:30 AM - 4:00 PM Eastern Standard Time (ET). Also note that because the CBOE is in Chicago, for the CBOE, these times are 8:30 AM - 3:00 PM Central Time.
Trading Cut Off:	The last day to trade equity options is on the third Friday of the expiration month. The last time to trade on this day is 4:00 PM ET (3:00 PM CT).
Exercise Cut Off:	The last day to exercise equity options is on the third Friday of the expiration month. The last time to exercise on this day is 5:30 PM ET (4:30 PM CT).
	Regarding these times, please remember that the Options Clearing Corporation is based in Chicago (it started as part of the CBOE), and operates on Central Time. To translate these times into Central Time, **subtract** 1 hour.

8b. OPTIONS CLEARING CORPORATION RULES

Options Clearing Corporation Rules **Options Disclosure Document**	The Options Clearing Corporation (O.C.C.) has a number of rules by which customers and registered representatives must abide. Before opening an options account, the O.C.C. requires that the customer receive an "Options Disclosure Document" published by the O.C.C. The date it is furnished to the customer is entered on the New Account Form. The disclosure document explains the basic option strategies; their risks and uses. It also outlines these important rules:
Next Day Settlement	Trades of options are settled regular way **next business day**.
Maintenance Of Records	The O.C.C. keeps the record of who has long option positions and short option positions in the name of the brokerage firm. The list is updated daily as of the settlements for that day. If a customer decides to exercise, he notifies his brokerage firm, who notifies the O.C.C.
Assignment Of Exercise Notices	When the O.C.C. receives an exercise notice from a brokerage firm, it selects a short contract to be exercised on a **random order** basis. When the brokerage firm that has the short position receives that notice from the O.C.C., it is permitted to select the particular customer to be exercised on either a "**first-in, first-out**" or **random order** basis.
Settlement When Exercised	All assignments of exercise notices are based upon positions held at the close of business the previous day. If an exercise occurs, this results in a regular way stock trade in the underlying security. Thus, if a call writer is exercised, the stock must be delivered **2 business days** after exercise date. If a put

writer is exercised, he or she must pay the strike price to buy the stock **2 business days** after exercise date.

Position Limits

A person who accumulates a large number of contracts has "control" over 100 times that number of shares of stock. The O.C.C. limits the number of positions that any individual can take (or group of individuals "**acting in concert**"). The limit varies depending on the trading volume of the underlying stock - the higher the trading - the higher the limit.

This limit is applied to each "side" of the market, with the following exhibit showing that the:

"**UPSIDE**" of the market consists of: Long Calls and Short Puts;

"**DOWNSIDE**" of the market consists of: Long Puts and Short Calls.

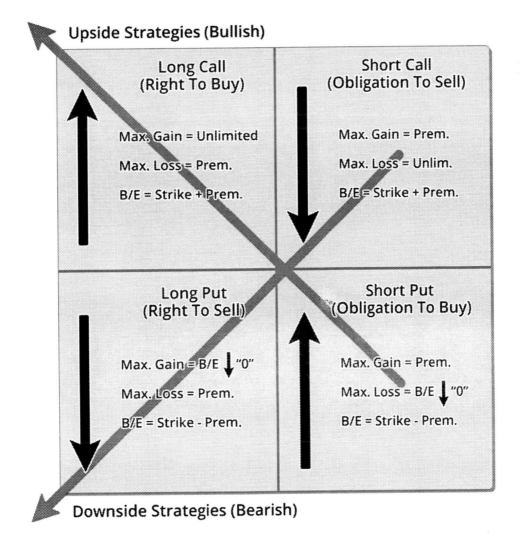

For example, with a 100,000 contract position limit:

100,000 long calls and 100,000 long puts do not exceed the limit and are acceptable;

100,000 long calls and 100,000 short puts **EXCEED** the limit and are **NOT** acceptable.

Position Limits

The actual position limits depend on the trading volume of the underlying security - there are 5 tiers based on trading volume. The more actively traded issues have higher option contract position limits than less actively traded ones.

Position Limit Aggregation Rules

Any accounts that are under "common control" are aggregated to determine if there is a position limit violation. Control is deemed to exist for:

- all owners in a joint account;
- each general partner in a partnership account;
- accounts with common directors or management; and
- an individual with authority to execute transactions in an account.

The most common situation where this comes up is a registered representative who exercises discretionary authority over a number of customer accounts - these would be aggregated to see if there is a violation of position limits.

Exercise Limits

Exercise Limits: In addition to position limits, there are limits on the number of contracts that can be exercised within any **5 business day** (1 working week) period. Exercise limits also vary depending on the trading volume of the underlying stock, but you do not have to know the specific limits.

No Adjustments For Cash Dividends

Adjustments to Contracts: Option contracts are **not** adjusted for cash dividends. When a stock goes ex dividend, the strike prices are left alone.

2:1 Or 4:1 Splits - Number Of Contracts Up / Strike Reduced

Contracts **are** adjusted for stock splits and stock dividends. For whole share splits that are either 2:1 or 4:1, the strike price is reduced and the number of contracts is increased.

For example, ABC stock splits 2:1.

Before: 1 ABC Jan 60 Call
After: 2 ABC Jan 30 Calls

Fractional Split - No Change To Contract But "Deliverable" Is Adjusted

For fractional splits and stock dividends, there is no change to the terms of the contract as it is traded. Instead, if there is an exercise, the "deliverable" is adjusted.

For example, ABC stock "pays" a 20% stock dividend.

Before: 1 ABC Jan 60 Call
After: 1 ABC Jan 60 Call

Strike Price And Multiplier Are Unchanged

The contract remains with a strike price of 60 and a multiplier of 100. If there is an exercise of the contract, then the delivery amount and price are "fixed" to reflect the value of the stock dividend or fractional stock split.

Adjustment To Deliverable

For the 20% stock dividend, the adjusted deliverable will be:

$$100 \times 1.2 = 120 \text{ shares at } \$60/1.2 = \$50$$

Note that after the deliverable adjustment, the aggregate exercise value of the contract does not change. Before, the contract covered 100 shares at $60 = $6,000 of stock. After, the contract covers 120 shares at $50 = $6,000 of stock.

Also note that because the contract strike is not adjusted, but the actual market price is adjusted on "ex" date, it might appear that these unadjusted contracts are "in" or "out" of the money when they really are not. For these contracts, simply comparing the strike price to the market price will not work to determine whether the contract is "in" or "out" of the money.

Covered Writing Positions

Writers of naked options assume large risk positions and are required to make large margin deposits to the Options Clearing Corporation to protect the brokerage firm. A "covered" writer is covered against this risk and hence does not have to put up margin on the short option position.

The following positions cover the sale of options by a customer:

"Covered Call Writing Positions"
Short Call (Unlimited Upside Risk)

1. **Long the underlying stock (or equivalent security such as a convertible or warrant)** (a "covered call writer")

2. **Long a call at the same strike price or lower that expires in the same month or after the short call** (creating a "debit" or long call spread)

   Please note that being "long a call" with a nearer expiration will **not** cover a short call. This makes sense, because the long call might expire, and the remaining short call is "naked" for the time left until expiration.

3. **Long an escrow receipt for the stock** (the stock is held in a bank vault - not with the broker)

4. **Bank guarantee letter** (the bank will pay if the customer can't upon exercise)

1. **Short the underlying stock position** (creating a "covered put writer")

2. **Long a put at the same strike price or higher that expires in the same month or after the short put** (creating a "debit" or long put spread)

   Please note that being "long a put" with a nearer expiration will not cover a short put. This makes sense, because the long put might expire, and the remaining short put is "naked" for the time remaining until expiration.

3. **Bank guarantee letter / Cash escrow receipt**

   Since the writer of a put is obligated to buy the stock if exercised, having cash equal to the strike (purchase) price on deposit covers a short put.

8c. LONG TERM STOCK OPTIONS (LEAPs)

The CBOE and other exchanges introduced an equity options product in late 1990, in an effort to increase investor interest in stock options trading. These contracts are "long term" equity options, with a longer life than the 9 month maximum for regular stock options.

LEAPs

30 Month Expiration

So-called "LEAPs" - Long-term Equity AnticiPation options are issued at the end of May with an expiration 30 months later. For example, at the end of May 2017, LEAPs will be issued for January 2020. At the end of May 2018, LEAPs will be issued for January 2021, etc.

They allow investors to position themselves for market movements that are expected over a longer period of time. LEAPs trade alongside the regular stock options, and have much higher time premiums since their expiration is much longer.

8d. EQUITY OPTION FINANCIAL LISTINGS

OPTION & N Y CLOSE	STRIKE PRICE	CALLS-LAST			PUTS-LAST		
		SEP	OCT	DEC	SEP	OCT	DEC
Delta	**90**	6.40	8.50	r	1.70	2.75	4.25
94.25	95	3.15	5.50	8.40	3.40	4.75	7.25
94.25	100	1.40	3.40	6.25	7.25	7.75	9.50
94.25	105	.45	1.90	4.75	11.00	12.00	13.00
Disney	**55**	6.15	6.40	r	.20	.50	1.25
60.13	60	1.75	2.90	5.00	1.25	1.90	3.00
60.13	65	.25	.90	2.65	4.85	5.25	r

(Note: **r** means not traded)

Listed options are quoted daily in the newspapers.

The listing gives the name of the underlying stock and its closing market price that day, followed by the strike price of the option. Then the listing gives the closing prices (premiums) of the 3 call and 3 put contracts trading closest to expiration.

For example, Delta Airlines December 100 Calls last traded at $6.25, or $625 per contract.

Option Type

The table is broken into the two **"types"** of options - puts and calls.

TYPE

OPTION & N Y CLOSE	STRIKE PRICE	CALLS-LAST			PUTS-LAST		
		SEP	OCT	DEC	SEP	OCT	DEC
Delta	**90**	6.40	8.50	r	1.70	2.75	4.25
94.25	95	3.15	5.50	8.40	3.40	4.75	7.25
94.25	100	1.40	3.40	6.25	7.25	7.75	9.50
94.25	105	.45	1.90	4.75	11.00	12.00	13.00
Disney	**55**	6.15	6.40	r	.20	.50	1.25
60.13	60	1.75	2.90	5.00	1.25	1.90	3.00
60.13	65	.25	.90	2.65	4.85	5.25	r

(Note: **r** means not traded)

Option Class

All contracts of one type on an underlying issue are termed a **"class"** of options. For example, all Delta Airlines calls constitute a "class."

CLASS

OPTION & N Y CLOSE	STRIKE PRICE	CALLS-LAST			PUTS-LAST		
		SEP	OCT	DEC	SEP	OCT	DEC
Delta	**90**	6.40	8.50	r	1.70	2.75	4.25
94.25	95	3.15	5.50	8.40	3.40	4.75	7.25
94.25	100	1.40	3.40	6.25	7.25	7.75	9.50
94.25	105	.45	1.90	4.75	11.00	12.00	13.00
Disney	**55**	6.15	6.40	r	.20	.50	1.25
60.13	60	1.75	2.90	5.00	1.25	1.90	3.00
60.13	65	.25	.90	2.65	4.85	5.25	r

(Note: **r** means not traded)

Option Series

Options of the same class with the same strike price and expiration are termed an option "**series**." For example, all Delta Airlines September 90 Calls constitute a "series."

SERIES

OPTION & N Y CLOSE	STRIKE PRICE	CALLS-LAST			PUTS-LAST		
		SEP	OCT	DEC	SEP	OCT	DEC
Delta	**90**	6.40	8.50	r	1.70	2.75	4.25
94.25	95	3.15	5.50	8.40	3.40	4.75	7.25
94.25	100	1.40	3.40	6.25	7.25	7.75	9.50
94.25	105	.45	1.90	4.75	11.00	12.00	13.00
Disney	**55**	6.15	6.40	r	.20	.50	1.25
60.13	60	1.75	2.90	5.00	1.25	1.90	3.00
60.13	65	.25	.90	2.65	4.85	5.25	r

(Note: **r** means not traded)

(Note: These options tables are an "older" format that is still tested on Series 7. The new format presents the same information in a "vertical" format instead of a horizontal format, but gives the same information. In addition, options tables are now presented in decimal pricing.)

For example, Disney, as listed above, would show in the new format as:

OPTION	STRIKE	EXP	CALL	PUT
Disney	55	Sep	6.15	.20
60.15	55	Oct	6.40	.50
60.15	55	Dec	r	1.25
60.15	60	Sep	1.75	1.25
60.15	60	Oct	2.90	1.90
60.15	60	Dec	5.00	3.00
60.15	65	Sep	.25	4.85
60.15	65	Oct	.90	5.25
60.15	65	Dec	2.65	r

(Note: **r** means not traded)

Answer the following questions to understand the tables (use both the old **and** new formats):

A customer buys 1 Disney Dec 60 Put. The cost is?

Answer: Premium = 3 = $300 per contract

The time premium on the Disney Dec 60 Put is?

Answer: Since the market price of the stock is $60.15, this put is out the money. The entire 3 point premium is "time."

The time premium on the Disney Oct 65 Put is?

Answer: The market price is $60.15, so the 65 put is "in the money" by $4.85. The total premium is $5.25, so the "time" premium is $.40.

Which of the following is trading "at parity"?

a. Disney Sept 65 Call

b. Disney Sept 65 Put

c. Disney Oct 60 Call

d. Disney Oct 60 Put

Answer: b A contract is trading "at parity" if the premium equals intrinsic value. In this case, the market is giving no value to the remaining time left to the contract. Of the 4 choices, the Sept 65 Put is trading at $4.85. Since the market price of Disney is $60.15, this contract is "in the money" by $4.85.

What is the cost to buy 10 Disney Dec 60 straddles?

Answer: A long straddle is the purchase of a put and call at the same strike and expiration. The Dec 60 Call is at 5. The Dec 60 Put is at 3. The cost per straddle is $8 or $800. The cost for 10 straddles is $8,000.

Which of the following is a "debit" spread?

a. Buy Sept Disney 60 Call / Sell Oct Disney 60 Call

b. Buy Oct Disney 60 Call / Sell Dec Disney 60 Call

c. Buy Oct Disney 65 Put / Sell Sept Disney 65 Put

d. Buy Oct Disney 65 Put / Sell Dec Disney 65 Put

Answer: c In a debit spread, the purchase must be **more** expensive than the sale. A call with a closer expiration is cheaper than a farther expiration, so **a, b,** and **d** are incorrect - they are credit spreads. Choice **c** is a debit spread - the near option (the Sept) is cheaper and is being sold. The far option (the Oct) is more expensive and is being purchased.

EQUITY (STOCK) OPTIONS SECTION EXAMINATION

1.

The last time to trade an equity option that is about to expire is:

a. 2:00 PM Central Time; 3:00 PM Eastern Time; on the 3rd Friday of the expiration month

b. 3:00 PM Central Time; 4:00 PM Eastern Time; on the 3rd Friday of the expiration month

c. 4:00 PM Central Time; 5:00 PM Eastern Time on the 3rd Friday of the expiration month

d. 5:00 PM Central Time; 6:00 PM Eastern Time on the 3rd Friday of the expiration month

2.

In determining whether there has been a violation of position limits, long calls will be aggregated with:

I Long Puts
II Short Calls
III Short Puts

a. I only
b. II only
c. III only
d. I, II, III

3.

The maximum "legal" life on a regular stock option contract is:

a. 6 months
b. 9 months
c. 12 months
d. 30 months

4.

The O.C.C. assigns exercise notices on a:

a. first in; first out basis
b. last in; first out basis
c. random order basis
d. method of reasonable fairness

5.

Exercise limits on stock option contracts cover a time period of:

a. 5 business days
b. 10 business days
c. one calendar month
d. nine calendar months

6.

The November stock option contracts of a company assigned to Cycle 1 have just expired. Which contracts will commence trading on the CBOE?

a. December
b. January
c. April
d. July

7.

A customer purchases an equity option contract at 1:00 PM Eastern Standard Time on Tuesday, October 10th in a regular way trade. If the customer wishes to exercise, the customer may place an exercise notice with the Options Clearing Corporation:

a. immediately

b. no earlier than 10:00 AM Eastern Standard Time, the next business day

c. no earlier than 10:00 AM Eastern Standard Time, on the 3rd business day following trade date

d. no earlier than the Friday immediately preceding the third Saturday of the expiration month

8.

ABC corporation is trading in the market for $51. The corporation declares a 25% stock dividend. After the ex date, the holder of 1 ABC Jan 50 Call will have:

   a.   1 ABC Jan 50 Call

   b.   1.25 ABC Jan 50 Calls

   c.   1 ABC Jan 40 Call

   d.   1.25 ABC Jan 40 Calls

9.

When the O.C.C. receives an exercise notice from a brokerage firm, it selects a short contract to be exercised on a:

   a.   method of reasonable fairness

   b.   LIFO basis

   c.   FIFO basis

   d.   random order basis

10.

Which of the following are "classes" of options?

   I   ABC Calls

   II   ABC Puts

   III   ABC Jan 50 Calls

   IV   ABC Jan 50 Puts

   a.   I and II

   b.   I and III

   c.   II and III

   d.   III and IV

11.

Trading in a stock is suspended. Which statement is **TRUE** regarding the trading of listed options on that stock?

   a.   Only opening transactions are permitted

   b.   Only closing transactions are permitted

   c.   Both opening and closing transactions are permitted until the contracts expire

   d.   Trading will be halted in options contracts on the suspended stock

12.

Regular way trades of all of the following securities settle next business day **EXCEPT:**

   a.   Listed stocks

   b.   Listed stock options

   c.   U.S. Government securities

   d.   Agency securities

13.

A customer sells 1 ABC Jan 55 Call. To cover the position, the customer could:

   a.   buy 1 ABC Jan 50 Call

   b.   sell 1 ABC Jan 50 Put

   c.   buy 1 ABC Jan 60 Call

   d.   sell 1 ABC Jan 60 Put

14.

All of the following are standardized for listed option contracts **EXCEPT:**

   a.   strike price

   b.   contract size

   c.   premium

   d.   expiration

15.

Stock options contracts:

   I   are American style

   II   are European style

   III   can be issued at any time

   IV   can be exercised at any time

   a.   I and III

   b.   I and IV

   c.   II and III

   d.   II and IV

EQUITY (STOCK) OPTIONS EXAMINATION EXPLANATIONS

1. The best answer is **b**. The largest equity options market is the Chicago Board Options Exchange, which is on Central Time. Thus, cut-off times for options are stated in both Central Time and Eastern Time. Options are traded during the same hours as the NYSE. Trading on the NYSE stops at 4:00 PM (Eastern Time), which is 3:00 PM Central Time, so options trade until 4:00 PM Eastern Time, 3:00 PM Central Time. Trading takes place through the third Friday of the month.

2. The best answer is **c**. Long calls and short puts constitute the "up" side of the market. Long puts and short calls constitute the "down" side of the market. Position limits are applied to each "side" of the market.

3. The best answer is **b**. Legally, the maximum life of a regular stock option contract is 9 months. Currently, the way that options are issued, the actual maximum life is 8 months. Longer term stock options, known as LEAPs (Long Term Equity AnticiPation options) have a maximum life of 30 months.

4. The best answer is **c**. If an option contract is exercised by a holder, a writer is selected by the Options Clearing Corporation to perform on the contract on a random order basis.

5. The best answer is **a**. Exercise limits are applied to all exercises occurring within a 5 business day period - the same as 1 calendar week.

6. The best answer is **d**. The options cycles are:

Cycle 1	Jan	Apr	Jul	Oct
Cycle 2	Feb	May	Aug	Nov
Cycle 3	Mar	Jun	Sep	Dec

Cycle 1 contracts are issued for the months of Jan - Apr - Jul - Oct. One can always get a contract for this month, next month, and the next 2 months in the Cycle. In November, prior to expiration, the contracts that will trade are November (this month), December (next month), January and April (the next 2 months in the cycle). After November contracts expire, the contracts that will trade are December (this month), January (next month), April and July (the next 2 months in the cycle).

7. The best answer is **a**. An exercise notice may be placed by a customer immediately upon the purchase of a call or put contract. However, the Options Clearing Corporation does not handle the exercise until the morning of the next business day (which is also the day that the customer must pay for the option contract). This procedure is followed because the Options Clearing Corporation does not receive the report of the purchase of the option until the close of trading on the day that the contract is purchased. The O.C.C. opens the next day with the customer recorded as being "long" that contract, and can now assign an exercise notice to a writer.

8. The best answer is **a**. This is a stock dividend of 25%. The OCC does not adjust the contract on ex date. Only if there is an exercise, then the OCC adjusts the "deliverable." The contract holder owns 1 ABC Jan 50 Call. If the contract is exercised, the holder will receive 100 x 1.25 = 125 shares; at a price of $50/1.25 = $40.

9. The best answer is **d**. If an option contract is exercised by a holder, a writer is selected by the Options Clearing Corporation to perform on the contract on a random order basis.

10.   The best answer is **a**.   A class of option consists of all options of one type on an underlying security. For example, all ABC calls are a "class;" all ABC puts are a "class." In contrast, an options "series" would be all ABC Jan 50 Calls - a series is a class of option on the same underlying stock with the same strike and expiration.

11.   The best answer is **d**.   If trading in a stock is suspended, say on the New York Stock Exchange, the exchange where the option trades will also stop trading in the option contracts. This must occur because there is no longer any way to price the option contracts if there is no current market for the underlying stock. Any holders of outstanding options can still exercise their contracts during a trading halt, since this is performed through the Options Clearing Corporation and does not occur on the exchange floor.

12.   The best answer is **a**.   Regular way trades of U.S. Government and agency issues settle next business day. Regular way trades of options settle next business day. Regular way trades of listed stocks settle 2 business days after trade date.

13.   The best answer is **a**.   The only way to cover a short call with another option contract is to buy an option that allows for the purchase of the stock (meaning a call option). The option must have the same strike price or lower (allowing the stock to be purchased at the same price or cheaper) as that of the contract which is sold and must have the same expiration or longer than the contract sold. Thus, to cover the short Jan 55 Call, a long Jan 50 call is good because the strike price is lower; a long Jan 60 call is not good because the strike price is higher.

14.   The best answer is **c**.   Exchange traded option contracts have standardized contract sizes (e.g., 100 shares of stock), expiration dates, and strike prices. The premium or "price" of the option is determined minute by minute in the trading market.

15.   The best answer is **b**.   The very first options contracts were single stock options, which started trading on the CBOE in 1973. All single stock options are "American Style" - these are options that can be exercised at any time. In contrast, European style options can only be exercised at expiration and not before.

All options contracts can be traded anytime until expiration. Options contracts can only be issued based on the cycles set by the Options Clearing Corporation.

SECTION 9: INDEX OPTIONS

9a. OVERVIEW

The "idea" behind individual stock options is carried one step further with index options. A market "index" is composed of a number of issues traded. For example, the Standard and Poor's 500 Index is composed of the 500 largest companies (based on market capitalization) headquartered in the United States. If one believes that the market as a whole will rise, instead of picking calls on individual stocks, why not buy a call on the index instead? If one thinks the market as a whole will fall, why not buy a put on the index?

Index options are considered by some people to be gambling. This is not really true. Assume that one is a portfolio manager, with $100,000,000 invested in NYSE issues. One can protect the portfolio against a drop in the market by purchasing individual puts on each stock position. Alternatively, one can buy index puts as a hedge - which is simpler and cheaper. Maybe the manager believes that the market will stay flat and wants to earn some extra income during this time period. Why not sell index calls against the portfolio for the added premium income?

All of the strategies that were discussed using equities as the underlying security apply to **all** option contracts - including index options.

We all should know the name of the most widely quoted index - the Dow Jones Industrial Average. It consists of 30 industrial stocks listed on the NYSE, such as IBM, GE, Exxon, American Express, etc. The DJIA is the index one always hears quoted in the news - such as "The Dow was up 20 points today." It would make sense that an index option would be traded on the DJIA, but Dow Jones and Co. did not (until October of 1997) allow its name to be put on an index option because it believed that "gambling" using its index could have a negative effect on its value.

Standard And Poor's 100 Index (OEX)

Traded On CBOE

The very first index option was introduced in 1983 by the Chicago Board Options Exchange (about 10 years after stock options first started trading in that market). At that time, the CBOE attempted to license the DJIA, but was rebuffed by Dow Jones. Instead, the CBOE went to Standard and Poor's to license the S&P 500 index. Standard and Poor's problem with the licensing was that if the contract was a failure, it could reflect badly on their index, so a compromise was struck. A sub-index of 100 stocks out of the 500 was created, called the S&P 100 index. An index option was created by the CBOE called the "OEX" - as in Options Exchange Index - that started trading in 1983.

OEX - American Style

Very Actively Traded Option On CBOE

Trading in this index option exploded after introduction, and the other exchanges that trade options quickly came out with products for this marketplace. The OEX became the most actively traded option contract in the world. It was modeled after traditional stock options, in that it is an "American Style" option - that is, one that is exercisable at any time.

Standard And Poor's 500 Index (SPX)

Traded On CBOE

SPX - European Style

With the success of the OEX, the CBOE was able to license the full S&P 500 index, and introduced the "SPX" index option in 1984. First introduced as an American Style option, it was changed to a "European Style" option about 6 months later. A European Style option is one that is exercisable only at expiration. These contracts are more attractive to institutional writers, since there is no risk of an unexpected exercise. This contract has also been very successful - the SPX now surpasses the OEX in trading volume.

Major Market Index (XMI)

Traded On AMEX

The American Stock Exchange came up with an index that mimics the DJIA - it is called the Major Market Index and consists of 20 stocks, most of which are in the DJIA. The Major Market Index, known as the "XMI" index, tracks the DJIA with 99% accuracy.

Dow Jones Industrial Average Index (DJX)

Traded On CBOE

In October of 1997, Dow Jones and Co. finally decided to license its Dow Jones Industrial Average to the Chicago Board Options Exchange, stating at the time that it believed that the options market had matured enough, and that investors had become sophisticated enough, to allow trading of options on the index. The Dow Jones Industrial Average Index option (DJX) covers the 30 stocks in the industrial average. As of this writing, the DJX option is still not being tested on Series 7.

OEX, SPX, And XMI - "Broad Based"

The most popular index options, by far, are the OEX and SPX. The XMI has not been as successful. These are all termed "broad based contracts" since they measure a cross section of the market. Also note that, while not currently tested, the DJX option is off to a relatively strong start, with trading volumes that are much greater than the essentially equivalent XMI option.

"Narrow Based"

Other index options were devised using sectors of the market - such as an airlines index, an energy index, etc. These are termed "narrow based contracts" and have been relatively unsuccessful.

9b. OEX (S&P 100) INDEX OPTION

The OEX index option is traded on the Chicago Board Options Exchange and it mirrors price movements in the broad market. Instead of covering 100 shares, the contract is said to have a "multiplier" of 100.

If a holder of an index call exercises, he is not delivered 100 bundles of the 100 stocks in the index at the strike price. Similarly, if the holder of an index put exercises, he does not sell 100 bundles of the 100 stocks in the index at the strike price.

Exercise Settles In Cash At Closing Index Value

Exercise of index options results in a settlement in cash. If the holder of a call or put exercises, the writer must pay to the holder the difference between the strike price and the closing index value that day. Since the OEX option is American style, it can be exercised at any time. Also note that as a general rule, all of the other index options are European style - and can only be exercised at expiration. In reality, very few contracts are ever exercised. Positions are closed by making offsetting trades in the market.

Following is a financial listing for OEX contracts:

S & P 100 Index (Chicago)

Option & NY Close	Strike Price	Calls - Last			Puts - Last		
		Sep	Oct	Nov	Sep	Oct	Nov
495.54	490	11.75	14.75	17.50	5.50	11.00	14.50
495.54	495	8.50	12.25	14.75	7.65	11.75	16.40
495.54	500	6.00	10.50	r	10.40	17.40	r
495.54	505	4.00	7.50	11.00	13.00	19.00	r

Total Call Vol: 64,749   Call Open Int: 229,354   r: Not Traded
Total Put Vol: 53,995   Put Open Int: 220,087

A customer who believes that the market will rise can buy an OEX Call. Assume a customer takes the following position:

> Buy 1 OEX Sep 490 Call @ $11.75
> OEX Close: 495.54

The customer pays a premium of $11.75 times a multiplier of 100 equals a total cost of $1,175 for the contract. Trades settle next business day.

The contract covers a "value" of 490 index strike price times a multiplier of 100 = $49,000. If this customer decided to exercise the contract (which technically cannot happen until the trade settles the next day), he does not take delivery of the index! The seller is obligated to pay to the holder:

Contract Price =	490	x	100	=	$49,000
OEX Close =	495.54	x	100	=	$49,554
Paid by seller to holder					$554

Upon Exercise, Seller Pays Buyer "In The Money" Amount Computed Based Upon Closing Index Value

If an index option is exercised, the seller must pay the holder the **next** business day. Notice that the seller pays the holder the closing index value. If a call holder exercised during this day when the OEX was at 515.82 at 1:00 PM and then the market fell sharply to close at 495.54, the cash settlement would be calculated from the **closing price** - not the price at the moment of exercise.

Options

The OEX (or SPX) is used by portfolio managers who wish to hedge or get extra income. Assume that a portfolio manager runs a $1,000,000 portfolio of "blue chip" stocks. To protect against a fall in the market, the manager can buy OEX Puts. Assume the manager decides to buy the following:

Existing portfolio: $1,000,000 "Blue Chip" stocks
Hedge: Buy 20 OEX Sept 500 Puts @ $10.40

Matching Number Of Contracts To Hedge Portfolio

Since each contract covers 500 x 100 = $50,000 of value, 20 contracts must be purchased to hedge the portfolio. If the market drops, the portfolio cannot be "put" to the writer. Instead, the cash profit on the put contracts will offset the loss in value of the portfolio.

Beta - Measures Volatility

Assume that one has a portfolio that tracks the market, but it consists of more volatile stocks. The measure for volatility is called the "**beta**." If one's portfolio moves as fast as the market as measured by the S&P 500 index, the portfolio has a beta of 1; a beta of 2 means the portfolio is twice as volatile; 3 means 3 times as volatile, etc.

Can Use Beta Weighted Contracts To Hedge Against Systematic Risk

To hedge a $1,000,000 portfolio with a beta of 2, one needs **twice** the number of contracts. (Remember, if the index falls, one's portfolio falls twice as fast.) Matching portfolio "betas" allows for hedging against "market risk." This is the risk that the market will drop, taking the portfolio value with it. Market risk is also known as "systematic risk."

Cannot Hedge Against Unsystematic Risk

Hedging with index contracts does not protect against "unsystematic risk." This is the risk that a specific security may turn into a bad investment.

As a second example, assume that it is believed that the market will stay flat for the next few months. The portfolio manager decides to generate extra income from the portfolio by selling 20 OEX Sep 500 Calls @ $6 (collecting $600 x 20 contracts = $12,000). If the market rises, any gain on the portfolio will be offset by an equal loss on the short calls (but one wouldn't do this if it was thought that the market will rise). If the market drops, the calls expire and the premiums are kept as a partial hedge against stock losses in the portfolio.

From the chart, also notice that the trading volume of puts and calls for that day is given, as well as the open interest (the number of contracts to be closed prior to expiration). Some analysts gauge the strength of the market by the:

$$\text{Put / Call Ratio} = \frac{\text{Put Volume}}{\text{Call Volume}} = \frac{53,995}{64,749} = .83$$

Normally, fewer puts are traded than calls, and the ratio stays around .50. This means that in normal conditions, twice as many calls trade as do put contracts. If the ratio increases above .50, proportionately more puts are being traded - a bearish sign. If the ratio decreases below .50, proportionately more calls are being traded and is bullish.

Put / Call Ratio Used To Determine If The Market Is "Overbought" Or "Oversold"

In reality, the put/call ratio is used as a market indicator to show when a market is either "oversold" or "overbought" and therefore ready for a turnaround. If the put/call ratio is very high, this means that the market is currently "oversold" and would have a difficult time going any lower. Thus, the market is ripe for a turnaround and is ready to move higher. Our ratio above would give this indication.

On the other hand, if the ratio is very low, this means that the market is "overbought" and would have a difficult time going any higher. Thus, the market is ripe for a turnaround and is ready to move lower.

9c. OEX / SPX LEAPs

OEX / SPX LEAPs / Long Term Index Options

A newer type of index option is a contract with a long life. On the CBOE, these are known as "LEAPs" - Long-term Equity AnticiPation options. LEAPs cover both the OEX and SPX indexes. Both of these products expire in December of each year, and contracts are issued for each of the two Decembers after the current year.

Index LEAP Maximum Life Is About 36 Months

For example, in the beginning of December of 2017, index LEAPs are available with December '17 (about to expire), '18, and '19 expirations. After the Dec '17s expire, the '18s and '19s still trade; and in January of 2018, LEAPs are issued with a Dec '20 expiration. Thus, the maximum life on these contracts is 35 months (but this is tested as 36 months). The LEAP contract is issued in the same "style" as the regular index option. Thus, OEX LEAPs are American style options; while SPX LEAPs are European Style Options.

If LEAP contracts on indexes are exercised, the writer must pay the holder the "in the money" amount (identical to the exercise of regular index options). For LEAP index contracts, the multiplier is 100.

Below is a comparison of the OEX, along with its LEAP variant, to a regular stock option:

	Stock Option	OEX Option
Multiplier:	100	100
Trade settlement:	Next day	Next day
Exercise settlement:	2 business days Delivery of stock	Next day Delivery of cash
Maximum life:	9 months	4 months (each of next 4 upcoming months)
Style:	American	American
LEAP max. life:	30 months	36 months
LEAP style:	American	American
Trading cut-off:	4:00 PM ET	4:15 PM ET
Expiration:	3rd Friday of month @ 11:59 PM ET	

9d. OTHER INDEX OPTIONS

Major Market Index (XMI)

Major Market Index (XMI) contract traded on the AMEX. It consists of 20 stocks and mimics the Dow Jones Industrial Average. With the advent of the DJX option on the CBOE, this contract will probably be discontinued, since it has a very small trading volume.

Value Line Contract (VLE)

Value Line (VLE) Index contract traded on the Philadelphia Exchange (PHLX). The Value Line index consists of approximately 1,700 common issues, selected from the NYSE, AMEX, and OTC markets. This contract would be useful to a portfolio manager whose securities mirrored this selection. This contract has been unpopular, and will probably be discontinued. The multiplier is 100.

Narrow Based Contracts

A variety of narrow based index options contracts are traded on the various exchanges. These contracts are either country specific or industry specific. Examples of these narrow based contracts are:

CBOE:	Mexico Index (MEX) Technology Index (TXX)
AMEX:	Japan Index (JPN) Pharmaceutical Index (DRG)
PHLX:	Gold / Silver Index (XAU) Oil Service Index (OSX)

Narrow Based Contracts Have Higher Betas

Most Contracts Other Than OEX Are European Style

It is not necessary to memorize these for the examination, but, for example, it should be known that these portfolios will tend to have higher "betas" than broad based indexes; and that they are available, though not very actively traded, in the market. In contrast to the OEX (Standard and Poor's 100 Index option), which is American style, the other contracts, including the XMI, SPX and narrow based contracts, and any LEAPs on these contracts, are typically issued in European style only.

9e. VIX OPTIONS

VIX - Volatility Index Options

"VIX" is the trading symbol for S&P Volatility Index Options. This is a benchmark index that gauges investor sentiment - commonly referred to as a "fear gauge."

VIX Based On SPX Expected Volatility Over Next 30 Days

The index is derived from real-time S&P 500 Index option (SPX) bid and ask quotes. It reflects investors' consensus view of expected stock price volatility over the upcoming 30 days. It uses a formula to derive expected volatility excluding changes in underlying price, dividends, interest rates and time to expiration (these are the regular determinants of the option premium).

What is truly odd about the "VIX" contract is that it is an option on a futures contract. In 2003, the CBOE started the "CFE" - the Chicago Futures Exchange - to electronically trade futures and options on futures. However, the CFE uses the CBOE's electronic trading platform to trade, so the contract is deemed to be "SEC" regulated and not CFTC regulated - hence it is a securities product that can be tested on Series 7!

VIX Value Of "0" Implies Flat Market

A VIX value of "0" implies no market volatility over the next 30 days - that is no daily change in the S&P 500 Index. An extreme VIX measure (the VIX has tended to range between 15 and 50) implies high volatility. However, historically, the S&P Index is not very volatile - rarely moving more than 5% in a given day. Very low VIX levels imply that the market is calm and the next likely market move is upwards. Very high VIX levels indicate heightened investor fear and the next market move is likely to be down (when the equities markets "collapsed" in the fall of 2008, the VIX reached its highest recorded value ever - over 80).

VIX Negatively Correlated To Stock Price Movements

During normal market conditions, the VIX is negatively correlated to the price movements of the S&P 500 Index. The "idea" here is that when VIX values are rising (increasing market volatility), this is an indicator of increased "fear" and an impending market decline.

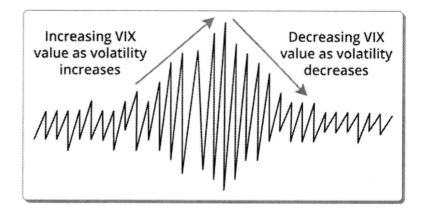

Conversely, when VIX values are falling (decreasing market volatility), this is an indicator of increased "confidence" and an impending market rise.

CBOE statistics show that over the past 15 years, during days of sharp price movement in the S&P 500 Index, when stock prices dropped on average 4%, the VIX went up by 17%; and on days when the S&P 500 Index rose by 4%, the VIX dropped by 9% (all numbers are rounded). Thus, the VIX could be used as a "catastrophic hedging tool" for stock portfolios.

The index allows risk managers and hedge funds to trade "volatility," and market makers that trade "volatility" can use these options to hedge their positions.

This option contract differs from standard index options in that the:

- contracts available are the upcoming 2 months plus 1 more upcoming month based on the February quarterly cycle (either Feb., May, Aug., or Nov.);

- contract is a 30-day benchmark of expected market volatility as measured by SPX options' prices. Exercise settlement is based upon a monthly calculation of expected market volatility over the upcoming 30 days. It is based on SPX options that will expire exactly 30 days prior to the third Friday of the following calendar month;

- exercise settlement calculation is not performed on the Friday that is 30 days prior to expiration, but the Wednesday morning before. Options exercises settle on this Wednesday, so that the expiration does not coincide with the regular index option exercises (which occur on the third Friday). Exercise settlement is in cash, on the business day following the calculation;

- last day to trade an expiring contract is the Tuesday before the monthly Wednesday morning exercise-settlement value calculation;

- underlying value of the VIX option is the forward value (expected future value) of SPX options expiring 30 days later. A June VIX

contract measures implied market volatility for the July following; a July VIX contract measure implied market volatility for the August following, etc.

This option contract is the same as regular index options in that the:

- contract multiplier is $100;

- contract is only issued in European style;

- contract trades between 9:30 AM and 4:15 PM ET (8:30 AM and 3:15 PM CT);

- exercise settlement occurs in "cash" the next business day, with the writer paying the holder any "in the money" amount.

9f. INTEREST RATE INDEX OPTIONS

Options Based On Yield Movement

The CBOE created interest rate index options, using the movement of Treasury security interest rates as the "price" reference. These were discontinued in 2011 due to lack of retail investor demand, but the index values are still calculated daily, and they can be reinstated by the CBOE if there is sufficient demand.

Interest rate index options were available based on the yield of the most recently auctioned:

- 13 week Treasury Bill (IRX option)
- 5 year Treasury Note (FVX option)
- 10 year Treasury Note (TNX option)
- 30 year Treasury Bond (TYX option)

Premiums Move Opposite To Price-Based Options

These are a minor test item, with maybe 1 or 2 questions on the exam. The key points that must be known about interest rate index options are:

The contract value tracks interest rate movements - if market interest rates rise, call premiums rise and put premiums fall; and vice-versa.

To speculate on interest rate movements, for the maximum profit, one could buy calls (rising interest rates) or buy puts (falling interest rates).

To hedge an existing Treasury security position:

if long Treasury securities, when market interest rates rise, values fall. To have an offsetting profit from an interest rate index option when interest rates rise, buy calls.

if short Treasury securities, when market interest rates fall, values rise. To have an offsetting profit from an interest rate index option when interest rates fall, buy puts.

(Note that these hedging positions are the opposite of other options because they are based on interest rate movements, which move inversely to price movements.)

The contracts trade like any other option with regular way settlement occurring next business day.

The contract multiplier is 100.

The contracts are European style, with exercise settlement occurring next business day in cash (no delivery of the underlying Treasury securities).

INDEX OPTIONS
SECTION EXAMINATION

1.

A customer buys 1 OEX Jan 500 Call @ $5 when the index closes at 501. The maximum potential loss is:

   a. $500

   b. $505

   c. $5,000

   d.   unlimited

2.

Index options expire:

   a.   each week

   b.   each month

   c.   every three months

   d.   every nine months

3.

Index calls would be purchased by a customer who:

   a.   is bullish on the direction of the market

   b.   is bearish on the direction of the market

   c.   believes that interest rates will rise

   d.   believes that interest rates will fall

4.

A customer sells 1 XMI Dec 530 Put @ 8 when the index is at 529.00. The customer is exercised when the index closes at 525.00. The writer is obligated to:

   a.   deliver cash

   b.   receive cash

   c.   deliver stock

   d.   receive stock

5.

A customer sells 1 XMI Dec 530 Put @ $8 when the index is at 529.00. The customer is exercised when the index closes at 525.00. The writer must pay:

   a. $30,000 to the holder

   b. $5,000 to the holder

   c. $1,000 to the holder

   d. $500 to the holder

6.

Which of the following are **TRUE** statements regarding index options?

   I   Upon exercise, the writer must pay to the holder the "in the money amount"

   II   Settlement upon exercise occurs next business day

   III   Settlement is based on the index value at the time of exercise

   IV   The maximum risk for an index option writer is the loss of the premium

   a.   I and II

   b.   II and III

   c.   I, II, III

   d.   II, III, IV

7.

The manager of a $400,000 aggressive stock portfolio wishes to hedge with OEX 400 Put contracts. The portfolio has a beta of 1.5. To hedge, the manager will buy:

   a.   10 OEX puts

   b.   15 OEX puts

   c.   10 OEX calls

   d.   15 OEX calls

8.

The maximum life of an index LEAP contract is:

   a.   12 months

   b.   24 months

   c.   36 months

   d.   48 months

9.

The sale of index calls against a portfolio of listed securities is a:

a. covered writing strategy
b. naked writing strategy
c. horizontal spread strategy
d. bullish strategy

10.

A customer buys 1 OEX Jan 550 Put @ $10 when the index is at 548.25. The maximum potential gain for the customer is:

a. $1,000
b. $53,825
c. $54,000
d. $55,000

11.

The VIX Index Option:

a. is negatively correlated to the S&P 500 Index
b. is positively correlated to the S&P 500 Index
c. is delta neutral when compared to the S&P 500 Index
d. has no correlation to the S&P 500 Index

12.

Which statements are **TRUE** about the VIX Index option contract?

I The contract value is based upon the price movement of the S&P 500 Index option
II The contract value is based upon the price volatility of the S&P 500 Index option
III The contract is offered in American style
IV The contract is offered in European style

a. I and III
b. I and IV
c. II and III
d. II and IV

13.

A client who believes that current economic events will make market conditions more stable over the upcoming 30 days could profit by:

a. buying VIX calls
b. selling VIX calls
c. buying VIX debit call spreads
d. selling VIX puts

14.

Which of the following index options would be considered "broad based"?

I Oil and Gas Index
II Major Market Index
III Standard and Poor's 100 Index
IV Standard and Poor's 500 Index

a. IV only
b. II and III only
c. II, III, IV
d. I, II, III, IV

15.

Which of the following index options would be considered "narrow based"?

I Oil and Gas Index
II Major Market Index
III Standard and Poor's 100 Index
IV High Technology Index

a. IV only
b. I and IV only
c. II and III
d. I, II, III, IV

INDEX OPTIONS EXAMINATION EXPLANATIONS

1. The best answer is **a**. The customer pays a premium of $5. Since the multiplier on the contract is 100, the total premium is $500. This is the maximum potential loss.

2. The best answer is **b**. Index options expire monthly. Contracts extend out for each of the next 4 months.

3. The best answer is **a**. Index calls are purchased by a customer who believes that the market will rise. Index puts are purchased by a customer who believes that the market will fall.

4. The best answer is **a**. If an index option is exercised, the writer is obligated to pay the holder the "in the money" amount in cash the next business day.

5. The best answer is **d**. The put has a strike price of 530. Upon exercise, the index closes at 525, therefore the put is "in the money" by 5 points or $500. The writer must pay this amount to the holder.

6. The best answer is **a**. If an index option is exercised, the writer must pay the holder the "in the money" amount the next business day. There is no delivery of the stocks that are in the index - these are termed "cash settled options." The index value is computed as of the close the day of exercise. The writer of an index call has unlimited risk; the writer of an index put has increasing risk as the market drops.

7. The best answer is **b**. Each OEX 400 Put contract covers $40,000 of stock (multiplier of 100 x 400 strike price). To hedge a $400,000 portfolio, 10 contracts are necessary. Since the portfolio is 1.5 times as volatile as the index (beta of 1.5), 1.5 x 10 contracts = 15 contracts are needed to provide a complete hedge.

8. The best answer is **c**. The maximum life of an index LEAP contract is 36 months (as compared to a maximum life of 30 months for an equity LEAP contract).

9. The best answer is **b**. If the writer of index calls is exercised, he does not deliver the stocks in the index - he delivers cash. Index call writing against a portfolio of securities is therefore considered to be a "naked" writing strategy. As with any "income writing" strategy where the call writer owns the physical instrument or an equivalent, the writer expects the market to remain neutral or is mildly bearish.

10. The best answer is **c**. If the index drops to "0," the writer must pay the holder 550 x 100 = $55,000. Since the holder paid 10 points ($1,000) in premiums, the maximum potential gain is $54,000.

11. The best answer is **a**. The VIX option measures volatility of the S&P 500 Index, and rising volatility is associated with bear markets. When the S&P 500 Index is falling, the VIX will be rising (meaning that volatility is increasing). "Delta neutral" is an advanced option strategy that is not covered on the Series 7 exam.

12. The best answer is **d**. The VIX option is an up-to-the-minute market estimate of expected price volatility using real-time SPX (S&P 500 Index) option bid/ask quotes. The VIX calculates expected SPX price volatility over the next 30 days. The contracts are available in European style, not American style. (The very first index option, the OEX, is American style, since it was modeled after stock options. All of the later index options are European style).

13. The best answer is **b**. The VIX option is based on market volatility. Increased levels of volatility will increase the VIX value - so buy VIX calls, buy VIX call (debit) spreads, sell VIX puts or sell VIX put (credit) spreads. Decreasing volatility will lower the VIX value - so buy VIX puts, buy VIX put (debit) spreads, sell VIX calls or sell VIX call (credit) spreads.

14. The best answer is **c**. For an index option to be considered to be "Broad Based," it must have companies in the index covering a broad spectrum of industries. Thus, the Major Market Index, and the Standard and Poor's 100 and 500 Indexes, are all broad based. Examples of narrow indexes are oil and gas; gold; and airline stock indexes; as well as country indexes, such as the Mexico and Japan indexes.

15. The best answer is **b**. For an index option to be narrow based, it must be country specific or industry specific. Examples of narrow indexes are oil and gas; gold and silver; high technology; and airline stock indexes; as well as country indexes, such as the Mexico and Japan indexes. For an index option to be considered to be "Broad Based," it must have companies in the index covering a broad spectrum of industries. Thus, the Major Market Index and the Standard and Poor's 100 Index are broad based.

SECTION 10: FOREIGN CURRENCY OPTIONS

10a. FOREIGN CURRENCY MARKET OVERVIEW

Interbank Market

Unregulated

Foreign currency values relative to the dollar affect U.S. business activity and therefore the financial markets. Foreign currencies are traded in the "interbank" market. Trading is unregulated between domestic and foreign banks, in very large units (usually $5,000,000 minimum).

For each foreign currency trade, the buyer and seller negotiate the price and settlement terms. Settlement can be:

- **Spot market**: Settlement and delivery in 1 or 2 business days. (The more active the trading in the currency, the quicker the settlement time.)

- **Forward contract**: Settlement later than "spot," usually months in the future.

Floating Exchange Rates

Central Bank Trading

Because exchange rates "float," the value of currencies is determined in the marketplace. Central banks are big players in this market and can easily drive prices up or down for the short term. If a country feels its currency is undervalued, it will buy the currency in the market. If it feels the currency is overvalued, it will sell the currency in the market.

However, long-term price trends reflect the changing economic fortunes of each country. As a country's economy strengthens and its interest rates rise, currency values rise. As a country's economy weakens and its interest rates fall, currency values fall. Because long-term prices are based on the country's economic performance, fiscal and monetary policies of each country are determinants of price direction.

24-Hour Trading

Trading occurs 24 hours a day, with no systematic trade reporting taking place.

Options On Foreign Currencies

Options on foreign currencies are traded on the Philadelphia Stock Exchange (PHLX). They can be used to speculate on the direction of the currencies' values. For example, if you believe that the Japanese Yen will strengthen, buy yen calls. If you believe that the Canadian Dollar will weaken, buy Canadian dollar puts.

Importers and exporters can also use these contracts. Suppose an importer needs to pay for a shipment expected in 2 months from Britain in Pounds. To protect against the Pound rising (and hence costing more dollars), he can buy Pound calls and lock in a fixed cost for the currency.

Options

Assume an exporter will be paid in Euros when a shipment arrives in 2 months. To protect against a fall in that currency (meaning the currency is worth less in dollars), buy Euro puts.

Options on foreign currencies are not popular - most people prefer to trade the futures and options on futures instead, since these markets are more liquid.

10b. CURRENCY OPTION CONTRACTS

The PHLX currency options contracts that must be known for the Series 7 exam are:

Foreign Currency	Contract Size	Premium
Australian Dollar	10,000	
Canadian Dollar	10,000	
British Pound	10,000	Multiplier of
Swiss Franc	10,000	100
European currency (EURO)	10,000	
Japanese Yen	1,000,000	Multiplier of 100

These are the six major world currencies and the contracts are sized to appeal to the "smaller" investor - the contract sizes are much smaller than currency futures contracts and options on futures (which are not securities and thus are not on this exam).

Below is a sample quote for a PHLX EURO (the symbol is XDE) contract:

1 PHLX XDE Nov 145 Call @ 2.10
(Market = 146.00)

The customer will pay a premium of 2.10 times a multiplier of 100 = $210 for the contract.

This contract allows the holder to buy the EURO at a price of 145 cents ($1.45). Since the market price is $1.4600, the contract is "in the money" by $.0100.

To breakeven the EURO must climb above 145 + 2.10 premium or above $1.4710.

If the EURO rises in value from 146 to 147 ($1.46 to $1.47), this is an increase in value of $.01 x 10,000 units of currency = $100. All other things being equal, this increase in value would directly result in an increase in the premium from 2.10 to 3.10, which equals an increase from $210 to $310 - again, a $100 increase in value.

This example shows that the basics of options apply to **all** types of contracts. Also note that the PHLX states that the multiplier on the larger Japanese Yen contract is also "100" - but they add a "00" to the computation. Thus, a $.01 move in the Japanese Yen contract equals (.00)01 = $.0001 x 1,000,000 = $100 - the same as for the contracts that are sized in 10,000 units of currency.

Trades Settle Next Business Day

European Style

Foreign currency option trades settle next business day through the Options Clearing Corporation. The contracts are available only as "European Style" - which can be exercised only at expiration (but can still be traded). European style options are more attractive to institutional writers of contracts that do not want an unexpected exercise.

The contracts are essentially similar to index options. If the contract is "in the money" at expiration, the holder could perform a closing trade to realize the profit, or could exercise at expiration, with the last day to trade being the third Friday of the month, just like stock and index options.

Exercise Settlement In Cash

Exercise settlement results in a delivery of cash (U.S. dollars) from writer to holder the next business day, again just like index options. The settlement value is based on the 12:00 Noon "Buying Rate" determined by the Federal Reserve on the third Friday of the month (last trading day for that month, just like stock and index options).

Also note that an exercise of the "previous" generation of PHLX currency options could be settled by delivering the foreign currency - this is no longer the case.

For example, assume that a customer has purchased 1 PHLX Mar XDC (Canadian Dollar) 100 Put @ 2.10 when the Canadian Dollar is at 99. Just prior to expiration, the Canadian Dollar falls to 95 and the premium on the contract rises to 5.00 (intrinsic value only since there is no "time" left to the contract). The customer performs a closing trade. The profit is:

Closing sale proceeds	$500 (5.00 x 100)
Opening purchase cost	<u>$210</u> (2.10 x 100)
	$290 Profit

For example, assume that a customer has purchased 1 PHLX Mar XDC (Canadian Dollar) 100 Put @ 2.10 when the Canadian Dollar is at 99. The Canadian Dollar falls to 95, and on the 3rd Friday in March, the exercise settlement value is set at 95.00. The customer exercises the contract.

As a result of the exercise, the writer must pay the holder the "in the money amount" of 5 x 100 = $500. Since a premium of 2.10 x 100 = $210 was paid for the contract, the profit is $290 ($500 - $210).

The specifics on foreign currency option contracts traded on the PHLX are:

Contract size:	10,000 units of currency except for Japanese Yen, which cover 1,000,000 units of currency
Multiplier:	100
Settlement of trades:	Next business day
Settlement of exercise:	Writer pays the holder the "in the money" amount the next business day
Expiration type:	European (exercise only at expiration)
Trading cut-off:	4:00 PM ET on the 3rd Friday of the month
Expiration date:	11:59 ET on the 3rd Friday of the month
Trading hours:	9:30 AM - 4:00 PM ET (same as equity options; in contrast, index options trade until 4:15 PM)

FOREIGN CURRENCY OPTIONS SECTION EXAMINATION

1.
When reading the morning news reports, you see that Great Britain has discovered oil in the North Sea, while Canada is suffering from labor shortages. An appropriate strategy is to buy:

   I   British Pound Calls
   II Canadian Dollar Calls
   III British Pound Puts
   IV Canadian Dollar Puts

   a. I and II
   b. I and IV
   c. II and III
   d. II and IV

2.
Canadian Dollar Feb 80 Calls on the PHLX are quoted at 1.25. Canadian Dollars are trading at 80.25. The contract size is 10,000 dollars (Canadian). What is the total premium for 10 contracts?

   a. $1.25
   b. $12.50
   c. $125.00
   d. $1,250.00

3.
A customer buys 1 PHLX British Pound 180 Call @ 5.00 when the Pound is trading at 181. Later, the Pound is trading at 189 and the contract is closed at intrinsic value. The profit is: (Contract size = 10,000 Pounds)

   a. $300
   b. $400
   c. $800
   d. $900

4.
A foreign currency trader has bought 1,000,000 Canadian Dollars in the spot market at 92. To hedge, the trader buys 100 PHLX Jul Canadian Dollar 92 Puts @ 1.75. The position will be profitable at which price?

   a. .9025
   b. .9200
   c. .9375
   d. .9400

5.
Which contract is at parity?

   a. British Pound Jul 155 Call @ 6 when the Pound closes at 160
   b. British Pound Jul 155 Put @ 1 when the Pound closes at 160
   c. Canadian Dollar Oct 81 Call @ 3 when the Canadian Dollar closes at 84
   d. Canadian Dollar Oct 81 Put @ 3 when the Canadian Dollar closes at 79

6.
A customer buys 1 PHLX Canadian Dollar Jan 98 Call @ 2 and 1 PHLX Canadian Dollar Jan 98 Put @ 3 when the Canadian Dollar is trading at $.9875. The contract size is 10,000 Canadian Dollars. The maximum potential loss is:

   a. $200
   b. $300
   c. $500
   d. unlimited

7.
A customer buys 1 PHLX Canadian Dollar Jan 98 Call @ 2 and 1 PHLX Canadian Dollar Jan 98 Put @ 3 when the Canadian Dollar is trading at $.9875. The contract size is 10,000 Canadian Dollars. The breakeven points are:

   a. $.93 and $1.03
   b. $.95 and $1.00
   c. $.96 and $.91
   d. $1.01 and $1.03

Options

8.
Upon exercise of a Japanese Yen World Currency call option, the holder will:

    a.   receive U.S. Dollars
    b.   deliver U.S. Dollars
    c.   receive Japanese Yen
    d.   deliver Japanese Yen

9.
An option contract that is exercisable at any time until expiration date is a(n):

    a.   spot contract
    b.   American contract
    c.   European contract
    d.   cash contract

10.
Performance on exercise of foreign currency option contracts is guaranteed by the:

    a.   exchange where the currency option trades
    b.   writer of the contract
    c.   Options Clearing Corporation
    d.   International Monetary Market

11.
Which option exchange trades foreign currency options?

    a.   Chicago Board Options Exchange
    b.   American Stock Exchange
    c.   Philadelphia Stock Exchange
    d.   All of the above

12.
Foreign currency options expire on the:

    a.   Friday before the third Wednesday of the month
    b.   Friday after the third Wednesday of the month
    c.   second Friday of the month
    d.   third Friday of the month

13.
All of the following investors are likely to trade foreign currency options **EXCEPT:**

    a.   foreign corporations with multinational operations
    b.   individuals with large U.S. dollar holdings
    c.   individuals with large foreign currency holdings
    d.   U.S. corporations with multinational operations

14.
An exporter of goods to Japan is going to receive 1 million Japanese Yen in payment. To protect against a decline in the Yen, the customer would hedge by purchasing how many World Currency contracts?

    a.   1
    b.   10
    c.   100
    d.   1,000

15.
A customer buys 1 Euro Feb 142 Call and sells 1 Euro Jan 142 Call. The position is profitable if:

    a.   the spread between the premiums widens
    b.   the spread between the premiums narrows
    c.   both contracts are exercised
    d.   both contracts expire "out the money"

FOREIGN CURRENCY OPTIONS EXAMINATION EXPLANATIONS

1. The best answer is **b**. If Great Britain has discovered oil reserves, its currency can be expected to strengthen. To profit, buy British Pound calls. If Canada is having labor problems, its economy is in trouble, weakening the currency. To profit, buy Canadian Dollar puts.

2. The best answer is **d**. World Currency options are standardized, using a multiplier of 100 applied to the premium. A premium of 1.25 x multiplier of 100 = $125 total premium per contract. Since 10 contracts are purchased, 125 x 10 contracts = $1,250 total premium.

(Another way of doing this - but not necessarily recommended - is contract size = 10,000 units of currency x a premium of 1.25 cents ($.0125) = $125 per contract x 10 contracts = $1,250.)

3. The best answer is **b**. The contract was purchased at a premium of 5 x a multiplier of 100 = $500. It was closed (sold) at a premium of 9 - the intrinsic value of the contract, therefore the profit is 900 - 500 = $400. The contract is "in the money" by 9 points because the holder has the right to buy the British Pound at 180 ($1.80) when the British Pound is trading at 189 ($1.89).

4. The best answer is **d**. The trader bought the Canadian Dollars at 92 and paid a premium of 1.75 for the put option, for a total cost of .9375 - the breakeven point. To be profitable, the price must rise above .9375. The only answer above .9375 is .9400 - Choice **D**.

5. The best answer is **c**. A contract trades "at parity" when the premium equals intrinsic value. The CD Oct 81 Call has intrinsic value of 3 (since the market is 84). Since the premium is 3, the contract is at parity.

6. The best answer is **c**. The customer paid 2 per call + 3 per put = 5 x 100 multiplier = $500 paid per straddle. If the Canadian Dollar does not move from 98, both the call and put expire "at the money" and the total premium paid is lost. This is the maximum potential loss.

7. The best answer is **a**. To breakeven on a long straddle, the total premium must be recovered, either moving up on the call or down on the put. To recover 5 cents total premium paid on the call, the market price must move to 98 + 5 = 103 = $1.03. To recover 5 cents on the put, the market price must move down to 98 - 5 = 93 = $.93.

8. The best answer is **a**. If there is an exercise of a foreign currency option, settlement is the same as for exercise of index options. If a PHLX World Currency option is exercised, the writer must pay the holder the "in the money" amount the next business day. There is no delivery of the foreign currency upon exercise.

9. The best answer is **b**. "American" style options are exercisable at any time until expiration. "European" style options are only exercisable on the expiration date, not before.

10. The best answer is **c**. The O.C.C. (Options Clearing Corporation) guarantees performance on listed options contracts. If the writer fails to perform, the O.C.C. will make good on the contract.

11. The best answer is **c**. Trading of foreign currency options in the United States takes place only on the Philadelphia Stock Exchange. (Do not confuse this with the futures market for trading of foreign currency futures and options on futures.)

12. The best answer is **d**. Foreign currency options, which are traded on the PHLX, have the same expiration as all of the other listed options - the third Friday of the month at 11:59 P.M. Eastern time.

13. The best answer is **b**. Any multinational corporation will trade foreign currencies, either to acquire currency for payment in a particular country or to hedge transactions against fluctuations in currency values. Similarly, individuals with large foreign currency holdings are likely to use the foreign currency markets to hedge their positions. Individuals with U.S. dollar holdings have no need for the foreign currency markets - since they are not exposed to currency exchange risk.

14. The best answer is **a**. PHLX World Currency options cover 10,000 units of currency, with the exception of the Japanese Yen contract, which covers 1,000,000 units of currency. Since this customer is long 1,000,000 Japanese Yen, and each put contract covers 1,000,000 Yen, only 1 contract is needed to hedge the long foreign currency position from a market decline.

15. The best answer is **a**. The February expiration must be the month immediately following January. It cannot be the other way around, because then the time between the 2 expirations would be 11 months (February followed by January 11 months later). Since the maximum life of regularly issued options is 9 months, this cannot be the case. Thus, the February expiration must be later than the January expiration, with the February expiring 1 month after the January. The customer is buying the "far" expiration (February) and selling the "near" expiration (January) in this calendar spread. Because of its higher time value, the far expiration must be more expensive, so this is a debit spread. Debit spreads are profitable if the spread between the premiums widens. Then the positions can be closed out at a larger net credit.

In this case, exercising both contracts will not result in a gain because the strike price is the same for both. If both contracts expire, the customer loses the net debit. If both contracts are exercised, the customer buys Euros at $1.42 and delivers them for $1.42, incurring commission costs without any gain on the currency.

TRADING MARKETS

Trading Markets

TRADING MARKETS

TRADING MARKETS

This page intentionally left blank

SECTION 1: TRADING MARKET BASICS

1a. DEFINITIONS OF THE TRADING MARKETS

Negotiable securities trade in specific "markets." The overall marketplace for securities is divided into the:

- **Primary market**: new issues being sold to the public for the first time
- **Secondary market**: trading of issued securities

The primary market will be covered in the New Issues Chapter. This chapter deals with the "secondary" market - trading of issued securities.

Secondary Market Subdivisions

The secondary market is divided into 4 submarkets. These are called the:

- **First market;**
- **Second market;**
- **Third market;**
- **Fourth market.**

The names of the markets follow the chronology of each market's founding. These markets must be known for the examination.

However, a tidal wave of change sweeping through the securities industry is blurring the distinctions between these markets. This is occurring due to "demutualization" of exchanges, making them for-profit public companies, instead of member-owned not-for-profit businesses. The markets are consolidating, as the larger "publicly-owned" markets, such as the NYSE and NASDAQ Stock Market buy out the smaller markets or are bought out themselves. (The NYSE itself was bought by ICE - the Intercontinental Exchange - at the end of 2013.) This allows them to spread their fixed costs over a much larger trading base, making them more efficient and profitable. A description of each of these markets follows.

1b. FIRST MARKET - EXCHANGE TRADING

First Market

Trading On Exchange Floors

First Market: The first market is trading of exchange listed securities on the floor of the stock exchange. This was the first market, as the New York Stock Exchange (NYSE) is over 200 years old. The largest stock exchange with a physical trading floor, by far, is the NYSE, followed by the American Stock Exchange (AMEX), now renamed the NYSE-MKT.

Trading Markets

These exchanges have specific listing standards for companies that wish their stocks to be traded, both requiring that companies have a **national** investor base to be listed. As of this writing, on average 1 billion shares change hands on the NYSE each day, spread among about 2,500 listed companies. This is a very active trading market.

The American Stock Exchange, now owned by the NYSE and renamed the NYSE-MKT, is much smaller and generally trades national companies that do not meet NYSE listing standards. The NYSE is positioning NYSE-MKT as its incubator market for smaller growth companies. On average, 100 million shares change hands on the NYSE-MKT each day, spread among approximately 400 listed companies, including about 150 exchange traded funds.

There are also regional stock exchanges which trade companies specific to that region, and they may also trade some NYSE and NYSE-MKT listed issues (so called "dual listings"). These exchanges are:

Regional Stock Exchange	Daily Volume
Chicago (Midwest)	70,000,000
Pacific (ARCA)	20,000,000
Philadelphia	10,000,000
Boston	20,000,000
Cincinnati	20,000,000

As the securities industry continues its consolidation, in 2008, the NYSE purchased the AMEX and has moved AMEX stock and options trading to separate areas on its trading floor, renaming the equities market as the NYSE-MKT and keeping the AMEX name for the options market. The NYSE already owns the Pacific Stock Exchange, now renamed the ARCA (as in Archipelago) exchange. The NYSE purchased Archipelago (an electronic trading network that owned the Pacific Exchange) in 2006. The NASDAQ Stock Market bought the Philadelphia and Boston Stock Exchanges in 2007. All of these are being run as separate operating subsidiaries. Note that these "regional" exchanges must still be known for the exam.

Dual Listing

Historically, dual listings occurred because when a company was small, it would list on a "local" stock exchange; and then when it got big enough, it would list on the NYSE (the "Big Board"). When this happened, the NYSE allowed the company to remain listed on the "local" stock exchange as well.

However, note that such "dual listings" generally do not occur between the NYSE, NYSE-MKT, or NASDAQ (covered following). The NYSE and NASDAQ are the two dominant securities markets in the U.S.; with the NYSE-MKT being much smaller (though still larger than the regionals). Each of these 3 dominant markets competes intensely with the others for listings.

Until recently, the NYSE, NASDAQ, and NYSE-MKT markets required "exclusivity" for each of their listings. However, the SEC viewed this as "anti-competitive" and these rules have been rescinded. Thus, over time, competition among these markets is increasing as each begins to trade the others' listings.

Thus, a trade for an NYSE listed issue will not necessarily take place on the floor of the New York Stock Exchange. It might take place on a "regional" exchange that dual lists the stock or it might take place "OTC" - Over-The-Counter - in the so-called Third Market (covered later in this section).

Because of this competition, the NYSE's market share trading its own stocks is actually about 40%. The other 60% represents trades of NYSE-listed issues that take place on regional exchanges or OTC.

CQS - Consolidated Quotation Service

To promote competition among these market centers for trading of NYSE listed issues and NYSE-MKT (AMEX) listed issues, there is a centralized electronic quotations service called "CQS" - the Consolidated Quotation Service. CQS was established under SEC-mandate to impose competition on the NYSE. Prior to its establishment, there was no central source for quotes for the NYSE and AMEX (NYSE-MKT) listed issues. Instead, one had to go to each market separately to view that market's quote. This made it hard to "comparison shop" quotes for stocks that were dual listed or that were quoted OTC in the Third Market (covered following). Also note that NASDAQ was not included in CQS at the time, because it was in its first years of operation and was very small.

Quotes For NYSE And AMEX (NYSE-MKT) Issues

CQS provides current price quotes (not actual trade reports) for exchange listed securities, regardless of the source of the quote. Thus, these quotes might come from the NYSE market maker, a market maker on a regional exchange that dual lists the stock, or from an OTC "Third Market Maker" in that issue.

Once a trade occurs in any of these market centers in an exchange-listed issue, it is reported to the "Consolidated Tape." There are 2 tape feeds:

Network A Tape-Trades Of NYSE Listed Issues

Network A Tape: Reports trades of NYSE-listed issues, regardless of the market center where the trade takes place.

Network B Tape-Trades Of NYSE-MKT And Regional Exchange Listed Issues

Network B Tape: Reports trades of NYSE-MKT-listed issues, regardless of the market center where the trade takes place. It also reports trades of stocks listed on the other regional exchanges, such as the PHLX.

Thus, when a trade is reported across the NYSE "tape," the trade did not necessarily take place on the floor of the NYSE - it may have taken place on a regional exchange or OTC.

NASDAQ Stock Market

The NASDAQ Stock Market was recognized by the SEC as an "exchange" in late 2006. NASDAQ started in 1971 as "NASD Automated quotes," where NASD stood for the National Association of Securities Dealers. At that time, the system only provided each dealer's quote with the telephone number, and retail member firms telephoned the dealers to trade. With the advent of computerized trading and the Internet, NASDAQ became a fully-linked electronic market in 2003 and also tightened its listing standards to compete with the NYSE.

NASDAQ is a different type of exchange. Rather than having a physical trading floor, it consists of a computer trading network. Just like the NYSE, NYSE-MKT and regional exchanges, it has minimum listing standards for the stocks that it trades. NASDAQ lists about 3,000 issues, and averages about 1 billion shares traded each day.

NASDAQ is not part of CQS - it was too small when CQS was created in 1979 for it to be included. By 2006, when NASDAQ became a recognized stock exchange, it was the largest exchange by trading volume. As part of the process of becoming an exchange, NASDAQ had to show its own consolidated quotes and publish a real time tape of its trades (called the Network C Tape).

UTP - Unlisted Trading Privileges

Trading Of NASDAQ Listed Issues By Exchanges And ECNs

Similar to the situation for NYSE-listed issues, where the NYSE actually only trades about 40% of its listed issues, NASDAQ also has about a 40% market share trading its own stocks. The NYSE trading floor gets competition from regional exchanges and OTC market makers that trade NYSE listed issues. The NASDAQ Stock Market gets competition from exchanges that trade NASDAQ issues under a so-called "UTP" plan - Unlisted Trading Privileges. In addition, electronic order matching services known as ECNs (Electronic Communications Networks, covered later in this section) compete with the NASDAQ Stock Market.

UQDF - UTP Quote Data Feed

Quotes For NASDAQ Issues

To promote competition among these market centers for trading of NASDAQ listed issues, there is a centralized electronic quotations service called "UQDF" - the UTP Quotation Data Feed. UQDF provides current price quotes (not actual trade reports) for NASDAQ listed securities, regardless of the source of the quote. Thus, these quotes might come from the NASDAQ market maker, a market maker on the NYSE, a regional exchange market maker that trades the stock via an Unlisted Trading Privilege Plan, or an ECN.

Once a trade occurs in any of these market centers in a NASDAQ-listed issue, it is reported to the "Consolidated Tape," known as the Network C Tape.

Network C Tape - Trades Of NASDAQ Listed Issues

Network C Tape: Reports trades of NASDAQ-listed issues, regardless of the market center where the trade took place.

To recap, the Network A Tape reports trades of NYSE-listed issues, wherever the trade took place; the Network B Tape reports trades of NYSE-MKT (AMEX)-listed issues and regional exchanges listed issues, wherever the trade took place; and the Network C Tape reports trades of NASDAQ-listed issues, wherever the trade took place.

Options Trading

Options also trade on exchange floors. The largest options exchange, by far, is the Chicago Board Options Exchange (CBOE). The exchanges that trade options, listed in order of trading volumes, are:

Chicago Board Options Exchange	(CBOE)
Philadelphia Stock Exchange	(PHLX)
American Stock Exchange	(AMEX)
Pacific Stock Exchange (ARCA)	(PSE)

NYSE Bond Trading

Bonds are generally traded over-the-counter. However, the NYSE does very limited trading of corporate bonds for those companies listed on the NYSE.

1c. SECOND MARKET - OTC TRADING

Second Market

With NASDAQ now considered to be a stock exchange (even though it has no physical trading floor), the second market is where over-the-counter trading of stocks that are not listed on NYSE, NYSE-MKT, or NASDAQ (or a regional exchange) occurs.

Over-The-Counter Trading Of Unlisted Stocks

The second market developed in the early 1900s with the invention of the telephone. Instead of needing an exchange floor to meet and trade, trading could now take place over the phone. The OTC market for equity securities consists of the OTCBB and the Pink OTC Markets.

OTCBB

OTCBB: Stands for the Over-The-Counter Bulletin Board. This is a "display facility" run by FINRA. It is not an exchange because it cannot execute trades and is not an SRO (a "Self-Regulatory Organization" under SEC oversight). The OTCBB displays quotes for publicly traded companies that are not listed on an exchange. These are companies that cannot meet exchange listing standards or that have been delisted (for example, the company is bankrupt).

Trading Markets

Pink OTC Markets

Pink OTC Markets: This is the "great granddaddy" of the OTC market, started in 1913. It used to publish the "Pink Sheets" - OTC stock quotes printed on pink paper. It was bought by a private equity group, transitioned to the web, and is now renamed the "Pink OTC Markets."

The stocks quoted "OTC" are mainly speculative "penny stocks" and delisted companies. Also, there are legitimate foreign companies that do not want to comply with exchange listing requirements - for example, Nestle and Daimler AG are quoted in the Pink OTC Markets. There are over 6,000 issues quoted in the OTCBB and Pink OTC Markets.

No Options Trading

"Over-The-Counter"

Generally speaking, options don't trade over-the-counter. The OCC only guarantees standardized options contracts that are created on exchanges. The only OTC options are custom derivative contracts that are not included on this exam.

Most Corporate Debt, All Government And All Municipal Debt Is Traded OTC

Almost all corporate bond trades and all corporate commercial paper transactions take place OTC. U.S. Government bonds and municipal bonds also trade OTC, but these are not regulated by FINRA. These are "exempt" securities from federal regulation and hence FINRA oversight. The government securities market is loosely regulated by the Federal Reserve through its relationship with the primary U.S. Government dealers (covered in the Debt chapter). The municipal securities market is regulated by the MSRB - the Municipal Securities Rulemaking Board.

Primary Market Is OTC

Finally, remember that the entire new issue equity market (the primary market) is an OTC market. New equity issues are initially sold to the first investors OTC. Then the securities are either listed on an exchange or trade OTC.

1d. THIRD MARKET - OTC TRADING OF EXCHANGE LISTED ISSUES

Third Market

The third market is trading of exchange listed securities which takes place "off the trading floor" through over-the-counter market makers.

Over-The-Counter Trading Of Exchange Listed Securities

The third market developed in the 1960s, but really did not come into prominence until the 1980s. At that time, the NYSE had a rule that if a member firm had an order to buy or sell an exchange listed stock during the hours the exchange was open, the trade had to be performed on the exchange floor. Because of this rule, virtually all trades were funneled to the exchange floor and there were no competing marketplaces to perform trades in NYSE listed issues.

This NYSE rule was deemed to be "anti-competitive" and was modified in 1979 (remember that this is the same year that CQS was created, putting NYSE quotes on the same screen as the quotes for that stock from competing markets, including Third Market Makers) under SEC pressure and finally was dropped at the end of 1999. Thus, NYSE listed issues can now be traded anywhere.

Starting in the 1980s, as new companies were listed by the NYSE, these could be traded anywhere - not only on the floor of the NYSE. It was at this point that the so-called "Third Market" - that is FINRA (formerly NASD) member firms that are making markets in NYSE-listed issues - started to become active. These "Third Market Makers" would trade NYSE-listed issues at narrower bid-ask spreads than the market makers on the NYSE floor, attracting orders away from the exchange floor.

Furthermore, during the 1980s, a global market developed trading NYSE listed issues. In response, "Third Market Makers" began to stay open 24 hours. Imagine that a trader in London wants to buy 1,000 shares of GE at 10:30 AM London Time (5:30 AM New York Time). The NYSE doesn't open for 4 hours, so the trader calls a Third Market Maker such as Jefferies & Co., or Weeden and Co. and performs the trade.

Probably the most famous (or infamous) "Third Market Maker" was Bernard Madoff. Before he ran his $60 billion "Ponzi Scheme" fraud (for which he is now in jail for the rest of his life), his company, Bernard Madoff and Co., was a legitimate trading firm and one of the first 3rd market makers. Madoff "invented" payment for order flow (discussed following) as a way of attracting trading business from retail member firms.

So, who really dislikes the Third Market Makers? Well, that would be the NYSE, NYSE-MKT (AMEX) and NASDAQ Markets. Third Market Makers represent serious competition for these exchanges. They will often trade at slightly better prices than the exchange to grab an order that would otherwise be routed to the exchange. They stay open 24 hours a day, and grab orders from institutions that wish to trade when the exchanges are closed. They will "pay" for orders sent to them by retail member firms (in essence, giving up a little bit of the market maker's profit to the retail member firm that placed the order).

To compete with the Third Market, the exchanges (NYSE, NYSE-MKT and NASDAQ) are moving towards staying open 24 hours; will now pay for order flow; and will compete keenly on price of execution. So the SEC views this as a success, because competition between the markets is good for investors.

Payment For Order Flow

The SEC requires that member firms route their orders to the market that is posting the best available price. So if a Third Market Maker is offering an NYSE listed stock for a cheaper price than can be obtained on the NYSE floor, then the order must be sent to the Third Market Maker.

But what happens if both the Third Market Maker and the NYSE are offering the stock at the same price? Then another issue comes up. Some market makers have a policy of "paying for order flow" - that is, they actually pay a small amount to the retail member firm that directs the order to that market maker. In essence, the market maker is rebating some of its profit on executing that order back to the retail member firm that sent it the order.

In the real world, what often happens is that whoever is the dominant market maker in that security sets the price and moves it according to market conditions; and the other smaller market makers continuously match that price. In such an environment, a retail member firm will then simply send the order to the market maker that will pay the most for it!

Payment For Order Flow Disclosed On Customer Confirm

The SEC permits this practice, because it believes that such competition will ultimately result in a lower execution cost for the customer. It requires that any payment for order flow that is made be disclosed on the customer's trade confirmation. It also puts disclosure rules on broker-dealers that accept payments for order flow and markets that make these payments. These are part of Regulation NMS, covered following.

1e. FOURTH MARKET - ECNs / ATSs

Fourth Market - Direct Trading Between Institutions Over-The-Counter

The fourth market is direct trading of securities between institutions, without the use of a broker. This market also developed in the 1960s, because at that time the NYSE had fixed commission rates (these were abolished under Federal Law in 1975). Under the fixed commission rates, institutions did not get discounts for large trades, so the "cost" of trading for these firms was quite high. Instinet ("Institutional Network") was created at that time as an electronic bulletin board for banks, insurance companies, mutual funds, etc. to list offerings of securities to sell, or bids for securities they wished to buy. The subscriber simply called the listing firm directly to trade, bypassing the brokers and large commissions.

In 1975, when fixed commissions were abolished, brokers started giving large discounts on institutional trades. The main reason for Instinet's existence was eliminated and it never developed into a large marketplace for this reason. Instinet was purchased in 1987 by Reuters. Reuters used the system as the basis for a global electronic trading system that it was developing. Instinet was repositioned by Reuters as an institutional intermediary, brokering institutional trades at much lower cost. This proved to be a very successful strategy, and Instinet volumes grew wildly - to the point where it was executing more trades in NASDAQ securities than NASDAQ itself (though it was not as successful at eroding the NYSE's market share trading NYSE issues).

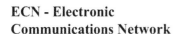

ECN - Electronic Communications Network	Instinet is the first of what are now called "ECNs" - Electronic Communications Networks, that match customer buy and sell orders 24 hours a day on an agency basis. Other major ECNs are Island (which has been purchased by Instinet with the combined entity called INET) and Archipelago. ECNs have been capturing an ever-larger share of NYSE and NASDAQ trading, and are becoming a major competitive force in the marketplace.
NASDAQ Purchases INSTINET/ISLAND	Both the NYSE and NASDAQ responded to the growth of ECNs in a similar fashion. In mid-2005, NASDAQ announced that it was buying INET (Instinet and Island); and the NYSE announced that it was buying Archipelago.
NYSE Purchases ARCHIPELAGO	In the case of NASDAQ, the issue was simple - Instinet and Island had captured about 50% of NASDAQ trading volume because their trading technology was superior to NASDAQ's and their trade pricing was much cheaper. NASDAQ figured that once it completed the purchase (which closed in January 2006), it could drop many of its more expensive and slower trading systems and achieve large cost savings. In the case of the NYSE, the worry was that using human floor traders would be quickly outmoded by electronic trading, especially when a new SEC Regulation - Regulation NMS (covered following) - took effect in 2006.
Regulation ATS	The SEC wrote Regulation ATS in the year 1998, specifically to address the growth of ECNs. Regulation ATS requires Alternative Trading Systems, which include ECNs, member firm internal crossing systems and dark pools (covered later in this chapter), to register with the SEC and be regulated as broker-dealers (as opposed to registering as an exchange and being regulated as such). Exchanges are SROs - Self-Regulatory organizations, that create rules for their members and can discipline their members for rule violations. ATSs are not SROs - they have no rules for their users other than the types of orders that can be placed and they cannot discipline their users, other than restricting access to their systems.
ECN Must Link If It Trades 5% Of NMS Issue's Volume	Regulation ATS requires that any ATS:

- that displays orders to anyone other than ATS employees; and

- that has average daily trading volume in an NMS security (either an NYSE, NYSE-MKT or NASDAQ listed issue) of 5% of aggregate volume in that issue for 4 of the last 6 months;

- must link with a national securities exchange so that the ECN's quote is displayed and can be accessed under Regulation NMS (covered following).

Because of Regulation ATS, the ADF - Alternate Display Facility - was created to display ECN quotes if the ECN was not going to post its quote in an exchange order book such as the NASDAQ System.

After Hours Market	Third Market Makers and ECNs stay open 24 hours a day and execute a large percentage of their trades when the NYSE, NYSE-MKT and NASDAQ are closed. Customers who trade outside of regular exchange trading hours should be aware that:
Thin Trading	The "after hours" market is much less liquid - order flow is very limited and getting an execution is much more difficult and can be more costly;
Greater Price Volatility	There is much greater price volatility in the "after hours" market, because of the limited order flow.

1f. REGULATION NMS

SEC Regulation NMS	SEC Regulation NMS (National Market System) is a comprehensive update to the "patchwork" of SEC rules that have been enacted from 1975 until now to foster competition between market centers in trading of "National Market Securities."

Regulation NMS consists of Rules 600 - 612. Some of these are "new" rules, and others are simply the renumbering of existing rules. There are 3 basic new rules that impact market participants (Rules 610 - 612):

1. All market centers (defined as an order execution facility of any exchange or NASDAQ) are required to establish and enforce policies to prevent "trade throughs" - which is an execution of an order in that market at an inferior price to that displayed in another market. This is covered under Rule 611.

   Rule 611 requires that trade execution occur at the best price within 1 second, instead of the 90 seconds that was permitted at that time (it is now reduced to 10 seconds). Human-based floor trading works great when you have 90 seconds to fill an order; but is not so great if you only have 1 second to complete the fill! To comply with this rule, the NYSE has become a "hybrid" market, offering both human-based trading and electronic trading via the Archipelago purchase. Human based floor trading will continue because there are "opt out" provisions from the "trade-through" rule - for example, an institution might want a human trader on the NYSE floor to "work" a large block order that is not easy to fill via an automated system.

2. Under Rule 610, market centers must provide a "level playing field" when providing access to their markets (e.g., market access fees must be consistent across all market participants and cannot favor one firm over another). Each market must provide for automated access and execution that does not favor one group of users over another.

3. Sub-penny pricing is prohibited unless the stock trades below $1.00. All limit orders and displayed quotes for NMS securities (NYSE,

NYSE-MKT and NASDAQ) must be in increments of pennies. This is covered under Rule 612.

In addition, other "older" SEC rules are now incorporated into Regulation NMS. Specifically:

Rule 602: Exchanges Must Collect And Display Bids And Offers

Rule 602: Covers quotes disseminated by market participants. It requires each exchange to establish a mechanism for collecting bids, offers, and quotation sizes from broker-dealers and for disseminating this data to "quotations vendors" (for example, Bloomberg buys quotes and provides them to subscribers). The rule also obligates broker-dealers to promptly communicate changes in bids and offers to the exchange.

Rule 604: Limit Order Display Rule

Rule 604: Requires that exchanges and market makers display customer limit orders publicly, so that they can be accessed by all investors. Before the existence of an electronic centralized limit order book, market makers would keep customer limit orders in a separate file and they would not be displayed. The market maker would simply display its current quote in NASDAQ, because the system did not have the capability of displaying more than 1 quote per market maker and it had no capability of displaying customer orders. Thus, the true level of buying and selling interest in the marketplace was unknown to the public.

The "Limit Order Display Rule" required that if a market maker received a customer limit order that was better-priced than its own quote, it had to display that customer order instead of its own quote. Thus, the best prices were always shown in the market.

With the advent of electronic order books that permit each order to be entered separately, sequenced, and displayed (this did not happen until 2003), compliance with this rule is assured. Note that if a customer specifically requests that an order not be displayed, the rule permits this exception - for example, an institution with a large order can send it to a dark pool where it will not be displayed.

Rule 605: Market Center Order Execution Report

SEC Rule 605 under Regulation NMS requires that market centers prepare, and make available to the public, monthly standardized reports summarizing their order executions. Included in the report is data on:

- Effective spreads (a comparison of the bid-ask spread of the inside market versus that of actual trade executions - narrower is better);

- How market orders of various sizes were executed relative to the public quote;

- Speed of execution;

- Fill rates; and

- Price improvement or disimprovement.

Reports are only compiled for each stock exchange and NASDAQ and registered Alternative Trading Systems, such as DirectEdge ECN. Note that OTCBB and Pink Sheet security executions are excluded from these reports.

Rule 606: Reports To Customers On Order Routing And Payment For Order Flow

Most market makers have a policy of "paying for order flow" - that is, they actually pay a small amount to the retail member firm that directs the order to that market maker. In essence, the market maker is rebating some of its profit on executing that order back to the retail member firm that sent it the order.

In the real world, what often happens is that whoever is the dominant market maker in that security sets the price and moves it according to market conditions; and the other smaller market makers continuously match that price. In such an environment, a retail member firm will then simply send the order to the market maker that will pay the most for it!

The SEC permits this practice, because it believes that such competition will ultimately result in a lower execution cost for the customer. However, it does attach strings if firms engage in this practice under Rule 606 of Regulation NMS.

The requirements of the rule are:

Disclosure Of Payment For Order Flow

The fact that the firm received a payment for order flow must be disclosed on the customer trade confirmation;

Disclosure On Request Of Routing Of Customer Orders In Prior 6 Months That Were "Non-Directed"

The firm, on request of the customer, must disclose the identity of the market to which the customer's orders were routed for execution in the preceding 6 months along with the time of execution. (These are known as "non-directed" orders, since the customer did not tell the broker the specific market where the order was to be executed, so the member firm could route the order to wherever it wanted.)

Quarterly Report Detailing Order Routing Procedures

In addition, the rule requires member firms to prepare a quarterly report that is publicly available that details the:

- Percentage of customer orders that were "non-directed";

- Identity of the 10 largest markets or market makers, to whom non-directed orders were routed and any other venue that received 5% or more of the firm's orders; and

- Member firm's relationship with that market maker (for example, many larger retail member firms own their own market maker subsidiaries to whom they route orders); and

- Arrangement, if any, for payment for order flow or profit-sharing.

Because of this rule, member firms cannot have "hidden" arrangements with market makers to favor them in return for "payment for order flow" - everything is out in the open and is fully disclosed. Thus, customers can make informed decisions about how retail member firms are routing and executing their orders.

Rule 607: Customer Notice Of Payment For Order Flow

Rule 607: Requires each broker-dealer to notify each new customer at account opening, and annually thereafter of:

- its policy regarding receipt of payment for order flow, including a statement as to whether any payment for order flow is received for
- routing customer orders and a detailed description of the compensation received; and
- the broker-dealer's policies for determining the routing of each customer order that is the subject of payment for order flow.

The "new" rules incorporated into Regulation NMS are:

Rule 611: Trade Through Rule

A "trade through" occurs when an order is executed in a given market at a price that is inferior to that currently being posted by another market center. In a perfect world, this would not occur, since all trades are subject to "best execution" requirements. However, older systems that attempted to link markets were less than perfect and they produced a high level of "trade throughs" that current computer software technology would eliminate.

Applies To All NYSE, NYSE-MKT And NASDAQ Stocks

The new "trade through" rule applies to NYSE, NYSE-MKT and NASDAQ listed issues. These are now called the "NMS" stocks. Any order execution facility that executes orders internally in its market, even if its quote is not the NBBO (National Best Bid and Offer, also known as the "inside market"), must execute that trade at the NBBO. Thus, the rule forces the exchanges to update their linkages to other markets to attempt to eliminate "trade-throughs." The quotes that must be protected under the rule are "immediately accessible" automated quotes. These quotes must be accessible within 1 second. Thus, executable orders will now be filled at the best price available in all markets for that security, within 1 second.

Rule Applies To All National Securities Exchanges

The "trade through" rule applies to all national securities exchanges, the NASDAQ Market, ECNs such as Archipelago, OTC market makers and block positioners, and any broker-dealer that executes trades internally, **regardless** of whether they are posting a quote for that issue. Thus, broker-dealers must have internal policies and procedures in place to ensure that "trade-throughs" do not occur.

Rule 610: Market Access

There are multiple trading venues for equity securities.

For example, NYSE securities are traded on the NYSE floor, on regional exchanges, in the Third Market, and also there is limited trading via ECNs. Currently, about 60% of NYSE trading takes place "off the floor."

NASDAQ securities are traded via the NASDAQ System, unlinked ECNs quote NASDAQ securities in the ADF (Alternate Display Facility) and trade them, NASDAQ securities are traded on regional exchanges on a "UTP" basis (Unlisted Trading Privilege). Currently, about 60% of NASDAQ trading occurs outside of the NASDAQ System.

Because of this market fragmentation, there has been an increasing incidence of "locked" and "crossed" markets - evidence of imperfect linkages between market venues because those quotes should have traded with each other. Competing market centers offer different types of access and speeds of execution. For example, System trades of NASDAQ stocks are completely automated (a "fast market") whereas a NASDAQ stock traded via a UTP plan on a regional exchange might be handled manually (and thus, slowly).

Quoting Market Centers Must Offer Automated Executions

The rule requires quoting market centers and quoting market participants to offer automatic execution of orders, and they cannot discriminate by offering members faster automatic execution than that offered to non-members.

Furthermore, each exchange must establish and enforce rules that eliminate locked or crossed markets across all market venues; and must have rules that prohibit members from engaging in patterns of locking or crossing markets.

Rule 612: Sub-Penny Quoting

While the NYSE, NYSE-MKT and NASDAQ quote stocks in minimum price increments of \$.01, the ECNs display quotes in their proprietary systems in "sub-pennies." These quotes are effectively hidden from the public, because the public display of these orders rounds them to the nearest penny. However, broker-dealer routing software accesses the unrounded quotes, so there is a "hidden" market where securities trade at prices that are not transparent to the public.

The SEC is not too crazy about the fact that these superior sub-penny quotes on alternative markets are not available to the average investor. Furthermore, by using "sub-penny" pricing, market professionals can "step-ahead" of customer limit orders, without the customer being aware of this.

No Sub-Penny Quotes For NMS Stocks Priced At \$1 Or More

So the SEC solution is simple - no sub-penny pricing on NMS stocks trading at \$1.00 or more - the minimum quote increment is \$.01. For stocks that are trading for less than \$1.00, the minimum quote increment is set at \$.0001.

Customer Limit Orders Cannot Be In Sub-Penny Increments

As part of the enforcement of this rule, the SEC requires that all customer limit orders for NMS stocks be in increments of \$.01. Any limit orders that are in increments of \$.001 (or more decimal places) must be rejected.

Also note that Rule 612 does not apply to non-NMS stocks, such as OTCBB or Pink Sheet issues. These may be quoted by member firms in sub-penny increments.

1g. BROKERS AND DEALERS

In order to function, markets must be liquid. Orders to buy and sell must be filled at all times. It is the function of the dealers to make markets in securities. Dealers are expected to maintain an inventory of each security in which they make a market: to buy if a customer wishes to sell, and to sell if a customer wishes to buy.

Dealer Quotes In Bid And Ask

Spread

Dealer quotes are in terms of Bid and Ask. The Ask price is the price at which the dealer will sell the security. The Bid price is the price at which the dealer will buy the security. To make a profit, the Ask price is always higher than the Bid - the difference is the **spread** - the dealer's gross profit margin. For example, a dealer quotes ABC stock at:

	Bid	Ask
ABC	13.00	13.50

The dealer is offering ABC stock at $13.50 to any buyer. The dealer is willing to buy ABC stock at $13 from any seller. The spread is 50 cents. For each "round turn" (a buy and sell), the dealer earns 1/2 dollar.

Active Markets Characterized By Narrower Spreads

The more active the trading market, the narrower the spreads become. This makes the market more "efficient" and is better for customers, since the "spread" gives the customer a built-in loss (the customer in this example buys at $13.50, but can only sell for $13) that is recovered only if the market price moves up.

Specialists

DMMs Are Dealers On The NYSE

On stock exchange floors (First Market), the dealers are called Specialists, also called DMMs (Designated Market Makers). There are 6 Specialist firms handling the approximately 3,000 NYSE listed issues, so each DMM firm handles about 500 different stocks. The Specialist/DMM is the sole market maker in that stock.

Specialists

DMMs Do Not Deal With The Public

Specialist/DMM firms are prohibited from dealing with the public. They are wholesalers of securities and only deal with the retail members of the NYSE. Retail members (firms such as Merrill Lynch, Morgan Stanley, etc.) accept customer orders and go to the exchange floor to execute the trade with the Specialist/DMM. For acting as a middleman (broker), the retail firm earns a commission.

The NYSE has relabeled the Specialist firms as "DMMs" - Designated Market Makers. It felt that the "Specialist" name had a negative connotation, implying a sort of "insider" status to the general public. (The names of the DMM (Specialist) firms are not generally known, because they don't deal with the public - they only deal with retail member firms.) Some DMMs are Barclays, Virtu Capital Markets, and KCG (Knight Capital Group).

The NASDAQ Stock Exchange, as a networked "virtual" market, operates quite differently. It uses a system of competing market makers. The two biggest NASDAQ market makers are KGC and UBS. In addition, retail member firms often have separate trading subsidiaries that act as NASDAQ market makers. Market makers register with FINRA, must maintain minimum capital and must quote the stock during regular market hours (9:30 AM-4:00 PM ET - the same as NYSE hours). For example, Apple (Symbol: AAPL) is one of the most heavily traded NASDAQ stocks with over 20 market makers competing at any time. NASDAQ uses an electronic linkage system called the NASDAQ Market Center or NASDAQ System (covered later in this chapter) which displays all market maker quotes and all customer limit orders that cannot be immediately executed. Members can electronically access the book and trade against those orders.

NASDAQ feels that the system of competing market makers narrows spreads and makes for a more efficient market. This contrasts with the exchanges' view that the market should be concentrated in the hands of one DMM.

Second Market Is Negotiated

The non-NASDAQ market for stock trades is not electronically linked. The OTCBB and Pink OTC Markets are "display facilities" only. Their systems display market maker quotes for these unlisted stocks, but to trade, one must "negotiate" with the market maker posting the quote. This is the case because there is no rule requiring that these quotes be posted in "real time" - and the market may have moved since the quote was shown in the system. To negotiate an OTC stock trade, either the telephone is used; or Pink OTC markets has an internet-based trade negotiation application that can be used.

Thin Trading

In the non-NASDAQ "Second Market," there are competing market makers in each stock, but the level of competition is not that great. Unlike NASDAQ, where there can be 10 or 20 competing market makers in an actively traded stock, here the trading is thin and there are usually only 2 or 3 (and sometimes only 1) market makers in each issue.

NASDAQ And OTC Market Makers Can Act As Either

Market Makers in either NASDAQ or OTC stocks can also deal with the public. On the exchanges, the DMM firms are prohibited from dealing with the public - only the retail members are allowed to take customer orders. OTC firms are called broker/dealers because they can handle either function.

Broker Earns A Commission	Assume that a customer wishes to buy Apple stock and goes to a small broker/dealer who is not a market maker. The small broker/dealer gets the best quote for Apple from the NASDAQ System and electronically buys from that market maker. Assume that the NASDAQ market maker posting that best quote is KCG, which does not deal with retail clients. For acting as middleman, matching the retail customer to the best market maker, the small broker/dealer charges a commission. In this transaction, the small broker/dealer is acting in the "broker" function - a middleman - matching the customer to the best market.
Dealer Earns A Mark-Up	Assume that a customer wishes to buy Apple stock, and his firm is UBS, which not only has a retail distribution channel, but also is a large NASDAQ market maker. The firm will sell Apple to the customer from its inventory directly (which it must do at the "best price"). The firm is acting as a "dealer" and is allowed to "mark-up" the stock to the customer. When acting as a dealer, OTC firms earn mark-ups.
In OTC Transactions, Firm May Act As EITHER A Broker OR A Dealer	In each OTC transaction, the firm can act either as broker or dealer - it cannot be both at once. When acting as a broker, a commission is earned. When acting as a dealer, a mark-up is earned. As a comparison, on exchanges, all customer transactions are handled through brokers. Customers cannot contact DMMs directly - DMMs trade only with retail members.

1h. ORDER TICKET INFORMATION

To place an order in the secondary market, a registered representative fills out an order ticket (this is done electronically). The information on the order ticket is used to wire the order to the exchange or to the firm's over-the-counter trading desk. Following is a sample copy of an order ticket:

ACME Securities, Inc.		ORDER TICKET		
(Buy) Sell Long Short Exempt	Size 100	(Day) Spec. Inst. GTC DNR Discret.		
Name of Security ABC Common		Price Mkt	Stop Stop Limit	
Customer Name Smith		Account Number 01487		
R R Number 333	Date 3/17/2017	Manager Approval		

The order ticket must specify the following:

- **Buy or sell -** When stock is bought, a long position is being taken. In this case the customer is buying, so "Buy" is circled on the ticket.

- **Sell long -** If a customer sells a long position, it is termed a long sale. Then "Sell" is circled on the ticket.

- **Sell short -** If a customer sells borrowed shares, he or she is taking a short stock position. In this case, both "Sell" and "Short" are circled.

Short Sale Fundamentals

To understand the mechanics of a short sale, one must have a basic understanding of customer margin accounts (covered in detail in the next section). When a customer opens a margin account, buying securities with credit extended by the brokerage firm, the brokerage firm takes all of the securities held in the account as collateral for the loan, and keeps them in the name of the brokerage firm.

Short Sale Example

Customer #1 buys 100 shares of ABC stock in a margin account. When opening a margin account, the customer signs a margin agreement and a loan consent agreement. By signing the margin agreement, the customer pledges the securities in the account to the brokerage firm as collateral for the margin loan. Such shares are held in "Street Name," with a common depository name being "Cede and Co." By signing the loan consent agreement, the customer permits his or her shares to be loaned out on short sales.

The brokerage firm deposits the 100 shares of ABC stock in its vault.

Customer #1 stock position in firm's vault

Customer #2 comes into the same brokerage firm and wishes to sell 100 shares of ABC stock "short." The brokerage firm goes to its vault and "borrows" the 100 shares of ABC owned by Customer #1, selling these shares for Customer #2. An "IOU" is placed in the vault, representing the borrowed shares that Customer #2 owes Customer #1.

IOU

Customer #2 has borrowed 100
shares of ABC stock from Customer
#1 and promises to replace these
shares upon demand.

Customer #2
"IOU" to
Customer #1
for borrowing
his shares

During the period of the "stock loan," Customer #2 pays any dividends on the borrowed shares to Customer #1 (because the issuer now sends dividend checks to the person who bought the shares that were sold short). At a later date, Customer #2 buys back the ABC shares and the firm replaces them in the vault. During this whole time Customer #1 never knew that the shares were missing!

The brokerage firm has the right to lend these securities to anyone else. If another customer wishes to sell short this stock, the brokerage firm simply "borrows" the first margin customer's securities and sells them (this is a "short sale"). At a later date, the shares are repurchased by the second customer and replaced in the vault.

Short Sales Subject To Regulation SHO

Short sales of stock in all markets are subject to SEC Regulation SHO. Regulation SHO (as in SHOrt sale) basically requires that every order ticket to sell be marked as either a "long sale" or a "short sale"; and that if the sale is "short," the securities to be borrowed must be "located" by the broker and the borrowed shares delivered on settlement. In addition, Regulation SHO has many other provisions, which are covered later in this section.

Order Size

The size of the order is specified: The number of shares of stock (in this case 100 shares), or number of option contracts or number of bonds to be traded. If an order is for more than a round lot (100 shares for stock), then it is assumed that the customer will accept a partial execution if the whole order cannot be filled. For example, if a customer wants to buy 400 shares at 30 and the trader can only get 300 shares at 30, then 300 shares will be bought.

Day Order

The duration of the order is specified: An order is assumed to be a day order if nothing is said on the ticket. In this case "Day" is circled. Day orders are canceled at the end of the day if the order is not filled.

Good Til Canceled (GTC)

The order can be entered "GTC" - Good Til Canceled. It used to be the case that exchange order books accepted GTC orders. In 2016, both the NYSE and NASDAQ changed their rules and will only accept Day orders. Member firms take GTC orders onto their internal systems and route them to the appropriate exchange each day as a new day order, until the order is filled or cancelled. Orders can be entered by a customer with special instructions such as "Good Thru the Week" or "Good Thru the Month," if the firm's internal system support these order types.

Trading Markets

Other special instructions are:

AON

AON: "All or None" - either the entire order is filled or the order is not executed. Depending on the duration specified in the order, a trader is free to attempt an entire execution again and again until the order expires.

FOK

FOK: "Fill or Kill" - either the entire order is filled on the first try or the order is canceled. There can be no extra attempts at executing the order.

IOC

IOC: "Immediate or Cancel" - either part or all of the order is filled on the first try and the balance is canceled. There can be no extra attempts at executing the order.

Either / Or

Either/Or: An "Either / Or" order specifies **two** possible trades, e.g., "**Either** Buy 500 ABC at $40 **Or** Sell 500 ABC at $60." If one side of the order is filled, the other side is canceled. If one side of the order is partially filled, the remaining amount applies to both orders. For example, if 300 shares were purchased at $40, the remaining order would be "Either Buy 200 ABC at $40 or Sell 200 ABC @ $60."

Not Held

Not Held: Not held is used in conjunction with an order to be filled at the market price. A simple market order is to be filled immediately at the prevailing price. If the order is marked "Not Held," the trader is free to "hold back" and determine the best time and price of execution during that day. If the trader believes the market will rise and it is a buy order, he would fill the order immediately. If he believes that the market will fall, he will hold back and wait until later in the day. Firms with astute traders may encourage customers to place market orders "not held" - but the customer has no recourse if he doesn't like the price or time of execution.

Discretionary

Discretionary: The registered representative is placing an order where the customer has not specified the security and size of the order. The registered representative has chosen this under a power of attorney granted by the customer. Discretionary accounts are covered in the Customer Accounts section.

DNR

DNR: "Do Not Reduce" - On ex-date, when the price of the stock is adjusted by the exchange, certain orders held on member firm's internal systems are also reduced to reflect the loss of the dividend or any other distribution. This is covered in detail at the end of this chapter.

At The Opening

At The Close

At The Opening or At The Close: An order placed "At the opening" is to be filled at the opening price or else canceled. An order placed "At the close" is to be filled at the closing price, otherwise the order is canceled.

Security Name

Name of Security: The ticket specifies the name of the corporate security to be traded - in this case, ABC common. If the trade were in preferred stock, the ticket would say "Pfd." If the trades were warrants, it would say "wts," etc.

Execution Price **Market Order**	Price of Execution: In this case, the order is a "MKT" or market order, to be filled at the prevailing market price. Notice that no specific price is being specified in the order.
Limit Order	If a price is specified, e.g., "Buy 100 ABC @ 42," the price is the limit. A limit order to buy is to be filled at that price or better (lower). A limit order to sell is to be filled at that price or better (higher).
Stop Order; Stop-Limit Order	Stop and Stop-Limit: In addition to market and limit orders, orders may be placed to "stop a loss." These are stop or stop limit orders and are covered later in this section.
Manager Approval	In addition, the customer name and account number are on the order, as well as the date, registered representative number (so the registered representative gets credit for the trade), and a space for the manager's initialing of the order.
Order Ticket Must Be Completely Filled Out	The order ticket must be completely filled out. An order ticket that does not include the customer name or account number cannot be accepted. This makes sense because, once the order is filled, the representative could check to see whether the stock's price has moved favorably, in which case the representative could place the trade in his or her personal account by entering that account number!
Alterations To Executed Order Ticket Prohibited Unless Manager Approves In Writing	Alterations to the order ticket after it is written out are prohibited. Again, the issue is that if the stock's price has moved favorably, the representative could take the order out of that customer's account and move it to his or her personal account. Under FINRA rules, any alteration to an executed order ticket:

- must be approved in writing by a branch manager or compliance officer of the firm;
- must be documented in writing with the essential facts relating to the order and the reasons for the change.

Written Cancel And Re-Bill Record Maintained For Any Alterations	The written record of such an account change is called a "Cancel and Re-Bill" record. A Cancel and Re-Bill record is not only required to move a trade from one customer account to another unrelated account; it is needed to move a trade between related accounts as well (e.g., moving a trade from "John Doe Cash Account" to "John Doe Margin Account").

1i. TYPES OF ORDERS

There are four basic order types:

- Market order;
- Limit order;
- Stop order;
- Stop Limit order.

Market Order

Market Not Held

A market order is to be filled immediately at the prevailing market price. There is no price specified on the order. A market order - NOT HELD is to be filled at whatever time and price the trader thinks best - but it must be completed that day. Thus, market orders do not carry over to the next day.

Limit Order Specifies A Price

Limit orders specify a price at which to buy or sell. To understand how these orders (and stop orders) are used, you must focus on the security's price at the time the order is placed.

Buy Limit Order

Placed Below Current Market

Assume that XXX stock is now trading at 70. A customer wishing to buy XXX stock at this price would simply place a market order. But what if the customer only wants to buy at 65 or lower? The order would be placed as:

Buy 100 XXX @ 65 GTC
(Buy Limit order)

A limit order to buy has been placed (the price is the limit). The order was placed GTC, because it would be canceled at the end of the day if it were a Day order.

If the market falls to 65 or lower, the order will be filled. Thus, limit orders to buy are placed **BELOW** the current market and are executed only if the market **DROPS**. Again, with XXX trading at 70, a registered representative has a customer who wishes to sell XXX stock that he owns (a long sale) if the price reaches 75. The following order would be placed:

Sell 100 XXX @ 75 GTC
(Sell Limit order)

Sell Limit Order

Placed Above Current Market

A limit order to sell has been placed (the price is the limit). The order was placed GTC, because it would be canceled at the end of the day if it were a Day order. If the market rises to 75 or higher, the order will be filled. Thus, limit orders to sell are placed **ABOVE** the current market and will be executed only if the market **RISES**.

Specialist Acts As "Broker's Broker"

Limit orders to buy and sell are given to the Specialists (now called DMMs - Designated Market Makers) on stock exchange floors. The DMM is at the center of trading and executes these orders for the retail firms. In this case, the DMM is acting as a broker for another brokerage firm, "a broker's broker."

For performing this function, the retail firm shares its commission with the DMM. So, in addition to acting as a dealer, DMMs handle limit orders for retail firms, acting as a "broker's broker."

NASDAQ System Electronic Limit Order Book

Non-NASDAQ OTC Limit Order File

The NASDAQ System, covered later in this chapter, maintains an electronic book of limit orders, against which electronic executions are routed. For OTC trading of smaller non-NASDAQ issues, OTC trading desks at each firm keep an electronic file of limit orders and execute them if the market price moves to the customer's limit.

To summarize for limit orders:

Stop Order - Stops A Loss At Trigger Price Turns Into A Market Order

There are 2 types of stop orders - "Sell stops" to stop a loss on a long stock position in a falling market, and "Buy stops" to stop a loss on a short stock position in a rising market.

Sell Stop Order

Used To Limit Loss On A Long Stock Position

Assume that XXX is now trading at 70 and the registered representative has a customer who owns XXX stock, purchased at that price. The customer tells the registered representative that he wishes to sell if the market drops to 65, to "stop" any further loss. If the registered representative entered the following order, he or she would be in trouble with the customer:

Sell 100 XXX @ 65 GTC
(Erroneous order)

Since XXX is now trading at 70, someone will be only too happy to buy the stock from this customer at 65. The buyer could then turn around and sell it for its true value of 70. This order is entered in error. A limit order to sell has been entered at a price lower than the market. Limit orders to sell can only be entered above the market (see prior diagram). This order would be returned to the registered representative for correction. The registered representative reenters the order as:

Sell 100 XXX @ 65 Stop GTC
(Sell Stop order)

The stop on the order tells the trader that this order cannot be executed until the market reaches the specified price (65). Once a trade occurs at 65 or lower, this order is triggered and turns into a market order. Since the exchanges no longer accept stop orders, they are only taken by member firm's internal systems. When the order is triggered, the member firm routes the newly-created market order to the appropriate exchange to be filled. The order enters the market queue of orders and is then filled based on its position in the queue. The fill price can therefore be higher or lower than the $65 stop price that triggered the order.

Placed Below Current Market

Sell stop orders are used to limit losses on long stock positions in falling markets. Thus, they are always placed **BELOW** the current market and are executed if the market **FALLS.**

Again with XXX now trading at 70, assume that the registered representative has a customer who has sold short XXX stock at that price. The customer tells the registered representative that he wishes to buy in, if the market rises to 75, to "stop" any further loss. If the registered representative entered the following order, he or she would be in trouble with the customer:

Buy 100 XXX @ 75 GTC
(Erroneous order)

Since XXX is now trading at 70, someone will be only too happy to sell the stock to this customer at 75 (since he or she can buy it at its true value of 70). This order is entered in error. The registered representative has entered a limit order to buy at a price higher than the market. Limit orders to buy can only be entered below the market (see prior diagram). This order would be returned to the registered representative for correction. The registered representative reenters the order as:

Buy 100 XXX @ 75 Stop GTC
(Buy Stop order)

Buy Stop Order

Used To Limit Loss On A Short Stock Position

The stop on the order tells the trader that this order cannot be executed until the market reaches the specified price (75). Once a trade occurs at 75 or higher, this order is triggered and turns into a market order. Since the exchanges no longer accept stop orders, they are only taken by member firm's internal systems. When the order is triggered, the member firm routes the newly-created market order to the appropriate exchange to be filled. The order enters the market queue of orders and is then filled based on its position in the queue. The fill price can therefore be higher or lower than the $75 stop price that triggered the order.

Placed Above Current Market

Buy stop orders are used to limit losses on short stock positions in rising markets. Thus, they are always placed **ABOVE** the current market and are executed if the market **RISES.**

To summarize for stop orders:

Open Buy Stops

MARKET PRICE

Open Sell Stops

Orders to buy at a stop price are filled if the market: **RISES**

Orders to sell at a stop price are filled if the market: **FALLS**

Stop Limit Order

If a simple stop order is triggered, it becomes a market order to be filled on the next trade. If an order is entered stop limit, when the stop price is hit, the order is to be filled at the limit price or better. If the market never hits the limit price, the order will never be executed. The limit price at which the order is to be executed can be different from the stop price.

Sell Stop Limit

For example, a customer wishes to sell 100 shares of ABC if the market falls to 30, but doesn't want to sell for any less than 28. The order to be placed is **not** "Sell 100 ABC @ 30 Stop" because when triggered it turns to a market order and the stock may be sold for less than 28.

The appropriate order is "Sell 100 ABC @ 30 Stop Limit 28." If the price falls to 30, the order is triggered. It turns into a limit order to sell for 28 - meaning sell for 28 or higher.

Buy Stop Limit

For example, a customer wishes to buy 100 shares of ABC if the market rises to 30, but doesn't want to buy for any more than 32. The order to be placed is **not** "Buy 100 ABC @ 30 Stop" because when triggered it turns to a market order and the stock may be bought for more than 32.

The appropriate order is "Buy 100 ABC @ 30 Stop Limit 32." If the price rises to 30, the order is triggered. It turns into a limit order to buy for 32 - meaning buy for 32 or lower.

Trading Markets

OSLOBS

OBLOSS

If we put together the diagram for limit orders and stop orders, the composite picture is found below:

Orders Above The Current Market Are OSLOBS

The orders that are always placed **ABOVE** the market are open sell limits and open buy stops (**OSLOBS**). The orders that are always placed **BELOW** the market are open buy limits and open sell stops (**OBLOSS**).

Orders Below The Current Market Are OBLOSS

You must memorize OSLOBS (above market) and OBLOSS (below market). These will be used later in the book.

1j. FURTHER DISCUSSION OF STOP AND LIMIT ORDERS

Customers use stop orders to limit losses on stock positions and technical analysts use stop orders to profit from market price movements. Technical analysts use stock price movements and trading volumes to determine when to buy and sell. They are often called "chartists" because of the charts that they use to analyze stock price movements. Following is a chart of ABC stock's price movements for the past 3 months:

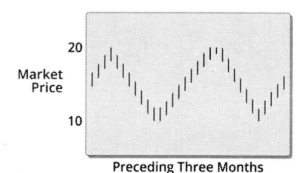

Resistance Level

Breakout Is Bullish

A chartist looking at this diagram sees that as the stock moves up to $20, people are willing to take their profits and sell. The stock appears to have "resistance" at $20. If the stock moves above $20, the theory is that all the sellers have been cleared out, and there are still buyers for the stock. If there are more buyers than sellers, the price will rise strongly. Thus, a break through a resistance area is bullish.

Support Level

Breakout Is Bearish

The chartist also sees that as the stock moves down to $10, people feel the stock is cheap and are willing to buy. The stock appears to have "support" at $10. If the stock moves below $10, the theory is that all the buyers have been cleared out, and there are still sellers for this stock. If there are more sellers than buyers, the price will fall sharply. Thus a break through a support area is bearish.

The chart now shows:

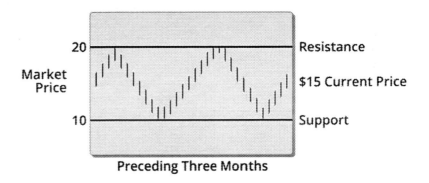

The technical analyst believes that if the price breaks the resistance level, the price will move up sharply. He only wants to profit from this potential price movement - he is not concerned with the current trading range of $10 - $20 a share. He wants to buy if the price moves to $21. He cannot place a simple order to buy the stock at $21 (a buy limit order) because it would be filled right now at the current $15 price. In addition, that order is **wrong**. Buy limit orders are placed below the market, not above. To buy above the current market price, he must place a buy stop order.

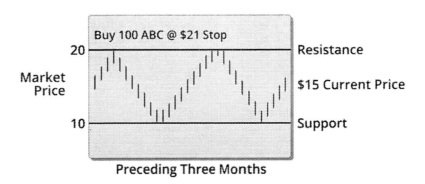

Assume that the market moves up from the current price of $15. Following is the trading sequence and how the order is handled:

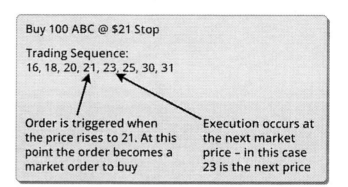

Once·the market moves to $21 or higher, the stop price is triggered, and the order becomes a market order to buy. The customer buys at the next trade of $23. He now owns the stock and hopefully can enjoy the expected continued price rise.

Instead of placing a stop order, the customer could have placed a buy stop limit order. If this were done, the result is found below:

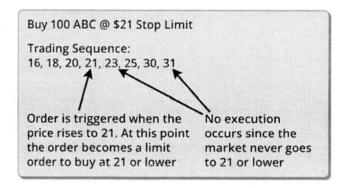

When the market moves to $21 or higher, the order is triggered. But instead of becoming a market order, it now becomes an order to buy at 21 or lower (the limit price). Since the price never went back down to 21, the customer never buys the stock. If the trading sequence were different and the price moved back to 21 or lower, the order would be filled.

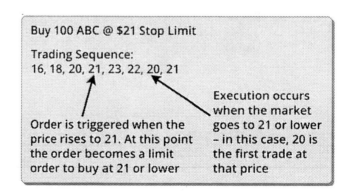

The technical analyst also believes that if the price breaks the support level, ·the price will move down sharply.

He only wants to profit from this potential price movement - he is not concerned with the current trading range of $10 - $20 a share. He wants to sell if the price moves to $9. He cannot place a simple order to sell the stock at $9 (a sell limit order) because it would be filled right now at the current $15 price. In addition, that order is **wrong**. Sell limit orders are placed above the market, not below.

To sell below the current market, he must place a sell stop order. In addition, to profit from the expected price fall, the analyst wants to sell borrowed shares, and buy them back at the lower price later on. This is a short sale.

Assume that the analyst places the following order to sell the stock short if it breaks the support level.

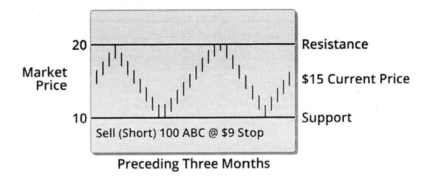

Assume that the market moves down from the current price of $15. Following is the trading sequence and how the order is handled.

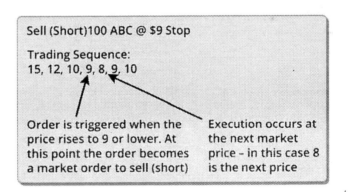

When the market moves to 9 or lower, the order to sell is triggered and becomes a market order. The order can be filled on the next trade. Hopefully, the price will now drop dramatically, and the trader can buy back the stock (covering the short position) at a cheaper price.

TRADING MARKET BASICS
SECTION EXAMINATION

1.
A customer has asked his registered representative to sell 100 XYZ if the market falls to 50, but he does not want to sell for less than 45. The proper order is:

   a.   Sell 100 XYZ @ 50 Stop Limit
   b.   Sell 100 XYZ @ 45 Stop Limit
   c.   Sell 100 XYZ @ 50 Stop 45 Limit
   d.   Sell 100 XYZ @ 45 Stop 50 Limit

2.
The First Market includes trading in:

   a.   unlisted issues
   b.   new issues
   c.   NYSE issues
   d.   OTC issues

3.
A trade takes place directly between a bank and an insurance company without the use of a broker. This trade took place in the:

   a.   First Market
   b.   Second Market
   c.   Third Market
   d.   Fourth Market

4.
All of the following information must be on an order ticket before it can be entered **EXCEPT**:

   a.   size of transaction
   b.   execution price if the order is not a market order
   c.   commission
   d.   customer account name and/or number

5.
A customer places an order to buy bonds. The order reads "Buy 5M ABC 9s M '35 @ 90 GTC." The customer has entered a:

   a.   stop order to buy at 90
   b.   limit order to buy at 90
   c.   market order to buy
   d.   stop limit order to buy

6.
A customer places an order to buy bonds. The order reads "Buy 5M ABC 9s M '35 @ 90 GTC." Which statement is **TRUE** about this order?

   a.   The order will be canceled at the end of the day if an execution is not possible
   b.   The order must be executed at a price of 90% or better
   c.   If executed, the customer will pay $4,500 for the bonds
   d.   The customer is establishing a short position with this order

7.
In a falling market, which orders will be executed?

   I   Open Buy Stops
   II   Open Buy Limits
   III   Open Sell Stops
   IV   Open Sell Limits

   a.   I and II
   b.   III and IV
   c.   I and IV
   d.   II and III

8.
A customer has a gain on a long stock position that he wishes to protect. The appropriate order is:

   a.   buy stop order
   b.   sell stop order
   c.   sell limit order
   d.   market order

9.

A customer has a gain on a short stock position that she wishes to protect. The appropriate order is:

a. buy stop order
b. buy limit order
c. market order
d. sell stop order

10.

The First Market is a(n):

a. auction market
b. negotiated market
c. unregulated market
d. primary market

11.

An investor has bought 500 shares of a volatile growth stock and wishes to limit downside loss. Which strategies are appropriate?

I   Place a buy stop order
II Place a sell stop order
III Buy 5 put contracts
IV Sell 5 put contracts

a. I and IV
b. II and III
c. I and III
d. II and IV

12.

An investor has sold short 500 shares of ABC at $60. The stock has since declined to 38. All of the following can be used to protect the gain **EXCEPT**:

a. place a buy stop order at $40
b. buy 5 ABC 40 puts
c. buy 5 ABC 40 calls
d. sell 5 ABC 40 puts

13.

A technical analyst has identified a resistance level for ABC stock at $50 and a support level at $40. The stock is currently trading at 45 and the analyst expects the stock to break the support level. Which order is appropriate to profit if the support level is broken?

a. Sell 100 ABC @ Market
b. Sell (short) 100 ABC @ $39
c. Sell (short) 100 ABC @ $39 Stop
d. Sell (short) 100 ABC @ $41 Stop

14.

A technical analyst has identified a resistance level for ABC stock at $50 and a support level at $40. The stock is currently trading at $45 and the analyst expects a breakout on the upside. What order is appropriate to profit from this movement?

a. Buy 100 ABC @ Market
b. Buy 100 ABC @ $49 Stop
c. Buy 100 ABC @ $51 Stop
d. Buy 100 ABC @ $51

15.

Which statement is **TRUE**?

a. AON orders can be executed in part or in full
b. FOK orders can be executed in part or in full
c. AON orders are canceled if the entire order is not executed
d. FOK orders are canceled if the entire order is not executed

16.

Trades of NASDAQ listed securities that take place in all markets are consolidated and reported through the:

a. Network A Tape
b. Network B Tape
c. Network C Tape
d. Network D Tape

17.

An order placed "market - at the close" will:

    a.   either be executed at the closing price that day or will be canceled

    b.   be executed as close to the closing price that day

    c.   be executed as close to the closing price the next trading day

    d.   be executed during the day at the discretion of the trader

18.

The Second Market is the:

    a.   trading of OTCBB stocks

    b.   issuance of listed stocks

    c.   trading of listed stocks on the floor of an exchange

    d.   issuance of listed and unlisted stocks

19.

The Third Market trades:

    a.   listed and unlisted stocks between institutions without the use of a broker

    b.   listed securities on the trading floors of regional exchanges

    c.   unlisted securities over-the-counter

    d.   listed securities over-the-counter

20.

An "efficient" market is characterized by:

    I   Narrow Spreads
    II   Wide Spreads
    III   Low Trading Volume
    IV   High Trading Volume

    a.   I and III

    b.   I and IV

    c.   II and III

    d.   II and IV

21.

The Second Market is a(n):

    a.   auction market

    b.   negotiated market

    c.   unregulated market

    d.   primary market

22.

Retail member firms that route orders to market makers in return for compensation earn:

    a.   mark-ups

    b.   mark-downs

    c.   commissions

    d.   payments for order flow

23.

Under Rule 606 of Regulation NMS, all of the following must be disclosed to customers by member firms upon request **EXCEPT**:

    a.   which market received the customer order

    b.   whether the order was directed or non-directed

    c.   the time of execution of the order

    d.   the best market for the security at the time of execution

24.

An order for a New York Stock Exchange listed issue is routed by the member firm to a Third Market Maker rather than to the exchange floor. This practice is:

    a.   prohibited

    b.   permitted only if the customer consents

    c.   permitted only if an attempt to fill the order on the NYSE fails

    d.   permitted if the price offered by the Third Market Maker is better

25.

The "after hours" market is characterized by:

I Narrow Spreads
II Wide Spreads
III Low Trading Volume
IV High Trading Volume

a. I and III
b. I and IV
c. II and III
d. II and IV

26.

Which of the following is **NOT** an ECN?

a. INSTINET
b. ISLAND
c. ARCHIPELAGO
d. PENINSULA

27.

Under SEC Rule 606 of Regulation NMS, broker-dealers are required to compile statistical information on routing of customer non-directed orders to market venues, and make this information available to customers:

a. monthly
b. quarterly
c. semi-annually
d. annually

28.

The "trade-through" rule of Regulation NMS:

a. prohibits an order from being routed to a market that will pay for the order
b. prohibits a market maker on an exchange from executing a trade at an inferior price to that posted by another market at that moment
c. requires member firms to execute any order received within 1 second of execution
d. requires member firms to use automated clearing and settlement of all trades

29.

If a customer directs that a marketable order be sent to a specific trading venue, then the trade must be:

a. rejected
b. sent to the NYSE for execution
c. sent to the market specified by the client
d. sent to the market with the largest display size

30.

An NMS stock is current quoted at $16.10 Bid - $16.30 Ask. A customer wishes to place an order to buy 1,000 shares of the stock at $16.111. The registered representative should:

a. refuse to accept the order
b. route the order to an ATS
c. route the order to an exchange
d. accept the order and round the price to $16.11

31.

The SEC regulation that requires market centers to accept automated executions that do not discriminate against any class of users of their systems is:

a. Regulation NMS
b. Regulation ATS
c. Regulation SHO
d. Regulation M

32.

ECNs trade:

I listed stocks
II listed and OTC stocks
III by matching buy and sell orders for a small fee
IV by routing orders to exchange floors for payment for order flow

a. I and III
b. I and IV
c. II and III
d. II and IV

33.

An NMS stock is quoted at $30.50 Bid; $35.75 Ask. Which quotes can be accepted by an SRO for this stock?

I $30.55 Bid
II $30.555 Bid
III $30.65 Ask
IV $30.655 Ask

   a.   I and III
   b.   I and IV
   c.   II and III
   d.   II and IV

34.

Under Regulation ATS, any ECN that accounts for what percentage of the trading volume in a listed stock must show its quotes either through an exchange or a display facility?

   a.   1%
   b.   2%
   c.   4%
   d.   5%

35.

A customer places an order to buy 1,000 shares of ABC stock at the market in his cash account. The order is executed and, when reporting the trade back to the customer, the registered representative notices that the trade was executed in the customer's margin account. Which statement is **TRUE**? The registered representative can move the trade to the customer's cash account:

   a.   to correct the error without needing to take any additional action since these accounts are related to each other

   b.   as long as a signed statement requesting the transfer is obtained from the customer

   c.   as long as a cancel/rebill record is created that documents the reasons for the account designation change and the manager approves in writing

   d.   as long as FINRA is sent a quarterly report detailing all account designation changes whenever transactions were placed in incorrect customer accounts

TRADING MARKET BASICS EXAMINATION EXPLANATIONS

1. The best answer is **c**. An order to sell that is placed **BELOW** the market must be a sell stop order (sell limit orders are placed above the market). The customer wants to sell if the market falls to 50, so the order is "Sell 100 XYZ at 50 Stop." If triggered, this order becomes a market order to sell (which will happen at the prevailing market price). But the customer has also specified that he doesn't want to sell for less than 45 per share, meaning there is a limit on the execution price. The proper order is "Sell 100 XYZ at 50 Stop 45 Limit."

2. The best answer is **c**. The First Market is trading of listed stocks on an organized stock exchange - like the NYSE, AMEX (now renamed the "NYSE-MKT") or NASDAQ exchanges. Exchanges have listing standards for the companies that trade there and accessible order books, where orders can be posted and traded against.

Any companies that do not meet exchange listing standards ("unlisted securities") are quoted in either the OTCBB (Over The Counter Bulletin Board) or the Pink OTC Markets. These constitute the Second Market. Both the OTCBB and Pink OTC Markets are classified by the SEC as "quotations vendors" - they are not exchanges. To trade an OTCBB or Pink OTC Markets stock, the trade must be negotiated, usually over the phone. New issues are sold for the first time in the Primary Market.

3. The best answer is **d**. The Fourth Market is direct trading of securities between institutions on ECNs (Electronic Communications Networks) such as Instinet or Archipelago. The systems bypass brokerage firms, and therefore brokerage commissions. Instead, the ECN charges a small matching fee.

4. The best answer is **c**. The commission is calculated after the trade is executed - it is not on the order ticket that is used to enter the order. The ticket must include the size of the trade, desired execution price, and customer identification.

5. The best answer is **b**. Since a price is specified with no other qualifications, this is a limit order to buy $5,000 face amount ("5M") of 9% bonds maturing in 2035. The customer wants to pay 90% of par for the bonds or less. Open buy limit orders are executed if the market drops.

6. The best answer is **b**. Since a price is specified with no other qualifications, this is a limit order to buy $5,000 face amount ("5M") of 9% bonds maturing in 2035. Since this order was entered "GTC" - "good til canceled" - the order stays open until execution is possible. The customer is attempting to establish a long position with this order and wants to buy for 90% of par or less if possible. If executed, the customer is buying $5,000 par value of bonds at 90% = $4,500 or less.

7. The best answer is **d**. The orders that are executed if the market drops are "OBLOSS" - Open Buy Limits and Open Sell Stops. The orders that are executed in a rising market are "OSLOBS" - Open Sell Limits and Open Buy Stops.

8. The best answer is **b**. The customer will "lose" the gain on a long stock position if the market begins to fall. To sell out the position in a falling market, the order must be a sell stop order (placed below the market). To sell out a long position in a rising market the order would be a sell limit order.

9. The best answer is **a**. The customer will "lose" the gain on a short stock position if the market begins to rise. To buy in the position in a rising market, the order must be a buy stop order (placed above the market). To buy in a short position in a falling market the order would be a buy limit order.

10. The best answer is **a**. The first market is trading of listed stocks on the floor of an exchange. Exchanges started as pure "auction" markets, where an open outcry auction determined the price of a stock. With the advent of computerized trading, the NYSE is now a "hybrid" market that offers both a computerized matching market and an auction market that is done both electronically and manually.

NASDAQ, as the first "virtual" exchange, does not use the auction model. It simply uses computerized matching.

The over-the-counter market (e.g., OTCBB and Pink Sheets), by comparison, is a negotiated market.

11. The best answer is **b**. To limit loss on a long stock position, the investor wants to sell if the market drops. To sell in a falling market, the appropriate order is a sell stop order. Another strategy that would work is the purchase of a put contract, giving the investor the right to sell at the strike price should the market drop.

12. The best answer is **b**. The investor has a gain on the short stock position that will evaporate as the market rises. To protect the gain, the stock must be bought in if the market begins to rise. A buy stop order is executed in a rising market, and would be appropriate to close the short position if the market rises. The purchase of a call allows the stock to be bought in at the strike price if the market rises, protecting the gain. If a put is sold and the market rises, the put will expire worthless, and the writer will keep the premium received. This amount of premium received will reduce any loss on the short stock position if the market rises. The purchase of a put will not protect the gain, since it allows the stock to be sold at the strike price. If exercised, the long put will cause the customer to have sold the stock **TWICE.**

13. The best answer is **c**. A stock breaks a "support" level as the market falls. If the stock breaks this level ($40), the investor feels that the price will plummet. To profit, he wants to sell short if the market breaks $40 on the downside, so the order is to sell (short) @ $39 Stop. The order must be a sell stop because it is placed lower than the current market. If the market falls to $39, the order is triggered and becomes a market order to sell short. The order can then be executed on the next trade. Once the short stock position is established, the customer believes that the price will plummet, and that the stock can be purchased later to cover the short sale at a much lower price for a profit.

14. The best answer is **c**. A stock breaks a "resistance" level as the market rises. If the stock breaks this level ($50), the investor feels that the price will rocket upwards. To profit, he wants to buy if the market breaks $50 on the upside, so the order is to buy @ 51 Stop. The order must be a buy stop because it is placed above the current market. If the market rises to $51, the order is triggered and becomes a market order to buy. The order can then be executed on the next trade. Once the long stock position is established, the customer believes the price will skyrocket, so that it can be sold at a higher price for a profit.

15. The best answer is **d**. A "fill or kill" order is to be executed in full or the order is canceled. An "all or none" order is to be executed in full, but if trader can't fill the order, he is free to attempt execution at a later time. These orders cannot be executed in part.

16. The best answer is **c**. Reports of trades of NASDAQ issues are made through the Network C Tape, regardless of the market venue where the trade took place. The Network A Tape reports trades of NYSE-listed issues, regardless of the market venue where the trade took place. The Network B Tape reports trades of NYSE-MKT (AMEX) and regional exchange-listed issues, regardless of the market venue where the trade took place. There is no Network D Tape.

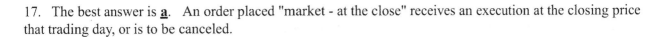

17. The best answer is **a**. An order placed "market - at the close" receives an execution at the closing price that trading day, or is to be canceled.

18. The best answer is **a**. The Second Market is over-the-counter trading of securities that are not listed on a stock exchange. For equities, the Second Market is the OTCBB (Over-The-Counter Bulletin Board) and the Pink OTC Markets. The First Market is trading of listed stocks on an exchange. Choices **B** and **D** are definitions of the primary (new issue) market - not the secondary (trading) markets.

19. The best answer is **d**. The "Third Market" is over-the-counter trading of exchange listed securities. It can be viewed as a competitor for the exchanges as a place to execute trades of exchange listed stocks. Third Market Makers are OTC firms such as Jefferies and Co. and Weeden and Co. that stay open 24 hours a day and capture much of their trading volume in NYSE-listed issues when the NYSE is closed.

20. The best answer is **b**. An efficient market is one where there is a high trading volume, so that liquidity risk is minimized. As trading volume increases, dealer spreads will narrow, since the dealer doesn't have to make as much on each trade to be profitable.

21. The best answer is **b**. The Second Market is trading of unlisted securities "over-the-counter." This is a negotiated market. For example, a stock quoted in the OTCBB is actually traded by picking up the phone, calling the market maker posting the quote, and negotiating a price.

22. The best answer is **d**. If a retail member firm chooses a market maker to execute its orders in return for compensation from that market maker, then the retail firm is earning so-called "payment for order flow." The SEC permits this practice, subject to the retail member firm always executing its trades at the best available price.

23. The best answer is **d**. Rule 606 of Regulation NMS covers reports that broker-dealers must prepare on their order-routing procedures.

It requires that, upon customer request, a member firm must disclose:

- The markets to which the customer's orders were routed to during the past 6 months;
- Whether the orders were directed (that is, the customer specified the market where the order was to be filled) or non-directed (the member firm chose the market where the order was to be filled); and
- The time of execution of the orders.

There is no requirement to disclose the best market available for that security at the time, since SEC rules require that execution must occur at the "best market."

24. The best answer is **d**. SEC rules require that execution must occur at the "best market." If a stock is traded in multiple markets, then the order must be routed by the member firm to the market that is posting the best quote.

25. The best answer is **c**. After hours trading is characterized by much lower trading volumes than during the regular trading day and, correspondingly, dealer bid-ask spreads are much wider.

26. The best answer is **d**. ECNs - Electronic Communications Networks - only accept orders for actively traded securities - that is, NYSE listed and NASDAQ stocks. Essentially they are electronic matching services,

matching customer buy and sell orders for a very low fee (often as low as $1 per trade). ECNs do not act as dealers - only as agents, earning a fee on each successful transaction. ECN volumes have been growing, as institutions use them to reduce trading costs. The major ECNs are Island, Instinet and Archipelago. (Also note that in 2006, the NYSE purchased Archipelago, and NASDAQ purchased Instinet and Island (which had merged into INET), and are running them as separate trading systems).

27. The best answer is **b**. SEC Rule 606 of Regulation NMS requires broker-dealers to compile and report statistical information on their order routing procedures for all customer trades every quarter. Do not confuse this with another part of the rule that requires that broker-dealers give to their customers an annual notice that the customer can, on request, get detailed information on the routing of that customer's orders over the prior 6 months.

28. The best answer is **b**. The trade-through rule of Regulation NMS requires that any "fast market" (NYSE, AMEX and NASDAQ) must either execute a trade within 1 second at the best price posted for a given security at that moment; or must route that order to the market that is posting the better price (this could be a Third Market Maker or an ECN). Thus, market makers are prohibited from "trading through" another market's better priced quote.

29. The best answer is **c**. If the customer directs that the trade be sent to a specific trading venue, follow the customer's instructions. When the trading venue gets the order, it must either fill the order at the best price available in all markets; or it must re-route the order to the better-priced market (the "trade-through" rule); so the customer will get the best price, no matter where the order is actually sent!

30. The best answer is **a**. Rule 612 of Regulation NMS does not allow sub-penny orders to be entered for NMS stocks. The order must be refused under SEC rules (or the representative can tell the customer to enter it as $16.11, but this is not given as a choice).

31. The best answer is **a**. Rule 610 of Regulation NMS requires all market centers to electronically link and provide automated execution within 1 second for orders that are executable. It also mandates that market centers cannot discriminate against customers who access their quotes.

32. The best answer is **a**. ECNs (Electronic Communications Networks) attempt to match large institutional orders. They only do this for listed stocks (NYSE, NYSE-MKT (AMEX) and NASDAQ). They don't do OTC stocks (OTCBB or Pink Sheet issues) because the market is too thin. For each match, the ECN earns a small fee.

33. The best answer is **a**. Rule 612 of Regulation NMS does not allow sub-penny quotes or orders to be entered for NMS stocks.

34. The best answer is **d**. Under Regulation ATS, any ECN (Electronic Communications Network) or ATS (Alternative Trading System) must register with FINRA as a broker/dealer (therefore it comes under some market regulation). Once an ECN is big enough (5% of the trading volume in a given stock in the past 6 months), it must publicly display its orders so that they can be accessed and traded against electronically.

35. The best answer is **c**. FINRA requires that anytime there is a change of account name or designation relating to an executed order, a written record must be made of the change. This is called a "Cancel-Rebill" record. A branch manager or compliance officer must know the reasons for the change and must approve the

change in writing. Such a record must be created for any change of account designation - even for something as minor as moving a trade from a customer's cash account to the same customer's margin account.

This page intentionally left blank

SECTION 2: NYSE TRADING

2a. LISTING AND DELISTING RULES

To be listed on the NYSE, a corporation must meet the following minimum standards (only a general understanding is required for the examination):

Listing Standards

For Initial Public Offerings there are 3 tests to be met to be listed:

- At least 400 holders of round lots of 100 shares; and
- At least 1.1 million shares outstanding; and
- Minimum market capitalization of $60 million.

For companies moving their listing from another market, there are 2 alternative sets of tests that can be met to be listed:

- At least 400 holders of round lots of 100 shares or 2,200 shareholders; and
- Minimum 100,000 share monthly trading volume for the last 6 months; and
- Minimum market capitalization of $100 million.

    or

- At least 500 stockholders; and
- Minimum 1 million share monthly trading volume for the last 12 months; and
- At least 1.1 million shares outstanding; and
- Minimum market capitalization of $100 million.

In addition, to be listed, the issuer must have either:

- At least $10 million in aggregate pre-tax earnings over the past 3 years, with a minimum of $2 million in each of the preceding 2 years;

    or

- At least $25 million in operating cash flow over the past 3 years (only for companies with at least $100 million in revenues and $500 million global market capitalization);

    or

- At least $75 million of revenues in the most recent year and $750 million global market capitalization.

Delisting Conditions

The exchange will consider delisting if any of 3 conditions are met:

- The total number of stockholders falls below 400;

    or

- The total number of shareholders falls below 1,200 and average monthly trading volume falls below 100,000 shares;

    or

- The number of publicly held shares falls below 600,000.

Also, the exchange will consider delisting a company if its share price falls below $1.00 or if its market capitalization falls below the thresholds set by the NYSE (which vary for different types of companies).

In addition, the exchange will consider delisting for many other reasons. For example, if the company:

- substantially reduces its scope of operations;
- files for bankruptcy;
- fails to maintain its registration with the SEC;
- issues a class of non-voting common stock;
- fails to solicit proxies for annual meetings.

Finally, the exchange can also delist a company for a variety of reasons, such as failure to keep good accounting practices, inability to meet debt obligations, failure to make adequate disclosures to the public, etc.

2b. HOW THE EXCHANGE FUNCTIONS

NYSE Classic

Arca ECN

The NYSE operates both a "traditional" floor-based trading market named "NYSE Classic," and a computer order matching engine - the Arca ECN (the shortened name for the Archipelago Electronic Communications Network that the NYSE purchased in 2006).

SuperDisplayBook

The "NYSE Classic" system routes orders electronically to either floor brokers on their hand-held devices or the NYSE Specialist/DMM (Designated Market Maker) in that stock. The DMM maintains the book of open orders, which can be traded against by both the floor brokers and the DMM. This electronic trading book is called "SuperDisplayBook."

Floor Brokers

$2 Broker

Floor brokers are employees of each brokerage firm. The floor brokers work for the retail brokerage firms, executing customer orders. If the floor brokers are very busy, the firm can have a "$2 broker" perform the trade. $2 brokers are independent brokers who assist brokerage firms, helping them execute trades. The name stems from the fact that they used to be paid $2 per trade.

Floor Broker Can Only Act As Agent	Floor brokers act as agent only, attempting to get the best fill for their customers. This means that a floor broker must always put the client's interest first. Floor brokers are prohibited from exploiting their time and place advantage to their own benefit through proprietary or discretionary trading.
Specialist **DMM** **Exchange Member**	Specialists/DMMs are exchange members that are the market markers in NYSE listed issues. There is only 1 Specialist/DMM firm per stock. The DMM stays at the trading post for the stock, and executes market orders that arrive electronically via SuperDisplayBook; and also executes limit orders that are electronically placed on the DMM's book (covered later in this section) via SuperDisplayBook. The DMM also trades with floor brokers who either access the DMM's quote electronically or who physically come to the trading post. Below are examples of orders that arrive via SuperDisplayBook and how they are handled:
Market Order Execution By DMM	A large market order to buy would be routed electronically directly to the DMM in that stock. At the same time, the order can also be electronically accessed by the floor brokers. The order is either filled by the floor brokers or the DMM, with either of these having the obligation to get the best price. It might be possible for the DMM or floor broker to "improve" the matching prices for the customer that placed the buy order. (Such price improvement is not typically available with a pure automated order matching system, which is the other NYSE trading platform - the Arca ECN).
Market-Not Held Order Execution By Floor Broker	A market-not held order would be routed to a floor broker by SuperDisplayBook and not to the DMM under NYSE rules. This is a market order that is not held to an immediate execution. The floor broker can access the SuperDisplayBook to fill the order or can take the order to the trading post and attempt a fill with either the DMM or another floor broker. The floor broker acts in a pure agency capacity and attempts to "work" the order to get the best price, since he or she is "not held" to an immediate execution at the market. Again, because there is a human being filling the order, there is the possibility of getting "price improvement" on the order.
Limit Order Placed On Specialist's/DMM's Book	A limit order to sell would be routed directly via SuperDisplayBook to the Specialist/DMM in that stock and would be placed on the Specialist's/DMM's book of open orders. If the market moves up to, or through, the limit price, the Specialist/DMM is obligated to fill the order for the customer at the limit price (or better, if the Specialist/DMM can get the seller a higher price than the limit specified).

Trading Markets

| **SuperDisplayBook Reports Trade To Tape And Entering Firm** | Once the trade is executed, SuperDisplayBook reports the trade over the Consolidated Tape and reports the trade back to the firm that entered the order. |

The "benefit" of having human interaction in these orders is that the NYSE always attempts to get customers "price improvement" if this is possible. And the NYSE "Classic" SuperDisplayBook system was built to allow this.

Arca ECN

However, with the increased use of computerized algorithmic trading by large institutions and hedge funds, who value speed and accuracy of execution of large size orders at the current market price over the possibility of getting a marginally better price, the NYSE needs a system that has the capability to automatically match and execute trades of relatively large size. This is the purpose of the Arca ECN - which is basically a super-computer located in Mahwah, New Jersey, where member firms can co-locate their servers and feed orders into the system at lightning speed and get virtually "instant" order matching and execution.

For the examination, most of the questions center on floor trading rules - not on the Arca ECN. These procedures are covered next.

SuperDisplayBook

To understand how SuperDisplayBook functions, let's start with an order to Buy 100 Shares of XXX stock at the market. This is written on an order ticket (this can be an electronic order ticket) and entered on the SuperDisplayBook system. (Now you know that SuperDisplayBook handles market orders.) The system routes the order directly to the DMM's trading post.

DMM's Quote - Bid And Ask In Cents

The DMM maintains his quote on a computer screen. Assume that, currently, the DMM is quoting XXX at 70.03 (Bid) - 70.05 (Ask). The DMM is willing to buy the stock at $70.03 per share; and is willing to sell the stock at $70.05 per share. The DMM has the system programmed to automatically execute at the ask quote and the execution is reported back directly to the originating firm.

The DMM is free to change his quote at any time. If he receives an overflow of buy orders, the quote will be raised; an overflow of sell orders will result in the quote being lowered. He is given the responsibility for maintaining an "orderly" market in the stock, so that price changes are gradual.

The advantages of the SuperDisplayBook system are that it is fast and inexpensive to run. The system is constantly being enlarged and can handle orders of very large size (for example, at this writing, market orders are accepted up to 999,999 shares and limit orders are accepted up to 3,000,000 shares).

DMM's Book Of Limit Orders

The system also accepts limit orders for execution if the market rises or falls. These are maintained on an electronic "book" run by the DMM.

In March 2016, the NYSE ceased accepting stop orders on its system. Member firms may accept them into their own systems, and when elected, route them to the NYSE as either a market order (if a stop order was elected) or a limit order (if a stop limit order was elected). You still must understand stop and stop limit orders for the exam since they can be accepted by member firms.

To understand how the book operates, imagine that the "book" is empty - there are no existing orders to buy and sell. The stock is XXX and the DMM is opening the stock that morning at 70.03 - 70.05, a quote that he considers to be "fair and orderly." The empty book looks as follows:

BUY	SELL
70.08	
70.07	
70.06	
70.05	
70.04	
70.03	
70.02	
70.01	
70.00	

Specialist's Quote Currently Is: 70.03 - 70.05

(Please note that this is a very "basic" presentation of the book. The actual Specialist/DMM book is much more complex, and its details are not tested.)

Orders now come in through the system that are lower and higher than the current market. An order comes from Merrill to buy 100 shares at 70.00. Since the Specialist/DMM is asking 70.05 for the stock, the order cannot be filled and is entered on the book.

Another order comes in from Goldman Sachs to buy 200 shares at 70.01. Since the Specialist/DMM is asking 70.05 for the stock, the order can't be filled and is placed on the book for execution at a later date.

An order comes in from Fidelity to sell 500 shares at 70.06. Since the Specialist/DMM is willing to buy at 70.03, this order cannot be filled and is placed on the book for future execution.

After a number of orders have been entered, assume the book looks as follows:

BUY		SELL
	70.08	200 RJames Day 300 Wells Fargo Day
	70.07	200 MorganStan Day
	70.06	500 Fidelity Day
	70.05	
	70.04	
	70.03	
300 Janney Day	70.02	
200 Goldman Day	70.01	
100 Merrill Day	70.00	

Specialist's Quote Currently Is:
70.03 - 70.05

The stock is currently trading at 70.03 Bid - 70.05 Ask. If the price moves down, the Specialist/DMM will buy the stock for Janney, then Goldman and finally Merrill. If the stock moves up, the Specialist/DMM will sell the stock for Fidelity, Morgan Stanley, Raymond James and finally Wells Fargo.

Customer Orders On Book Have Priority

The Specialist/DMM is free to trade for his own account at any price where the book is clear. Before he can buy at 70.02 for his own account, he must fill the Janney order. Before he can sell for his own account at 70.06, he must fill the Fidelity order.

Registered representatives don't see the book. If a registered representative accesses his or her quotations terminal, the following will be shown for XXX stock:

XXX Cmn
70.02 - 70.06
3 x 5

There are 300 shares bid at 70.02 and 500 shares offered at 70.06. These are the next orders to be filled on the Specialist/DMM book if the market rises or falls. The source of this quote is highlighted on the book below:

BUY		SELL
	70.08	200 RJames Day
		300 Wells Fargo Day
	70.07	200 MorganStan Day
	70.06	500 Fidelity Day
	70.05	
	70.04	
	70.03	
300 Janney Day	70.02	
200 Goldman Day	70.01	
100 Merrill Day	70.00	

First Order OUTSIDE Current Trading Range

Current Trading Range

First Order OUTSIDE Current Trading Range

Size Of Market

If a customer wants to buy XXX stock, there are 500 shares offered at 70.06 (from Fidelity, which doesn't show on the screen). If a customer wants to sell XXX, the registered representative can tell him that currently 300 shares are bid at 70.02 (from Janney, which doesn't show on the screen). Thus the "size" of the current market is 3 x 5 - 300 shares bid (at 70.02) and 500 shares offered (at 70.06).

Quotes Are Firm For The Indicated Size

Also note that these quotes are "firm" for the indicated size. Thus, a customer that wishes to buy at the market can purchase up to 500 shares at 70.06. Any size that the customer wishes to purchase that is larger than 500 shares offered at 70.06 would be subject to the movement of the market.

Orders Filled On FIFO Basis

Orders that are received at the same price are handled on a "first in - first out" basis. For example, there may be a stack of 22 different orders to buy if the price falls to 70.02. If the market moves to this price, the Specialist/DMM fills the orders in the sequence they were received. If the market moves back up before all the orders are filled, the remaining orders sit on the book until they can be executed.

2c. OTHER SPECIALIST FUNCTIONS

Specialist/DMM Positive Obligation

The Specialist/DMM, as the assigned market maker in the stock, is obligated to make a continuous market in the stock. If there are customers that wish to sell and there are no other buyers for that stock, then the Specialist/DMM must "step-in" and buy that stock into its inventory account. If there are customers that wish to buy and there are no other sellers for a stock, then the Specialist/DMM must "step-in" and sell that stock out of its inventory account. This is called the Specialist's/DMM's "positive obligation" - that is, the obligation to be the buyer or seller of last resort.

Trading Markets

Specialist/DMM Negative Obligation **Auction Market**	On the other hand, if there are buyers and sellers ready to trade at a given price, then the Specialist/DMM has a "negative obligation" not to interposition itself between these willing traders. The Specialist becomes the "auctioneer" - conducting an orderly auction between the floor brokers that wish to buy and those that wish to sell. Thus, if the market is active, then the Specialist/DMM should not be performing many trades for its own account. Note, however, that the Specialist/DMM can still execute trades from its book as the market moves, since these are trades for the account of customers.
Stopping Stock Specialist/ DMM Courtesy Function	The Specialist/DMM can perform a courtesy function known as "stopping stock." Assume a floor broker has an order to buy 10,000 shares of GE at the market - not held. The floor broker goes to the Specialist/DMM and asks for a quote. The Specialist/DMM says "GE is 30 to 30.25." The floor broker thinks the ask price is a bit high, and wants to see if there are any other floor brokers at the post who might wish to sell for less. As a courtesy, the Specialist/DMM says "You are stopped at 30.25 for 10,000."
"s/t" - Stopped Stock **Price Guarantee**	The trader is now free to try and get a better price, but if he can't, he can return to the Specialist/DMM a short time later and get the stock at the "stopped" price of 30.25. Thus, the Specialist/DMM has "guaranteed" the price. The trade comes across the tape with the symbol "s/t" for stopped instead of "s" (these symbols are discussed immediately following).
Specialist/DMM Can Only Stop Stock For Public Orders	Stopping stock can only be done for orders from public customers - stock cannot be stopped for member firms' own trading accounts. The Specialist cannot stop stock indefinitely - only for short time periods.
Specialist/DMM Acts As Odd Lot Dealer	Another "courtesy" function performed by DMMs on the NYSE floor is the handling of "odd lots" - orders for less than 100 shares. The Specialist/DMM does not place "odd lot" orders on the book for execution. Rather, the Specialist/DMM simply buys and sells these units from its inventory, charging the customer the current market price plus an "odd lot differential" - which is an extra fee to cover the higher cost of handling these transactions.

2d. THE CONSOLIDATED TAPE

Consolidated Tape	As trades are performed on the floor of the exchange, it is required that the sell side of the trade report to the Consolidated (Network A) Tape within 10 seconds of the trade. Thus, during the hours when the NYSE is open (9:30 AM - 4:00 PM Eastern Standard Time), there is a running tape of actual trades.

The tape is called "Consolidated" because trades in NYSE listed issues that take place in any market are reported to the tape via computer linkups. For example, if a trade in a NYSE-listed issue takes place on the Pacific exchange (now actually renamed the "ArcaEx" as in Archipelago Exchange, since Archipelago has bought this marketplace - but this may not be reflected on the exam) in the Third Market, or on Instinet, these trades are included in the tape during the hours that the NYSE is open.

Executing Member Reports Trade Within 10 Seconds

Whether the stock is listed on the NYSE, NYSE-MKT (the market formerly known as AMEX), NASDAQ or is an OTC issue, executing members must report the trade within 10 seconds.

Network A - NYSE

The Network A tapes reports all NYSE-listed trades; the Network B tape reports all NYSE-MKT and regional exchange listed trades.

Following is a sample of the Network A Tape:

New York Stock Exchange Composite Tape

....C.............	IBM.............	GM.............	F.............
32.50	2s 114	30s 70.06	99s 48

...MMM.....C pfd........	ABC.............	PDQ wt....
62.88	87.25	2s/s 18.13	1.05

....C. SLD.................	T. OPD.......IBM...........
5s 32.40	41.75	10,000s 113

....C.............................	F.............
32.25	32.30...32.30	2s.3s.4s .48.25

Stock Symbol

Reading across the tape in sequence, here is what has occurred. A round lot of Citigroup (C) traded at 32.50. A round lot is 100 shares.

"s" = Round Lots Of 100s

Two hundred shares of IBM traded at 114. If a trade is for more than 1 round lot, the symbol "s" appears next to the price. 2s = 2 round lots of 100.

30 round lots of GM traded at 70.06. 30 x 100 shares per lot = 3,000 shares.

99 round lots of Ford traded at 48. 99 x 100 = 9,900 shares.

1 round lot of 3M traded at 62.88.

1 round lot of Citigroup preferred traded at 87.25.

"s/s" = Round Lots Of 10s	The symbol "s/s" is unusual. It is used to designate what are termed "cabinet" stocks. These are either extremely expensive stocks like Berkshire Hathaway (which trades for around $200,000 per share) or almost defunct companies that have not been delisted and have very little trading volume. They trade in round lots of 10 shares. The orders used to be kept in cabinets on the side of the exchange floor - hence the name. Therefore, 2 round lots of 10 shares of ABC stock changed hands at 18.13. 1 round lot of PDQ warrants (100 warrants) traded at 1.05.
SLD - Out Of Sequence	C. SLD 5s at 32.40 means that 500 shares of Citigroup were "sold," but were reported out of sequence. This is not a current price - the trade, in error, was not reported to the tape when it occurred, and is now being reported late.
OPD - Opening Delayed	T. OPD at 41.75 means that American Telephone and Telegraph (ATT) stock had a delayed opening. The stock did not start trading at the opening of the market, due to an imbalance of buy and sell orders, usually due to some important news that became known after the market closed the previous day. In this case, the Specialist/DMM can delay the opening of the stock while he gives indications of the likely opening price to the market. He adjusts the indications of the opening price until there is a relatively equal balance of buy and sell orders at the opening. Thus, if there is a large overage of buy orders, the Specialist/DMM will adjust the opening price higher to attract more sellers; conversely, if there is a large overage of sell orders, the Specialist/DMM will adjust the opening price lower to attract more buyers.
Block = 10,000 Shares	Once a trade hits 10,000 shares, it is considered a "block" trade. The full amount of the "block" is printed on the tape (with an "s" following, which may be confusing). Therefore, this trade of 10,000s IBM at 113 is a trade of 10,000 shares - **not** 10,000 units of 100 shares. 100 shares of Citigroup changed hands at 32.25, followed by another 100 shares at 32.30, followed by another 100 shares at 32.30. Notice how these trades were reported in "shorthand." Following these trades were 200 shares of Ford, followed by a 300 share trade and then a 400 share trade, all at 48.25. Again, these trades were reported in "shorthand." As an example of a difficult type of question about trade reporting on the tape, try this problem:

> The last trade in Citigroup took place at 32.50. A customer places an order to sell short 100 shares of Citigroup at 32.25 Stop Limit GTC. The trades that take place after the order is placed are shown on the tape. At what price is the order elected (triggered)? What is the first trade where the order could be executed?

To understand what is happening, you must first identify that this is a sell (short) stop order. Sell stop orders are placed lower than the current market and are triggered as the market falls. This order is similar to the example used for the technical analyst - it is used to establish a short position below a support area in the belief that the market will drop further.

The trading sequence is:

32.50   This is the trade prior to entering the order

32.50   Nothing happens because the market has not fallen to the stop price of 32.25.

C. SLD   (Ignore this trade; it is out of sequence.)
32.40

32.25   This trade triggers the order since the market has fallen to the stop price of 32.25. The order now becomes a limit order to sell at 32.25 (meaning sell for at least that amount).

32.30   The order can be executed, since a sale can be made at 32.30, which is better than the limit price to sell of 32.25.

2e. SPECIFIC NYSE TRADING RULES

Rule 76 - Prohibits Crossing Of Orders Within Firm

Order Must First Be Exposed To Exchange Floor

Rule 76 - states that if a member firm holds an order to buy a security from one customer and an order to sell a security from another customer at the same price, the order cannot simply be "crossed" within the firm. The security must first be offered in the trading market at $.01 (the minimum price change for NYSE listed stocks) more than the bid held by the firm. If the offer is not taken, **then** the cross may be performed.

Rule 77 - Prohibited Practices

Rule 77 - prohibits any person on the trading floor from offering to:

- Bet on the course of the market;

- Buy or sell dividends;

- Buy or sell privileges to receive or deliver securities;

- Buy or sell securities "at the close";

- Buy or sell securities at a "stop" price away from the current market.

Rule 78 - Prohibits Prearranged Trades

Rule 78 - prohibits prearranged trades to sell, coupled with an offer to buy back at a stated price.

Rule 92 - Requires Customer Orders Get Priority Over Equivalent Orders For Firm Account	Rule 92 - requires that a customer order receives priority over an order for the firm's trading account or any person associated with that firm. If a firm holds a customer order to buy stock at a stated price, the firm cannot execute an order to buy for its own account at the same price or lower **unless** the customer order is executed first. Similarly, if a firm holds a customer order to sell stock at a stated price, the firm cannot execute an order to sell for its own account at the same price or higher **unless** the customer order is executed first.

Finally, if the firm has a market order from a customer, it must execute the customer order before a market order can be filled for the firm or an associated person.

Rule 410 - Requires Records Of Trades To Be Kept For 3 Years	Rule 410 - requires that records of orders transmitted to the floor be kept for 3 years, with the preceding 2 years records kept readily accessible. The order record must include the terms of the order, the time the order was transmitted, and the time the order was executed. If the order is canceled, the time of cancellation must be placed in the record.

Rule 411 - If A Trade Is Reported With An Error, Customer Gets Actual Price	Rule 411 - states that if a transaction is reported erroneously, the customer must pay the actual price of the trade. If a trade is reported, but was not actually executed, then the trade is not binding. Also, the rule requires member firms to record customer transactions in accounts no later than settlement date.

Rule 435 - Prohibited Practices

Rule 435 - prohibits a member firm from:

- Effecting trades of excessive frequency or of excessive size in an account;

- Effecting trades at successively higher or successively lower prices to create a misleading appearance of activity in the stock;

- Participating in any manipulative operation;

- Circulating rumors of a sensational nature which might be expected to influence market prices;

- Changing the price on a transaction before settlement date;

- Loaning money with stocks, bonds, or securities as collateral (unless the provisions of Regulation T of the Federal Reserve Board are followed, which will be covered in the following section).

Most Block Trades In NYSE Listed Stocks Are Handled Today By OTC Block Trading Desks

The NYSE auction market is designed to handle a large volume of relatively small trades. In order to properly execute large block trades (mainly institutional orders), the NYSE allows its retail members to maintain an OTC block trading desk. If a customer wishes to trade a very large block of stock that cannot be handled through SuperDisplayBook (e.g., the system only takes limit orders up to 3,000,000 shares), the block trading desk will simply take that position into the firm's inventory. Again, note that such a practice is subject to the SEC's "best price" execution requirements, meaning that the price given to the customer must be at least the same, or better than, the best quote available in the market. In this manner, large institutional orders are quickly and easily executed.

Block Positioning

These so-called "block-positioners" are adding liquidity and price stability to the market, since they free the specialist to handle the regular order flow. Hence, "block positioning" is permitted and regulated by the NYSE, and is an integral part of the marketplace.

2f. OTHER ITEMS RELATED TO NYSE TRADING

Definition Of Long Sale

When filling out an order ticket, all purchases are "long," but sales are either "long" or "short." A customer sells stock long when he "owns" the stock.

A sale is considered to be long if:

- The customer owns the stock and will deliver on the sale on settlement;

- The customer owns a convertible security, has given orders to convert, and will deliver on the sale on settlement;

- The customer owns rights, warrants

For example, if a customer owns a call option on a stock and wishes to sell that stock, it is a short sale unless the option is exercised and the stock will be delivered by settlement.

Customer Position Is "Long" To Extent Of Net Position

The next factor in whether a sale is "long" or "short" stems from the fact that a customer is only considered to be "long" a security to the extent of his "net" long position.

To illustrate, consider the following: At year end, customers, in the past, often would "sell short against the box" securities that they owned to "lock in" a capital gain and also to defer taxation to the next tax year. Under tax law revisions of 1997, deferral of taxation of the gain is generally prohibited; deferral is only permitted if very specific tests are met (these tests are covered in the Taxation section).

Assume a customer owns 100 shares of GM purchased at $40 and the stock is worth $50 at year end. Also assume that the customer can meet the tests required to defer taxes if he or she chooses to go "short against the box." If the stock is sold "long," meaning delivered on the sale, the customer must pay tax on a $10 capital gain. Instead, the customer borrows another 100 shares of GM and sells those shares.

Since this customer can meet the specific tests that allow the tax deferral of the gain, the sale of the borrowed shares does not result in a taxable gain at that point. The customer has created the following position:

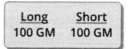

At a later date, the customer can use the long position to cover the borrowed shares, and will pay tax at that point. The sale of the borrowed shares is technically a short sale, since the customer is not delivering stock that he or she owns.

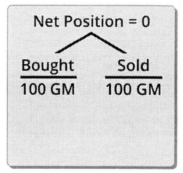

Since the customer is borrowing shares to sell, this is a short sale.

After the short sale, the customer's net position is ZERO.

Assume that instead of delivering the GM shares held to cover the short position, the customer wants to sell those shares. Technically, the customer has no long position (the net is "0"), so the sale is a short sale. This looks as follows:

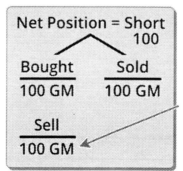

Since the net position is ZERO when the new sale occurs, the sale is technically "SHORT"

After the short sale, the customer is left with a short position in GM stock that must be covered by purchasing the shares at a later date.

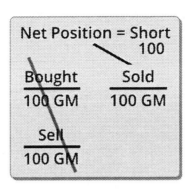

After the short sale, the customer is left with a SHORT position of 100 shares.

Best Execution Requirement

Finally, remember that if a customer places an order for an NYSE listed issue, the order is no longer required to be sent to the NYSE floor for execution. The member firm is obligated to route the order to the trading market (also called "trading venue") that can give the best execution.

Payment For Order Flow

Thus, if a Third Market Maker or an ECN such as Instinet is offering a better price than the NYSE Specialist/DMM, then the order must be routed to that marketplace. On the other hand, if all of the markets have the same quote, the member is free to choose where it wants the order routed; and is permitted to accept "payment for order flow" from market makers in return for sending orders - however, payment for order flow must be disclosed to customers.

Private Trading Prohibited

Note, however, that all orders must be executed in the public market - firms are not permitted to do these trades "privately"; nor can they internalize their trades and simply match them "in house" without giving the public access to their order flow.

2g. REGULATION SHO

In mid-2004, the SEC approved a new short sale regulation, called "Regulation SHO." The intent of the rule is to have a uniform federal rule that can be applied to all securities markets and to curb the potentially manipulative practice of "naked short selling."

Basic Short Sale Rule Was Eliminated

The basic premise of the original "short sale rule" that dates back to the 1930's - that is, short sales can only be effected when the market is rising (short sales could only be executed on an uptick), was rescinded effective July 2007. The SEC, after a 2 year test, had determined that the potential to manipulate stocks downward in price by relentless short selling was no longer an issue.

Short Sale Rule Reinstated In 2010

However, in 2010, the SEC reversed course due to unprecedented market volatility experienced in 2008 - 2010 and issued a "short sale rule" that is specific to each stock (Rule 201 covered following).

| **Short Sale Definition - Sale Of Shares Not Owned By Seller** | Rule 200 of Regulation SHO defines a "short sale" as: |

- the sale of a security that the seller does not own; or

- any sale that is settled by the delivery of a security that the seller does not own; or

- any sale that is settled by the delivery of a security borrowed by the seller or borrowed for the account of the seller.

Long Sale Definition - Sale Of Shares Owned By Seller And Delivered On Settlement

In order to be considered to be "long" a security:

- the seller must own the stock and deliver on settlement; or

- if the seller owns a convertible or derivative security, the seller must convert or exercise and deliver the underlying security on settlement.

Sale Of Shares To Be Received From Conversion Or Exercise Is A Long Sale

Also, the SEC has added a provision to the rule, explicitly stating that if a customer is long a convertible security; or long an option or warrant; and the customer has either tendered the shares for conversion or has exercised the option or warrant; then the sale is considered to be long, even if the security cannot be delivered by settlement. This recognizes the fact that the transfer agent may take a longer amount of time to handle the conversion or exercise than the 3 business days needed for regular way settlement.

Only "Long" To Extent Of Net Long Position

In determining whether an order ticket to sell is marked "long" or "short," a customer is only considered to be "long" to the extent of the seller's net long position in the security. Consider the following position held by a customer:

Long: 1,000 ABCD   Short: 1,000 ABCD

Short Against The Box

This customer is "short against the box" 1,000 shares of ABCD - meaning that the customer has sold 1,000 shares of ABCD short against 1,000 shares being held long by the firm (in the firm's box, or vault). This is a strategy that is used to lock-in a gain on an appreciated stock position.

This customer has a "net long position" of "0." If the customer places an order to sell any of the ABCD position, this is a technical short sale, and the short sale rule would apply.

Now consider the following position held by a customer:

Long: 1,000 ABCD   Short: 600 ABCD

This customer has a net long position of 400 ABCD shares. If the customer places an order to sell 1,000 shares of ABCD, the order to sell would be: Sell 400 Long and Sell 600 Short. The short sale portion of the order is subject to the provisions of Regulation SHO.

Marking Sell Order As Long	Rule 200 of Regulation SHO requires that every order ticket to sell be marked either:
Marking Sell Order As Short	• Long Sale: when the seller is delivering securities that are owned on settlement.
	• Short Sale: when the seller is delivering securities that are borrowed on settlement. Short sales are subject to the provisions of Regulation SHO.
Short-Exempt Order Ticket Marking	There used to be a provision for marking an order ticket "sell short - exempt," that was meant to be used where a short sale was being effected, but the sale was not subject to the "uptick" requirement. This is now used for short sales that are exempt from the provisions of Rule 201, covered next.
Triggered If Stock Price Falls By 10%	Rule 201 of Regulation SHO was put in place due to market volatility that was experienced in specific stocks.
Can Only Sell Short ABOVE Best Bid For Rest Of The Day And The Entire Next Day	Once a specific stock's price drops by 10% or more from the previous day's closing price, a circuit breaker is triggered for that security and, for the remainder of that day and the entire next day, a short sale is only permitted at a price above the national best bid for that security.

> For example, if ABCD closes at $20 and the next day, a trade occurs at $18 or lower, the circuit breaker is triggered. If a short sale at the market is entered the next business day when the NBBO is: $17.50 - $17.75, it can only be executed at $17.51 or higher.

The rule only applies to NMS stocks (NYSE, NYSE-MKT and NASDAQ). It does not apply to OTCBB or Pink Sheet issues. Furthermore, the short sale rule does not apply to:

- Short sales effected above the national best bid;

- Technical short sales where the seller actually owns the security but delivery is delayed;

- Odd lot transactions; and

- Arbitrage transactions.

Short Exempt	These transactions are designated on the order as "short exempt" - meaning that they are exempt from the Rule 201 circuit breaker.

Rule 203 of Regulation SHO specifically addresses a potentially manipulative practice on the part of hedge funds, where these investors have shorted stock without first having borrowed the shares to make delivery. This is known as "naked short selling." If the shares are "difficult to borrow," then the trade may not settle because the seller "fails to deliver" the stock to the buyer on settlement.

Borrowed Securities' Location Must Be Determined Prior To Short Sale	The rule requires short sellers in all equity securities to locate the source from which the shares can be borrowed before effecting a short sale. The "locate" requirement must be documented in writing prior to effecting the short sale.
Locate Requirement	Specifically, Rule 203 states that a broker-dealer cannot execute a short sale for its own account or for the account of another person unless:

- the security has been borrowed or an arrangement has been entered into to borrow the security; or
- there are reasonable grounds to believe that the security could be borrowed and delivered on settlement.

Easy To Borrow List - Updated Daily	To meet the "reasonable grounds" test, a broker-dealer can create a list of "easy to borrow" securities that is less than 24 hours old. These "easy to borrow" securities are readily available and are unlikely to create a fail to deliver on settlement.
Threshold Securities Are "Hard To Borrow"	The rule also requires the exchanges to create a daily list of securities that are "hard to borrow." These are known as the "threshold" securities. A "threshold list security" is one which has:

- a clearing short position at NSCC (National Securities Clearing Corporation division of DTCC) of 10,000 shares or more; and
- this clearing short position represents at least 1/2% of the total shares outstanding.

List Is Updated Daily	To be on the list, the security must meet these tests for 5 business days. The NYSE and NASDAQ update the list every day.
Threshold List Includes NASDAQ, OTCBB And Pink Sheet Issues	Basically, a threshold list security is one that has a large outstanding short position - the SEC and FINRA do not want large outstanding short positions that cannot be covered to build over time. Note that the NASDAQ threshold list covers not only NASDAQ securities, but OTCBB and Pink Sheet issues as well.
Buy-In Of Undelivered Shares If On Threshold List For 13 Consecutive Settlement Days	If a customer sells short a security and fails to deliver on settlement, the rule requires that the position be bought in. Because of the mandatory buy-in requirement, large outstanding naked short positions in "difficult to borrow" securities should not occur. Regulation SHO's wording requires that the buy-in occur if the security is on the threshold list for "13 consecutive settlement days" following the trade date. (Note: With "T+2" settlement starting September 5th, 2017, this buy-in rule should be shortened by 1 business day to 12 consecutive settlement days. However no rule change has been filed and it remains at 13 consecutive settlement days.)

2h. CIRCUIT BREAKER RULES

The "circuit breaker" rules are intended to stop a catastrophic market drop. The rules have 2 levels - market-wide circuit breakers and single-stock circuit breakers.

Market-Wide Circuit Breakers

The market-wide circuit breakers apply to all NMS stocks - NYSE, AMEX and NASDAQ. The markets will close after the Standard & Poor's 500 Index drops by a given percentage from the prior day's closing value. These are called:

- Level 1 Drop: 7%
- Level 2 Drop: 13%
- Level 3 Drop: 20%

Level 1 Or 2 Drop Before 3:25 PM - 15 Min. Close

A Level 1 or Level 2 drop that occurs before 3:25 PM will cause the market to close for 15 minutes.

Level 1 Or 2 Drop After 3:25 PM - No Close

A Level 1 or Level 2 drop that occurs after 3:25 PM will not affect the market (in the past, when markets were shut near the close, it pretty much led to investor panic, hence no closing of the markets).

Any Level 3 Drop - Close For Rest Of Day

A Level 3 Drop at any time of day will cause the markets to close for the remainder of the day.

Single-Stock Limit Up - Limit Down - Rule

The single-stock circuit breakers are designed to stop erratic trading in a single stock, usually due to faulty computer algorithms. The "limit up - limit down" rule tracks each NMS stock's price movement in 5-minute windows.

Actively Traded Issues Capped At 5% Up Or Down Move From Prior 5 Minute Average Price

Tier 1 Stocks: (Actively Traded NMS Issues): Trades that are 5% above or below the average price of the proceeding 5-minute window are prohibited for stocks included in the S&P 500 Index, Russell 1,000 Index and specified ETFs.

Less Actively Traded Issues Capped At 10% Up Or Down From Prior 5 Minute Average Price

Tier 2 Stocks: (Less Actively Traded NMS Issues): Trades that are 10% above or below the average price of the preceding 5-minute window are prohibited for all other listed stocks.

(Also note that the percentage bands are doubled during opening and closing periods; and broader bands apply to stocks priced at $3 or less.)

If Trades Unable To Occur In Price Band Then Trading Stops For 5 Minutes

If trades are unable to occur within the price band for 15 seconds (this is called a "fundamental price move"), then the stock will stop trading for 5-minutes to let the market digest the news that is causing the price movement.

Trading Markets

NYSE TRADING
SECTION EXAMINATION

1.

Specialists (DMMs) on the New York Stock Exchange can perform which of the following functions?

- I   Act as a market maker
- II Act as a broker's broker
- III Handle odd lot transactions
- IV Act as an underwriter

- a.   I and II only
- b.   III and IV only
- c.   I, II, III
- d.   I, II, III, IV

2.

All of the following are true about the NYSE automated trading system **EXCEPT**:

- a.   market orders are accepted
- b.   limit orders are accepted
- c.   any size order is accepted
- d.   day orders are accepted

3.

Under NYSE rules, every "responsible broker or dealer" who communicates bids and offers on the exchange floor (also known as "addressing the crowd") must comply with all of the following rules **EXCEPT**:

- a.   any bid or offer for less than the normal trading unit has no standing in the trading crowd
- b.   the highest bid and the lowest offer have precedence in all cases
- c.   bids and offers must be publicly announced
- d.   bids and offers are set by floor officials during unusual situations

4.

The Specialist (DMM) performs all the following functions **EXCEPT**:

- a.   trades for his own account
- b.   executes orders for other brokers
- c.   executes odd lot orders
- d.   participates in new issue syndicates

5.

Which of the following movements in the Standard and Poor's 500 Index before 3:25 PM would **INITIATE** the market-wide "circuit breaker"?

- a.   1,200 to 1,176
- b.   1,200 to 1,140
- c.   1,200 to 1,116
- d.   1,200 to 1,080

6.

The Network A Tape shows the following:

ABC	DEF	PDQ
2s 40.25	52.38...52.25...52.13	4⅝18.00
DEF SLD	**EGE**	**DEF**
53.00	10,000 s 41.00	52.50

Regarding the trade of EGE stock, which statement is **TRUE**?

- a.   10,000 round lots of 10 shares traded
- b.   10,000 round lots of 100 shares traded
- c.   10,000 round lots of 1,000 shares traded
- d.   10,000 shares traded

7.

Trades of NYSE listed issues are reported via the:

- a.   Network A Consolidated Tape
- b.   Network B Consolidated Tape
- c.   Network C Consolidated Tape
- d.   Network D Consolidated Tape

8.

A customer places an order with a member firm that is "Good through the month." The person responsible for canceling the order if it remains unexecuted after the month is up is the:

a. customer

b. Specialist (DMM)

c. member firm

d. NYSE

9.

A Specialist (DMM) on the NYSE is quoting ABC stock as follows:

$50.05 - $50.06
30 x 60

The Specialist/DMM receives an order via Super Display Book to buy 6,000 shares of ABC at the market. The Specialist/DMM will:

a. place the order on his book for execution

b. fill 3,000 shares at $50.05 and place the unfilled portion of the order on his book

c. fill 6,000 shares at $50.05

d. fill 6,000 shares at $50.06

10.

On the New York Stock Exchange, which of the following persons will handle odd lot transactions?

a. Specialist (DMM)

b. Floor Broker

c. $2 Broker

d. Competitive Trader

11.

If a member firm routes a customer market order for an NYSE listed issue to the NYSE's automated trading system, the order will be sent to:

a. Super Display Book

b. Single Book

c. OTCBB

d. Pink OTC Markets

12.

Which of the following statements are **TRUE** regarding the Super Display Book system?

I Orders are routed directly to the NYSE DMM for execution

II Only round lots are permitted; odd lot orders cannot be entered into the system

III Member firms prefer to use the system because it is more efficient and cheaper than manually handling the orders

IV Executed trades are directly reported to the member firm that entered the order

a. I and IV only

b. II and III only

c. I, II, III

d. I, II, III, IV

13.

The following trade comes across the tape:

ABC pf
$25 \frac{5}{8} 18.50$

Which statement is **TRUE**?

a. 2,500 shares traded at 18.50

b. 25 round lots of 10 shares traded at 18.50

c. 2,500 shares were sold short at 18.50

d. 2,500 shares were stopped at 18.50

14.

Under the provisions of Regulation SHO, before a security can be "sold short," it must be determined that the security:

a. can be borrowed and delivered by settlement

b. has been traded on an + tick or a 0+ tick

c. is not on the threshold list

d. is subject to the short interest reporting rule

15.

The DMM (Specialist) on the NYSE, just prior to market opening, has orders to sell 100,000,000 shares of ABC stock at the open, but only has orders to buy 5,000,000 shares. Because of the extreme order imbalance, the DMM, at the open, displays "ABC - OPD" on the Network A Tape. Which statement about this is **FALSE**?

    a.   The NYSE has delayed the opening of the stock

    b.   Other markets are permitted to trade the stock

    c.   This is a non-regulatory trading halt

    d.   Any other market that wishes to trade the stock during the halt must get prior FINRA approval

16.

A floor broker goes to the trading post to buy 10,000 shares of ABC at the market-not held. The Specialist (DMM) says to the trader "One hundred shares are stopped at 19." This means that:

    a.   the trader is stopped from trading with anyone else

    b.   trading has been stopped in the issue

    c.   the Specialist/DMM has guaranteed that the price will not change for a short period

    d.   the Specialist/DMM will not trade with anyone else at the $19 price

17.

All of the following statements are true regarding the Super Display Book system **EXCEPT**:

    a.   orders are routed directly to the NYSE DMM for execution

    b.   odd lot orders cannot be entered into the system; only round lots are permitted

    c.   customers must request use of the system, otherwise the trades are directed to floor brokers

    d.   executed trades are directly reported to the member firm that entered the order

18.

Assuming that the Standard and Poor's 500 Index closes at 1,230, the U.S. listed equities markets will close its market for the balance of the day if the index declines below:

    a.   1,169

    b.   1,144

    c.   1,070

    d.   984

19.

If a customer sells short a security that is on the "threshold list" and the member firm fails to deliver the security on settlement, the:

    a.   customer's account will be frozen for 90 days

    b.   security must be bought-in no later than 13 consecutive settlement days from trade date

    c.   customer's account must be restricted under Regulation T

    d.   customer's margin requirement will be increased from 50% to 100% of the sale amount

20.

An NMS stock can only be sold short on an up bid if its price falls by at least:

    a.   1%

    b.   2%

    c.   5%

    d.   10%

21.

Under NYSE rules, a company moving its listing from another market must meet which requirements?

I   2,200 shareholders

II   4,400 shareholders

III   Average monthly trading volume of 100,000 shares

IV   Average monthly trading volume of 1,000,000 shares

a.   I and III

b.   I and IV

c.   II and III

d.   II and IV

22.

Third Market Makers must report their trades of exchange listed stocks to the Consolidated Tape:

a.   within 10 seconds of execution during all hours of the day

b.   within 10 seconds of execution during the hours that the NYSE is open

c.   at the close of the trading day

d.   at the opening of the trading day

23.

Under Regulation SHO, a "threshold" security is one that:

a.   cannot be sold short under any circumstances but long sales are permitted

b.   can only be sold short at a price that is $.01 lower than the preceding trade

c.   if sold short and not delivered within 13 business days of the trade, buy-in is required

d.   if sold short on a down-tick, must be immediately bought-in on an up-tick

24.

A corporation is making a tender offer for all of its common shares. Which of the following customers **CANNOT** tender the shares?

a.   Customer A, who is long 100 shares of ABC in a custodian account

b.   Customer B, who is long 100 shares of ABC in a cash account

c.   Customer C, who is long 200 shares of ABC, and short 100 shares of ABC in a margin account

d.   Customer D, who is long 100 shares of ABC, and short 200 shares of ABC in a margin account

25.

All of the following trade securities on the New York Stock Exchange **EXCEPT**:

a.   Two dollar broker

b.   Floor brokers

c.   Specialist (DMM)

d.   Registered Representative

NYSE TRADING EXAMINATION EXPLANATIONS

1. The best answer is **c**. Specialists (now renamed DMMs - Designated Market Makers) cannot deal with the public, so they cannot act as underwriters. They are wholesale members of the NYSE who deal only with other member firms. DMMs act as market makers and broker's brokers. DMMs also act as the odd lot dealers for trades of NYSE listed stocks that are less than a round lot.

2. The best answer is **c**. The Super Display Book system cannot handle any size order: there are maximum order sizes (e.g., 3,000,000 shares for limit orders). The system accepts market and limit orders. It no longer accepts stop orders, but member firms can take stop orders into their internal systems. It no longer accepts GTC orders and only will take Day orders. If a member firm wishes, it can take a GTC order into its internal system and route it to the NYSE as a new Day order each day, until it is either filled or it expires.

3. The best answer is **d**. Under NYSE trading rules, bids and offers must be for the minimum 100 share size trading unit; the highest bid and lowest offer have priority (the same as NASDAQ's "inside market" - now renamed the NBBO - National Best Bid and Offer); and all bids and offers must be publicly announced (no secret bids and offers, or side deals allowed). Bids and offers are always set by market participants; they are not set by floor officials (the regulators) under any circumstances.

4. The best answer is **d**. The Specialist (now called the DMM - Designated Market Maker) is a dealer on the exchange floor trading for his own account. He trades both round lots and "odd" lots (units of less than 100 shares for all stocks except "cabinet" stocks - very high priced stocks that trade is round lots of 10 instead of 100). The Specialist/DMM also acts as agent for other brokers, running a book of open orders to be filled if the market moves up or down.

The Specialist/DMM does not participate in new issue syndicates; this is handled by retail firms who deal with the public. All new issues are initially sold over-the-counter, so the Specialist/DMM on an exchange could not participate in these offerings. Once an initial public offering is completed over-the-counter, the stock trades either on an exchange or over-the-counter.

5. The best answer is **c**. Under the circuit breaker rule, if the Standard and Poor's 500 Index moves down by 7% or more from the prior day's closing price, the listed equity markets will be shut down for 15 minutes. After reopening, if the index falls by a total of 13% or more from the prior day's closing price, the markets will close again for 15 minutes. This is intended to allow investors to calmly evaluate market conditions, so that a "domino effect" of panic selling does not occur. Finally, after reopening, if the index falls by a total of 20%, the markets will close until the next day.

Also note that any 7% or 13% drop that occurs after 3:25 PM will not close the markets - they will stay open until the 4:00 PM close. This is the case because funds base their NAVs on closing prices, and it was felt that having a lack of pricing to investors would be overly disruptive. On the other hand, any 20% drop at any time will shut the markets until the next day, since such a dramatic price drop is usually caused by a major news event.

6. The best answer is **d**. The symbol "s" stands for a round lot of 100 shares. Up to 9,900 shares is reported in this fashion (e.g., 99s = 9900 shares traded). However, trades of 10,000 shares or higher are reported by showing the full trade amount - with the "s" to confuse you!! A trade of 10,000 shares is 10,000s. A trade of 15,000 shares is 15,000s. A trade of 5,000 shares, however, is 50s.

7. The best answer is **a**. The Network A Consolidated Tape reports all trades of NYSE listed issues, wherever they occurred. The Network B Consolidated Tape reports all trades of NYSE-MKT (AMEX) and regional exchanged listed issues, wherever they occurred. The Network C tape reports trades of NASDAQ listed issues wherever they occur. There is no Network D tape.

8. The best answer is **c**. Since the Specialist (now renamed the DMM or Designated Market Maker) only accepts "Day" orders on his book, if a customer wants an order canceled at the end of a month, this is the responsibility of the member firm that entered the order. An order with a "Time in Force" longer than that day is taken into the firm's internal order system and would be routed to the NYSE as a new "Day" order each day by the member. If the order is not executed by the end of the month, would be canceled by the member.

9. The best answer is **d**. The Specialist (now called the DMM - Designated Market Maker) is quoting the stock at $50.05 Bid with a size of 30 (good for 30 x 100 = 3,000 shares); and $50.06 Ask with a size of 60 (good for 60 x 100 = 6,000 shares). These are the next orders to be filled on the Specialist's/DMM's book. If the Specialist/DMM receives a market order to buy for 6,000 shares, the Specialist/DMM will fill that order at the current ask price of $50.06.

10. The best answer is **a**. Odd lot transactions on the NYSE are handled by designated "Odd Lot" dealers - who happen to be the Specialists (Designated Market Makers) in the assigned stocks.

11. The best answer is **a**. The NYSE's automated trade execution system is Super Display Book, which replaced the older SuperDOT (Designated Order Turnaround) system in late 2009. The comparable NASDAQ system was Single Book, which has now been renamed the "NASDAQ Market Center Execution System," and is now simply called the "NASDAQ System." OTCBB is FINRA's "Over-The-Counter Bulletin Board," where dealers post quotes for non-NASDAQ issues.

12. The best answer is **d**. All of the statements are true regarding the Super Display Book System. It is an electronic order entry, order matching, and trade reporting system. The system can only handle round lots (100 shares or more), with limits on the maximum order size permitted (e.g., 3,000,000 shares for limit orders). Odd lots (orders for less than 100 shares) cannot be entered into the system - these are handled by a separate order entry system to the DMM - Designated Market Maker. Over 90% of NYSE trading now goes through Super Display Book. Firms prefer to use it because it is cheaper and faster than having a floor trader manually handle the order.

13. The best answer is **b**. The symbol s/s stands for round lot units of 10. These are the infrequently traded "cabinet stocks" - so-called because the orders are kept in cabinets on the side of the exchange floor. "25 s/s 18.50" means that 25 round lots of 10 (250 shares) traded at $18.50. An example of a cabinet stock is Berkshire Hathaway - a stock that trades for about $200,000 per share, so 10 shares are pretty expensive!

14. The best answer is **a**. Regulation SHO (as in SHOrt sale rule) requires that, prior to effecting a short sale for a customer, it must be affirmatively determined that the security can be borrowed and delivered on settlement. This "locate" requirement must be documented.

Under Regulation SHO, any securities that are sold short that are on the "threshold" list of hard-to-borrow securities on trade date, if not delivered on settlement, must be bought-in no later than "13 consecutive settlement days" from trade date.

(Note: With regular way settlement moving to 2 business days from 3 business days on September 5th, 2017, this rule should be changed to 12 consecutive business days. When, and if, the rule change occurs, we will reflect it in the study material.)

15. The best answer is **d**. OPD stands for "Opening Delayed." This is a non-regulatory halt, which is quite different from a "halt" imposed by a regulator, such as the SEC or FINRA. For example, in the "good old days," the NYSE would routinely delay the opening of trading in a stock if there was a large opening order imbalance (many more opening sell orders than buy orders). During the halt, the Specialist/DMM would attempt to round up matching buy orders, so that there could be an orderly opening. The NYSE learned that this was not such a great idea, because institutions that could not trade the stock on the NYSE simply went to regional exchanges, Third Market Makers and ECNs to do their trades instead. So each time the NYSE did this, they lost market share! Needless to say, they don't do this anymore - except in test questions of course!

16. The best answer is **c**. When a Specialist (now renamed the DMM - Designated Market Maker) "stops stock," he gives a guaranteed price for a short time period to a floor broker. The floor broker is free to try and get a better price, but if he fails, he can return to the Specialist/DMM for the stock at that price. This can only be done for public orders.

17. The best answer is **c**. The NYSE Super Display Book system is an electronic order entry, order matching, and trade reporting system. The system can only handle round lots (100 shares or more), with limits on the maximum order size permitted. Odd lots (orders for less than 100 shares) cannot be entered into the system - these are handled via a separate order entry system to the DMM - Designated Market Maker. Over 90% of NYSE trading now goes through Super Display Book. There is no requirement for customers to request the use of the system - firms prefers to use it because it is cheaper and faster than having a floor broker manually handle the order.

18. The best answer is **d**. Under the "circuit breaker" rule on the U.S. equities markets, if theStandard and Poor's 500 Index falls by a cumulative 20% in a single day, the market will be shut for the balance of the day. If the Standard and Poor's 500 Index closes at 1,230, a 20% drop is 246 points. 1,230 - 246 = 984.

19. The best answer is **b**. Regulation SHO requires that if a security that is on the exchange's "threshold list" (list of hard-to-borrow securities) is sold short and the seller fails to deliver on settlement, then the member firm must buy-in the position no later than 13 consecutive settlement days from trade date.

(Note: With regular way settlement moving to 2 business days from 3 business days on September 5th, 2017, this rule should be changed to 12 consecutive business days. When, and if, the rule change occurs, we will reflect it in the study material.)

20. The best answer is **d**. If an NMS (National Market System stock - NYSE, NYSE-MKT (AMEX), or NASDAQ listed) falls by 10% or more, it can only be sold short on an "up bid" for the remainder of that trading day and the entire next trading day. Thus, it can only be sold short into a rising market. This stops the relentless short selling of stocks with the intent of driving market prices down - a market manipulation.

21. The best answer is **a**. Under NYSE rules, the numerical standards for a company wishing to move its listing from another market include 2,200 or more shareholders, with an average monthly trading volume of 100,000 shares for the past 6 months. Also, there must be a national interest in trading the stock and the company must agree to distribute proxies to be listed.

22.   The best answer is **b**.   Third market makers are over-the-counter firms who trade exchange listed stocks in competition with the exchange Specialists (now renamed DMMs - Designated Market Makers).

Equity trade reporting rules are consistent for all markets - trades must be reported by the executing member within 10 seconds of execution during regular market hours.

23.   The best answer is **c**.   Regulation SHO (as in SHOrt sale rule) prohibits "naked" short selling. Before a short sale can be effected for a customer, the member must make an affirmative determination that the securities can be borrowed and delivered by settlement.

If the security is "difficult to borrow," it is placed on the exchange's threshold list. If a security on the threshold list is sold short, and there is a "fail to deliver" on settlement, Regulation SHO requires that the member firm buy-in the position in no later than "13 consecutive settlement days" from trade date.

(Note: With regular way settlement moving to 2 business days from 3 business days on September 5th, 2017, this rule should be changed to 12 consecutive business days. When, and if, the rule change occurs, we will reflect it in the study material.)

24.   The best answer is **d**.   Under the "short tender" rule, tendering shares for a customer who is in a "net" short position in a security is prohibited. Tenders are permitted only to the extent of the customer's net long position. Customer **C** is net long 100 shares and can tender. Customer **D** is net short 100 shares and cannot tender. Customer **A** is long 100 shares and can tender - the fact that the shares are held in a custodian account is of no relevance. Customer **B** is long 100 shares in a cash account and can tender as well.

25.   The best answer is **d**.   The Specialist (now renamed the DMM - Designated Market Maker) is the assigned market maker in a security on the NYSE floor. The Floor Broker handles orders as agent for retail member firms. The Two Dollar Broker executes orders for retail member firms, usually when its Floor Brokers are too busy. Registered representatives cannot trade securities - they can enter orders on behalf of customers to be executed by traders in the market.

This page intentionally left blank

SECTION 3: NASDAQ MARKET / OTC MARKET

3a. OVERVIEW

NASDAQ

NASDAQ started in 1971 as part of the OTC market. At that point, it had a basic system that could display market maker quotes in real time. However, way back then, there was no internet and no electronic linkages. The only way to trade was to pick up the phone and call the market maker. In 2003, NASDAQ introduced its first fully integrated electronic display and trading system, and the SEC recognized it as a "stock exchange" in late 2006.

OTC Stocks

Any stocks that cannot meet NASDAQ's listing standards are quoted in OTC "display facilities." These display market maker quotes, but not necessarily in real time. Additionally, they have no ability for anyone to access and trade against the quotes electronically. To trade, a communication link must be established either over the phone or the internet, and the price is negotiated.

The display facilities are the OTCBB and Pink OTC Markets:

OTCBB

Companies that cannot meet NASDAQ listing standards, but which are current in their SEC filings, are included in another electronic marketplace called the OTCBB - Over-The-Counter Bulletin Board. Companies included in the OTCBB must be registered with the SEC and must be current in their SEC filings. The OTCBB distributes its quotes through NASDAQ Workstations, but it has nothing to do with NASDAQ, nor does it have anything to do with the Pink Sheets (covered next).

Pink Sheets

Companies that cannot meet NASDAQ listing standards that are not current in their SEC filings, or that choose not to make SEC filings, cannot be quoted in the OTCBB. Instead, quotes for these might be found in the "Pink OTC Markets," which is a private company that posts quotes of very thinly traded OTC issues. Often included in the "Pink Sheets" are companies in bankruptcy, penny stocks, foreign companies that don't wish to comply with SEC disclosure rules and DPPs (Direct Participation Programs, which are very thinly traded tax shelter vehicles).

In addition to stocks, the following securities trade or are issued in the OTC market:

- Corporate bonds not listed on an exchange
- Municipal bonds
- U.S. Government and agency debt
- Money market instruments
- Bank and insurance company issues
- American Depositary Receipts

In addition, all new issues are initially sold OTC. After issuance, the securities are either listed on an exchange or traded over-the-counter. Mutual funds and limited partnerships are also sold as new issues OTC, but these do not trade. Mutual funds are redeemable with the sponsor, while limited partnership interests are normally non-negotiable. They can only be sold by a limited partner if the manager (general partner) in the limited partnership venture permits.

3b. NASDAQ STOCK MARKET

NASDAQ Stock Market

The NASDAQ Stock Market is an "electronic" networked marketplace with no physical trading floor that lists equities, rights, warrants, and convertible bonds (but no options). It is subdivided into the:

NASDAQ Global Market (Formerly "NMS")

NASDAQ Global Market: NASDAQ Global Market is the "upper tier" of NASDAQ listed equities (and equivalents) that meet tougher listing standards. There are about 2,800 issues in the "NGM." Note that the former name for the Global Market was the NASDAQ National Market System or "NMS" and this is still tested.

NASDAQ Capital Market (Formerly Small Cap Market)

NASDAQ Capital Market: The "lower tier" of NASDAQ listed equities (and equivalents) that meet easier listing standards. There are about 500 issues in the NASDAQ Capital Market. Note that the former name for the Capital Market was the NASDAQ Small Cap Market.

Market Regulator Is FINRA

The regulator for NASDAQ is FINRA. Note that the regulator is completely separate from, and independent of, the markets.

Network C Tape NASDAQ Trades Reported Within 10 Seconds

Trades in all NASDAQ issues are reported to the Consolidated "Network C" Tape. The FINRA rule for NASDAQ (and OTC) trade reports is that the executing member must report within 10 seconds.

NASDAQ Open From 9:30 AM - 4:00 PM ET

The NASDAQ Market regular trading hours are the same as the New York Stock Exchange - 9:30 AM - 4:00 PM Eastern Time. During these hours, NASDAQ market makers are obligated to make a market in their assigned issues.

(Please note that NASDAQ also has formal "Before Hours" and "After Hours" trading sessions in which members may participate, but they are not obligated to participate.)

3c. LISTING AND DELISTING RULES

Types Of Securities Included On NASDAQ

(Note that only a general understanding of the listing and delisting rules is required for the exam.) The following securities are eligible for inclusion in the NASDAQ system:

- Common stocks;
- Preferred stocks;
- Convertible bonds;
- Warrants;
- Rights;
- American Depositary Receipts.

Securities Not Traded On NASDAQ

Please note that all of these securities are equities or equity equivalents. The securities that are **NOT** traded on NASDAQ include:

- Stock options;
- Non-Convertible corporate bonds;
- Municipal bonds;
- Government and Agency bonds.

NASDAQ is positioning its Global Market stocks against the NYSE's listed issues. Note that the NYSE has about 3,000 listed issues, and the NASDAQ Global Market has about 3,000 listed issues, split between the larger capitalization Global "Select" Market and the regular "Global Market" that has less stringent listing standards.

Global Select Listing Standards

Global Select listing standards are similar to the NYSE's requirements. These listing standards are shown below.

For Initial Public Offerings there are 3 tests to be listed:

- At least 450 holders of round lots of 100 shares or 2,200 shareholders; and
- At least 1.25 million shares outstanding; and
- Minimum market capitalization of $70 million.

For companies moving their listing from another market, there are 2 alternate sets of listing standards:

- At least 450 holders of round lots of 100 shares or 2,200 shareholders; and
- At least 1.25 million shares outstanding; and
- Minimum market capitalization of $110 million.

or

- At least 550 stockholders; and
- Minimum 1.1 million share monthly trading volume for the last 12 months; and
- Minimum market capitalization of $100 million and minimum shareholder's equity of $110 million.

Global Select Continued Listing Standards

NASDAQ will delist a Global Select company if it cannot meet either of 2 sets of minimum continued listing standards. These are:

- At least 400 stockholders; and
- At least 750,000 shares outstanding; and
- Minimum shareholder's equity of $10 million; and
- Minimum market capitalization of $5 million; and
- Minimum share price of $1; and
- At least 2 market makers in that security.

or

- At least 1.1 million shares outstanding; and
- Minimum market capitalization of $15 million; and
- At least $50 million of total assets and $50 million of annual revenue; and
- Minimum share price of $1; and
- At least 4 market makers in that security.

Note for the exam that the specific initial and continued listing standards do not have to be memorized. However, a general understanding is required. For example, it should be known that:

- Initial listing standards are more stringent than continued (minimum) listing standards; and
- Delisting occurs if a company falls below minimum standards; not if it falls below initial standards.

Global Market Listing Standards

For the regular Global Market issues, the listing standards are much lower, with 3 alternate listing standards. Again, the actual listing standards are not tested, but it should be known that the initial listing standards include:

- Minimum Stockholder's Equity;
- Minimum Revenues and Total Assets;
- Minimum Number of Outstanding Shares;
- Minimum Market Capitalization;
- Minimum Share Price;
- Minimum Number of Shareholders; and
- Minimum Number of Market Makers.

The continued (minimum) listing standards look at the same items, but with lower amounts. For example, the minimum share price to be listed on the Global Market is $5. The continued listing minimum share price is $1. Therefore, a company will be delisted from the Global Market if its share price falls below $1.

Capital Market Listing Standards

The NASDAQ Capital Market listing standards are lower still than the Global Market requirements.

For any company to be listed on the NASDAQ Market, whether it be classified as Global Select, Global Market, or Capital Market, the issuer must meet high standards of corporate governance. These include:

- having a minimum representation of outside independent directors on the Board;
- having an Audit Committee;
- holding annual shareholder meetings and soliciting proxies;
- providing annual and quarterly financial reports;
- giving shareholders voting rights; and
- having a Code of Conduct, that, in addition, addressed conflicts of interest.

3d. HOW THE MARKET OPERATES

Any OTC member is allowed to register as a market maker in an issue, if minimum requirements are met. There is no restriction on retail firms acting as market makers (as is the case on the NYSE). Assume that a registered representative has a customer who wishes to buy 100 shares of ABCD stock. The registered representative's firm is a small OTC broker-dealer which does not make a market in ABCD stock.

NASDAQ Levels I And II

As a FINRA member, the firm is connected to the NASDAQ system. The system is divided into 2 Levels. Level I is a "summary" of the market intended for use by registered representatives; Level II lists all market makers and their quotes and is used by trading desks.

(Note: NASDAQ Levels I and II are now incorporated into the newest trading platform "The NASDAQ Market Center," or simply the "System." The 2 NASDAQ levels must still be known for the exam.)

To buy 100 shares of ABCD stock for the customer, the firm's trading desk will access Level II of the NASDAQ System. The screen shows the following (Note - This is simplified to introduce basic concepts - the complete NASDAQ System Level II screen is shown later in this section):

NASDAQ Level II Screen

	BID	ASK
Raymond James	10.00	10.50
Morgan Stanley	10.20	10.60
UBS Cap. Mkts	10.25	10.60
Wells Fargo Sec.	10.15	10.75

Firm Quotes

There are 4 market makers in ABCD stock, each showing their bid and ask quotes. The NASDAQ stock market, like exchanges, quotes stocks in minimum trading increments of 1 cent. On the NASDAQ system, the quotes are "firm," with FINRA requiring a minimum quote size of 100 shares.

Inside Market

The trading desk will buy from the dealer offering the best price - and the best ask price is from Raymond James at $10.50. If the customer wanted to sell, the best bid price is from UBS Capital Markets at $10.25. We have just identified the "inside" market for ABCD stock - the highest bid and lowest ask. These are the prices at which the next trades would take place. These are highlighted on the screen following:

NASDAQ Level II Screen

	BID	ASK
Raymond James	10.00	10.50
Morgan Stanley	10.20	10.60
UBS Cap. Mkts	10.25	10.60
Wells Fargo Sec.	10.15	10.75

NASDAQ Level I summarizes the "best" prices in the market:

Level I NASDAQ

ABCD Cmn
10.25 - 10.50

NASDAQ Level 1 (Inside Market)

The Level I screen gives the inside market for the stock. From this screen, the registered representative can tell the customer that the stock is currently offered at $10.50 (the customer can buy at this price) and bid at $10.25 (the customer can sell at this price).

NASDAQ System

The trading desk is going to buy 100 shares for the customer from Raymond James at $10.50. NASDAQ has an automatic order display and trade execution system called the NASDAQ System (covered in detail later in this section). By using touch screens, the trader accepts Raymond James' offer and the trade is executed. The firm has bought the 100 shares at $10.50.

The firm now confirms the trade to the customer. The confirmation is sent out the next business day, and it states the following:

> **Confirmation**
>
> We bought for your account:
> 100 ABCD Cmn @ 10.50 + .50 Com = $11 = $1,100 Due
>
> We acted as an agent in this transaction

Broker Earns Commission

The firm acted as a middleman and earned a commission. The amount of the commission is disclosed on the confirm. (The same disclosure is made for all NYSE trades).

Assume that a customer of Raymond James wants to buy 100 shares of ABCD stock. The customer does not know that Raymond James makes a market in the stock (nor should he really care). The order goes to the Raymond James trading desk and Raymond James fills the order directly out of its inventory of ABCD stock. The confirmation would show:

> **Confirmation**
>
> We sold to you as principal:
> 100 ABCD Cmn @ 11 Net = $1,100 Due
>
> Raymond James is a market maker in this security and took a mark-up of .50 in the transaction

Dealer Earns Mark-Up

Raymond James sold the stock directly to the customer, acting as a dealer. Dealers are allowed to "mark-up" the stock to the customer from the "inside" price. (Inside prices are only for other FINRA firms, not customers). The customer pays a net price, including the mark-up of $.50.

The rule on principal transactions is that the mark-up (which must be "fair and reasonable" - this is discussed in a later section) is included in a net price and is not disclosed to the customer **unless** the security is traded on NASDAQ (as in this example). On the NYSE, there are no principal transactions with customers - the only dealers are the DMMs (Specialists) and they only deal with retail firms - not customers. The NYSE has an inherent advantage here because all customer trades are agency trades where the commission must be disclosed. OTC customers in principal transactions don't know how much the dealer is earning - and this undermines the credibility of the marketplace.

In response to this, FINRA now requires that if an OTC principal transaction is done in a NASDAQ stock, the mark-up must be disclosed on the confirmation (remember, there are approximately 3,000 NASDAQ issues). In effect, this makes the NASDAQ market a full equivalent and competitor for NYSE listing. For all other non-NASDAQ OTC issues (either OTCBB or Pink Sheets), in principal transactions, the mark-up still is not required to be disclosed.

To summarize:

OTC and Exchange Agency Trades:	**Commission disclosed**
OTC Principal Transactions in NASDAQ Issues:	**Mark-up disclosed**
All Other Non-NASDAQ OTC Principal Transactions:	**Mark-up NOT disclosed**

3e. THE NASDAQ MARKET CENTER

The NASDAQ Stock Market is composed of a network of various trading systems that link market makers with order entry firms. Most of these are accessed electronically, however trading still takes place by direct telephone contact in more thinly traded issues.

The original NASDAQ System started in 1971 and displayed electronic quotes of market makers, but all trading occurred via the telephone. In the 1990s, NASDAQ began electronic trading with a system known as "SOES" - the Small Order Execution System. This system was revamped and enlarged and the newer "SuperSOES" system was rolled-out in 2001.

The "missing piece" to the puzzle was that the NASDAQ system still did not have the capability to store and show limit orders placed either by market makers or customers. This was addressed with the 2002 roll-out of SuperMontage - which incorporated a "CLOB" - an electronic Centralized Limit Order Book - for NASDAQ issues, along with completely automated "locked-in" trading ability.

NASDAQ spent big money to build SuperMontage, and the target was the INSTINET/INET ECN, which had captured about 50% of NASDAQ trading volume. INET captured such a large share of NASDAQ trading volume by having cheap automated trading against a limit order book before NASDAQ developed its SuperMontage system. NASDAQ found that it was hard to recapture market share lost to INET, and it purchased INET in 2006, basically buying back its market share.

NASDAQ Market Center SingleBook

Along with the previous purchase of a smaller ECN, BRUT, NASDAQ has merged these 3 platforms - SuperMontage, INET, and BRUT, into the NASDAQ Market Center Single Book. This merged system was rolled out in the first quarter of 2007.

NASDAQ Market Center AKA System

NASDAQ has since dropped the use of the Single Book name and now calls its automated order book the "NASDAQ Market Center" or simply the "System." Note, however, that the Single Book name may still show on the exam.

NASDAQ System

NASDAQ TOTALVIEW

SIRI

GET STOCK

SIRI go

Aggregate
☑ by Price
☑ by MPID

LAST MATCH		TODAY'S ACTIVITY	
Price	.5731	Orders	16,555
Time	14:20:19	Volume	2,526,814

BUY ORDERS			SELL ORDERS		
MPID	SHARES	BID	ASK	SHARES	MPID
NSDQ	1,000	.5734	.5736	800	NSDQ
NSDQ	930	.5730	.5785	500	NSDQ
NSDQ	1,000	.5708	.5789	100	NSDQ
NSDQ	1,000	.5700	.5790	94,420	NSDQ
UBSS	5,090	.5700	.5800	107,353	NSDQ
NSDQ	1,000	.5676	.5800	86,450	UBSS
UBSS	1,000	.5660	.5830	1,000	NSDQ
UBSS	5,900	.5653	.5850	15,000	NSDQ
NSDQ	1,000	.5627	.5850	5,000	UBSS
UBSS	9,300	.5625	.5860	5,000	NSDQ
UBSS	46,050	.5624	.5890	30,753	NSDQ
NSDQ	5,000	.5617	.5900	337,965	NSDQ
NSDQ	1,000	.5615	.5900	6,900	UBSS
NITE	100	.5610	.5910	4,300	NSDQ
NSDQ	2,000	.5608	.5920	50,322	UBSS

NASDAQ Market Center	The NASDAQ Market Center (aka System) is a completely automated trading platform. The System displays, for all NASDAQ securities, both Global Market and Capital Market, all limit orders that have not been executed along with their size and price. In addition, the System displays orders for the other NMS securities (NYSE and NYSE-MKT listed) as NASDAQ competes with exchange trading floors.

The System arranges the orders into the "Buy" (bid) side and "Sell" (ask) side and sequences them based on price and time priority.

- Buy orders are sequenced from high bid on down; and
- Sell orders are sequenced from low ask on up.

Orders can be entered in the Book for either round lots, odd lots, or mixed lots (an order larger than a round lot that has an odd lot component - say an order for 143 shares). However, the system only displays orders that aggregate to 100 shares or more. (Note, in contrast, the NYSE system only displays round lots.) The market participant that entered the order shows under "MPID" - the Market Participant I.D.

This is a display for "SIRI" - Sirius Satellite Radio Corp. Currently, the highest bid is at $.5734 for 1,000 shares and the lowest ask is $.5736 for 800 shares. This is the "NBBO" - National Best Bid and Offer or inside market for the issue.

(Note: This exhibit shows quotes to 4 decimal places. Under current rules, stocks that are priced under $1 can be quoted in sub-pennies. If the price is $1 or more, orders and quotes can only be accepted in penny increments.) |
| **Attributable Quote Shows MPID** | For each of these, note that the "MPID" is "NSDQ." NASDAQ allows a market maker to maintain quotes either on an "attributable" or "non-attributable" basis. If a market maker wishes to disclose its identity, its MPID shows, such as the 5th buy order in the exhibit. It shows 5,090 shares bid from UBS at $.5700. |
| **"NSDQ" MPID = Anonymous Quote** | If the market maker wishes to remain anonymous, it can enter the quote under the MPID "NSDQ" and keep its identity hidden from other market participants. This is the case with both market makers whose quotes make up the NBBO. |
| **Orders And Quotes Time Stamped**

Orders Filled FIFO | Orders and quotes that are entered in the System are time stamped upon receipt. The time stamp determines the ranking for execution purposes, since orders at the same price level are filled on a FIFO (First In, First Out) basis.

As each automatic execution occurs against the displayed quote, the size of the quote is reduced by the fill amount - this is termed "decrementation." Market makers are obligated to maintain a firm 2-sided quote during Regular Market Hours, so the issue arises as to what happens when the market maker's quote is decremented to "0." |

Reserve Size Can Be Used To Refresh Quote

One feature of the system is "Reserve Size" which allows the market maker to specify that when the quote is decremented to "0," a reserve quote at the same price of at least 100 shares will be displayed. Thus, a market maker can maintain "hidden liquidity" in the System.

Maximum Order Size Is 999,999 Shares

Orders entered into the System can be for any size, up to a maximum of 999,999 shares. As is the case with all orders, it must be specified if the order is a: Buy, Sell (Long), or Sell (Short) and Sell Short (Exempt).

System Accepts Market, Limit, And Marketable Limit Orders

The system accepts market orders, limit orders, and marketable limit orders (a limit order placed at the current inside market price). It does not accept stop or stop limit orders.

Supporting the NASDAQ System are systems to enter the orders into the book; and systems to report trades that occur against the book. These are:

OATS - Order Audit Trail System

OATS, FINRA's Order Audit Trail System, provides for the electronic capture of order information for NASDAQ equity securities. OATS reports are also now required for all orders for NYSE, NYSE-MKT issues and OTC issues. Each Reporting Member must, immediately following receipt or origination of an order, record the details of the order in OATS. Also required to be recorded are the details of any order modification or cancellation. Thus, there are no more paper order tickets. All order information is recorded and time stamped electronically, including any changes to standing orders.

This data is used to match the order details to the trade execution that results via the ACT - Automated Confirmation of Trade System (covered next).

ACT System

The Automated Confirmation of Transactions Service ("ACT") is a NASDAQ system that provides reporting and dissemination of last sale information on equity securities traded "over-the-counter." The market venues that must report trades to ACT are:

- NASDAQ (both Global Market and Capital Market);
- OTCBB and Pink Sheets;
- Third Market (OTC trades of listed equities);
- Fourth Market (ECNs).

For NASDAQ stocks, trades that occur are reported through the NASDAQ TRF (Trade Reporting Facility) that is run by ACT. Under FINRA rules, the executing party must report the trade within 10 seconds of execution. ACT also reports the trades for the other markets shown in the list via separate TRFs. This is covered later in this section.

3f. ACT / TRF

ACT started as a trade comparison and reporting service for OTC equity trades. When NASDAQ became its own stock exchange in 2006, ACT was divided into separate feeds, covering each of the OTC markets. The trade feeds are called "TRFs" - Trade Reporting Facilities.

Essentially, the TRF is broken down into 4-feeds with similar rule sets. These are the:

NASDAQ TRF: Reports of trades of NASDAQ listed issues

NYSE TRF: Reports of trades of NYSE-listed issues that occur OTC between 2-Third Market makers

ORF: The "Over-The-Counter" reporting facility which reports trades of OTCBB and Pink Sheet issues

ADF/TRACS: The Alternate Display Facility which reports trades of NASDAQ and NYSE listed issues that occur on ECNs and ATSs (Alternative Trading Systems) through a system called TRACS

Trades Reported Within 10 Seconds

As a general rule, ACT participants must report trades within 10 seconds of execution. Transactions not reported within this time frame are designated as "late." Reports of trades into ACT can be made either by:

- ACT Market Makers; or
- ACT Order Entry firms.

Executing Member Reports Trade

Only the "executing member" side of the trade is required to report to ACT. ACT sends this report to the contra-party to the trade to either be accepted or declined. All trade reports are priced excluding mark-ups, mark-downs, commissions, and any other related charges.

ACT Display Of Trade Detail - Confirmed Within 20 Minutes

The reporting party enters its record of the trade into ACT; and the contra-party is obligated to review the trade report on-line; and accept or decline; within 20 minutes. Thus, unmatched trades, that are time-consuming and costly to resolve, are minimized.

ECN Trading

The 4th Market is trading of large blocks of stock by institutions on ECNs (Electronic Communications Networks) such as Instinet or Lava. ECNs are FINRA member broker-dealers that accept agency orders from customers to buy and sell. They attempt to "match" these orders internally, or with other market participants - and in doing so, earn a matching fee. ECNs operate 24 hours a day, and collectively account for over 1/2 of the trading in NASDAQ securities.

ADF

ECNs can either choose to "link" into a display book system such as the NASDAQ System and display their quotes there; or they can use a separate stand-alone Display Book called the ADF - Alternate Display Facility - which shows quotes from ECNs that were not linked (that is, not posting quotes) NASDAQ. Since these ECNs are competing with NASDAQ, they most often choose not to "link" and will show their quotes only in the ADF.

TRACS

If a trade results, the trade must still be reported, but this is done through an "ADF-only" system called TRACS - Trade Reporting and Comparison Service - which feeds the trade to the appropriate tape (Network A for an NYSE-listed issue; Network B for an NYSE-MKT-listed issue; Network C for a NASDAQ-listed issue).

Dark Pools

An evolution of the ECN is the "dark pool." Dark pools are operated by the larger broker-dealers (e.g., Goldman Sachs) and there are some that are independent companies (e.g., Liquidnet). They allow institutions to buy or sell very large blocks without displaying their orders in the ADF or in a display system such as the NASDAQ System. They are called dark pools because the size of the trade and the identity of the institution are not displayed. This avoids the problem that could occur where the display of a very large order in such a system, by itself, could move the market. If there is a match in a dark pool and a trade results, it still must be reported to the appropriate tape.

3g. OTC TRADING RULES AND TERMS

Firm Quote

Unless otherwise stated, quotes given by OTC market makers are "firm" - meaning the dealer will honor the quote for the stated size. For NASDAQ stocks, all quotes in the NASDAQ System must be firm.

Good For 100 Shares If NASDAQ Issue

If no size is stated for a NASDAQ stock, it is assumed that the quote is only good for 100 shares.

In the OTCBB or Pink Sheets, dealers can place quotes that are Firm, Unfirm, BW or OW. Regarding the last three of these:

Unfirm Quote

A quote shown in the OTCBB or Pink Sheets that is subject to negotiation.

BW (Bid Wanted)

A "Bid Wanted" posting, indicating that the dealer wants to sell a position and is looking for a bidder (buyer). This would only occur for a very thinly traded illiquid issue.

OW (Offer Wanted)

An "Offer Wanted" posting, indicating that the dealer wants to buy a position and is looking for a seller. This would only occur for a very thinly traded illiquid issue.

Trading Markets

Regarding OTCBB and Pink Sheet issues, if a trader contacts a dealer over the phone, the dealer may give a quote verbally. If nothing is stated, it is assumed that the quote is "Firm." If the dealer puts a qualification on the quote, then that changes the terms of the quote. These verbal qualifications are:

Subject Quote

An OTC (non-NASDAQ) dealer can give a "subject" quote - meaning the quote is subject to confirmation. This quote is an approximate price and can be changed.

Nominal Quote

A "nominal" quote is really no quote. It is the dealer's guess at a current price, but he is not willing to trade at that quote.

Workout Quote

A "workout" quote is an approximate quote - the dealer has to work out the exact price at which he will trade.

As stated previously, transactions can be effected "over-the-counter" either on a principal basis or on an agency basis. The types of principal transactions are:

Types of Principal Transactions	
Long / Short position	Taking a long or short position for the dealer's inventory.
Position trading	Selling a security out of inventory direct to a customer with a mark-up. Buying a security into inventory direct from a customer with a mark-down.
Riskless or Simultaneous trade	Performing a "riskless" principal trade - after receiving a buy order from a customer, the dealer **then** purchases the stock into inventory and resells it to the customer. Since the dealer wasn't holding the security when the order was received, there is no "risk" to the dealer of falling prices giving him an inventory loss.
Arbitrage	Taking an arbitrage position - simultaneously buying and selling short the same or equivalent security, such as a convertible bond, with different market makers to lock in a temporary price differential.

Types of Agency Transactions	
Broker transaction	Buying or selling for a customer through a dealer, earning a commission.
Crossing **Must Be Effected At Current Market Price**	"Crossing" two customer orders, earning a commission on each. For example, if a market order to buy and a market order to sell come in at the same moment from two different customers for the same stock and amount, the firm can simply cross them at the current market price. Please note that it is prohibited for the firm to execute these trades at a price that is "away from the current market."
Dual agency **Proceeds Transaction**	"Dual agency" trades occur when a customer wishes to perform what is known as a "proceeds" transaction. The customer directs the firm to sell one stock and use the proceeds to buy another. Because the firm is performing two transactions, the equivalent of two commissions is earned.

Requirement To Find Best Available Market

When executing an order for a customer, the member must obtain the best available price in the market (the "inside" market). Among the factors to be considered in finding the best market are:

- The character of the market for that security (price; volatility; liquidity).

- The size and type of transaction.

- The number of markets checked.

- Location and accessibility of customer's broker-dealer to primary markets and quotation sources.

Customer Orders Have Priority Over Equivalent Orders For Firm's Own Account

When executing an order for a customer, the firm cannot give preference to orders for the firm's own account. For example, if a firm holds a customer order to buy 100 shares of ABC @ $21, and the stock becomes available at that price, the firm must buy the stock for that customer **before** it can buy the stock at that price for its own account.

Cannot Act As Both Broker And Dealer In Same Trade

FINRA prohibits a firm from acting as **both** an agent and principal in a given transaction - the firm can only wear one hat at any time.

Cannot Interposition

FINRA also prohibits a practice known as interpositioning. When a firm gets an order to buy or sell, the firm cannot go through a middleman firm, who in turn goes to the market maker. Therefore, a firm cannot interposition a second firm (who would earn a commission on top of the first firm's commission) between itself and the market maker.

Trading Markets

Backing Away From A Quote Is Prohibited	FINRA also explicitly prohibits "backing away" from a quote, that is, giving a firm quote and then failing to honor that quote.
Front Running A Customer's Order Is Prohibited	FINRA explicitly prohibits "front running" a customer's order - that is, when the firm is holding an order from a customer, the firm executes an equivalent transaction for its own account before executing the customer's order. Customer orders have priority.
If Firm Has Information Barriers In Place, Orders Received From Other Customers Are Not Considered To Be "Front Running"	When a firm receives a "block order" from a client that is likely to move the price of the stock, the temptation is always there to "front run" that block trade. This is, of course prohibited. However, FINRA has an exception in its front running rule that states that if the firm has effective information barriers in place that prevent the internal disclosure of customer order information, then any orders placed that come into the firm from the "other side" of the information barrier are permitted and do not violate the prohibition.
Trading Ahead Of Research That Will Be Distributed To Customers Is Prohibited	If a firm's research department is going to issue a report on a company that is likely to affect the market price of the issue, the firm's market making desk cannot alter its pre-existing inventory position in that issue based on advance knowledge of the recommendation. Once the recommendation is disseminated, the firm is not bound by this restriction.
Trade Shredding Is Prohibited	This is prohibited practice of splitting large orders into multiple smaller orders for execution for the purpose of maximizing "payments for order flow." Most payment for order flow arrangements are contingent on a minimum number of trades being sent to a market maker each month. To meet the minimum threshold, the order entry firm could attempt to split up larger orders - and splitting orders for this purpose is prohibited.
Market Manipulation	Manipulation of the market is prohibited in any form. Various ways in which members have been found to manipulate the market, and thus are violations are:
Trading Pools	Trading Pools: These are groups of traders who band together to trade a security at successively higher and higher prices. The "pool" participants take a long position in the security, and agree to rebate each other for losses incurred on the pooled transactions with each other. As the pool inflates the price of the issue and other investors see the frenetic trading activity, those outside investors jump in and buy; at which point the pool members jump out at an artificially high price. FINRA prohibits members from participating in such pools, from providing credit to such pools, and from managing such pools.

Wash Trades

Painting The Tape

Wash Trades: This is where a single member buys and sells a security, over and over, to create the appearance of trading activity with no actual change in ownership (so the trades are really a "wash" - hence the name). This is sometimes called "painting the tape," since a series of fictitious trades is being reported. Since false trades are being reported, this is a violation.

Marking The Close

Marking The Open

Marking The Close or Marking The Open:

- Marking The Close is trading at the close, or falsely reporting trades at the close, just to affect the stock's closing price.

- Marking The Open is trading at the open, or falsely reporting trades at the open, just to affect the stock's opening price.

Trading Markets

NASDAQ MARKET / OTC MARKET SECTION EXAMINATION

1.

Which of the following is a "firm" quote from a market maker?

- a. 12.50
- b. 12.50 workout
- c. 12.50 subject
- d. 12.50 nominal

2.

Over-the counter traders perform all of the following functions **EXCEPT**:

- a. establish spreads
- b. take positions
- c. give quotes
- d. perform clerical duties

3.

Comparing the first and second markets, which statement is **FALSE**?

- a. The First Market is an auction market
- b. The Second Market is a negotiated market
- c. The First Market has listing standards
- d. The Second Market has listing standards

4.

Which of the following persons trades securities over-the-counter?

- a. Two dollar broker
- b. Market maker
- c. Specialist (DMM)
- d. Registered Representative

5.

The Specialist (DMM) accepts which of the following orders on his book?

- a. Day
- b. Good Through Week
- c. Good Through Month
- d. Good Til Canceled

6.

Which of the following can result in the establishment of a short position?

- I   Arbitrage transaction
- II   Sale of a security "against the box"
- III   Position trades of borrowed shares

- a. I only
- b. I and III
- c. II and III
- d. I, II, III

7.

The inside market found on NASDAQ Level I, is the:

- a. lowest bid and lowest ask
- b. lowest bid and highest ask
- c. highest bid and lowest ask
- d. highest bid and highest ask

8.

The NASDAQ Market Center Execution System (Single Book) is the automated trading and order maintenance system for which of the following?

- I   NASDAQ Global Market issues
- II   NASDAQ Capital Market issues
- III   Pink Sheet issues
- IV   OTCBB issues

- a. I only
- b. I and II only
- c. III only
- d. I, II, III, IV

9.

The OTCBB includes quotes for:

a. NASDAQ stocks

b. Non-NASDAQ Stocks

c. NYSE listed stocks

d. All of the above

10.

Under MSRB rules, yield to worst means that:

a. all municipal bonds quoted on a yield basis must be priced to the near-term in whole call date

b. municipal par bonds quoted on a yield basis must be priced to the near-term in whole call date

c. municipal discount bonds quoted on a yield basis must be priced to the near-term in whole call date

d. municipal premium bonds quoted on a yield basis must be priced to the near-term in whole call date

11.

The regular hours of operation of the NASDAQ system are:

a. 9:00 AM - 4:00 PM ET

b. 9:30 AM - 4:00 PM ET

c. 9:30 AM - 6:00 PM ET

d. 9:00 AM - 8:00 PM ET

12.

Which of the following are prohibited trading practices under FINRA rules?

I Backing away

II Interpositioning

III Marking to market

IV Using a correspondent

a. II only

b. I and II only

c. III and IV only

d. I, II, III, IV

13.

All of the following orders can be placed in the NASDAQ System (Single Book) **EXCEPT**:

a. market order

b. marketable limit order

c. limit order

d. not held order

14.

Interdealer transactions in which of the following are reported through ACT?

I NASDAQ Global Market Stocks

II NASDAQ Capital Market stocks

III Listed issues traded in the Third Market

IV OTC Bulletin Board Stocks

a. I and II only

b. III and IV only

c. I, II, III

d. I, II, III, IV

15.

Quotes placed by market participants in unlinked ECNs can be accessed through:

a. ATS

b. ADF

c. ACES

d. ACT

16.

A broker-dealer holds a limit order to buy 100 shares of ABC stock at $20.00 for a customer. Which of the following trades are acceptable?

I   The purchase of 100 shares of ABC for the firm's trading account at $19.50 prior to executing the customer's order

II   The purchase of 100 shares of ABC for the firm's trading account at $20.50 prior to executing the customer's order

III   The long sale of 100 shares of ABC out of the firm's trading account to the customer at $20.00

IV   The short sale of 100 shares of ABC out of the firm's trading account to the customer at $20.00

a.   I only

b.   I and II only

c.   III and IV only

d.   II, III, IV

17.

A member firm may use a third party to execute over-the-counter agency transactions for customer orders:

a.   under no circumstances

b.   if the resultant price is reasonably related to the inside market at that time

c.   if the resultant price is equal to the best available market at the time

d.   if the resultant price is better than the best available market at the time

18.

Which statements are **TRUE**?

I   TRF reports trades of NASDAQ issues listed in the NASDAQ System

II   TRF reports trades of NASDAQ issues listed in the ADF

III   TRACS reports trades of NASDAQ issues listed in the NASDAQ System

IV   TRACS reports trades of NASDAQ issues listed in the ADF

a.   I and III

b.   I and IV

c.   II and III

d.   II and IV

19.

A firm's market making desk, aware that the firm is about to publish a bullish research report on ABCD stock, purposefully increases its long position in order to satisfy anticipated retail demand. This action is:

a.   permitted without restriction

b.   permitted as long as the research report is released within 48 hours of the first trade made to increase the firm's position

c.   permitted as long as NASDAQ is notified, in writing, of the impending research report

d.   prohibited

20.

An index arbitrage trading desk places sequential buy orders at the market opening for securities included in the index to raise their price against the current index value. Which statement is **TRUE**?

a.   These transactions can only be effected on an upbid

b.   This is an illegal practice known as Marking To Market

c.   This is an illegal practice known as Marking The Open

d.   This is an illegal practice known as Painting The Tape

21.
When a firm "position trades," it:

    I   trades on an agency basis for customers

    II trades on a dealer basis for its own account

    III takes inventory positions, both long and short

    IV interpositions itself between a customer and another dealer

    a. I and II only

    b. II and III only

    c. IV only

    d. II, III, IV

22.
The "OATS" system is an:

    a. automated order routing and execution for customer market orders

    b. electronic trade negotiation system between dealers

    c. electronic order record maintenance system

    d. automated trade reporting and comparison system

23.
Which of the following will result in a "locked-in" trade?

    a. A market order placed for a NASDAQ issue quoted in the NASDAQ System (Single Book)

    b. A market order placed for an OTC equity issue quoted in the OTCBB

    c. A market order placed for an OTC equity issue quoted in the Pink Sheets

    d. All of the above

24.
The ACT system:

    a. is used to report backing away violations to FINRA for real-time resolution

    b. permits NASDAQ Order Entry firms to contract with a market maker to enter and maintain its limit orders

    c. routes market and limit orders electronically to market makers for locked-in execution and settlement

    d. intakes entries of completed trades for reporting, matching and clearance

25.
Trades of NASDAQ securities executed on an unlinked ECN are reported by:

    a. CAES

    b. TRACS

    c. ACT

    d. TRACE

26.
A member that has knowledge of a client order that has not been entered on a marketplace that could reasonably be expected to affect the market price of the security is prohibited from:

    I   entering a proprietary order for the purchase or sale of that security

    II soliciting an order from another person for the purchase or sale of that security

    III informing any other person, other than in the necessary course of business of the client order

    a. I only

    b. I and II

    c. II and III

    d. I, II, III

Trading Markets

27.

A bond trader believes that he has too much inventory in 25-year ABC corporation bonds. The dealer would most likely:

   a.   increase the mark-up on the bonds

   b.   hedge the bond positions

   c.   lower the reoffering yield on the bonds

   d.   place an "OW" for the bonds in Bloomberg

28.

Quotes found in the ADF are primarily bids and offers from:

   a.   NASDAQ market markers

   b.   Third market makers

   c.   ECNs

   d.   Designated market makers

29.

Dark Pools are:

   I   regulated as broker-dealers

   II   regulated as exchanges

   III   subject to Regulation ATS

   IV   not subject to Regulation ATS

   a.   I and III

   b.   I and IV

   c.   II and III

   d.   II and IV

30.

Quotes shown in the NASDAQ System (Single Book) are:

   I   Firm

   II   Unfirm

   III   1-Sided

   IV   2-Sided

   a.   I and III

   b.   I and IV

   c.   II and III

   d.   II and IV

NASDAQ MARKET / OTC MARKET EXAMINATION EXPLANATIONS

1. The best answer is **a**. An OTC quote is considered to be "firm" for 100 shares unless it is otherwise qualified. If a dealer gives a quote of 12 - 12.50, he is willing to sell 100 shares at 12.50 or buy 100 shares at 12. A workout quote is an approximate price - the final price must be "worked out." A subject quote is subject to confirmation. A nominal quote is a "guess" at a likely price - it is really no quote.

2. The best answer is **d**. OTC traders position trade (that is, trade for the firm's inventory account), establish spreads (the difference between the bid and ask quote that is the profit for the dealer), and give quotes to customers. Clerical duties are handled by clerks.

3. The best answer is **d**. Each exchange with a trading floor is an auction market (First Market). The over-the-counter market (Second Market) is a negotiated market. OTC equities are quoted in either the OTCBB or the Pink OTC Market. These "quotations vendors" have no listing standards. In contrast, each exchange has its own listing standards.

4. The best answer is **b**. Over-the-counter dealers are called market makers. Two dollar brokers and Specialists (now renamed DMMs - Designated Market Makers) trade on stock exchanges. Registered representatives cannot trade securities - they can enter orders on behalf of customers to be executed by traders in the market.

5. The best answer is **a**. The Specialist (now called the DMM - Designated Market Maker) only accepts "Day" orders on his book. If a customer wants an order with a longer "Time in Force," the member firm accepts it into its own internal system and feeds it to the exchange as a new order each day, until either the order expires or the "Time in Force" expires.

6. The best answer is **d**. Short positions are established in arbitrage transactions (the simultaneous purchase and short sale of a security in two different markets to lock in a temporary price difference). A short position is taken when a security is sold "against the box" - meaning that the long position is being held and an equivalent number of shares are being borrowed and sold to lock in a profit. Finally, position trades (position trading is trading for the firm account, using the firm's "positions") of borrowed shares are short sales.

7. The best answer is **c**. The "inside market" is the highest bid and lowest ask. These are the best prices at which to trade. (One wants to buy at the lowest price asked by dealers; one wants to sell at the highest price bid by dealers). Another name for the inside market is the "NBBO" - National Best Bid and Offer.

8. The best answer is **b**. The system for automated trading and order maintenance of NASDAQ issues (Global Market and Capital Market stocks) is the NASDAQ Market Center Execution System, or simply, the "System." The predecessor name was Single Book. OTCBB and Pink Sheet issues, which do not have listing standards, cannot be traded through the System.

9. The best answer is **b**. Over-the-counter stocks that are too small for NASDAQ are found on the OTCBB - the "Over-The-Counter Bulletin Board" (run by FINRA) or can be found in the privately run "Pink Sheets" - now renamed the Pink OTC Markets.

10. The best answer is **d**. When municipal serial bonds are quoted on a yield basis, the dealer must compute the dollar price shown on the customer confirmation. This dollar price must assure, that at a minimum, the customer will receive the promised yield. This is known as pricing to the "worst case" scenario.

For a premium bond, the "worst case" scenario is having the bond called early (which is the likely case). Bonds trade at a premium because market interest rates have dropped, so the issuer can refund the issue at lower current market rates by calling in the bonds. In this case, the bond is priced based on giving the customer the promised yield using the near-term in whole call date as the redemption date. If the bond were not called, the customer's actual yield would improve, because the annual loss of premium incorporated into the yield would be spread over a longer time frame.

For a discount bond, the "worst case" scenario is having the bond held to maturity (which is the likely case). Bonds trade at a discount because market interest rates have risen, so the issuer would not call these bonds. In this case, the bond is priced based on giving the customer the promised yield using the maturity date. If the bond were called early, the customer's actual yield would improve, because the annual earning of the discount incorporated into the yield would be spread over a shorter time frame.

11. The best answer is **b**. NASDAQ's Regular Hours session is from 9:30 AM to 4:00 PM Eastern Time.

12. The best answer is **b**. FINRA rules prohibit backing away from quotes and prohibit interpositioning another firm between a customer and the best available market. All securities positions are marked to market daily under capital rules. A correspondent firm can be used to handle trades as long as the customer does not pay for this service. Any cost of using the correspondent firm must be given up out of the regular commission earned by the firm on that transaction.

13. The best answer is **d**. Single Book is the quotation and trading system for all NASDAQ issues - both Global Market and Capital Market. The system accepts market orders, marketable limit orders (a limit order at the current inside price) and limit orders that are away from the market. The system cannot accept orders that require human judgment for execution such as a market-not held order (where a trader uses his or her best judgment decide when to execute to get the best price). Finally, the NASDAQ system does not accept stop orders, as is the case with the NYSE DisplayBook system. Member firms take stop orders into their internal systems and feed them to the appropriate exchange if they are triggered.

14. The best answer is **d**. The "TRF" is the Trade Reporting Facility that is operated by the ACT system. Initially, the system was used for NASDAQ only. When NASDAQ became a registered stock exchange in late 2006, separate "TRFs" were created using ACT, which allowed NASDAQ to sell its Network C Tape (each exchange sells its tape - it's a big source of revenue for the exchange). The TRFs run by ACT include:

- NASDAQ TRF (reporting trades of NASDAQ stocks to the Network C Tape);

- NYSE TRF (reporting Third Market trades of NYSE listed issues to the NYSE Network A Tape. The NYSE feeds the trades that take place on its trading floor to this tape on its own);

- ORF (the Over-The-Counter Reporting Facility) which reports trades OTCBB and Pink Sheet issues;

- TRACS (Trade Reporting and Compliance Service) which reports trades of NYSE, NYSE-MKT (AMEX) and NASDAQ stocks that take place on ECNs that are not linked into an exchange. TRACS feeds the trade into the appropriate Network A, B or C Tape.

15. The best answer is **b**. An unlinked ECN is one that is not placing its quotes into Single Book. The SEC mandated that the FINRA provide an Alternate Display Facility ("ADF") to publicly display these quotes. Thus, to find the best market for a NASDAQ stock, both NASDAQ and the ADF must be checked.

16. The best answer is **d**. If a dealer holds a customer order, he or she cannot execute an order for the firm account that competes with that order - unless the customer order is executed first. Otherwise, the firm is "trading ahead" of the customer, which is prohibited. The customer has placed an order to buy 100 shares of ABC stock at $20. It is OK for the firm to buy the stock for its own account at $20.50 prior to executing the customer order, since the customer's limit price has not been met. However, the firm cannot buy for its own account at $19.50 until the customer order has been executed, since $19.50 is within the customer's limit. It is perfectly acceptable for the firm to sell the customer the stock at $20 out of its inventory account. It makes no difference whether the firm sells this stock long to the customer or if it sells the stock short to the customer. In trading accounts, firms routinely maintain both long and short positions.

17. The best answer is **d**. As a general rule, interpositioning a third firm between the customer and the market maker is prohibited unless it can be demonstrated that the use of the "middleman" firm will result in a better execution for the customer.

18. The best answer is **b**. The "TRF" is the Trade Reporting Facility that is operated by the ACT system. Initially, the system was used for NASDAQ only. When NASDAQ became a registered stock exchange in late 2006, separate "TRFs" were created using ACT, which allowed NASDAQ to sell its Network C Tape (each exchange sells its tape - it's a big source of revenue for the exchange). The TRFs run by ACT include:

- NASDAQ TRF (reporting trades of NASDAQ stocks to the Network C Tape);

- NYSE TRF (reporting Third Market trades of NYSE listed issues to the NYSE Network A Tape. The NYSE feeds the trades that take place on its trading floor to this tape on its own);

- ORF (the Over-The-Counter Reporting Facility) which reports trades OTCBB and Pink Sheet issues;

- TRACS (Trade Reporting and Compliance Service) which reports trades of NYSE, NYSE-MKT (AMEX) and NASDAQ stocks that take place on ECNs that are not linked into an exchange. TRACS feeds the trade into the appropriate Network A, B or C Tape.

19. The best answer is **d**. "Trading ahead of research" is prohibited. A member firm cannot alter its inventory position in anticipation of a research report that it is about to release. FINRA strongly suggests, but does not require, that member firms maintain a Chinese Wall between the firm's research department and trading desk.

20. The best answer is **c**. Marking The Open is trading at the open, or falsely reporting trades at the open, just to affect the stock's opening price. FINRA has disciplined program traders for "marking the open" violations. These firms attempt to arbitrage the difference between an index option's value (which can be based on market open, depending on the index option) against the actual prices of the securities that are included in the index. The illegal practice was placing sequential orders at the open for the securities in the index to either move their price up (or down), so that the index arbitrage position would show a profit.

21. The best answer is **b**. Position trading is trading for a firm's own account. The firm can take both long and short positions as it speculates in the market. Interpositioning is a prohibited practice under FINRA rules. If a customer wishes to buy or sell, a firm is obligated to go directly to the market maker. It cannot interposition another firm (another middleman) between the customer and the best available market.

22. The best answer is **c**. OATS stands for "Order Audit Trail System" - it is FINRA's system for electronic capture of order information. This information is later compared to the actual trade execution via the ACT system - Automated Confirmation of Trade system. OATS records of orders are now required for all U.S. equities markets - NYSE, NYSE-MKT (AMEX), NASDAQ and also for OTCBB and Pink OTC Markets issues.

23. The best answer is **a**. A "locked-in" trade is one in which all of the terms and conditions of the trade are accepted by buyer and seller. Once the trade is executed, last-sale reporting to NASDAQ and reporting to the clearance corporation (NSCC) are done electronically. System trades of NASDAQ stocks are "locked-in" - the NASDAQ System is both an automated quotation and execution system. Anyone who enters a quote or order into the System agrees to accept automated executions. Note that the previous name for the System was Single Book, and this may still show on the exam.

The OTCBB and Pink Sheets are quotation mediums only. There is no automated trading; rather, trades are still negotiated "over-the-phone" or "on-line" and thus, are not locked-in.

24. The best answer is **d**. The ACT system is where the details of completed trades are entered by market participants (The NASDAQ System does ACT reporting automatically; the information must be entered manually for OTCBB and Pink Sheet trades). The ACT system then reports the trade to the tape; to the contra-party to the trade for matching; and to the clearing corporation. FQCS - the Firm Quote Compliance System - is used to file reports of backing away violations (this is not tested on Series 7). ACES is the system that allows NASDAQ Order Entry firms to "pass through" their limit orders to NASDAQ Market Makers for order entry and maintenance. The NASDAQ Market Center Execution System is the automated quotations and execution system for trades of NASDAQ issues.

25. The best answer is **b**. An unlinked ECN is one that is not linked into the NASDAQ System or another exchange, so its quotes are shown in a separate system - the ADF - Alternate Display Facility. Trades of NASDAQ securities executed by unlinked ECNs are reported through TRACS - the Trade Reporting and Comparison Service. Trades of NASDAQ securities executed by linked ECNs are reported through the TRF - the Trade Reporting Facility that is part of NASDAQ's ACT system. TRACE is the FINRA system for reporting of corporate bond trades. CAES (Computer Assisted Execution System) is an older system used for Third Market trades.

26. The best answer is **d**. Consider this question to be a learning lesson in everything that is prohibited about "front running." Prior to entering a customer order that is likely to have market impact (meaning a big institutional order), a member firm cannot place an order in that security for the firm's account; cannot solicit others to place orders; and cannot inform others about the existence of the market-impact order so that they can "front run" it.

27. The best answer is **b**. The answer you are looking for - sell some of the bond position - is not here! The next best choice is to hedge the position in case prices fall, which can be done with options. Increasing the mark-up or lowering the reoffering yield will increase the price of the bonds, making them even harder to sell - so these are wrong answers. Placing an "OW" in Bloomberg is an "Offers Wanted." This indicates that the dealer wants to buy more of the bonds, which is not the case - he or she wants to sell them, not buy them! Rather, the dealer would want to place a "BW" - Bids Wanted - in Bloomberg, telling potential buyers that he or she is interested in selling.

28. The best answer is **c**. The "ADF" - Alternate Display Facility - was established under an SEC rule in 2002 as a place for ECNs that did not wish to place their quotes in the NASDAQ System because these ECNs felt that NASDAQ's order processing algorithms favored NASDAQ Market Makers over ECNs.

NASDAQ market makers post their quotes in the NASDAQ System. CQS - Consolidated Quotations Service - displays quotes for exchange listed issues (NYSE) from DMMs (Designated Market Makers) and Third Market Makers (firms such as Weeden and Jefferies that are OTC market makers in exchange listed issues, providing competition for exchange DMMs).

29. The best answer is **a**. An evolution of the ECN is the "dark pool." Dark pools are operated by the larger broker-dealers (e.g., Goldman Sachs) and there are some that are independent companies (e.g., Liquidnet). They allow institutions to buy or sell very large blocks without displaying their orders in the ADF or in a display system such as the NASDAQ System. They are called dark pools because the size of the trade and the identity of the institution are not displayed. This avoids the problem that could occur where the display of a very large order in such a system, by itself, could move the market. If there is a match in a dark pool and a trade results, it still must be reported to the appropriate tape.

The SEC wrote Regulation ATS (Alternative Trading System) in the year 2000, specifically to address the growth of ECNs, including dark pools. Regulation ATS requires Alternative Trading Systems, which include ECNs, member firm internal crossing systems and dark pools, to register with the SEC and be regulated as broker-dealers (as opposed to registering as an exchange and being regulated as such).

30. The best answer is **b**. The NASDAQ System only accepts Firm 2-Sided (Bid and Ask) quotes.

Trading Markets

This page intentionally left blank

SECTION 4: OPTIONS AND OTHER MARKETS

4a. MUNICIPAL AND GOVERNMENT BONDS

Trading of municipal and government bonds was covered in Municipal Debt section. Trading of government bonds was covered in the U.S. Government Debt section.

4b. LISTED OPTIONS TRADING

Chicago Board Options Exchange

Listed options are traded on exchanges - almost no trading occurs OTC. The principal options exchange is the Chicago Board Options Exchange (CBOE).

Listing Standards

Option contracts on equity securities of a specific issuer must be approved for trading by the SEC. To qualify for listed options trading, the issuer must be actively traded on the NYSE, AMEX, or NASDAQ markets. If the issuer is delisted from its primary market, then the options contract will be delisted from trading on the CBOE.

Stopped Issuance Of New Option Contracts

If the option contracts of an issuer have been, or are going to be, delisted, no new contracts can be issued. Regarding existing contracts, they will trade until their expiration, and can be exercised by the holder at any time until expiration.

Stopped Trading Of Underlying Stock

If trading in the stock stops on the principal exchange (usually because of an important news announcement), the trading in the option stops on the options exchange as well. This occurs because there is no longer a way to "price" the option if there is no known market price for the stock. A holder is still free to exercise the contract or let it expire.

Chicago Board Options Exchange

Trading Modeled On Futures Markets

The CBOE has a different structure from the stock exchanges, modeled on the "futures" markets that are based in Chicago. On stock exchanges, the specialist acts as the market maker and also acts as a "broker's broker" handling limit and stop orders via the "book," for other firms.

The CBOE splits this function between 2 different individuals - the Market Maker and the Order Book Official. Before discussing these individuals, we will start with the Floor Brokers on the CBOE.

Floor Broker

To execute a transaction on the CBOE, your firm will use a "floor broker" to handle the order. The floor broker may either be an employee of the member firm (the "nominee" of the firm) or may be an independent, whose business it is to execute transactions for retail firms on the trading floor.

Cannot Hold An Inventory	The floor broker will trade either with another floor broker, a Market Maker or an Order Book Official, earning a fee for each completed transaction. Floor brokers do not take inventory positions.
Can Accept ALL Orders **Find Best Available Market**	Floor brokers accept public orders and orders for member firm trading accounts. A floor broker can accept any type of order for execution. Floor brokers are under the obligation to obtain the best available price in the market for their customers.
	If a floor broker simultaneously holds a buy and sell order for the same contracts from two different customers, the floor broker cannot simply "cross" the orders at whatever price he sees fit. The price at which a cross is effected must reflect the prevailing market. To ensure this, the CBOE imposes a rigid procedure for crossing orders.
Crossing Orders	If a floor broker holds an order to buy an options contract at the market; and also holds an order to sell the equivalent contract at the market; he is only permitted to "cross" the orders if the following procedure is used:
	The floor broker must first request bids and offers for those contracts from the trading crowd, including the Order Book Official. The floor broker must then bid above the highest bid received by the minimum trading increment (5 cents); and must offer below the lowest offer received by the minimum trading increment (5 cents).
Must Announce Crossing By Public Outcry	If this higher bid and lower offer are not taken, he may cross the orders at such higher bid or lower offer by announcing by public outcry that he is crossing, and giving the quantity and price.
	Essentially, this procedure forces the floor broker to first attempt an execution with other traders before crossing the orders himself; and also forces the floor broker to cross the orders at a price that truly reflects the current market.
Market Maker	The market maker function is handled by registered "Market Makers" ("MMs") on the CBOE trading floor. These are individuals who trade for their own account in the security in which they are registered. Market Makers trade only with other participants on the floor, such as floor brokers - they cannot deal directly with the public.
	Market Makers must make a continuous market in the option contracts in which they are registered. For example, the IBM contract market maker must continuously make bids and offers on IBM contracts.
Minimum Quote Size Is 10 Contracts	These quotes are firm, and must be good for a minimum trading unit of 10 contracts. The profit to the market maker is the "spread" between his bid and ask quotes.

For example, the market maker might quote IBM Jan 100 Calls @ 4.00 - 4.50.

Any other trader on the floor who wishes to buy IBM Jan 100 Calls from this market maker may do so from the market maker at 4.50 Offered;

Anyone who wishes to sell IBM Jan 100 Calls may do so at 4.00 Bid by the market maker.

Market Maker Is NOT Allowed To Act As Floor Broker In Same Security

If a market maker is registered in a given security, he or she is **not** allowed to act as a Floor Broker in that security. However, the CBOE will permit a Market Maker, in say, IBM contracts, to act as a Floor Broker in another contract. For example, it is acceptable for the Market Maker in General Motors contracts to also register and act as a Floor Broker, executing trades of Disney contracts.

If a Floor Broker receives an order from a public customer that cannot be executed at the current market price, as quoted by the Market Maker, the order will be given over to the Order Book Official ("OBO").

Order Book Official

Exchange Employee

Accepts Limit Orders

Cannot Accept Stop Orders

The OBO is an exchange employee who works on a salaried basis, maintaining the book of **public** orders (not those from member firms' own trading accounts) and executing these trades when the market moves in the desired direction. As such, the OBO accepts limit orders, but unlike specialists on the stock exchanges, the OBO cannot accept stop orders or stop limit orders.

Will Accept Market Orders Before Opening

The OBO does not ordinarily accept Market orders during the course of the trading day - these are executed by Floor Brokers and never enter the "book." However, the OBO will accept market orders prior to the market opening, to be filled at the opening price.

Cannot Accept Spread Or Straddle Orders

OBOs are also prohibited from accepting spread and straddle orders on the book - these must be handled manually by the Floor Broker and are discussed in more detail below. Finally, OBOs are prohibited from acting as a dealer and cannot take inventory positions.

Designated Primary Market Maker (DPM)

In the past couple of years, the CBOE has changed its trading system to allow for a new participant - a "DPM" - Designated Primary Market Maker. DPMs are similar to stock exchange specialists. A Designated Primary Market Maker is appointed by the CBOE for given classes of options and acts as both market maker; floor broker; and order book official. Thus, similar to the NYSE Specialist, the DPM will maintain a bid and ask quote in each assigned option; and will handle the book of public limit orders. Unlike the NYSE Specialist system, there are still competing options Market Makers on the floor for these options classes. (Note: This information on DPMs is given to show how the market actually operates, but it is not currently tested.)

Order Priority

Public orders entered on the exchange have priority over orders for the account of member firms or market makers entered at the same price. Thus, the highest bid displayed by the Order Book Official (who only shows **public** orders on the book) will have priority, as will the lowest ask shown on the "book."

As stated before, trading procedures on the CBOE are also modeled on the futures markets. On the NYSE, the specialist decides at what price a stock should open each morning, based on the balance of buy and sell orders that has accumulated overnight. The opening is "orderly" because a price is set to fill those open orders, and then the normal stream of orders coming in at the opening is handled.

Trading Rotation

Daily Opening Rotation

On the CBOE, for each stock, there may be 20 or 30 option series to open (remember, each series has a different expiration and strike price). To open all the series for trading in an orderly manner, the OBO conducts a "trading rotation." He calls for Bids and Offers for each series, to establish opening pricing. After all series have gone through the rotation, the market is open to trade all series.

Closing Rotation On Day Prior To Expiration

A similar "closing" rotation may be gone through at the close of the day, and is **always** performed on the last trading day prior to expiration.

Note that the opening and closing rotations are only in **single** specified option contracts. Thus, during the rotation, only single orders can be filled. Combination spread and straddle orders, which require two or more contracts to be filled simultaneously, cannot be executed.

Spread And Straddle Orders

Certain order types are peculiar to the options markets. A spread or straddle order requires the execution of 2 trades to complete the position. These orders are entered on a single ticket specifying the two positions creating the spread or straddle. If it is a market order, the trades are executed at the prevailing premiums. If it is a limit order, the ticket specifies the **net** debit or credit desired for the spread or straddle. Premiums are not specified for each side of the spread or straddle. This gives the trader the needed leeway to get both positions in the market, as long as he satisfies the limit of the net debit or credit.

Spread Priority Rule

The CBOE also has a "spread priority rule," which states that during the trading day, spread limit orders have priority over single contract limit orders. In this way, it is easier for Floor Brokers to satisfy both sides of the position, thus creating the desired spread.

Accommodation Liquidations

$1 Net Premium

Cabinet Trades

The Options Exchanges also perform "accommodation" transactions for persons who have "worthless" options positions. Instead of letting the contract expire, the contract can be closed at a net premium of $1.00 per contract through this type of transaction. In this manner, there is a closing trade record, which is **very** useful for tax purposes. Accommodation transactions are also known as "Cabinet Trades," because the orders are placed in a "cabinet" for execution.

The rules for accommodation transactions are:

- Only orders for a premium of $1 per contract are permitted (these are limit orders).

- The orders are handled by the Specialist or Order Book Official, and are placed "in the cabinet" for execution.

- Orders to buy and sell the same contract at $1 are matched by the Specialist or Order Book Official on a First In, First Out basis.

- All cabinet trades must be marked as such, and must be reported following the close of each business day. Note that they are not reported to the "Tape," and are considered to be "off floor" transactions.

Cabinet trades are available for all closing transactions in worthless contracts - both for customer accounts and proprietary (firm trading) accounts. Thus, Order Book Officials, who normally **cannot** take orders for member firm proprietary accounts on the Book, are permitted to effect accommodation liquidations for member firm accounts.

Issuers Cannot Sell Calls Against Their Own Stock

The CBOE also has a rule prohibiting an issuer from selling calls on that company's stock. The worry is that, if the calls are exercised, the company will issue new shares to satisfy the exercise notice. This would dilute existing stockholder's equity; and such a move is not permitted unless the existing shareholders approve by vote; and would also require a prospectus offering by the issuer under the requirements of the Securities Act of 1933.

OSS

To help speed trading, the CBOE has an automated trading system called OSS - Order Support System.

As mentioned earlier, other markets trade options - AMEX, Pacific, Philadelphia and the New York Stock exchanges. Their procedures are similar to the NYSE rules covered previously.

4c. REGIONAL STOCK EXCHANGES

The regional stock exchanges were discussed early in the chapter. Trading procedures are similar to the NYSE and are not needed to be known for the exam.

Consolidated Quotations Service (CQS)

To foster competition between the various markets that "dual list" stocks, the Consolidated Quotations Service (CQS) was created. CQS lists the bid and ask quotes of **all** market makers in a given security. For example, Proctor and Gamble stock is listed on the NYSE; and is also traded on the Cincinnati Exchange. In addition, Third Market Makers (OTC firms) also trade the shares. All of these "market makers" are required to enter their bid and ask quotes into CQS.

Thus, anyone with access to a CQS terminal can enter the symbol for Proctor and Gamble and will see the current quotes of **every** market maker in that security; and thus can choose the best place to trade.

CQS Open Longer Hours Than NYSE

CQS is available for NYSE listed issues on one screen; and AMEX listed issues on another screen. Each quote shown on CQS is identified by a symbol designating the market where the quote comes from. It should also be known that CQS is open for a longer window of time than regular NYSE trading hours. Whereas the NYSE is open from 9:30 AM - 4:00 PM Eastern Time, CQS is open from 9:00 AM to 6:30 PM (since much Third Market and ECN trading, such as on Instinet, takes place "after-hours").

These symbols are:

New York Stock Exchange:	No symbol
NYSE-MKT (AMEX):	No symbol
Philadelphia Exchange:	X - (the "PhlX")
Pacific Exchange:	P - (Pacific)
Boston Stock Exchange:	B - (Boston)
Midwest (Chicago) Exchange:	M - (Midwest)
Cincinnati Exchange:	C - (Cincinnati)
NASDAQ:	T - (Third Mkt.)
Instinet:	O - (Other Mkt.)

Trades on these exchanges in NYSE-listed issues are reported into the Consolidated "A" Tape.

Trades on these exchanges in NYSE-MKT-listed issues and regional exchange listed issues are reported into the Consolidated "B" Tape.

Trades on these exchanges in NASDAQ-listed issues are reported to the Consolidated "C" Tape.

OPTIONS AND OTHER MARKETS
SECTION EXAMINATION

1.

The Order Book Official:

   I   is similar to a dealer
   II is an exchange employee
   III is a market maker
   IV records and executes public orders

   a. I and III
   b. I and IV
   c. II and III
   d. II and IV

2.

Which statements are **TRUE** about the CBOE Order Support System?

   I   The order is directed to the brokerage firm's communication post on the exchange floor
   II The order is directed to the trading post
   III Execution notices are sent directly from the trading post to the brokerage firm

   a. I and III
   b. II and III
   c. I only
   d. I, II, III

3.

The Consolidated Quotations Service is open during the hours of:

   a. 9:00 AM ET - 4:00 PM ET
   b. 9:30 AM ET - 4:00 PM ET
   c. 9:00 AM ET - 6:30 PM ET
   d. 9:30 AM ET - 6:30 PM ET

4.

On the CBOE, customer good-til-canceled orders are handled by the:

   a. Specialist (DMM)
   b. Market Maker
   c. Order Book Official
   d. Floor Broker

5.

All of the following may trade for their own account on the floor of an options exchange **EXCEPT** a:

   a. market maker
   b. competitive option trader
   c. registered option trader
   d. floor broker

6.

Quotes from all of the following sources are found on the Consolidated Quotations Service **EXCEPT**:

   a. New York Stock Exchange
   b. Boston Stock Exchange
   c. Philadelphia Stock Exchange
   d. NASDAQ Stock Market

7.

When an exchange stops trading in a stock, the options exchange:

   a. keeps trading in the option
   b. exercises all outstanding option contracts
   c. lets all outstanding option contracts expire
   d. stops trading in the option

8.

The "spread priority rule" affords precedence to:

    I   One-on-one transactions
    II Sales of covered calls and puts
   III Simultaneous purchase and sale of option positions

    a. I only
    b. II only
    c. I and III
    d. I, II, III

9.

Floor brokers on the Chicago Board Options Exchange:

    I   can accept all orders
    II can only accept orders that are "away" from the market
   III can maintain bid and ask quotes
   IV cannot maintain bid and ask quotes

    a. I and III
    b. I and IV
    c. II and III
    d. II and IV

10.

The "crossing" of customer orders by a Floor Broker on the CBOE floor is:

    a. a prohibited practice
    b. permitted only if the floor broker could not execute each of the orders with other market participants
    c. permitted only if a Floor Official approves
    d. permitted without restriction

OPTIONS AND OTHER MARKETS EXAMINATION
EXPLANATIONS

1. The best answer is **d**. The Order Book Official is an employee of the Chicago Board Options Exchange who runs the book of public orders. The "OBO" does not make a market in the option contracts - this function is performed by the "MM" - Market Maker. The "OBO" performs the book function for option contracts.

2. The best answer is **b**. All automated trading systems function in a similar fashion. Orders are routed directly to the trading post, eliminating the need for the order to be wired to the communication post on the exchange floor and then written by hand to be given to a floor broker. The execution report is sent directly to the originating firm; it does not go through the firm's communication post.

3. The best answer is **c**. The Consolidated Quotations Service ("CQS") presents bid and ask quotes for exchange listed stocks - for both NYSE and AMEX (NYSE-MKT) listed issues.

For NYSE listed issues, CQS shows the quote of the NYSE Specialist (now called the DMM - Designated Market Maker), regional exchange quotes where the stock is "dual listed," and third market maker quotes (remember, the third market is OTC trading of NYSE listed securities and currently accounts for about 40% of NYSE trading volume).

CQS is open longer than the NYSE. The NYSE trades from 9:30 AM ET - 4:00 PM ET, however CQS is open from 9:00 AM to 6:30 PM. Much "third market" trading of NYSE listed issues happens before the NYSE opens or after it closes; and the longer hours of CQS helps facilitate third market trading. Also note that the NYSE is trying to expand its trading hours to compete, but has not yet done so.

4. The best answer is **c**. The CBOE splits the specialist function into two. The order book official handles the book of customer limit orders. The market maker acts as the dealer in that option contract.

5. The best answer is **d**. On the Options Exchanges, floor brokers, and order book officials, handle trades as agent only. They accept orders from the public for execution but do not trade for their own account. Market makers on the exchange floor make markets in option contracts and are buying and selling for their own account. Registered options traders and competitive options traders are individuals that trade on the floor for themselves to add liquidity to the market. They can take positions and carry them.

6. The best answer is **d**. The Consolidated Quotations Service shows Bid and Ask quotes for exchange listed stocks, for all market makers in those stocks. These include the Specialist/DMM (Designated Market Maker) on the stock's principal exchange; any Specialist quotes from regional exchanges that dual list the stock; and the quotes of OTC Third Market Makers in that stock. CQS was created in 1979, when NASDAQ was in its infancy - so it was not included.

The UQDF (UTP Quote Data Feed) aggregates and displays quotes for all market makers in NASDAQ issues. UTP stands for "Unlisted Trading Privileges." Not only do NASDAQ market makers quote and trade NASDAQ stocks, but exchange Specialists (DMMs) are now permitted to compete and trade NASDAQ stocks under a "UTP" plan.

7. The best answer is **d**. When an exchange stops trading in a stock, the options exchange stops trading in the option (since there is no longer a way to price these "derivative" securities, whose price is based on the price movements of the underlying stock).

8. The best answer is **c**.   The spread priority rule gives priority to "combination" orders (e.g., spreads and straddles) that require 2 positions to be filled at 1 net debit or credit. Choice III describes a spread position and falls under the rule. A "one-on-one" transaction describes an order that requires one trade followed by another (e.g., a long straddle requires the purchase of a call and the purchase of a put) and also falls under the rule. The sale of covered calls and puts does not fall under the rule.

9. The best answer is **b**.   The floor broker is an individual who executes transactions for retail member firms on the CBOE. The floor broker can trade with another floor broker, a Market Maker or an Order Book Official, earning a fee for each transaction. Floor brokers cannot maintain a bid-ask quote - they cannot be market makers. They can accept all orders, and are obligated to find the best available market. Regarding orders that are "away" from the market, that is, orders that cannot be executed immediately, these orders would be placed on the Order Book Official's book of open orders.

10. The best answer is **b**.   The crossing by a Floor Broker of 2 customer orders at the same time does not expose those orders to the market. To make sure that the orders are exposed, the Floor Broker must attempt an execution on the trading floor prior to being permitted to cross the orders himself.

SECTION 5: CUSTOMER DISCLOSURE AND SETTLEMENT RULES

5a. OVERVIEW

The regulators of each marketplace have their own rules and regulations for disclosure to customers and settlements. FINRA sets rules for the NYSE, NYSE-MKT (AMEX), NASDAQ and OTC equity markets; the MSRB (Municipal Securities Rulemaking Board) sets rules for the municipal bond market; the CBOE sets rules for the Chicago Board Options Exchange. The essential features of the rules are similar for all of these organizations, but there are distinctions which should be committed to memory.

This section is arranged so that the "general rule" is covered first, followed by the distinctions for each regulating body.

5b. DISCLOSURE ON CUSTOMER CONFIRMATIONS

Confirmations Sent No Later Than The Completion Of The Transaction

Confirmations of customer trades must be sent to customers no later than "the completion of the transaction" under FINRA rules. This is a legalistic wording that covers both cash and regular way settlements in 1 rule. In practice, this is applied as follows:

Confirmation For Regular Way Trade Sent No Later Than Day After Trade Date

Regular Way Trade Settlement: The confirmation must be sent no later than the day after trade date. Since the trade settles in 2 business days, this gives the customer plenty of time to remit payment for a purchase transaction.

Confirmation For Cash Trade Sent On Trade Date

Cash Settlement: The confirmation must be sent on trade date. Since the trade settles the same day, the customer must receive the confirmation that day for a purchase transaction in order to know the amount to pay.

(Both cash and regular way settlement are covered later in this section.)

The information on the confirmation details the specifics of the transaction and tells the customer how much he or she must pay or will receive on settlement date.

Trading Markets

Confirmations for securities transactions must include:

- Customer name and address;

- Firm name, address and telephone number;

- Name of security purchased or sold;

- Size and price of trade;

- Accrued interest if a bond trade;

- If the trade is an agency trade, the commission must be disclosed;

- If the trade is a principal transaction, the mark-up or mark-down is not disclosed except for principal transactions in NASDAQ stocks;

- Whether a payment for order flow was made;

- Trade date and settlement date;

- CUSIP number ("Committee on Uniform Securities Identification Procedures" I.D. number).

Also included on the confirmation is the type of account in which the trade occurred (such as a cash account or margin account).

A record of the time of the trade and the name of the other party to the trade must be kept and made available to the customer on written request.

The MSRB requires additional disclosure for municipal bond transactions. The following must be added:

Name of issuer, interest rate, maturity date, if callable this must be indicated, if a limited tax G.O. bond, this must be indicated, if a revenue bond, the source of the revenue must be indicated.

Yield and Dollar Price of the Transaction - the dollar price that is computed must be the **LOWER** of the price to maturity or the price to call. This results in the following pricing guidelines:

For transactions in non-callable issues effected on a yield basis, the security is priced to maturity.

Generally, Discount Bonds Are Priced To Maturity

Premium Bonds Priced To Near Term Call Date

For transactions in callable issues effected on a yield basis, discount bonds are priced to maturity while premium bonds are priced to the near term call date. Thus, the customer is always given a dollar price that ensures he or she will, at a minimum, get the promised yield.

Only "In Whole" Calls Considered When Pricing Municipal Issues

For pricing callable bonds, only "in whole" call dates are considered. These are dates established in the Bond Contract where an entire maturity may be called. Partial calls and sinking fund call dates are **NOT** considered, since it is not known specifically which bonds might be called (the bonds to be called are picked by random selection).

Extraordinary Calls Are Not Considered When Pricing Municipal Issues

Furthermore, any extraordinary mandatory calls or extraordinary optional calls are **NOT** considered. For example, if mortgages backing housing bonds are prepaid, the issuer usually has the option of calling in bonds. This is an extraordinary optional call and would **NOT** be considered - after all, who knows when, and if, this might happen? As another example, if a hurricane destroys a hospital backed by a revenue bond issue, a catastrophe call covenant may require the bonds that financed the facility to be called. Again, this extraordinary mandatory call would **NOT** be considered.

Disclose Call Date Used For Pricing And Other Optional And Mandatory Call Dates

The call date used for pricing the bond must be disclosed, as must all other optional or mandatory call dates. Please note, again, that "extraordinary call" dates are never disclosed, however, since no one knows when they might occur!

If the resultant dollar price computed using the guidelines above is either a discount or a premium, both the yield and dollar price must be shown on the confirmation. On the other hand, if the securities are to be purchased at par, only the dollar price is shown; no yield disclosure is required (which makes sense, because the yield can't be anything other than the stated coupon rate).

Additional information on the confirmation is:

The "dated date" for new issues (this is the legal issue date of the security, from which date interest starts accruing, even if the security is physically issued at a later date);

Statement as to whether the securities are "fully registered," "registered to principal only," or "book entry." (If nothing is said, it is assumed that registered are being delivered.);

If the securities are subject to Federal taxation or subject to the Alternative Minimum Tax;

If the securities are "called" or "pre-refunded," the date of the call or prerefunding and the amount of the call or the prerefunding price (e.g., call premium) must be disclosed;

If the bonds are "original issue discount," this must be disclosed;

Trading Markets

If the securities are not in normal units (normal units are $1,000 denominations or multiples up to $100,000 per bond).

Any additional information requested by a customer after receiving a confirmation (such as the time of the trade, or name of the other party to the trade since these must be made available to the customer) must be provided within 5 business days of the request.

5c. FAIRNESS OF PRICING TO CUSTOMERS

Commissions and mark-ups charged to customers must be fair and reasonable.

On the exchanges, all trades are "agency" trades and commissions are competitively determined by the brokerage firm.

OTC transactions can either be effected on an agency basis, where the member firm is a middleman, matching a customer order to the best market; or the firm can act as a principal, buying the security into; or selling the security out; of its inventory account. In this case, a mark-down or mark-up is charged.

FINRA and the MSRB have specific rules on fairness of pricing to customers. Both regulators' rules essentially require that commissions charged in agency trades; and mark-ups and mark-downs charged in principal transactions be "fair and reasonable."

5% Policy Applies To Both OTC And Exchange Trades

The FINRA 5% Policy states that 5% is a guideline - not a rule - for commissions charged on exchange trades and commissions or mark-ups charged on OTC transactions. The charge must be "fair and reasonable" under the circumstances of the trade. To determine a fair and reasonable commission or mark-up, all of the following are considered:

- Type of security involved (for example NASDAQ Global Market stock trades would have a lower percentage than a high yield bond trade);

- Availability of the security (a thinly traded stock is more difficult to buy or sell and could justify a higher percentage);

- Price of the security (the higher the price, the lower the percentage);

- The total dollar amount of the trade (the higher the dollar amount, the lower the percentage);

- Disclosure of the amount of mark-up or commission to the customer before the trade (this, however, doesn't justify a higher amount);

- Pattern of mark-ups (that this mark-up is consistent with other similar trades made by your firm);

- Nature of member's business (if your firm gives full service, it may justify a higher percentage).

Mark-Up Or Mark-Down From "Inside Market"

The basis for determining the percentage is always the inside (current highest bid and lowest ask) market. It is not based on the dealer's cost of the securities. When a security is purchased for a customer in a principal transaction, the security is "marked-up" in price from the "inside ask" (lowest asked) price. When a security is sold for a customer in a principal transaction, it is "marked-down" from the "inside bid" (highest bid) price.

Under this policy, a 1% mark-up or mark-down might be unreasonable under the circumstances; and an 8% mark-up or mark-down might be entirely reasonable.

Policy Does Not Apply To Municipal Securities Or New Issues

The policy applies to **all** exchange and over-the-counter transactions except for trades in municipal securities, which are covered under a separate MSRB rule following. The policy also does **not** apply to New Issues sold under a prospectus - including investment companies such as mutual funds and variable annuities.

The types of transactions to which the policy applies are:

- Trades effected on the NYSE or NYSE-MKT (AMEX) floor; (FINRA is the regulator for both exchanges and the OTC market);

- Trades effected in NASDAQ stocks (NASDAQ is a virtual exchange). On NASDAQ, trades can either be agency or principal. In a NASDAQ agency trade, the commission must be disclosed and in a NASDAQ principal transaction, the mark-up must be disclosed;

- OTC Agency Trades (commission is disclosed);

- OTC Principal Trades (mark-up or mark-down included in net price and is not disclosed);

- Riskless or Simultaneous Trades (where the dealer, at the same moment, gets an order to buy a security for one customer; and an order to sell the same security for another customer - the dealer may "cross" these trades at the current market price);

- Proceeds Transactions (where the customer tells you to liquidate a position and use the proceeds to buy another position. You earn a doubled commission or mark-up, called a "combined" commission or mark-up. This must, of course, be fair and reasonable.)

MSRB - Fair Prices To Customers

The MSRB states that prices charged to customers in municipal bond transactions must be "fair and reasonable."

Each broker-dealer, whether executing a trade on an agency or principal basis, must be diligent in establishing the market value of the security and the reasonableness of the compensation. The rules states that:

Trading Markets

a dealer effecting an agency transaction must exercise the same level of care as if it were acting for its own account;

a fair price bears a reasonable relationship to the prevailing market price of the security;

dealer compensation on a principal trade is based on current market value, not dealer cost; and

reasonable compensation differs from fair pricing (a dealer that buys a security for a customer at an "above market" price and then charges a very small (or no) commission has still violated the rule).

Factors To Consider For Both Principal And Agency Trades

The factors to be considered for **BOTH** principal and agency trades are:

1. Best judgment of the fair market value of the securities when the trade occurs, and if applicable, the value of securities exchanged or traded in connection with the transaction;

2. Expense of filing the order;

3. The fact that the firm is entitled to a profit;

4. Availability of the security;

5. Total dollar amount of the transaction (larger transactions for institutions should have a lower mark-up or commission per bond); and

6. Value of services rendered in effecting the trade.

Factors To Consider Only For Principal Trades

The factors to be considered that **ONLY** apply to principal trades are:

1. Most important of all is that the yield should be comparable to that of other securities of similar quality, maturity, coupon rate and block size then available in the market;

2. Maturity, rating and call features of the security, including the impact of information from ratings agencies about potential rating changes;

3. Nature of the dealer's business; and

4. The existence of material information about a security through EMMA or other industry sources.

Factors To Consider Only For Agency Trades

The factors to be considered that **ONLY** apply to agency trades are:

1. The price of the transaction; and

2. Amount of any other compensation received in connection with this transaction (e.g., a proceeds transaction, where the customer directs

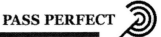

the broker to sell one security and use the proceeds to buy another. Two commissions are charged because the two trades are tied together, each commission should be lower).

5d. SETTLEMENT DATES

Regular Way - 2 Business Days

"Regular Way" settlement of all stock, corporate bond, and municipal bond transactions is 2 business days after trade date.

Regular Way - U.S. Governments & Options

"Regular Way" settlement of U.S. Government securities and listed options is next business day.

Cash

"Cash" settlement is same day settlement, before 2:30 PM ET. Prices that sellers receive for cash settlements are typically lower than for regular way settlements because of the difficulty of arranging the settlement on that day.

Seller's Option

"Seller's Option" settlement is used when the seller needs more time to deliver than "regular way" (2 business days) settlement allows. Settlement will be made when the seller gets the securities, but not before the 3rd business day after trade date. The seller gives the buyer 1 day's notice, and settlement takes place the next business day. "Buyer's Option" settlement is also available for a buyer who can't pay by the regular way settlement date.

When, As, And If Issued

"When, As, and If Issued"(WAII) settlement is used for new securities whose issuance is announced, but the certificates are not yet available for trading. Trades are performed on a "WAII" basis. If there is a problem and the issue is canceled, the trades are canceled as well. A confirmation is sent out when the "WAII" trade is performed specifying the price and trade date, but there is no settlement date since the securities aren't available as yet. When the certificates are finally issued, the exchange, or NASDAQ sets a settlement date (typically 2 business days after the certificates are issued). For municipal bonds, the settlement date is set by the underwriter, usually at 2 business days after the certificates are issued.

"T" - "S" - "R"

The MSRB uses distinct terminology for settlements:

- T = Transaction date
- S = Settlement date
- R = Receipt of confirmation, or other notice

Therefore, a regular way trade in a municipal bond settles "T+2"; cash settlement occurs on "T"; Customer confirmations must be sent "T+1."

5e. COMPARISONS AND DK NOTICES

Comparisons Dealer To Dealer

Aside from sending confirmations to customers on the day after trade date, comparisons must be sent to the "contra" broker (the other side of the trade). The contra broker receives a comparison from your firm, and your firm receives one from his firm. The comparison is matched against the trading record to see if all the terms agree so that settlement can proceed. Comparisons for virtually all securities are now generated on a "real time" basis during the trading day.

Comparisons Sent Day After Trade

The information on the comparison details the specifics of the trade: trade date, settlement date, size of trade, security traded, execution price, CUSIP #. There is no customer information or commission information, since this is a dealer to dealer "trade comparison."

DK - Don't Know Notice

Assume your firm receives a comparison for a trade executed at $50 per share and the comparison shows the trade at $60 per share. To clear the record, your firm will "DK" the comparison and send it back with its record of the trade. "DK" means don't know. The two firms then review the trading records and clear the discrepancy so that regular way settlement can take place. DKs are required to be resolved within 20 minutes of receiving the mismatched trade report.

5f. GOOD DELIVERY OF SECURITIES

On settlement, the securities are delivered and paid for. The securities must be delivered in "good" form to the buying firm at their offices or clearing house. If the securities are not in good form, they can be rejected and settlement will not take place.

For good delivery, the following conditions must be met:

Registered securities must be endorsed on the back by the registered owner in exact name. This endorsement is called an "assignment." Often, securities are not endorsed on the certificate itself, but rather on a "stock power" or "bond power." In this case, the brokerage firm is registered as the owner of the security, and has transferred ownership with the "stock power" to the customer. If the customer signs the "power," the security can now be transferred with a new "stock power" to another customer. In this way, the certificate doesn't have to be canceled and replaced after each trade.

Signature Guarantee

Medallion Signature Guarantee Program

The signature is not acceptable to the transfer agent unless it is guaranteed. Signature guarantees can be made by commercial banks and NYSE firms. If the signature turns out to be counterfeit, any loss is the guarantor's problem. Also note that signature guarantees are now standardized under the "Medallion" signature guarantee program - so any "Medallion" member can guarantee a signature.

Registered to principal bonds must have a proper assignment and a signature guarantee. These bonds have bearer coupons attached, and since only the face amount is registered, all unpaid coupons must be attached. Certain older municipal bonds fall into this category.

Bearer bonds must be delivered with all unpaid coupons attached (even if the bond is in default). No assignment or signature guarantee is required since the bonds are held by the "bearer."

Stock certificates must be delivered in round lots of 100 shares, or multiples of 100 on one certificate. If certificates of less than 100 are used, they must add up to units of 100.

> For example, for a 400 share trade, 1 certificate of 400 shares is good, 4 certificates of 100 shares are good, 8 certificates of 50 shares are good (two 50s = 100), 10 certificates of 40 are not good since 40 + 40 + 40 = 120.

Registered bonds must be delivered in $1,000 minimum face amount or multiples of $1,000, up to a maximum of $100,000 per bond.

Bearer bonds are only acceptable in $1,000 and $5,000 denominations. (Any other amount is a counterfeit bond.)

For municipal bond trades, if nothing is stated at the time of the trade, and the bonds are available in either bearer or registered form, delivery is expected in registered form.

Securities cannot be accepted if mutilated unless they are accompanied with a validation letter from the transfer agent or issuer stating that the securities will be accepted.

Municipal bonds must be delivered with a legal opinion unless identified at the time of the trade as "ex legal"- meaning coming without the opinion (there are virtually no municipal bonds trading that are "ex legal").

Insured municipal bonds must be delivered with proof of insurance.

DRS - Direct Registration System

Book Entry Registration

Important note: All these rules are still in place for delivery of physical certificates, which exist for thousands of stock and bond issues. However, the industry is now moving towards "paperless" registration, where there are no more physical stock certificates issued. This is called "DRS" - the Direct Registration System, which is run by Depository Trust Corporation (DTC). DTC maintains custody of most physical securities, and clears and settles trades through its National Securities Clearing Corporation (NSCC) subsidiary.

DRS allows the investor to be registered directly on the books of the transfer agent without a physical certificate being issued (saves money and time). Instead of the physical certificate, the investor gets a "statement of ownership" - essentially an account statement. These securities positions are moved electronically when a trade occurs.

When Hurricane Sandy hit lower Manhattan in October 2012, the vaults of DTC, which are located, ironically, on Water Street, were flooded out and all the certificates kept there were ruined. DTC made an emergency request to the SEC to not have to replace the physical certificates and, instead, simply replace them in electronic form. This will accelerate the move away from physical securities.

5g. DUE BILLS AND DUE BILL CHECKS

If a distribution has been declared by the Board of Directors, the Exchange or NASDAQ will set an appropriate "ex-date," when the price of the security will be adjusted for the distribution. Consider the following: A customer buys a stock before the ex-date and expects to get the dividend. But settlement is delayed, and the trade settles after the record date. Since the buyer wasn't on record with the transfer agent, he isn't mailed the dividend for which he paid.

Due Bill Used To Claim Payment Due

The dividend has been mailed to the seller, who shouldn't have gotten it. Your firm will send a "due bill" to the contra broker to claim the dividend. The other broker then sends your firm a "due bill check" for the dividend amount. Due bills are required when a trade takes place before ex-date (meaning "cum" the distribution) but settlement does not take place until after the record date.

5h. EX-DATES

When a corporation decides to make a distribution (for example, a cash dividend) or if the corporation is going to issue "preemptive rights" to its existing shareholders, it makes an announcement. Below is a sample announcement:

Monday, March 31, 20XX

The Board of Directors of Acme Manufacturing Company today declares a dividend of 50 cents per share to stockholders of record on April 15, 20XX. The dividend will be paid on April 30th, 20XX.

The Board of Directors has set the:

Declaration Date

Declaration Date: The date the dividend is declared.

Record Date	Record Date: The date on which the corporation takes the shareholder names and addresses from the transfer agent records for mailing the dividend.	
Payable Date	Payable Date: The date the dividend checks will be mailed by the corporation's transfer agent.	

These dates show on the calendar as:

APRIL						
S	M	T	W	T	F	S
30	31	1	2	3	4	5
6	7	8	9	10	11	12
13	14	15	16	17	18	19
20	21	22	23	24	25	26
27	28	29	30	1	2	3

Declaration Date — 31

Record Date — 15   Payable Date — 30

Regular Way Settlement Is 2 Business Days And Trade Must Settle By The Record Date To Receive Dividend

Once the distribution is announced, FINRA has some work to do. To be an owner of record for the distribution, a customer must have paid for the stock by the close of business on the 15th (the record date). If the trade settles on the record date or before, the buyer will be on record as of the evening of the 15th and will be mailed the dividend.

If Trade Settles After Record Date, Do Not Receive Dividend

Regular way settlement occurs 2 business days after trade date, so that the last day to buy and get the dividend is 2 business days prior to the record date. If the stock is bought after this date, the trade will settle after the record date and no dividend is received.

APRIL						
S	M	T	W	T	F	S
30	31	1	2	3	4	5
6	7	8	9	10	11	12
13	14	15	16	17	18	19
20	21	22	23	24	25	26
27	28	29	30	1	2	3

Last day to buy stock regular way and receive dividend — 11

Record Date — 15

Trading Markets

Cum-Dividend

If a customer buys on the 11th or before in a regular way trade, he or she will get the dividend. The stock is trading with the dividend - "cum-dividend."

Ex-Dividend

If the customer buys on the 14th or later, he or she does not get the dividend - the stock is now trading "ex-dividend."

APRIL

Last day to buy stock regular way and receive dividend

First day stock trades without dividend

Record Date

If a customer buys on the 10th, the trade will settle on the 14th, regular way, and the customer will get the dividend. If the customer buys on the 11th, the trade will settle on the 15th, and since the record book list is taken that night, the customer will get the dividend. If the customer buys on the 14th, the trade will settle on the 16th, and the customer will not be on the record book for the dividend, since the list was taken the previous night.

On Ex-Date, FINRA Tells Exchange To Reduce The Price Of The Stock

As of April 14th, any purchaser in a regular way trade does not get the dividend. FINRA sets this date as the "ex-dividend" date and tells the exchange to reduce the price of the stock by the amount of the distribution when the stock opens for trading, since purchasers no longer qualify for the payment.

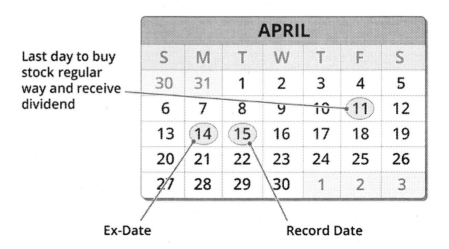

Last day to buy stock regular way and receive dividend

Ex-Date

Record Date

Ex-Date For Cash Dividends Is 1 Business Day Prior To Record Date

The "ex-date" is set by FINRA as 1 business day prior to the record date. (Remember, if one buys the stock 2 business days prior to the record date, the trade will settle on the record date and that person will get the distribution.)

Assume that Acme stock was trading at $20 on the 11th. As of the 14th (the "ex"-date), the stock will open for trading at a price reduced by the $.50 dividend, so it opens at $19.50.

Reduction on ex-date is done for a very simple reason. It stops traders from making windfall profits. If there was no reduction, a day trader could buy the stock on the 11th (getting on the record book for the 15th) and then sell on the 14th (going off the record book on the 16th) and be on the record book for the one day necessary to get a $.50 dividend check. If there is no reduction, he could buy at $20 and then sell at $20 the next day and get a $.50 check for 1 day's investment.

With the reduction, he buys at $20 and sells at $19.50, but receives the $.50 dividend, so the end result is a "wash."

If a company declares a dividend in "sub-pennies" - for example, a dividend of, say, $.453 - the dividend amount is rounded up to the next highest penny ($.46 in this case) and the price is reduced by this amount.

Cash Settlement Ex-Date Is The Business Day After Record Date

If a cash settlement is used, the ex-date is set at the business day following the record date. The customer can buy up to, and including the record date, and since settlement occurs that day, he will be on record for the dividend. The day after the record date is the first day that the dividend would not be received, so this is the ex-date for a cash trade.

Ex-Date For Stock Splits Is Day After Payable Date

The ex-date for stock splits and stock dividends is handled differently because no cash payment is being made - only additional securities are issued. In this case, the ex-date is set at the business day after the payment date.

This creates an unusual problem, because the payment date is set weeks after the record date. If one buys the stock after the ex-date, that person will not get the additional shares. When ex-date comes, the price of the stock is dropped - and that person now has the same number of shares, each being worth less than before. This person doesn't deserve this loss, and can claim the additional shares from the seller with a due bill. Trades will take place with a due bill until the stock dividend or split is actually mailed to shareholders.

Any orders with a "Time In Force" (TIF) of more than 1 day are carried either on the order book of a member firm, which feeds it to an exchange when the market price moves to, or through the price of the order; or are maintained by the exchange itself on its internal order book. If there is a cash dividend, stock split, or stock dividend, the order itself must be adjusted to reflect this. The usual order adjustments are:

Only Orders Placed Below The Market Are Adjusted On Ex-Date For Cash Dividends

DNR = Do Not Reduce

Cash dividends: The stock price is reduced for the cash dividend and the orders that are placed lower than the current market (these are the ones that could become executable due to a dividend reduction) are reduced as well. The orders that are lower than the current market are: Open Buy Limits and Open Sell Stops ("OBLOSS"). If the customer does not want the order reduced, the customer must note "DNR" (Do Not Reduce) on the order. Also note that if the dividend is for a sub-penny amount, because orders are only accepted in round pennies, the convention is that the dividend amount is rounded up and then subtracted from the price.

All Orders Are Adjusted For Stock Splits And Stock Dividends

Stock splits and stock dividends: The number of shares is increased and the price is reduced. For example, for a 2:1 split, a standing order to buy 100 shares at $40 is adjusted to an order to buy 200 shares at $20. For stock splits and stock dividends, all orders both above the market (Open Sell Limits and Open Buy Stops - "OSLOBS") and below the market (Open Buy Limits and Open Sell Stops - "OBLOSS") are adjusted.

All Orders Are Canceled For Reverse Stock Splits

Reverse stock splits: A very rare event (typically used by companies that run the risk of delisting because their share price is approaching $1), all orders, both above and below the market, are canceled.

Since the exchanges no longer take orders with a TIF of more than 1 day, standing orders are maintained by the member firm and are routed to the exchange based on the order instruction. In this case, the member firm makes the adjustment. Also note that member firms holding such orders are free to make their own rules regarding adjustments.

5i. MARKS TO THE MARKET - BUY IN AND SELL OUT

Between trade date and settlement date, the price of a security can move sharply. The unsecured party can demand a "mark to market" for the dollar amount of the security's change in value. The mark to market must be met by the close of the next business day. The procedure only applies to transactions between dealer and dealer. It does not apply to transactions between dealer and customer. In practice, "marking to market" is rarely used between dealers.

On settlement, the securities may not be delivered. If this occurs, the buyer can give the seller a written notice of "buy-in." Upon receipt of the notice, the seller has 2 business days to deliver. On the third business day, the purchaser can buy in the position, charging any loss to the seller.

If the securities delivered are not paid for on settlement, the seller can "sell out" the position using the same notification procedure as for "buy-ins."

5j. REJECTION AND RECLAMATION

A rejection occurs when securities are delivered to a brokerage firm upon settlement and are refused for a valid reason. A reclamation occurs when a brokerage firm **accepts** delivery of securities on settlement and later determines that the delivery was not "good." The securities can be returned with a "Uniform Reclamation Form" attached that specifies the problem with the security. Upon receipt, the other firm must cure the deficiency and return the proper security.

For example, a security may be delivered that is missing an assignment; or that is missing a due bill check; or it may be the wrong security. The Uniform Reclamation Form is completed specifying the problem and is returned attached to that security. The receiving firm must cure the deficiency and return the proper security.

If a large shipment of securities is made to a firm and accepted, and it is later determined that some of the securities are not "good delivery," only those defective securities are reclaimed. The entire shipment is **not** reclaimed.

CUSTOMER DISCLOSURE AND SETTLEMENT RULES SECTION EXAMINATION

1.

Which of the following are disclosed on a customer confirmation?

    I   Commission if an agency trade was executed

    II Mark-up if a principal transaction in a non-NASDAQ OTC security

    III Inventory position of the dealer

    IV Amount of accrued interest for a bond trade

    a.   I and II

    b.   I and IV

    c.   II and IV

    d.   I, II, III, IV

2.

Which of the following information is disclosed on an options confirmation?

    I   Strike price

    II Type of option

    III Expiration date

    IV Open interest

    a.   I and II only

    b.   III and IV only

    c.   I, II, III

    d.   I, II, III, IV

3.

A customer has an open order to sell 1,000 shares of ABC at $50 Stop. ABC declares a 10% stock dividend. After the ex date, the adjusted order on the member firm's internal order entry system would be:

    a.   Sell 1,000 shares of ABC at 45.45 Stop

    b.   Sell 1,100 shares of ABC at 45.45 Stop

    c.   Sell 1,000 shares of ABC at 50.00 Stop

    d.   Sell 1,100 shares of ABC at 50.00 Stop

4.

Which information would be included on a When, As and If Issued trade confirmation for a bond trade?

    a.   Settlement date

    b.   Amount of accrued interest

    c.   Total transaction cost

    d.   Agent or principal transaction

5.

An open order is on the member firm's internal order entry system to sell 200 XYZ at 30 Stop GTC. The company has declared a 50% stock dividend. On the morning of the ex date, the order on the book will be:

    a.   Sell 300 XYZ at 20 Stop GTC

    b.   Sell 300 XYZ at 30 Stop GTC

    c.   Sell 300 XYZ at 40 Stop GTC

    d.   Sell 300 XYZ at 60 Stop GTC

6.

A customer places an order to sell 100 ABC at 12 Stop Limit, when ABC stock is trading at $13. The company is restructuring and has announced a special dividend of $2.85 to be paid to shareholders of record. On the ex date, the order will be:

    a.   canceled

    b.   reduced to $9.00

    c.   reduced to $9.15

    d.   executed at $12.00

7.

ABC stock has just closed at $70.50. A customer has an open order on the firm's internal order entry system to sell short 100 shares of ABC at 70 Stop. ABC stock goes ex dividend $.55. The order on the firm's order book the next morning will be:

    a.   Sell short 100 ABC at 69.45 Stop

    b.   Sell short 100 ABC at 69.50 Stop

    c.   Sell short 100 ABC at 69.55 Stop

    d.   Sell short 100 ABC at 70.00 Stop

8.

A "Right of Rejection" can be used when:

a. the buyer accepts delivery of securities that later prove to have a problem

b. the seller refuses to deliver securities by the settlement date

c. a trade settles after the record date and the buyer refuses to accept the securities because the price has fallen

d. the buyer refuses to accept securities on the settlement date because there is a problem with the securities

9.

An open order is on the member firm's internal order entry system to sell 400 XYZ at 40 Stop GTC. The company has declared a 25% stock dividend. On the morning of the ex date, the order on the book will be:

a. Sell 400 XYZ at 32 Stop GTC

b. Sell 400 XYZ at 40 Stop GTC

c. Sell 500 XYZ at 32 Stop GTC

d. Sell 500 XYZ at 40 Stop GTC

10.

Which of the following orders will be reduced on ex date for a cash dividend?

I   Buy 100 ABC @ 50

II Buy 100 ABC @ 60 Stop

III Sell 100 ABC @ 50 Stop DNR

IV Sell 100 ABC @ 60

a. I only

b. I and II

c. III and IV

d. II and III

11.

A dealer buys 10,000 shares of ABC common at $15 for its inventory. One week later the stock is quoted at $18 - $19, and a customer buys 100 shares from the dealer at a net price of $20. Under the FINRA 5% Policy, a fair and reasonable mark-up is based upon which price?

a. $15

b. $18

c. $19

d. $20

12.

An investor has 300 shares of stock that have split 3:1. Which statements are **TRUE**?

I   The investor will receive an additional 600 shares

II The investor will receive an additional 900 shares

III The investor will receive a replacement certificate for his original 300 shares

IV The investor will receive a sticker with a reduced par value to place on his or her original 300 share certificate

a. I and III

b. I and IV

c. II and III

d. II and IV

13.

On ex dividend date, which orders are reduced for cash dividends?

a. Orders placed above the current market

b. Orders placed below the current market

c. Orders placed at the current market

d. All of the above

14.

All of the following are considered in determining fair and reasonable compensation under the FINRA 5% Policy **EXCEPT**:

    a.   Size of the transaction

    b.   Level of service provided by the member firm

    c.   Profit to the dealer on the transaction

    d.   Total dollar amount of trade

15.

A simultaneous trade is performed on the OTC market. Under FINRA rules, the transaction is:

    a.   prohibited

    b.   allowed and must conform to the 5% Policy

    c.   allowed if a commission or mark-up is only charged on one side of the transaction

    d.   allowed if the combined mark-up does not exceed 8 1/2%

16.

ABC stock has just closed at $70.50. A customer has an open order on the firm's internal order entry system to sell short 100 shares of ABC at 70 Stop. ABC stock goes ex dividend $.55. The order on the firm's order book the next morning will be:

    a.   Sell short 100 ABC at 69.45 Stop

    b.   Sell short 100 ABC at 69.50 Stop

    c.   Sell short 100 ABC at 69.55 Stop

    d.   Sell short 100 ABC at 70.00 Stop

17.

An over-the-counter firm has traded stock with another dealer. Barring any unusual circumstances, settlement will take place in:

    a.   2 business days in clearing house funds

    b.   2 business days in Federal Funds

    c.   5 business days in clearing house funds

    d.   5 business days in Federal Funds

18.

A corporation in Toontown, Ohio declares a cash dividend on Tuesday, December 2nd, payable to holders of record on Monday, December 22nd. The local newspaper publishes the announcement on Wednesday, December 3rd, while Standard and Poor's reports the dividend on Wednesday, December 10th. The ex date for regular way trades will be set at:

    a.   Wednesday, December 17th

    b.   Thursday, December 18th

    c.   Friday, December 19th

    d.   Monday, December 22nd

19.

A mutilated security is considered a good delivery if validated by the:

    I   Issuer

    II   Contra-broker

    III   Customer

    IV   Transfer Agent

    a.   I only

    b.   I or IV

    c.   II or III

    d.   II or IV

20.

Which of the following open orders held by a member firm on its internal order entry system would be adjusted if the "ex" date for a cash dividend were tomorrow?

    I   Buy 100 ABC @ 50 Day

    II   Buy 100 ABC @ 60 Stop GTC

    III   Buy 100 ABC @ 50 GTC

    IV   Sell 100 ABC @ 60 GTC

    a.   III only

    b.   I and III

    c.   II and IV

    d.   I, II, III

21.
A bond trade takes place at 10:00 AM on Monday, July 10th for "cash." Settlement takes place:

a. before 2:30 PM on July 10th
b. before 2:30 PM on July 11th
c. during business hours on July 15th
d. during business hours on July 17th

22.
ABC corporation announces a 5:4 stock split to holders of record on Wednesday, November 15th, payable on November 30th. NASDAQ has set the ex date at December 1st. What is the first day that the stock will trade without a due bill attached?

a. November 10th
b. November 15th
c. November 30th
d. December 1st

23.
Which is **NOT** a good delivery for a 300 share trade of stock?

a. One 300 share certificate
b. Three 100 share certificates
c. Ten 30 share certificates
d. Thirty 10 share certificates

24.
On ex dividend date, which orders are reduced for cash dividends?

a. Orders placed above the current market
b. Orders placed below the current market
c. Orders placed at the current market
d. All of the above

25.
Which statements are **TRUE** regarding DK notices?

I   They are sent to customers
II They are sent to contra-brokers
III They are used to confirm the details of the trade
IV They are used to reconcile unmatched trades

a. I and III
b. I and IV
c. II and III
d. II and IV

CUSTOMER DISCLOSURE AND SETTLEMENT RULES
EXAMINATION EXPLANATIONS

1. The best answer is **b**. Customer confirmations must disclose the commission in an agency trade. The mark-up is not disclosed in principal transactions in OTC stocks (OTCBB or Pink Sheets) and is included in a net price. However, it must be disclosed for principal transactions in NASDAQ stocks. The confirmation does not disclose the inventory position of the dealer - this has no bearing on the customer. The amount of accrued interest on a bond trade must be on a confirmation, since the buyer pays this amount to the seller.

2. The best answer is **c**. Disclosed on an options confirmation are the type of option; the expiration; the strike price; the execution price and any commission; the trade date and settlement date. Open interest figures (the number of contracts that remain open that have yet to be closed by trading or exercise) are not disclosed.

3. The best answer is **b**. When there is a stock dividend or split, the order must be adjusted on the firm's internal order entry book on "ex date." The price of the stock is reduced and number of shares covered by the order is increased.

In this case, the 10% stock dividend results in a new price of $50/1.1 = $45.45. Adjusting the order for the 10% stock dividend would result in 1.1 x 1,000 = 1,100 share order.

4. The best answer is **d**. A "When, As and If Issued" trade occurs without knowing the settlement date. When the securities are finally issued, a settlement date is set. If the settlement date is unknown, the amount of accrued interest due is unknown (interest accrues up to, but not including settlement). If the amount of accrued interest is unknown, the total transaction cost is unknown. The confirmation would state whether the trade was performed by the firm as agent or dealer.

5. The best answer is **a**. To adjust the order for the 50% stock dividend, the number of shares is multiplied by a factor of 1.50 (since there are 50% extra shares) while the order price is divided by a factor of 1.50.

200 shares x 1.50 = 300

The price would change to:

$30 price / 1.50 = $20 adjusted order price

6. The best answer is **c**. On ex dividend date, all open orders placed lower than the current market are reduced for cash dividends (except for orders placed DNR - Do Not Reduce). The intent is to make sure that the order does not become executable due to the fact that the stock's opening price is reduced by the dividend amount. The order was originally placed at $12. The adjusted order price is $12 - $2.85 reduction = $9.15 adjusted order price.

7. The best answer is **a**. Orders placed below the market are reduced for cash distributions on ex date. The intent is to make sure that the order does not become executable due to the fact that the stock's opening price is reduced by the dividend amount. The orders below the market are OBLOSS - Open Buy Limits and Open Sell Stops. This is an open sell stop order. $70 - $.55 = $69.45. The adjusted order is: Sell Short 100 ABC at 69.45 Stop.

8. The best answer is **d**. When securities are delivered on settlement date, the buyer inspects the delivery to ensure that the proper securities are being delivered in "good form." If the buyer finds that the wrong securities are being delivered, or that there is a problem, such as the securities' not having a proper assignment; or a coupon bond missing coupons; then the buyer may reject the delivery. This is the "right of rejection."

9. The best answer is **c**. To adjust the order for the 25% stock dividend, the number of shares is multiplied by a factor of 1.25 (since there are 25% extra shares) while the order price is divided by a factor of 1.25.

   400 shares x 1.25 = 500 shares on the adjusted order (this is a round lot)

   $40 price / 1.25 = $32 adjusted order price.

10. The best answer is **a**. The orders that are reduced on ex date are those placed below the market - Open Buy Limit and Open Sell Stop orders. The intent is to make sure that the order does not become executable due to the fact that the stock's opening price is reduced by the dividend amount. However, an order with DNR on it (Do Not Reduce) will not be adjusted downwards on ex date.

11. The best answer is **c**. Under the 5% Policy, commissions and mark-up percentages are computed from the current market price (meaning the inside market), not from the dealer's cost. If a customer buys, any mark-up is calculated from the inside ask price of $19. If the customer sells, any "mark-down" is computed from the inside bid price of $18.

12. The best answer is **b**. Stock splits are mechanically handled by giving the stockholder a new certificate for the additional shares, as well as a sticker to place on his old shares reflecting the reduced par value per share. This is cheaper than having shareholders tender all old shares, canceling them, and issuing all new shares. Since this is a 3 for 1 split, for every share held, after the split, the investor will have 3 shares. Thus, for 300 shares held, after the split, the investor will have 900 shares. He or she will receive a new certificate for the 600 additional shares; and a sticker to place on the original 300 shares, reducing the par value per share.

13. The best answer is **b**. On ex dividend date, all open orders placed lower than the current market are reduced (except for orders placed DNR - Do Not Reduce). The orders placed below the current market are OBLOSS - Open Buy Limits and Open Sell Stops. The intent is to make sure that these orders do not become executable due to the fact that the stock's opening price is reduced by the dividend amount.

14. The best answer is **c**. Under the FINRA 5% Policy, any dealer profit or loss on that transaction is not considered in determining fair and reasonable compensation for effecting an over-the-counter transaction. The size of the trade, total dollar amount, and level of service provided by the firm are all considered.

15. The best answer is **b**. In a riskless or simultaneous trade, a dealer gets an order from a customer to buy a security, and then the dealer buys the stock into his inventory to sell to the customer. The dealer has no risk and in this case the mark-up must be disclosed to the customer. Of course, the amount of the mark-up must conform with the 5% Policy.

16. The best answer is **a**. Orders placed below the market are reduced for cash distributions on ex date. The intent is to make sure that the order does not become executable due to the fact that the stock's opening price is reduced by the dividend amount. The orders below the market are OBLOSS - Open Buy Limits and Open Sell Stops. This is an open sell stop order. $70 - $.55 = $69.45. The adjusted order is: Sell Short 100 ABC at 69.45 Stop.

17. The best answer is **a**. Generally, regular way settlement takes place in 2 business days in clearing house funds for all trades except U.S. Government securities and options. Trades of U.S. Government securities settle next business day in Federal Funds. Trades of options settle next business day in clearing house funds.

18. The best answer is **c**. The regular way ex date for cash dividends is set at 1 business day prior to record date. Since the record date is Monday, December 22nd, the ex date is 1 business day prior and is Friday, December 19th.

19. The best answer is **b**. A mutilated security is a "good delivery" if it is accompanied by a letter of validation from the issuer or transfer agent. It is not acceptable to have the customer or delivering broker tell you that the mutilated security is "OK."

20. The best answer is **a**. Only orders that are placed lower than the current market are adjusted on ex date for cash dividends. These are Open Buy Limit and Open Sell Stop orders (OBLOSS). The intent is to make sure that the order does not become executable due to the fact that the stock's opening price is reduced by the dividend amount.

Choice I is a Buy Limit order placed for the day. If it is not executed this day, it is canceled and thus would not be adjusted.

Choice II is an Open Buy Stop order. This is placed above the current market and is not adjusted.

Choice III is an Open Buy Limit order and would be adjusted.

Choice IV is an Open Sell Limit order, which is placed above the market and would not be adjusted.

21. The best answer is **a**. Cash settlement is same day settlement, before 2:30 PM.

22. The best answer is **d**. This is a hard question. The ex date for stock splits and stock dividends is unusual because it is set at the business day after the payable date. The record date to receive the extra shares is typically a month before the payable date. Someone who buys the shares settling after the record date will not get the extra shares. Yet on ex date the price is reduced, and that customer has the same number of shares, now worth less per share. The customer can claim the extra shares he deserves with a due bill. As of the morning of the ex date, any new purchaser buys at the reduced price and a due bill is not needed.

23. The best answer is **c**. To be a good delivery, certificates must be in round multiples of 100 shares on one certificate or must be delivered in certificates that add up to 100 share units. Certificates of 30 shares each are not good because $30 + 30 = 60$; $60 + 30 = 90$; and $90 + 30 = 120$. A round lot of 100 shares cannot be created from these units.

24. The best answer is **b**. On ex dividend date, all open orders placed lower than the current market are reduced (except for orders placed DNR - Do Not Reduce). The orders placed below the current market are OBLOSS - Open Buy Limits and Open Sell Stops. The intent is to make sure that these orders do not become executable due to the fact that the stock's opening price is reduced by the dividend amount.

25. The best answer is **d**. DK or "Don't Know" notices are sent dealer to dealer to reconcile unmatched trades. The dealer knows that there is a problem when he or she receives a comparison from the contra broker that does not agree with the trading record.

Topical Index

M